The Growth of the International Economy 1820–2000

Fully revised and brought up to date, *The Growth of the International Economy 1820–2000* remains the best available introduction to the study of the international economy as a mechanism for diffusing modern economic growth between nations. For the fourth edition, the authors have brought the story up to the year 2000, and have thoroughly revised the text by including new data and references.

Significant updates to the text include:

- globalization and the world economy
- the growth of regional trading blocs
- globalization and the financial crisis in Asia
- transition to the market in post-communist economies

Packed with new references and data, *The Growth of the International Economy* is an indispensable guide to the world economy as it enters the new millennium. This text is widely acknowledged as essential reading for first and second year undergraduates of economic history, international economics and applied economics.

A. G. Kenwood and **A. L. Lougheed** are Honorary Research Consultants in the Department of Economics at the University of Queensland.

D0542444

The Growth of the International Economy 1820–2000

An introductory text

Fourth edition

A. G. Kenwood and A. L. Lougheed

Routledge
Taylor & Francis Group

LONDON AND NEW YORK

First published 1971
by George Allen & Unwin (Publishers) Ltd
Second edition 1983
Third edition 1992

Fourth edition published 1999
by Routledge
2 Park Square, Milton Park, Abingdon, Oxon, OX14 4RN

Simultaneously published in the USA and Canada
by Routledge
711 Third Avenue, New York NY 10017

Routledge is an imprint of the Taylor & Francis Group

British Library Cataloguing in Publication Data
A catalogue record for this book is available from the British Library

Library of Congress Cataloging in Publication Data
Kenwood, A. G.
    The growth of the international economy 1820–2000 : an
introductory text / George Kenwood and A L Lougheed.—4th ed.
        p.   cm.
    Includes bibliographical references and index.
    1. International economic relations—History—19th century.
    2. International economic relations—History—20th century.
    3. Economic history—1750–1918.   4. Economic history—1918–
    I. Lougheed, A. L.   II. Title.
    HF1359.K465   1999
    337—dc21   98–33134
                           CIP

ISBN 10 0-415-19930-1 (pbk)
ISBN 10 0-415-19929-8 (hbk)

ISBN 13 978-0-415-19930-8 (pbk)
ISBN 13 978-0-415-19929-2 (hbk)

Contents

Part III
The post-1945 international economy

Figures

Tables

List of Abbreviations

ACP	African, Caribbean and Pacific (countries)
AFTA	ASEAN Free Trade Area
APEC	Asian Pacific Economic Community
ASEAN	Association of South Eastern Asian Nations
BENELUX	Belgium, the Netherlands, and Luxembourg
BIS	Bank for International Settlements
BIT	Bilateral Investment Treaty
BSFF	Buffer Stock Financing Facility
CACM	Central American Common Market
CAP	Common Agricultural Policy
CCFF	Compensatory and Contingency Financing Facility
CEEC	Central and Eastern European Country
CER	Closer Economic Relations
CET	Common External Tariff
CIS	Commonwealth of Independent States
CIT	Country in Transition
CMEA	Council for Mutual Economic Assistance
CPE	Centrally Planned Economy
DAC	Development Assistance Committee
EAGGF	European Agricultural Guidance and Guarantee Fund
EBRD	European Bank for Reconstruction and Development
EC	European Community/European Economic Community
ECB	European Central Bank
ECSC	European Coal and Steel Community
ECU	European Currency Unit
EDF	European Development Fund
EEA	European Economic Area
EEC	European Economic Community
EFF	Extended Fund Facility
EFTA	European Free Trade Association
EIB	European Investment Bank
EIF	European Investment Fund

EMEA	European–Mediterranean Economic Area
EMU	European Monetary Union
EPU	European Payments Union
ERM	Exchange Rate Mechanism
ESAF	Enhanced Structural Adjustment Facility
EU	European Union
FDI	Foreign Direct Investment
FEOGA	See EAGGF
FPEI	Foreign Portfolio Equity Investment
FPI	Foreign Portfolio Investment
GAB	General Arrangements to Borrow
GATT	General Agreement on Tariffs and Trade
GDP	Gross Domestic Product
G7	Group of Seven
GSP	Generalized System of Preferences
HIPC	Heavily Indebted Poor Country
IBEC	International Bank for Economic Co-operation
IBRD	International Bank for Reconstruction and Development (the World Bank)
IDA	International Development Association
IDB	Inter-American Development Bank
IFC	International Finance Corporation
IIB	International Investment Bank
IMF	International Monetary Fund
IPC	Integrated Programme of Commodities
ITA	Information Technology Agreement
LAFTA	Latin American Free Trade Area
LDC	Less Developed Country
MFN	Most Favoured Nation
MTN	Multilateral Trade Negotiations
NAB	New Arrangements to Borrow
NAFTA	North American Free Trade Association
NIC	Newly Industrialized Country
NIE	Newly Industrialized Economy
ODA	Official Development Assistance
OMA	Orderly Marketing Arrangement
OECD	Organization for Economic Co-operation and Development
OEEC	Organization for European Economic Co-operation
OPEC	Organization of Petroleum Exporting Countries
R&D	Research and Development
SAF	Structural Assistance Facility
SDR	Special Drawing Right
SEA	Single European Act
SEM	Single European Market

SRF	Supplementary Reserve Facility
STF	Systemic Transformation Facility
TNC	Transnational Corporation
U.K.	United Kingdom
UN	United Nations
UNCTAD	United Nations Conference on Trade and Development
U.S.	United States
U.S.S.R.	United Socialist Soviet Republics
VER	Voluntary Export Restraint
WTO	World Trade Organization

Introduction

The exchange of goods and services is the means through which independent economic units enter into economic relations with one another and become part of a local or national economic community. As exchange passes beyond a country's boundaries, national economic systems become parts of a broader regional, continental or world economy. Flows of commodity trade are not the only economic links forged between nations, however. People are also highly mobile, and the long evolution of trade from primitive barter to our modern worldwide network of commodity exchange has made necessary an intricate system of international credits, loans and investments. It is these flows of trade, labour and capital that constitute the vital processes of the international economy. Obviously, therefore, any study of the growth of the international economy must be concerned with the measurement and comparison of the rate at which these processes go on over time. It must also be concerned with examining the ways in which the international economic system is organized to carry out these vital processes, and how the structure, organization and functioning of these processes change as the international economy expands. In the final analysis, however, the international economy is studied not as an end in itself, but rather as a means to an end, for in studying its expansion in recent times, we are analysing one of the most potent causes of modern economic growth.

The international economy encourages national economic growth in two ways: by providing opportunities for international specialization; and by acting as a mechanism for diffusing between nations the apparatus and/or benefits of modern industrial technology. Since specialization implies trade and cannot occur without it, and since specialization and division of labour are a major cause of increased productivity and rising per capita real incomes, some comment is called for on the nature of the basis of trade between countries before we say something briefly about the international economy as a means of spreading industrialization.

International trade arises simply because countries differ in their demand for goods and services and in their ability to supply them. So far as supply is concerned, the basis for trade is to be found in the uneven distribution of economic resources among the nations of the world, coupled with the fact that commodities and services require different proportions of these economic resources in their production. This uneven distribution of resources is partly a matter of climate and geography, and partly a result of each nation's historical development, which has left it with a certain stock of capital and a population trained and educated in numerous techniques and skills. Whatever their origin, however, each country's endowment of land, minerals, skills, and machinery equips it to produce certain goods and services more efficiently (cheaply) than others. For differences in the relative supplies of different productive resources within a country will mean differences in their relative prices and therefore differences in the costs of producing various goods and services.[1] Considering these elements alone, each country would tend to specialize upon those products best suited to its factor endowment, which means those using little of its scarce factors but drawing heavily upon the cheap and abundant ones. Thus, differences in relative factor prices based on the relative abundance or scarcity of economic resources within countries will mean differences in international costs of production and therefore differences in commodity prices. It is these differences in commodity prices that are a basic cause of trade between nations.

However, the international structure of commodity prices and the pattern of foreign trade based on it are not fixed for all time. Over time, changes occur in the distribution of economic resources between countries that alter the comparative cost structure and modify the pattern of world trade. Any one country's factor endowment can change radically from internal causes, as technological progress occurs, as population changes, as domestic capital is accumulated, and as the economic extent of the land is modified. It can also change from external causes, by virtue of international movements of labour and capital and the spread of technical knowledge. The effect of such changes on a nation's relative factor endowment should be obvious. The principal basis for its specialization and the character of its trade are altered. In analysing the growth of the international economy, therefore, we must consider how changes in factor supplies, technical progress, increasing productivity, and changes in demand can transform the structure of comparative costs. For changes in comparative costs affect the pattern of international trade, while developments in international trade in turn influence the economic growth processes in the world economy that bring about changes in the international distribution of economic resources.

Whatever the structure of comparative costs at any particular point in time, the size of the trade flows between nations will also depend upon the existing level of transport costs. Since trade is based mainly on international price differences, it may be severely limited in situations where transport costs largely offset the price advantage of low-cost producers. In other words, the basis for trade, whether international or interregional, lies in comparative cost differences which are not neutralized by transport costs. It follows therefore that any reduction of transport costs due to technical improvements in the carriage of goods enhances the opportunities for trade by allowing international cost and price differences to become more apparent in world markets.

One apparent failure of the factor proportions theorem just outlined is that it does not provide an adequate explanation for the comparative advantage which industrialized nations appear to possess in different industries. This is brought out clearly by the fact that, in this century, trade has tended to expand fastest between the advanced industrial nations, many of which have roughly similar factor endowments. The need to explain the trade advantage of industrial countries has led consequently to an emphasis being placed on factors other than simple resource scarcity. One approach to the problem stresses the importance of economies of scale. The technical superiority of certain large indivisible units of capital or the use of specialized labour, both of which depend on the existence of large markets, suggests that a large country, especially one with a big population and high per capita incomes, will be more fruitful for the development of large-scale industry than a smaller country with a similar level of income. Hence, the scale economy explanation essentially asserts that the country with the largest domestic market tends to specialize in those commodities which exhibit the *greatest* scale economies.

The growth of trade between industrial nations has also been explained in terms of the technological gap between nations created by the discovery of new products and new processes of production. According to this theory, trade consists of the impermanent commerce which originates solely in the temporary technological superiority gained by the nation making the industrial breakthrough. In other words, the innovating country's export trade in the new product will last until such time as other countries adopt the new techniques or produce the new product on a scale sufficient to supply their domestic markets and make them independent of imported supplies. The period it will take for the manufacture of a new product to spread from one country to another will obviously depend upon a variety of factors, including the threat which new products pose to existing goods and the lure of the high profits to be earned in the new line of production. At the same time, technological gap trade may be prolonged by the fact that the innovating country enjoys a peculiar advantage in harvesting scale economies. This advantage arises because the markets for new products expand rapidly at first. The innovator can thus more confidently erect a large plant and secure an entrenched position in domestic and export markets than can successor firms abroad. In this respect the technological gap theory is an improvement on the scale-economy theory, since according to the former a small country which innovates may yet build a large plant, whereas the latter theory simply asserts that the country with the largest home market builds the biggest plant, regardless of when it begins production. Finally, it should be noted that while the technological gap theory implies that trade between industrial nations is only a temporary thing, the fact that innovation and technical progress are continuous processes means that trade between advanced industrial nations may well persist and even grow over time.

Another explanation of the rapidly expanding trade between industrial nations stresses the importance of domestic demand as a determinant of the products which a country will export. Only after the new product is firmly established in the domestic market, it is argued, will the entrepreneur be ready to respond to profit opportunities in foreign markets. Moreover, since income, more than any other variable, appears to determine the consumption and purchasing habits of broad sectors of the population, countries having similar income levels are likely to trade with each other more intensively than countries having different income levels. This explanation of the basis of trade between nations is, of course, dramatically opposed to the factor-endowment theory which implicitly argues that trade between capital-rich (high-income) and capital-poor (low-income) countries tends to be the more promising for the trading partners than exchange of goods between countries whose average income levels are similar, where labour and capital may be expected to be distributed in similar proportions. But having made this point, it should also be noted that none of the alternative theories just discussed completely dispenses with the factor proportions approach. Indeed, over time, a country's comparative advantage in certain industrial activities may be largely a matter of historical accident, in the sense that past international specialization based on relative factor endowment may lead to a strengthening and developing of natural skills, innovative capacity, and investment activity along lines which are different from those of other countries. Consequently, opportunities for technological gap trade may emerge and economies of scale assert themselves in the production of commodities and services which will have a ready market in other countries with similar income levels.

Whatever forms the basis of trade between nations, however, there is no doubting the gains from specialization, which come about because trade between countries provides the opportunity for an international division of labour that leads to a better allocation of economic resources and greater productive efficiency in every country. Indeed, it was these gains from trade, in the form of the extra output made possible by international specialization, and their distribution among trading nations, that formed the basis for the advocacy of a policy of free trade between countries during the nineteenth century. But past experience indicates that the emergence of a truly international economy did much more than just provide a large market suitable for increased specialization, for it also provided, through international flows of capital and labour as well as of goods, a mechanism for the diffusion of modern industrial technology and a means of transmitting economic growth from industrializing countries to the less developed areas of the world. In short, the expansion of the international economy after 1820 was a major cause of modern economic growth. But in emphasizing its functioning as an 'engine of growth', we should not forget the fact that an expanding international economy is both a cause and an effect of national economic growth. For while the technological diffusion and increased specialization facilitated by an expanding international economy may provide considerable stimulus to the economic growth of a country, that country's growth, in turn, may, through its increased demand for foreign goods, capital and labour, promote closer economic relations at the international level.

Given the main purpose of this book, which is to describe the growth and assess the economic significance of the international economy in the period between 1820 and 2000, its contents fall easily into three parts. The first part contains a discussion of the forces responsible for the expanding international flows of trade, labour and capital in the years up to 1913, and an examination of the functioning of the international economy as an 'engine of growth' during these years. The impact of World War I on the workings of the international economy is analysed in the second part, and in the light of this analysis an attempt is made to account for the partial collapse of the international economy during the 1930s. Finally, in the last part, we describe the latest phase in the development of the world economy, 1950–2000, a period which witnessed unparalleled economic expansion until the early 1970s and then persistent economic problems which have so far defied all attempts to eliminate them.

Recent attention to the topic of this book has produced the term 'globalization' to explain the process of international economic integration.[2]

NOTES

1 What is important is the relative, not absolute, supply of the factors of production. Thus, China is a country large in area, but, relative to its population's demand for food, land is scarce and capital is relatively even more scarce. On the other hand, Belgium may have a small population in absolute size, but its labour supply relative to the country's land and capital may be the most abundant factor.
2 For a comprehensive description of 'globalization' see International Monetary Fund, *World Economic Outlook*, May 1997, Chapters III and IV and Annex, Washington.

The international economy, 1820–1913

Chapter I

The causes of the growth of the international economy in the nineteenth century

To understand why a truly international economy first evolved during the nineteenth century it is necessary to examine the economic, technical and other changes which were responsible for the massive expansion of capital movements, migration and foreign trade that occurred during these years. For it was through these flows of money, men and goods that countries hitherto economically independent were fused into the international economy.

TECHNOLOGICAL PROGRESS: INDUSTRY AND AGRICULTURE

The industrial revolution, which began in Britain in the late eighteenth century and which spread first to Europe and then to the United States during the nineteenth century, enormously increased the opportunities for trade between countries, for the new technology presupposed a wide variety of resources and an expanding market. But except for a few favoured countries, such as the United States, most industrializing nations during the nineteenth century had to look outside their own borders for markets in which to sell the surplus output yielded by modern industry, and for the additional supplies of raw materials that were needed when domestic production of these inputs failed to keep pace with rising industrial demand. A similar situation arose in the new centres of primary production overseas, where the use of modern farming techniques produced agricultural surpluses for which markets had to be found abroad. At the same time, the apparatus of improved farming often had to be imported, along with the transport equipment necessary to the opening up of new areas of primary production.

Success in the search for foreign markets for manufactured goods depended very much on whether the new techniques resulted in a new product or in the cheapening of an existing one. Obviously trade in a new product will grow fastest when many countries are unable to produce it for themselves but want to consume it. For this reason, the rather limited spread of industrialization before 1913 must have given a powerful impetus to the growth of trade in industrial goods during the nineteenth century. On the other hand, where innovation involves the cheapening of old goods the effects on trade are often less clear. Thus, foreign trade in cheap machine-made articles often increased at the expense of trade in hand-made substitutes. This happened with British cotton textiles and Indian calicoes during the late eighteenth and early nineteenth century, though on balance the revolution in textile manufacturing that occurred in Britain at this time led to a net increase in the volume of cotton goods traded internationally. In other instances, however, where, for example, synthetic substitutes for natural products were discovered, a decline in trade could result from the introduction of the technical improvement.[1]

Taken generally, however, technical progress in the nineteenth century tended to be pro-trade biased. Innovation was widespread, and the opportunities for trade multiplied accordingly. Before 1870, the important innovating industries were textiles (especially cotton) and iron, with steam the new source of power. After 1870 the focus of technical change began to shift, as increasing emphasis came to be placed on the production of steel, machine tools, electrical engineering products, and chemicals. Electricity emerged as a new form of energy and the internal combustion engine as the basis of a new means of transport. The outcome of all these developments was a flood of new goods, including railway equipment, steamships, steel and electrical products, plant and machinery of all kinds, and a growing variety of other manufactured products. In addition, many of the articles already traded internationally became cheaper, especially cotton cloth. The result was a rapid expansion in foreign trade in manufactures.

Part of this trade in manufactures was necessarily of a temporary nature, since it was linked with the spread of industrialization. For, while technical progress in the form of new or cheaper goods undoubtedly favours trade, the diffusion of technology, by encouraging imitation in production and the substitution of domestically produced goods for goods previously imported, tends to be biased strongly against trade. Within a limited area the diffusion of the industrial revolution that began in Britain was fairly rapid. By 1850 it had penetrated into France and Belgium. Half a century later it had reached Germany, the United States, Sweden, Russia and Japan. In certain lines of foreign trade—for example, textiles and clothing—the trade reducing effect of technical diffusion soon became apparent. On the other hand, the spread of industrialization may have increased the world innovatory capacity, and there is some evidence of shifts in innovatory capacity occurring after 1870 from Britain to the U.S. and Germany. If increased innovation meant fresh opportunities for trade, shifts in the centre of innovatory activity were obviously important in influencing the geographical pattern of world trade. In short, despite the spread of industrialization, nineteenth century technical progress tended, on balance, to favour the expansion of world trade while at the same time bringing about changes in the direction and composition of trade between countries.

Besides providing expanding opportunities for the international exchange of manufactured goods, modern industrial technology also created increased opportunities for trade in raw materials. In the early stages of the industrial revolution, when textile production expanded rapidly, and machinery continued to be constructed largely of wood, agricultural raw materials dominated these exchanges, especially raw cotton and timber. Later on, however, as industrial technology continued to evolve, manufacturing industry came to rely more on minerals and relatively less on agricultural raw materials. This growing industrial dependence on mineral resources was reflected both in a widening of the range of minerals for which an industrial use was found and in the development of mass consumption of a few of them. While the output of coal and iron ore increased substantially throughout the nineteenth century, after 1850 the output of other metals, such as copper and zinc, grew even faster, and other previously little used minerals such as petroleum and aluminium, had achieved a considerable economic importance by the beginning of the twentieth century.

As industrial growth accelerated in the last quarter of the nineteenth century, the consumption of raw materials increased phenomenally. Between 1880 and 1913, petroleum production doubled every 8.6 years, copper every 13 years, pig iron, phosphates, coal and zinc every 15–17 years, and lead and tin every 20 years. In the circumstances, the tendency to exhaustion of the more readily available supplies of less common metals and fuels was to be expected, and their costs of production rose accordingly. In the search for new and cheaper supplies of minerals that followed, the United States emerged as a major producer, capable of supplying not only most of its own needs but also of providing a surplus for export to other industrial nations. Russia, too, possessed great, though widely dispersed, mineral resources, and Canada, South Africa, Australia, Chile, Malaya, and a number of other countries emerged as other important mineral producers. Indeed, a feature of the growth of world mineral production during these years was the constant shifting of the centre of world supply of these materials from one region to another. Such shifts were recorded for various minerals, including copper and iron ore, and for precious metals, such as gold. Quite obviously, these production shifts had important repercussions on the pattern of world trade, and they also exerted a significant influence on the international flows of labour and capital before 1914.

A similar situation to that found in mineral production developed in agriculture, when the spread of industrialization and the rapid growth of population brought about a phenomenal increase in the demand for foodstuffs and agricultural raw materials, a series of shifts in the geographical sources of supply and, consequently, great changes in the volume and commodity structure of foreign trade. Simultaneously, technological progress and the opening up of new regions cheapened many agricultural products and provided conditions under which mass markets could be supplied with many items formerly classified as luxuries. More and better farm implements and machinery, the use of chemical fertilizers, improved stock-breeding and new methods of checking plant and animal diseases—all made significant contributions to the growth of agricultural output. Many of these innovations originated in Europe and eventually diffused to countries overseas. Others were developed in the new farming regions themselves, where labour shortage, drought, short growing seasons and other problems called forth fresh invention and innovation to deal with them.

The growing demand for tropical products, which accompanied industrialization and the rise of real incomes in Europe and North America, led to a rapid expansion of plantation agriculture in the period after 1850. In the old established areas of European enterprise the growth of output was achieved primarily by the more efficient use of an abundant labour force. Elsewhere it was obtained either through improvements in peasant farming or through the spread of the plantation system, which brought with it better farming methods, higher-yielding plant strains, and the greater use of machinery, particularly in the preliminary processing operations. The plantation system also encouraged the introduction of new crops. Rubber trees, for example, were introduced into Malaya from Brazil in 1877. Rubber cultivation spread rapidly from there to the Netherlands East Indies and French Indo-China, and by the end of the century south-east Asia had become the chief source of the world supply of natural rubber. In contrast to rubber, the centre of world coffee production shifted in the opposite direction, from Asia to Latin America, following the emergence of Brazil as the world's greatest coffee producing country. Rice, sugar, tea, tobacco and cotton production were similarly affected by these production shifts as their output grew in response to the expanding demand for primary products in industrial Europe and North America.

TECHNICAL PROGRESS: TRANSPORT AND COMMUNICATIONS

Through cheapening and speeding up the movement of goods and people, improved transport and communications played a vital role in the growth of the world economy in the nineteenth century. By promoting the exchange of a growing volume of goods; by expanding markets, as well as opening up new sources of supply of many products; by permitting the concentration of certain types of production in fewer centres, thereby encouraging specialization and assisting the realization of economies of scale; and by allowing a greater interregional flow of men and capital, the new forms of transport and communications made possible that growing economic interdependence of the whole world which is so remarkable a feature of nineteenth-century economic development. Moreover, by making possible a significant relocation of economic activity throughout the world, transport improvements contributed substantially to the rising productivity that lay behind the growth of real incomes in the world economy during these years.

Of these improvements, the application of steam to land and sea transport was of critical importance. On land, steam was rapidly adapted to the railway, which quickly supplanted the existing means of transport. The earliest railways were built in Britain and the eastern United States, but they quickly spread, first to Europe and then to the other continents of the world. The extent of this dispersion in the nineteenth century is shown in Table 1.

In Europe the spread of the railway led to the formation of new states, such as Germany and Italy, and the creation of the large markets necessary for industrialization. In North America and Russia similar developments occurred, but on a grander scale. Here the railway permitted the political domination of whole continents by a single government while at the same time opening up the untapped wealth of virtually empty territories. Outside North America and Europe, railways were essentially instruments of the expansion of the world economy. Financed largely by European capital, the railways of Latin America, Asia, Africa and Australasia were built primarily to assist in the export of the continents' agricultural and mineral products and, since the abilities of the different countries in these continents to supply the required primary products varied, it is not surprising to find that railway developments were not uniform either within the continents or between them. In Latin America, only Mexico, Brazil, and Argentina had networks of any importance, whereas in Africa half the continent's railways at the end of the century were to be found in the Union of South Africa. In Asia, two-thirds of the railway mileage in operation at the end of our period were in India, where railways had been built chiefly to ensure political control of the sub-continent. Elsewhere in Asia, railway development had barely begun

Table 1 Railway route mileage, 1840–1910

	'000 miles		
	1840	1870	1910
Europe	2.6	65.4	212.1
North America	2.8	55.4	265.8
Latin America	0.1	2.4	60.7
Asia	—	5.1	59.5
Africa	—	1.1	23.0
Oceania	—	1.1	19.3
World	5.5	130.5	640.4

Sources: W. S. Woytinsky and E. S. Woytinsky, World Commerce and Governments (New York, 1955), p. 341; W. Woodruff, Impact of Western Man (New York, 1966), p. 253.

outside Japan, where over 7,000 miles of railway track had been built by 1914.

Compared to the railway, the steamship was slow to establish its supremacy at sea, where the relatively high standard of perfection achieved by the sailing-ship during the nineteenth century made it a formidable competitor. By 1869, however, the iron steamship had made serious inroads on the traffic of the sailing-ship. The coastal trade had earlier been taken over, while the ocean passenger service and the carriage of mail overseas also passed quickly to steam. With freight, progress was much slower. The steamship cut sharply into the North Atlantic carrying trade, but the Far Eastern trade remained exclusively the preserve of the sailing-ship. Here the opening of the Suez Canal in 1869, by providing a shorter route to the East, well served by conveniently located and efficient coaling stations, hastened the replacement of sail by steam. Later, the introduction of the compound engine, which significantly reduced coal consumption, and the conversion from iron to steel in ship-building that took place in the 1880s, made possible a continuous increase in the carrying capacity of the steamship and so increased its competitive power further. From 27m. tons in 1873, the amount of total world freight carried in steamships rose to 63m. tons in 1898, while the steamship proportion of the total world shipping tonnage grew from just over 12 per cent in 1870 to almost two-thirds of the total in 1900.

Despite the rapidly increasing demand for shipping in the nineteenth century, capacity grew sufficiently quickly to bring about a secular decline in ocean freight rates. This decline took place in two phases: between 1815 and 1851, and between 1870–3 and 1908–9. In the first period of decline, freight rates were particularly affected on outward cargoes (from Europe and the United Kingdom), on the Baltic and Mediterranean routes, and on the North Atlantic run. The causes of the decline in freight rates at this time included technological improvements in sailing-ship design and construction, the increased utilization of ships that resulted from improvements in cargo handling and dock facilities, the reduction of time in ballast, and increased knowledge, particularly of winds and currents. In the second period, the greatest decline occurred in the freight rates on long hauls. In bringing about this fall in rates, the steamship exercised a decisive influence, although the performance of sailing-ships continued to improve well into the last quarter of the nineteenth century. This lowering of transport costs was of vital significance for the growth of world trade, especially after 1870. Since only those goods that can bear transport costs and still be cheaper than some part of domestic production in the importing country will be traded, a reduction in transport costs will obviously widen the range of internationally traded goods by allowing foreign goods to become even lower in price relative to domestic production. By widening the range of international commodity exchange, and by permitting heavy or bulky products to enter into foreign trade, transport improvements provided a great stimulus to the growth of world trade in the nineteenth century.

In the task of cheapening and speeding up the movement of men and goods, the railway and steamship were supported by a series of developments in related activities. The growth of merchant fleets was accompanied by harbour improvements, the building of docks and warehouses, and the introduction of new machines and methods for the rapid handling of cargoes. Sea transport was also speeded up by the cutting of ship canals. Here the two outstanding feats were the opening of the Suez Canal in 1869, and of the Panama Canal in 1915. Other important developments during these years included the completion in 1872 of a new waterway connecting Rotterdam to the North Sea, the opening of the Manchester Ship Canal in 1894 and the Kiel Canal in 1895. The telegraph system was another development of immense significance for the growth of world trade. In particular, world commodity markets could become a reality only with the introduction of the telegraph and the spread of its use across the continents. By the turn of the century new developments in the field of transport and communications, of considerable significance for the future, were already apparent. The internal combustion engine offered an alternative form of land transport, although its ability to compete for traffic with the railways still seemed doubtful. The same could be said of aviation and the passenger traffic on the high seas. Meanwhile, oil began to be used to drive ships, although only some 2 per cent of world shipping was oil-fired in 1914. The telephone had emerged as an improvement on the telegraph, and the invention of the wireless set in 1896 was another step in the direction of bringing the peoples of the world closer together.

THE ACCUMULATION OF CAPITAL

The importance of capital accumulation for increasing production has long been recognized by economists. Capital accumulation facilitates the introduction of new techniques and provides tools and equipment for a growing population. It also brings about, through increases in the supply of tools and machinery per worker, the use of more efficient 'roundabout' methods of production. In particular, the process of industrialization, with its emphasis on more mechanized methods of production, a rapidly growing consumption of raw materials, and the need to supply wider markets, results in substantial additions being made to a country's stock of capital equipment. At the same time, technical progress and continued population growth make necessary a continuous increase in this capital stock if living standards are to be maintained or raised.

Any long-term analysis of the process of capital accumulation is made extremely difficult by the formidable conceptual problems involved in appropriately defining and measuring capital. Moreover, the task of amassing enough empirical evidence to justify definite conclusions concerning the changing level and structure of capital formation over time has barely begun. Yet while the available empirical data are limited to only a few countries, it is possible to use this material to make a few generalizations concerning the process of capital accumulation during the nineteenth century.[2] In Britain, for example, the transition from a pre-industrial to an industrial society was neither sudden nor did it involve any dramatic rise in the rate of capital accumulation. Most of the upward shift in the level of national investment associated with the industrial revolution in Britain seems to have occurred in the four decades between the mid-1830s and the mid-1870s, when capital formation rose from some 7–8 per cent of national product in the early 1830s to perhaps 14 per cent in the 1870s. This upsurge in the rate of capital accumulation was the result of heavy investment in domestic railways, the coal, iron and textile industries, shipping and its ancillaries, such as docks and harbours, plus substantial investment overseas. After 1875, capital accumulation continued at a high level, with the decline in the relative importance of railway investment being offset by much higher levels of investment in residential building activity and in industry, commerce and finance. Meanwhile, land as a percentage of total national capital declined continuously throughout the nineteenth century from being over one-half of the total capital stock in 1798 to just on 7 per cent of the total in 1912.

In other industrializing countries the process of capital formation and the consequent changes in the structure of the capital stock were similar to those experienced by Britain, although for various reasons the late industrializers probably achieved a high level of capital accumulation much more quickly than did Britain. But the demand for capital goods was not restricted to the industrial or industrializing countries. The spread of the railway to all corners of the globe set up a growing demand for railway equipment of all kinds, and efforts to exploit the natural resources of the newly settled continents created a heavy demand for agricultural machinery, mining equipment, and related types of capital goods. The consequent growth in the world stock of capital provided many fresh opportunities for international trade. The need of developing countries to import machinery and equipment during the early stages of industrialization created a growing demand for the manufacturing output of those countries already industrialized, as did the demand for capital goods by the primary-producing regions of the world. Moreover, differences in the rates of saving relative to investment possibilities in different countries provided profitable opportunities for lending capital on a large scale, which provided a means of financing the purchase of capital equipment needed by the various borrowing countries. In other words, the volume of world trade in the nineteenth century was kept at a high level by two closely connected facts: first, the fact that the new countries, whether industrializing or primary producing, keenly desired a type of good that the older industrialized countries were well fitted to supply, and, secondly, the fact that the old countries did not demand immediate payment for these goods, but were willing in effect to supply them on credit, so that the volume of trade was continuously larger than it would have been had it depended solely on the opportunities for simultaneous barter.

THE GROWTH OF WORLD POPULATION

Economic growth in the nineteenth century was also accompanied by a rapid increase of population. World population grew from just over 900m. in 1800 to approximately 1,600m. in 1900. At the same time, the distribution of world population changed in a number of significant ways as Table 2 shows.

Population grew fastest in the regions dominated by Europeans. In 1900 Asia still remained, as she does today, the most densely populated continent in the world. But in the nineteenth century her relative position had declined, as had that of Africa, because the populations in the other continents, especially North America and Europe (including Russia) were growing faster. The cause of the rapid increase of population in Europe was a familiar one, death rates were falling while birth rates continued at a high level. In North America, Latin America and Oceania, apart from high rates of natural increase, heavy inflows of migrant population, particularly from Europe, contributed to bringing about even faster rates of population growth in these regions than were to be found in Europe.

The rapidly growing world population had a number of important consequences for world trade. In itself a growing population would have meant some increased demand for those commodities already traded internationally.

Table 2 Growth and percentage distribution of world population, 1800–1900

	Numbers (millions)		Percentage distribution	
	1800	1900	1800	1900
Africa	90	120	9.9	7.5
North America*	6	81	0.7	5.0
Latin America	19	63	2.1	3.9
Asia†	597	915	65.9	56.9
Europe (including Russia)	192	423	21.2	26.3
Oceania	2	6	0.2	0.4
Total	906	1,608	100.0	100.0

Source: A. M. Carr-Saunders, World Population (Oxford, 1936), pp. 30–45.

Notes
* North America = north of the Rio Grande.
† Excluding Asiatic Russia.

Taken in conjunction with changes in the other factors of production, however, it greatly enhanced the possibilities of trade. For example, in Europe,
with the possible exception of Russia, the land–labour ratio became less
favourable as population grew, despite improved farming techniques and the
reclamation of waste lands. Land became scarce and rose in price, so that
agricultural products became more expensive relative to those obtained from
other countries overseas. As agricultural price differences widened, therefore,
the opportunities for trade increased correspondingly, while in those countries where the growth of domestic production of foodstuffs failed to keep
pace with the population increase, foreign imports had to be relied on increasingly to fill the gap. Moreover, the unfavourable land–labour ratio in Europe
had another consequence for the international economy. It forced people from
the land into the towns and, when domestic urban employment was unavail-
able, overseas to the new regions of primary production. In these areas, where
labour was short, the rapid growth of the indigenous population, aided by
immigration, served only to create more favourable conditions for the
exploitation of economic resources, particularly natural resources, which had
hitherto remained unworked partly because of the lack of labour.

THE SUPPLY OF NATURAL RESOURCES

Even if precise measurement of natural resources in economic terms is difficult, if not impossible, the available evidence suggests that a substantial
increase in the world supply of natural resources occurred during the nineteenth century.[3] Within Europe the supply was added to by the cultivation of
previously unworked land and the discovery and exploitation of new sources
of mineral supply. But by far the largest addition to the world supply of
natural resources came from the opening up of the vast, fertile and mineral-
rich continents of the Americas and Oceania. Virtually uninhabited, these
regions also afforded an enormous increase in living-space for the growing
flood of migrants from Europe. By 1800 the European-occupied areas in these
continents were already more extensive than the whole of western Europe,
whose settled area at this date has been put at between 650,000 and 790,000
square miles. In the course of the next hundred years a further 8–9m. square
miles was added to these European territories overseas, approximately an
eight to nine-fold increase in the occupied area, while the degree of land use
became, in every way, a great deal more intense.

Apart from people's willingness and ability to move to these new lands, the
key factors in opening them up included an increased knowledge of their
natural resources—land, minerals, climate, and so on—and their economic
accessibility, which largely depended on the availability of cheap and
adequate transport. Also important was a sufficiency of capital to clear
and work the land and exploit its mineral wealth. In all these respects the

Americas and Oceania were particularly fortunate, for they possessed a variety of natural resources, which, for the most part, were easily accessible and capable of development by known techniques requiring moderate amounts of capital.

In Asia and tropical Africa, on the other hand, the opening up of new lands and the development of new sources of raw materials was a much slower process than elsewhere. Climatic and topographical difficulties, inadequate knowledge, and institutional resistance to change provided the main obstacles to development in these regions. Where development in these continents did occur, however, the availability of natural resources appears to have been the chief factor influencing the location of what have been described as 'export economies'. Situated for the most part in the tropics, the location of these largely plantation and mining activities was determined not by the relative supply of the various factors of production which existed within a country's borders, but by the location of the least mobile factors of production, such as climate, soil conditions, or mineral deposits, and by accessibility to markets which, if overseas, meant access to ocean-going transport. Labour, capital and entrepreneurship were internationally mobile and could be applied almost anywhere in the world, so that choice of these industry locations was based on other cost considerations. The most fertile lands and the most promising mineral deposits could be chosen and those requiring the lowest transport costs worked first.[4]

THE GROWTH OF REAL INCOMES

Despite the high rates of population growth, there was a marked rise in real incomes in a number of countries as a result of the increase in productivity brought about by new production methods, better organization, and improved transport. While there are obvious difficulties in measuring this improvement in statistical terms that emphasize the approximate nature of the available national estimates, they suggest a three-fold classification of countries based on the annual rates of growth of real incomes which they experienced in the course of the nineteenth century. Heading the list are those primary producing countries which experienced rates of growth in real income per head in the region of 1½ per cent per annum. These included the United States, and Canada after 1850. Per capita real income in Argentina may also have risen this fast in the period after 1880. In Australia, on the other hand, the rate of growth of per capita real income was somewhat slower than 1½ per cent per annum, and that of New Zealand substantially so. In New Zealand, real income grew at 4.6 per cent per annum, but with population also growing rapidly (4.1 per cent per annum), there was only a 0.5 per cent rise in real income per head. The explanation of this slow growth of per capita income in New Zealand seems to be the high income level already attained by the mid-1860s, when average living standards appear to have been significantly higher than those in Australia, which in turn were significantly higher than those in either the United States or Britain. A further substantial rise in real income from such a high base with immigration running at a record level was clearly difficult. Australia's performance was similarly affected by a high initial per capita real income, but in addition she experienced a severe and prolonged depression in the 1890s which depressed average real income to such an extent that it did not regain its 1891 peak until 1909.

Angus Maddison's estimates of average growth rates of real GDP and GDP per capita for selected countries for the period 1870–1913 are shown in Table 3. In this group of countries, the performances of the United States are striking, as are, to a lesser extent, those of Germany, Austria and Sweden. Only for Australia, Belgium, the Netherlands and the United Kingdom are the average growth rates of per capita income 1 per cent or lower during these years. As was the case for New Zealand, Australia's low per capita growth rate was the result of heavy immigration and high rate of growth of population between 1870 and 1913.

Another group of countries, making up the greater part of Asia, Africa and

Table 3 Growth of real GDP and GDP per capita, 1870–1913 (selected countries)

Country	Annual average compound rates of growth	
	GDP	GDP per capita
Australia	3.5	0.9
Austria	2.4	1.5
Belgium	2.0	1.0
Canada	4.1	2.3
Denmark	2.7	1.6
Finland	2.7	1.4
France	1.5	1.3
Germany	2.8	1.6
Italy	1.9	1.3
Japan	2.3	1.4
Netherlands	2.3	1.0
Norway	2.1	1.3
Sweden	2.2	1.5
Switzerland	2.1	1.2
United Kingdom	1.9	1.0
United States	3.9	1.8
Arithmetic average	2.5	1.4

Source: Angus Maddison, *Dynamic Forces in Capitalist Development* (Oxford, 1991) Tables 3.1 and 3.2, pp. 49–50.

Latin America, had annual rates of growth of per capita real income of 0.5 per cent or less. Few statistics are available for these countries. In India, where conditions were more favourable to growth than anywhere else in Asia outside Japan, average per capita income rose at about 0.4 per cent over the period 1857–63 to 1896–1904. Elsewhere the world output appears to have grown fast enough to maintain a slowly growing population. Even if per capita real incomes grew in these countries during the nineteenth century, a rate of 0.5 per cent per annum would seem to be the upper limit to what was attainable given their prevailing economic circumstances. The one exception to this generalization was Japan whose total product grew at 3.2 per cent per annum over the period 1870 to 1913. After allowing for population growth, Japanese real income per capita grew at the relatively high rate of 1.9 per cent per annum.

Changes in income levels have much to do with changes in demand and consequently with changes in the structure of output and the composition of foreign trade. As incomes rise, there is an increased demand for capital goods, manufactured consumer goods, and services, and a relatively slow expansion in demand for food, textiles and clothing. Moreover, rising living standards, involving as they do changes in tastes, incomes and, consequently, in consumption patterns, not only influence the structure of domestic output but also affect the volume and composition of foreign trade. Thus, the shift in the diet of the United States and other Western nations from cereals towards meat and dairy products as the standard of living rose was important both for the domestic producers of these commodities and for the trade flows that existed between these countries. Another example associated with the rise in real incomes is the increased demand for colonial products. Items of trade, such as sugar, tobacco, tea, coffee, and cocoa, largely luxuries to previous generations, came to be regarded as necessities during the nineteenth century, while the consumption of tropical fruits also became important for the first time towards the end of this period.

The particular importance of the influence of per capita income levels on trade in manufactured goods has been stressed by S. B. Linder, who argues that exports can be developed only in those products for which there is a significant home market. In other words, countries typically export goods that fit into the standard of living attained by broad numbers of their own population. This certainly appears to have been the case with the manufactured consumer and producer goods exported by Britain during the nineteenth century, and it also fits the experience of most other countries too. Moreover, as C. P. Kindleberger has pointed out, Linder's theory may also apply to declining export markets. Thus, Britain lost the market for low-grade cotton textiles primarily because of foreign competition but partly because her living standards had risen to the point where these goods were unimportant items of consumption and domestic demand had shifted to higher qualities. On the other hand, the Japanese invasion of this export market was achieved by a textile industry which was supported by a growing domestic demand for low-grade cotton cloth. Linder's hypothesis that trade flows are related to the world structure of per capita incomes also leads us to expect large volumes of trade among nations with high per capita incomes and small trade flows between rich and poor countries, which is exactly what has tended to happen over the past 200 years or so. The general validity of Linder's theory has yet to be established empirically, but as the above necessarily limited observations show, it does have an attractive plausibility, particularly as an explanation of the rapid growth of trade in manufactures between high income countries.[5]

THE SPREAD OF ECONOMIC FREEDOM

The period between 1820 and 1913 was characterized by the gradual liberalization of controls over the flows of capital, labour and trade that were to link the countries of the world more closely together as the nineteenth century progressed. The gradual removal of restrictions on the movement of people, both within and between countries, while encouraging international migration, also gave to these movements of population their distinctive feature, namely, their quality as a free movement of individuals, almost entirely without control from either the receiving or sending countries and undertaken almost entirely by single individual or family units. Controls over financial transactions were also minimal. Short- and long-term capital could move unsupervised in any direction and these movements could take any form. Direct foreign investment was undertaken, and was often encouraged by the governments of the receiving countries. Foreign securities were freely traded on most stock exchanges. Repatriation of profits was unhampered, and the fear of confiscation of foreign investment almost completely absent. In the form of gold coins, foreign currencies mixed freely with the domestic currencies of many countries. Moreover, like migration, individuals (and enterprises) dominated international financial and commercial transactions before 1914, and only rarely were dealings conducted among countries acting as a whole. Finally, whereas international trade had to overcome tariffs during the latter part of the nineteenth century, these were exceedingly low by comparison with those introduced during the interwar years. Furthermore, quotas, import prohibitions and other quantitative restrictions on trade hardly existed before 1913, nor did ideas of economic self-sufficiency, towards the furtherance of which these restrictions on trade were often introduced.

   This increase in the degree and extent of economic freedom obviously contributed greatly to bringing about the formation of an international economy during the nineteenth century, although the true extent of that contribution is difficult to measure, because the spread of economic freedom was only one factor operating simultaneously with many others, and because in many instances its influence was dependent on the existence of these other factors for its full realization. For example, increased freedom to move was not in itself sufficient to generate mass migration, for, amongst other things, migration also depended on the existence of cheap and speedy transport facilities. This general conclusion is equally true of all the other influences at work taken individually. What is also apparent, however, is that, taken together, these influences brought about the powerful expansion of foreign trade, capital flows and population movements by means of which the integration of the international economy was achieved during the nineteenth century.

THE GROWTH OF INTERNATIONAL TRADE

Before turning to a consideration of the forging of the international links of capital, men and trade that constituted the growth of the international economy in the period since 1820, it is necessary to say something about the growth of foreign trade itself as a major cause of the economic growth of nations. In most countries export growth was a very powerful promoter of domestic economic growth and development. What is also clear from Table 4, which describes the long-run growth of the greater part of the world export trade over the period 1820 to 1989, is that the pace of world economic growth is very closely tied to the rate at which world trade grew during these years.

In the years up to 1913, the growth of world trade, as measured by the increase in the volume of exports of the world's leading industrial nations, averaged around 4 per cent per annum. It plummeted to a mere 1 per cent in the period 1913 to 1950, when two world wars and a worldwide depression severely restricted international trade. There followed a massive expansion of world trade in the third quarter of the twentieth century to reach a level more than twice that achieved in the period before 1913, as foreign trade restrictions were removed and the world experienced a period of sustained prosperity. In the economically-difficult years after 1973 the rate of growth of world trade slowed down considerably. Nevertheless, it still recorded a level somewhat higher than that reached in the years before 1913.

The final two rows of Table 4 show, respectively, the arithmetic average of the growth rates of the export trade of the 16 countries included in the table and the arithmetic average of the growth rates of Real Gross Domestic Product (GDP) of the same 16 countries. Comparing the two sets of data it can be seen that total output and the volume of exports move together, with export growth rates always higher than output growth rates, except in the period 1913 to 1950, when trade grew at half the pace of output as countries, under the impact of war and economic depression, increasingly depended on domestic production to satisfy their economic and wartime needs.

Table 4 Growth of world exports and world production, 1820–1996

Country	Annual average compound rates of growth					
	1820–70	1870–1913	1913–50	1950–73	1973–89	1990–96
Australia		4.8	1.3	5.8	4.5	8.0
Austria	4.7	3.5	–3.0	10.8	6.1	3.3
Belgium	5.4[a]	4.2	0.3	9.4	4.4	4.5
Canada		4.1	3.1	7.0	4.8	8.3
Denmark	1.9[b]	3.3	2.4	6.9	4.7	3.2
Finland		3.9	1.9	7.2	3.4	7.3
France	4.0	2.8	1.1	8.2	4.6	4.2
Germany	4.8[c]	4.1	–2.8	12.4	4.7	4.2
Italy	3.4	2.2	0.6	11.7	4.9	5.9
Japan		8.5	2.0	15.4	6.8	1.0
Netherlands		2.3[d]	1.5	10.3	3.6	4.1
Norway		3.2	2.7	7.3	6.7	5.8
Sweden		3.1	2.8	7.0	3.1	6.5
Switzerland	4.1	3.9	0.3	8.1	3.8	2.2
United Kingdom	4.9	2.8	0.0	3.9	3.9	5.0
United States	4.7	4.9	2.2	6.3	4.7	6.5
Arithmetic average, exports	4.2	3.9	1.0	8.6	4.7	5.0
Arithmetic growth of GDP	2.4	2.5	2.0	4.9	2.6	1.6

Sources: Angus Maddison, Dynamic Forces in Capitalist Development (Oxford, 1991), Table 3.2, p. 50 and Table 3.15, p. 75; World Trade Organization, International Trade, 1997; IMF, World Economic Outlook, May 1998, Table A3.

Notes:
a 1831–70; b 1844–70; c 1840–70; d 1872–1913.
The last column measures changes in exports of goods and services.

NOTES

1 Even so, certain other influences could offset the trade-reducing impact of the innovation. Thus, the Germans were responsible for a long series of major discoveries which led to synthetic dyes replacing those made from vegetable products. But the fact that by 1900 German producers controlled some 90 per cent of the world market in dyestuffs indicated a substantial increase of trade in the synthetic product, since consumers of dyestuffs in other countries were mainly dependent on German sources of supply.
2 For details of the available estimates of capital formation, see S. Kuznets, Modern Economic Growth (New Haven, 1966), pp. 75–81. The countries covered include Britain, Belgium, Norway, West Germany, the United States, Australia and Japan.
3 Difficulties of measurement arise for many reasons. For example, acreage will not do for land, since different areas of land vary significantly in their climatic features,

location and natural fertility. Moreover, once land is worked it becomes impossible to separate it from other factors, and especially from capital. Measurement over time is complicated by the fact that technical change may alter the economic value, if not the physical characteristics, of a given resource. Thus petroleum deposits became much more valuable following the invention of the motor-car. Finally, the fact that resource discovery and depletion may take place simultaneously makes it hard to decide whether the supply of natural resources available to a particular country has increased over time or not.

4 J. V. Levin, *The Export Economies* (Cambridge, Mass., 1960), Chap. IV.

5 S. Burenstam Linder, *An Essay on Trade and Transformation* (New York, 1961), especially Chap. 3. See also Kindleberger, *Foreign Trade and the National Economy* (New Haven, 1962), pp. 58–9. In a number of ways Linder's theory succeeds where the factor proportions theory fails. This is particularly so with respect to prediction of trade flows, where emphasis on differences in factor proportions lead to the false predictions of a large flow of trade between rich and poor countries, and declining trade among industrial countries.

SELECTED REFERENCES

Ashworth, W., *A Short History of the International Economy since 1850* (London, 1962), Chaps. 1–VI.

Habbakuk, H. J., and Postan, M. (eds.), *The Cambridge Economic History of Europe*, Vol. VI, 'The Industrial Revolutions and After, Part 1' (Cambridge, 1965), Chaps. I–IV.

Harley, C. K., 'Ocean Freight Rates and Productivity 1740–1913. The Primacy of Mechanical Inventions Reaffirmed', *Journal of Economic History* (Dec., 1988), pp. 851–76.

Headrick, D. R., *The Tools of Empire. Technology and European Imperialism in the Nineteenth Century* (Oxford, 1981).

Headrick, D. R., *The Tentacles of Progress. Technology Transfer in the Age of Imperialism, 1850–1940* (Oxford, 1988).

Kindleberger, C. P., *Foreign Trade and the National Economy* (New Haven, 1962).

Maddison, A., *Dynamic Forces in Capitalist Development* (Oxford, 1991).

Maddison, A., *Monitoring the World Economy, 1820–1992* (Paris, OECD, 1994).

North, D. C., 'Ocean Freight Rates and Economic Development 1750–1913', *Journal of Economic History* (Dec., 1958), pp. 537–55.

Woodruff, W., *Impact of Western Man* (New York, 1966), Chaps. V and VI.

Chapter 2

International long-term capital movements, 1820–1913

Specialization in production along the lines of comparative advantage was a major feature of the nineteenth-century international economy, and it was brought about partly by the mobility of capital (and labour) from country to country. In particular, the outflows of men and money from Europe to the vast, fertile and mineral-rich continents overseas helped provide the increased supplies of foodstuffs and raw materials needed to feed Europe's growing population and industry. Consequently the growth of trade and real income in the world economy that occurred at this time was determined in part by an international redistribution of capital and labour on a scale unique in history. Thus, during the century ending in 1913 some £9–10,000m. were invested abroad and some 45–46m. people moved overseas. This movement of capital and population from regions where they were relatively abundant to regions where they were relatively scarce was a necessary condition for the expansion of the international economy.

International movements of capital occur when the residents of one country acquire assets in another (or reduce their liabilities there). Transactions of this sort can occur in a number of ways. For example, a resident in Britain may purchase securities in an American business or the bonds of an American government; or he may export goods to the United States and leave the proceeds on deposit in that country; or, if he owns a business in the United States, he may 'plough back' the profits of the enterprise instead of withdrawing them as dividends. What all these transactions have in common is the fact that some person (an individual or a firm) resident in Britain acquires either the paper assets of, or property ownership rights in, the United States.

One basic distinction between different types of international capital movements is that between long- and short-term transactions. This distinction gives rise to problems of definition, but these can be safely ignored here by assuming that the foreign long-term capital investment discussed in this chapter consists of capital invested in the expectation that the investment will not be liquidated in the near future and that it will earn income over an appreciable period.[1] While it is our intention here to concentrate on an examination of foreign long-term capital movements in the nineteenth century, the methods adopted in compiling the estimates of foreign investment used in this chapter are such that the figures may occasionally include short- as well as long-term capital flows. This fact, however, does not weaken in any way the analysis that follows.

THE GROWTH OF FOREIGN INVESTMENT

At the beginning of the nineteenth century the total value of foreign investment was small, and its economic impact on both the borrowing and lending countries insignificant. It was a business activity undertaken almost exclusively by a few privileged European trading and financial organizations with foreign interests. From the end of the Napoleonic Wars, however, foreign investment assumed a new character and an increasing significance. This change came about for a number of reasons. The establishment and growth of specialized financial institutions in both borrowing and lending countries, such as commercial banks (operating in foreign exchange) and investment houses, made foreign investment easier and less risky, while the accumulation of savings by a middle class willing to invest them abroad supplied the funds needed for an expansion of foreign lending. The flow of funds from savers in one country to borrowers in another was also facilitated by the appearance of more sophisticated financial instruments, such as credit money and bills of exchange. In addition, capital markets, such as 'the City' in London, became much more diversified in their business dealings, thereby aiding the expansion of international trade and the growth of foreign investment.

From the end of the Napoleonic Wars until the mid-1850s about £420m. ($2,050m.) was invested abroad. By 1870 the total value of these investments had more than trebled. But the great era of international lending occurred after 1870, with the capital outflow becoming a flood during the decade before World War I. By 1900 foreign investments totalled £4,750m. ($23,000m.), and they rose rapidly during the next few years to reach £9,500m. ($43,000m.) in 1914.[2]

DIRECTION OF FOREIGN INVESTMENT

Capital exporting countries

Britain was the major source of supply of foreign capital during the nineteenth century, and France another foreign lender of substance during these years. After 1870, however, when the outflow of loanable funds from the capital-rich countries accelerated tremendously, Germany and the United States became major investing countries and, by 1914, together accounted for one-fifth of the total value of the assets owned abroad by all the capital exporting nations. Belgium, the Netherlands, and Switzerland formed another important group of countries willing to place large surplus savings at the disposal of investors in other countries. But as Figure 1(a) demonstrates, Britain remained by far the most important single source of foreign funds after 1870, with a record as a foreign lender unsurpassed in the whole history of international investment. Thus, between 1870 and 1914 the annual outflow of capital from Britain for investment overseas averaged approximately 4 per cent of national income. Even more striking is the fact that the annual outflow of capital from Britain averaged close to 7 per cent of her national income over the years 1905 to 1913, and reached a phenomenal 9 per cent in the latter year.[3]

Capital importing countries

Figure 1(b) shows the distribution of foreign investments in 1914 by recipient region. From it we see that Europe received the largest slice of this investment. Most European countries received some capital from abroad at one time or another during the nineteenth century, but by 1914 Russia and the Balkans (including Turkey) were the major borrowers, mainly from France and Germany. Next in order of size of capital inflow was North America. Two-thirds of its share went to the United States, and the remainder

Figure 1(a) Distribution of foreign investments, 1914, by investing regions

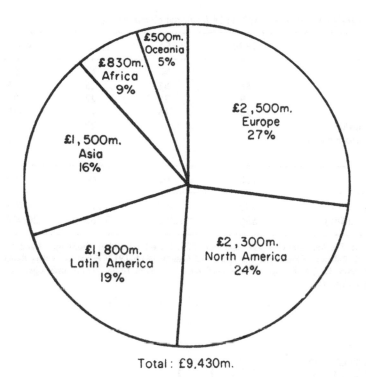

£500m.
Oceania
5%

£830m.
Africa
9%

£2,500m.
Europe
27%

£1,500m.
Asia
16%

£1,800m.
Latin America
19%

£2,300m.
North America
24%

Total: £9,430m.

Figure 1(b) Distribution of foreign investments, 1914, by recipient regions

Source: W. Woodruff, *Impact of Western Man* (London, 1966), pp. 154–5.

went to Canada. Argentina, Brazil and Mexico were the most attractive countries in Latin America for foreign investors, and together they accounted for over 80 per cent of the foreign capital directed to that region. In Asia the bulk of funds went to India, Ceylon, China and Japan, each of which received £200m. or more. By 1914, the Union of South Africa had absorbed approximately 60 per cent of the total funds entering Africa. Egypt accounted for another quarter to a third, and the colonies of Britain, France, Germany and Belgium for most of the remainder. Australia was the major recipient of funds exported to Oceania. If the countries comprising the 'regions of recent settlement'—the United States, Canada, Argentina, Uruguay, South Africa, Australia and New Zealand—are taken together, they absorbed about 40 per cent of the capital invested abroad by 1914.

Changing Direction of Investment

Table 5 and Figure 2 show the changing geographical pattern of British foreign investment over the period 1830 to 1914. The bulk of Britain's

Table 5 British foreign investment, 1830–1914 (regional distribution)

	1830	1854	1870	1914
	%	%	%	%
Europe	66	55	25	5
United States	9	25	27	21
Latin America	23	15	11	18
British Empire: India			22	9
Dominions	2	5	12	37
Other regions			3	9
Total	100	100	100	100
Total investment (£m.)	100	260	770	4,107
($m.)	536	1,266	3,750	20,000

Sources: L. H. Jenks, *The Migration of British Capital to 1875*, 3rd edn. (London, 1963), pp. 64 and 413; A. H. Imlah, 'British Balance of Payments and Export of Capital 1816–1913', *Economic History Review*, (August 1952), pp. 208–39; C. H. Feinstein, *Home and Foreign Investment, 1870–1973* (Cambridge, 1960); W. Woodruff, op. cit., pp. 154–5.

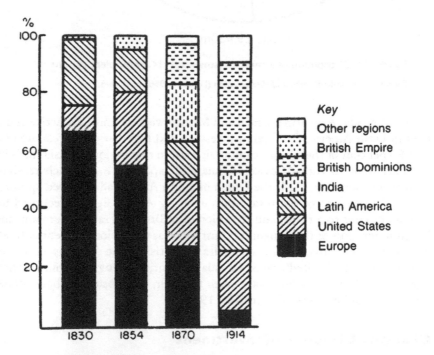

Figure 2 British foreign investment, 1830–1914 (regional distribution)
Sources: As for Table 5.

foreign investment in 1830 was to be found in Europe and Latin America, where British lending during the 1820s had been used primarily to stabilize currencies and to maintain the political *status quo*. In addition, the boom of the mid-1820s in Britain had stimulated substantial direct investment in Latin American mining activity. In the late 1820s, however, financial reverses in Europe and Latin America left much of the newly incurred debt in default, and consequently the British investor turned his attention to the United States, where canal and railway building financed by the issue of state and municipal securities created a demand for foreign funds. Unfortunately, North America proved little more reliable than South America as a borrower, and in the difficult years that followed the financial panic of 1837, the state governments were forced to stop interest payments and two states repudiated their debts outright. As a result of these further financial set-backs, and because domestic economic activity was running at a high level after 1845, interest in foreign investment waned in Britain during the 1840s, although the domestic railway boom of the mid-decade did give rise to railway construction by British contractors in Europe and the colonies. By the mid-1850s, therefore, the distribution of Britain's overseas investment had changed significantly. The share of the total to be found in Europe and in Latin America had declined, while that of the United States had increased substantially. The flow of funds to the rest of the world continued to be insignificant.

Between the mid-1850s and 1870 another major change in the regional distribution of British capital occurred. Empire countries increasingly attracted British funds away from Europe and Latin America, whereas the United States was barely able to maintain its relative share of the total capital outflow from Britain. These changing preferences of British investors were neither fortuitous nor largely the outcome of conscious political planning on the part of the investing country. Rather, they were the result of the changing circumstances confronting British railway builders and investors on the Continent who found their profits being squeezed by increasing competition from French, Belgian, and German entrepreneurs. In addition, the unsettled conditions in the United States prior to, and during, the Civil War combined to turn the British investor away from that country. By 1870 Empire countries accounted for a third of all British foreign investments. Investment had been heaviest in India, where some £95m. was invested in railways alone between 1845 and 1875, but the volume of investment in Canada, Australia and New Zealand was also growing during these years.

The trend towards investment in Empire countries intensified to such an extent after 1870 that close to one-half of the total British capital abroad in 1914 was located in these countries, with the bulk of it invested in the Dominion countries. Australasia during the 1880s and Canada after 1904 were the most attractive Empire regions for British investors during this period, while India's relative share declined considerably. The United States continued to receive a high proportion of British capital outflow, chiefly in the form of portfolio investment in railroad companies, and Latin American countries, especially Argentina and, to a lesser extent, Brazil, once again gained favour in the London capital market. On the other hand, Britain's European investments had become relatively unimportant by 1914, chiefly because the Continent had become better able to supply its own capital needs, and while the percentage share going to the rest of the world had trebled between 1870 and 1914, in absolute terms its amount remained small.[4]

French foreign investment during the period 1816 to 1851 amounted to 2,500m. francs (£98m.), the bulk of which was to be found in Spain, the Italian States and Belgium. There was some French investment in the United States in the late 1830s, but French capital played only a minor role in development there before 1880. Europe continued to absorb the largest share of the French capital outflow in the 30 years after 1851, while the Ottoman Empire and Egypt also emerged as major borrowers at this time. About a third of the new capital was invested in railway building, particularly in the Iberian and Italian peninsulas, in Central Europe, and in Russia. A large part of the foreign government loans was lost in the defaults of the 1870s, with losses particularly severe in the Near East, but by the early 1880s a revival of French foreign investment was well under way.

In the subsequent period up to 1914, the direction of the outflow of investible funds from France changed radically, as Table 6 and Figure 3 illustrate. The Mediterranean, Near Eastern, and Central European countries

Table 6 French foreign investment, 1851–1914 (regional distribution)

Region	Total investment as in:					
	1851		*1881*		*1914*	
	F.000m.	%	F.000m.	%	F.000m.	%
Mediterranean [1]	1.5	60	6.9	39	7.3	14
Central Europe [2]	0.3	12	3.1	18	4.1	9
Eastern Europe [3]	—	—	1.3	7	14.7	28
North-West Europe [4]	0.6	24	1.2	7	4.1	8
Near East [5]	—	—	3.5	20	5.9	11
Colonies	—	—	0.7	4	4.5	9
Western Hemisphere	0.1	4	0.9	5	8.3	16
Other regions	—	—	—	—	3.8	6
Totals (F.000m.)	2.5	100	17.6	100	52.7	100
(£m.)	98		688		2,073	

Source: R. E. Cameron, *France and the Economic Development of Europe 1800–1914* (Princeton, 1961), pp. 79, 85 and 486.

Notes: 1. Italy, Spain, Portugal. 2. Austro-Hungary, Germany, Switzerland. 3. Russia, Rumania, Greece, Serbia. 4. Belgium, Luxembourg, Netherlands, United Kingdom, Scandinavia. 5. Ottoman Empire and Egypt.

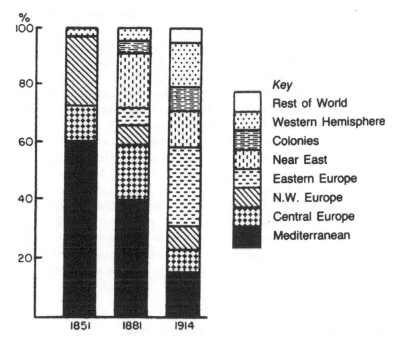

Figure 3 French foreign investment, 1851–1914 (regional distribution)

Source: As for Table 6.

lost their previous attractions for French investors who transferred their attentions towards Russia and the Balkans. In addition, from the late 1890s, non-European countries, chiefly in Latin America, increased their relative share of the available funds. In contrast to the attitudes of British investors, the French colonies were not considered favourably by French capital owners, and only Algeria, and to a lesser extent Indo-China, received the benefits of capital inflow. By 1914, therefore, approximately three-fifths of the total French capital outflow was located in Europe, 16 per cent in the Americas, and slightly more in Asia, chiefly in Turkey.

German foreign investment only assumed significance in the 1880s, when government securities issued by the Balkan countries, Turkey, Spain, Portugal and Italy, were subscribed to in Germany at a time when Paris hesitated to lend in these directions. In addition, loans were extended to Argentina, Venezuela and Mexico, and United States railroad bonds were also popular. Following the defaults associated with the financial crises of the 1890s, German foreign lending declined until the early years of this century when the German investor turned away from Europe and towards the United States and the German colonies. By 1914 about half the German foreign investments had been absorbed by European countries, with Austria-Hungary accounting for a substantial part of this capital, and the rest being fairly evenly spread over Russia, Turkey, the Balkans, Spain, Portugal, France and Britain. Of the 11,000m. marks (£540m.) invested outside Europe, about 70 per cent went to the Americas and Africa, and Asia (especially the German colonies there) obtained most of the remainder.

Before 1870, United States foreign investment was little more than $75m. (£15m.), and was mostly confined to direct investment in mining and manufacturing ventures in Canada, Mexico, and South America. By 1899, however, investment in Europe had considerable attractions for American businesses and 80 per cent of the $685m. (£140m.) held abroad, mainly in the form of direct investment, was located in Canada, Mexico and Europe. This proportion of total foreign placements of funds declined progressively after 1899 to 66 per cent in 1914, when the total United States foreign investment reached $3,514m. (£717m.). During this period of greatly accelerating foreign investment, South America and Asia became important recipients of United States direct investment. Manufacturing, the mining of industrial metals, and agricultural enterprises consumed the bulk of the capital outflow.

DETERMINANTS OF CAPITAL OUTFLOW

Before a country could undertake a massive foreign investment programme a number of conditions had to be fulfilled. First, a considerable degree of economic growth had to be achieved in the country to ensure that domestic savings were accumulated fast enough to provide the surplus of funds. Second, there had to exist abroad a number of government or business enterprises willing and anxious to borrow, or alternatively, numerous opportunities for profitable business ventures for direct investment. Third, some form of machinery was required to ensure that the transfer of funds from savers in one country to borrowers in another proceeded with a minimum of friction—in other words, a fairly diversified capital market was needed and one capable of undertaking foreign investment. Finally, an incentive to invest abroad had to present itself.

Undoubtedly the prospect of earning a higher rate of return on one's investment by placing it abroad rather than at home is a major determinant of the volume of foreign lending. For this reason we would expect to find that investment abroad tends to increase at times when domestic economic activity in the capital exporting country is depressed and investment at home is thus relatively unprofitable. On the other hand, investment in foreign extractive and other industries could be expected to rise at a time when business activity in the industrial capital exporting country was high and incomes rising, since foreign resources required tapping to feed domestic industries with raw materials and income earners required greater quantities of imported consumer goods, especially foodstuffs. However, attempts to establish statistically the nature of the relationship between expected rates of return and their effects on the volume of investment at home and abroad have not been very successful.[5] This is probably because of the very simple models used in these tests, which fail to consider the many other influences, including political factors, acting upon capital flows. Even so, changes in relative interest rates and rates of return on investments in the capital exporting and capital importing countries—after allowance for changing risk premiums—must have been important determinants of both the willingness to invest abroad and the desire and ability to borrow abroad during the nineteenth century.[6]

Another important determinant of the volume and direction of foreign investment during these years was the growth and altering structure of the international economy. The industrialization of Europe and the growth of its population created a steadily growing demand for raw materials and foodstuffs, much of which had to be imported. At the same time, important advances in technical knowledge, especially in transportation and communications, and the existence of underpopulated and land-rich countries in other continents provided the means whereby these demands could be met. The greater part of the foreign investment undertaken during the nineteenth century was concerned with promoting this international specialization between an industrial centre located in Europe (and, later, in the United States) and a periphery of primary producing countries. Apart from being suppliers of foodstuffs and raw materials, these peripheral countries were also important markets for manufactured goods. Their significance as markets provided another incentive for investment in them, especially after 1880, when, because of the industrialization of Germany and the United States and the spread of protection, Britain lost many of her traditional export markets in Europe and North America. Increasingly during these years British foreign investment was directed to the Empire, which also now became one of its most important export markets.

The amount of technical and capital assistance that can be used effectively by a country is often spoken of as its capacity to absorb capital. Obviously, while it is not possible to measure exactly what the 'absorptive capacity' of an individual country is at a particular time, it is possible to list certain conditions that are necessary for the productive utilization of capital, whether of domestic or foreign origin. Absorption capacity will be low, for example, when there are inadequate transport facilities, administrative and organizational bottlenecks, deficient qualities of entrepreneurship, a lack of complementary natural resources, scarcities of trained manpower, narrow localized markets, and so on. In respect of these conditions during the nineteenth century some countries, notably the United States, Canada, Australia, Argentina, Brazil, and a number of European countries, were better placed than others, for example, China, India, Egypt, and most of Africa. It is not surprising therefore to find that by 1913 almost two-thirds of the total foreign investment undertaken during the nineteenth century was to be found in the first-mentioned group of countries, whose capacity to absorb this capital was helped by the international flows of labour that accompanied these movements of foreign capital.

Institutional developments and the spread of protectionism were other important influences at work determining the volume and direction of foreign investment, especially after 1870. The growth and development of financial institutions in both lending and borrowing countries, the movement towards free trade by the 1870s (although reversed in later decades), and the establishment of the gold standard, all contributed in varying degrees to the marshalling of domestic savings in lending countries, the rapid transfer of these funds to borrowing countries, and the relatively efficient distribution of the acquired loans to the investors in the latter countries. Especially after the 1870s, foreign direct investment expanded for yet another reason, namely, to avoid high tariffs on imports by setting up factories in the tariff-raising countries. This was largely the reason for German direct investments in the United States, Russia, and a number of other European countries, for British direct investments in Europe and the United States, and for American investments in Canada and Europe.

Finally, political factors influenced foreign investment in a number of ways. Before 1850, British loans to Greece, Belgium and several Latin American republics were made partly because of the sympathy existing in Britain for the rebel states. However, this attitude did not prevent the British investor from advancing loans to other European governments for counter-revolutionary purposes or for other uses aimed at preserving the *status quo* in European politics. The pattern of French investment before 1850 was also largely determined by political considerations, as well as geographical proximity and cultural and religious affinities to the borrowing countries. In these years 95 per cent of French holdings of foreign government securities were those of Spain, Portugal, the Italian States, Belgium and Austria. After 1850, political considerations continued to exert some influence on the direction of foreign investment, but they became an important determinant only after 1890, when the need to build up military alliances in anticipation of a future power struggle led to numerous foreign loans being negotiated. The French invested heavily in Russian government securities, and by 1914 10,000m. francs (£390m.) was owed to French investors. For similar reasons, Russia also received substantial British loans in the years leading up to 1914. Much German investment at this time went to Austria-Hungary and certain of the Balkan countries. Moreover, the political rivalry which arose in Europe late in the nineteenth century manifested itself in a burst of imperialism and rapid colonization in much of Africa and Asia. This development was accompanied by a flow of funds into these regions either to exploit their natural resources or to establish European control over them.

THE USE OF FOREIGN FUNDS IN BORROWING COUNTRIES

During the nineteenth century, foreign investment went into three major fields: government loans, transport and communications, and manufacturing and extractive industries. Compared with most other capital-importing regions, European borrowing tended to be dominated by government loans. Frequently, in the first half of the century, these loans were used to support the extravagance or inefficiency of courts and governments, or for war, defence, insurrection, or counter-revolutionary purposes. Towards the end of the century, as the European power struggle gathered force, loans from the west European capital exporters to the governments of Russia, central Europe, and the Balkans tended once again to be utilized mainly for military purposes. Of greater economic significance, however, was the heavy investment in railway construction. From the 1840s the desire of railway builders, at first in Britain, and later in France and Germany, to cover the European continent with a railway network, provided most European countries with the usual economic (and military) benefits to be derived from improved transportation.

Foreign investment in railways was also important for the opening up of other continents. By 1914, $4,000m. (57 per cent) of the total United States foreign debt of $7,000m. was in the form of railway securities held abroad, more than half of them in Britain. The British also invested heavily in Indian, Canadian and Australian railways; while in Latin America, Asia and Africa railway building absorbed a large share of the investment funds flowing from Britain and Europe to these regions in the period after 1870. In addition to providing many countries with more unified domestic markets, this railway investment accelerated their integration into the international economy by allowing cheap and rapid transport, of commodities produced in the interior of each country, to the seaboard for shipment abroad. In this way international capital movements provided the basis for an expanding foreign trade.

If other forms of investment in public works were of minor significance when compared with the railways, they were nevertheless important to many countries. The provision of port facilities was a valuable supplement to the railway construction in the Great Plains regions. Canals were built in the United States in the 1820s and 1830s largely with the aid of British capital, and the provision of water and sewerage, roads, bridges, public buildings, telegraph and telephone facilities, gas and electricity financed with foreign funds formed important services for the inhabitants of countries which were experiencing the general benefits of expanding international investment.

For the most part the flow of funds into the manufacturing and extractive industries took the form of direct investment, the extent of which was small in the years before 1870. British capital and enterprise were involved in textile and iron manufacturing on the Continent at this time, and there was also some British capital invested in mining activities in Sweden, Italy and, later, Spain. French industrial investments were concentrated largely in Belgium and Germany, where they were to be found in mining, the metal-lurgical industries and glass manufacture. After 1870, however, the level of foreign investment in manufacturing and mining increased substantially. In Europe, Germany and France invested heavily in a wide range of manufacturing and mining enterprises in Austria, Italy, Spain and Sweden, but the most striking benefits to be derived from direct investment in Europe accrued to Russia, where a number of industries, including chemicals, metal fabricating, textiles and metal refining were financed by foreign capital after 1880. Foreign investment in oil production, and copper, gold and lead mining also contributed significantly to Russian development. As a result, Russia recorded one of the highest annual average rates of growth of gross national product in Europe between 1870 and 1914.

In the United States there was some private portfolio investment in manufacturing after 1870, where foreign investors, mainly British, contributed funds to such firms as U.S. Steel, Eastman Kodak, United Fruit Company, and General Electric. Direct investment by British, Belgian, and Dutch firms also went into American oil production, especially after 1901. In Canada, American direct investment expanded production in several spheres of manufacturing, chiefly steel, sugar refining, paper and pulp, and mineral refining.

Direct investment in mining and manufacturing also occurred in Latin America and, to a lesser extent, in Australasia and parts of Asia. But these investments remained of minor significance when compared with the much heavier foreign industrial investment in Europe and North America. Even in the latter continents, however, the importance of this type of investment should not be exaggerated. As we have already seen, the bulk of foreign lending went into railways and other forms of social overhead capital. Consequently, if foreign lending was of any great significance to the industrial development of the borrowing countries, it made its main contribution indirectly, in the sense that better transport facilities widened domestic markets and thereby encouraged the growth of manufacturing industry, and because the availability of foreign capital for investment in overhead capital meant that domestic capital resources were released for use in other forms of domestic economic activity, including manufacturing and mining.

In concluding this section a brief comment on foreign investment in primary production is relevant. British foreign investment in agricultural and pastoral industries tended to occur in an indirect manner, especially in Australasia and South America, where financial institutions, both British and domestic, accumulated savings through deposits in Britain and lent them to primary producers in the countries concerned. In addition, American direct investment was responsible for the establishment or expansion of agricultural industries in Canada, Mexico, Cuba and South America. Direct investment, of the colonial type, was instrumental in expanding plantation crops such as sugar, rubber, coffee, tea and cocoa, and in developing various mining ventures in Latin America, Africa, Asia, and Oceania. British, French and German investors were particularly active in these areas.

ECONOMIC CONSEQUENCES OF FOREIGN INVESTMENT

For capital-exporting countries there were risks involved in all types of investment, particularly those involving the postponement of interest payments and repudiation of debts. During several periods of the nineteenth century foreign investors either lost their capital through default or were compelled to wait many years before even interest payments were resumed. This happened to British investments in Europe and Latin America in the 1820s, in the United States in the 1830s, and in several areas of the world in the 1890s. French investors also burnt their fingers in the United States in the late 1830s and in Europe in the 1870s, and German investors were estimated to have lost through repudiation or default in the early 1890s as much as 10 per cent of their total capital abroad at the time.

The profitability of investing abroad to a large extent depended on the uses to which the funds were put in the recipient countries. If invested in economically useful and desirable fields, such as in overhead capital or in industrial enterprises located in the growth sectors of the borrowing economy, the likelihood of default was diminished (but not eliminated), for such investments favourably affected growth rates, and at the same time tended to expand exports (or more occasionally reduce imports), so that the means for paying income to foreign investors was provided by the use of the funds. Countries which 'wasted' their loans from abroad in uneconomic pursuits, such as wars, speculation, or to support the extravagance or inefficiency and corruption of courts and governments, tended on the whole not to provide such a mechanism for servicing the foreign debt. Thus, default or repudiation was often a virtual certainty. But while much foreign investment was lost in this way, the bulk of it was used productively, and the investment income from abroad, especially after 1870, was of such a size that it tended almost to equal or to exceed the total annual outflow of foreign capital. In other words, for most capital exporting countries during these years, and especially for Britain, the income receipts on past foreign investment provided the funds out of which new loans for foreign borrowers were provided.

The lending countries also received substantial indirect benefits from their foreign investments. For numerous non-European countries, foreign capital inflow led to an acceleration of international specialization of production, chiefly in the development of the Great Plains region. By lending surplus savings to these regions to set up railway systems and thereby directly effecting a rapid extension of the land frontier, European countries provided for themselves additional sources of supply of cheap foodstuffs and raw materials which ensured that the industrialization of their economies would take place with a minimum of friction and bottlenecks. Such benefits substantially outweighed the occasional losses through default and repudiation, for which irrational actions of the lenders themselves were partly to blame. Indeed, the speedy return of investors to foreign lending after each international financial crisis had passed is indicative of the benefits to be derived from such activity.

The benefits and costs of foreign investment to the investing country have been the subject of a continuing debate right up to the present. In particular, the question has been asked as to whether Britain's export of capital in the period before 1914, by limiting the availability of capital funds to domestic industry, was a major cause of the country's economic slowdown in the late nineteenth century and of its failure to exploit fully the new techniques emerging at that time. After an exhaustive review of the available evidence, Pollard concludes that it permits no clear-cut answer to the question whether benefits exceeded costs or vice versa.[7] In so far as such investment activity has a justifiable rationale, exporting capital to gain higher returns than can be earned at home may constitute an option for wealth now as against increasing domestic industrial strength and possibly greater wealth later. On the more general question of the overall costs and benefits of such investment, however, the studies undertaken to date have not produced an irrefutable conclusion one way or the other.

The economic impact of foreign lending on the capital-importing country depended on the uses to which the funds were put. In a number of countries capital inflows (accompanied by immigration) acted as a major force producing rapid and sustained economic growth so that by 1914 these countries were among the most economically, highly developed in the world. When countries used their foreign loans efficiently, the problem of servicing the debt incurred by borrowing, that is, of meeting the interest payments and the eventual repayment of the loan, was unlikely to produce any significant balance of payments difficulties. Thus over time, the only determinant of the borrowing country's capacity to repay was the loan's contribution to the productivity of the economy as a whole and the capacity of the system to skim away part of the increased productivity in taxes or pricing for transfer abroad. In so far as the loans to borrowing countries (largely primary producers) were used to increase the output of primary products and lower their costs of production, an expansion of exports could be expected which, as long as it grew faster than the long-run rate of growth of imports, would produce a balance of payments surplus out of which interest payments and debt redemptions could be met. Where foreign loans were wasted in uneconomic uses, balance of payments difficulties for the borrowing country were inevitable, followed by non-payment of interest on the debt and possibly even default.

Generally speaking, foreign investment bestowed other benefits upon many borrowing countries. It facilitated the diffusion of technological knowledge from the lending to the borrowing countries, thus increasing the likelihood of an increase in productivity. At the same time, the capital flows produced real flows of resources from lenders to borrowers by ensuring that the latter's imports of goods and services could continuously exceed exports for a considerable period of years. To the extent that capital goods increased relative to consumer goods in imports, the growth of productivity in the borrowing country was further enhanced. Thus, for many countries, the diversion of funds received into economically desirable avenues of investment assumed a major role in the development of their economies, even if, at times, the inflow exceeded the absorptive capacity of the industries concerned, and if, occasionally, sudden cessation of capital inflow led to short-run balance of payments crises. But as the loans made their impact felt on the economy and as each country's total production rose so too rose savings out of incomes. As time passed the rate of savings in many capital importing countries accelerated. Although for most countries the growth of domestic savings did not lead to a reduction of capital inflow, foreign capital tended on the whole to be used in certain different ways, especially in the provision of public works, so that the extra savings could be used to increase production in other sectors of the economy, for example, manufacturing and commerce. Nevertheless, there was often much overlapping of the two types of investment in certain industries. It remains true, however, that the ability of domestic income earners to accumulate savings stemmed in part from the use of foreign funds in the economy.

Finally, direct investment made some contribution to the growth of production in a number of countries. This was a particularly attractive form of foreign investment activity for industrializing countries in the nineteenth century because it provided a combination of capital with technological know-how and entrepreneurial ability. In the early stages of industrialization in both Europe and North America this type of investment played an important and valuable part. In primary producing countries, however, particularly those in Asia, Latin America, and Africa, the concentration of direct investment in export industries, such as plantation crops and mining, in general did little to improve local living standards, and most of the benefits derived from such ventures tended to accrue to the foreign investors in the capital-exporting countries.

With the exception of government loans used for military purposes and those frittered away on the upkeep of courts and other royal extravagances, the international capital flows in the nineteenth century aided the economic growth of both borrowing and lending countries. The recipient countries used the capital to construct social overhead capital and to increase their output of export products. The lending countries were at the same time able to intensify their movement towards industrialization by ensuring rapidly growing supplies of cheap raw materials to feed their factories, and of cheap foodstuffs for their increasing urban populations. The receipts of interest and dividend payments by the capital exporting countries rapidly grew to such levels as to provide a revolving fund out of which further capital was quickly made available for re-investment abroad. Although the mechanism of international investment occasionally broke down, when the whole period before 1914 is considered, the international flows of capital, and the benefits this investment produced in the form of high rates of economic growth in many countries and a rapidly rising volume of international trade, constituted one of the most significant forces at work in welding together the international economy during these years.

NOTES

1 Conventionally, capital lent for less than one year is said to be short-term; that lent for longer than this is described as long-term. The chief difficulty found in implementing this seemingly simple and clear-cut distinction is that the form of the commercial instrument used is not an entirely reliable guide for allocative purposes. Thus, nominally long-term investments, such as government bonds, may in fact be held for short periods if they are readily marketable. This has led some writers to think of the distinction in terms of the investor's motives. The definition used above is conceived largely in these terms.

   Long-term investment may also be classified into 'direct' and 'portfolio'. Direct investment occurs when a company in one country sets up a subsidiary, or acquires a controlling interest in a domestic business, in another country. Portfolio investment consists of capital flows from one country to another over the use of which the investors do not have any control, for instance investment in foreign government loans, in the purchase of a small proportion of share capital in a foreign company, or deposits in foreign financial institutions.

2 The total value of foreign investments is the gross amount owed by other countries to lending countries. Some lenders, for instance, the United States, were net borrowers during the period, since they borrowed much larger amounts of foreign capital than they lent abroad themselves.

3 In recent years, the conventional estimates of British foreign investment up to 1914 have been questioned (see, in particular, D. C. M. Platt, *Britain's Investment Overseas on the Eve of the First World War, The Use and Abuse of Numbers* (London, 1986). While Platt rightly stresses the distinction between investment *flows* over time and the *stock* of foreign investment at a point in time, he concentrates on the latter and argues that, in 1870, the stock of British foreign investment was £500m. as against the conventional estimate of £770m., and that, more importantly, in 1914, the total was £3,100m. and not £4,100m. Platt's approach has been criticized by W. P. Kennedy (see his review of Platt's book in *Economic History Review* (June, 1987), pp. 307–9). According to Kennedy, Platt does not appreciate fully the quality of Paish's work, too rapidly dismisses alternative evidence, and is

reluctant to undertake a serious examination of important sources of new evidence. Charles Feinstein has also questioned Platt's estimates and suggests that the 'true' figure would be much closer to the conventional estimate than to that of Platt (see his 'Britain's Overseas Investments in 1913', *Economic History Review* (June, 1990), pp. 288–95). Accepting these latter views, we have used the conventional estimates in this chapter.

4 It should be noted, however, that in the late nineteenth century an increasing volume of Continental funds found their way to the London capital market for investment chiefly in foreign issues and in shares quoted on the London Stock Exchange. See, for example, Ranald Michie, 'Different in Name Only? The London Stock Exchange and Foreign Bourses, c. 1850–1914', *Business History* (Jan., 1988), pp. 60–3, and L. E. Davis and R. A. Huttenback, *Mammon and the Pursuit of Empire, the Political Economy of British Imperialism* (Cambridge, 1986).

5 See, for example, A. I. Bloomfield, *Patterns of Fluctuation in International Investment before 1914*, Princeton Studies in International Finance, No. 21 (Princeton, 1968), especially pp. 35–40.

6 The relationship between capital movements and the terms of trade, which forms one aspect of this problem of relative rates of return in capital exporting and capital importing countries, is discussed in Chapter 10, pp. 155–9.

7 See Sidney Pollard, 'Capital Exports, 1870–1914: Harmful or Beneficial?', *Economic History Review* (Nov., 1985), pp. 489–514.

SELECTED REFERENCES

Business History Review (Autumn, 1974), especially articles by Franko and Stopford.

Cairncross, A. K., *Home and Foreign Investment, 1870–1913* (Cambridge, 1953).

Cameron, R. E., *France and the Economic Development of Europe 1800–1914* (Princeton, 1961).

Cottrell, P. L., *British Overseas Investment in the Nineteenth Century* (London, 1975).

Edelstein, M., *Overseas Investment in the Age of High Imperialism: the United Kingdom 1850–1914* (New York, 1982).

Feinstein, C., 'Britain's Overseas Investments in 1913', *Economic History Review* (June, 1990), pp. 288–95.

Feis, H., *Europe the World's Banker, 1870–1914* (New Haven, 1930).

Hall, A. R. (ed.), *The Export of Capital from Britain, 1870–1914* (London, 1968).

Hobson, C. K., *The Export of Capital* (New York, 1914).

Imlah, A. H., *Economic Elements in the Pax Britannica* (Cambridge, Mass., 1958).

Kindleberger, C. P., *A Financial History of Western Europe* (London, 1984).

Lewis, C. (assisted by K. T. Schlotterbeck), *America's Stake in International Investments* (Washington, 1938).

Michie, R., 'Different in Name Only? The London Stock Exchange and Foreign Bourses c. 1850–1914', *Business History* (Jan., 1988), pp. 46–68.

Milward, A., and Saul, S. B., *The Development of the Economies of Continental Europe, 1850–1914* (London, 1977).

Platt, D. C. M., *Britain's Investment Overseas on the Eve of the First World War, The Use and Abuse of Numbers* (London, 1986).

Pollard, S., 'Capital Exports, 1870–1914: Harmful or Beneficial?', *Economic History Review* (Nov., 1985), pp. 489–514.

Royal Institute of International Affairs, *The Problem of International Investment* (Oxford, 1937).

Saul, S. B., *Studies in British Overseas Trade, 1870–1914* (Liverpool, 1960).

Wilkins, M., *The Emergence of Multinational Enterprise: American Business Abroad from the Colonial Era to 1914* (Cambridge, Mass., 1970).

Woodruff, W., *Impact of Western Man* (New York, 1966), Chap. IV.

Chapter 3

International migration, 1820–1913

If the flow of capital from Europe constitutes a remarkable chapter in the history of international economic development, so does the emigration of labour that accompanied the outflow of capital. As we have just seen, the bulk of Europe's foreign investment in the nineteenth century went to relatively sparsely populated areas where labour was scarce. To these regions also went millions of emigrants from Europe. As entrepreneurs and workers, they complemented and helped to make productive the capital that was flowing to these new countries overseas.

EUROPEAN MIGRATION 1821–1913

When it comes to an examination of the volume, composition and direction of these intercontinental flows of population, difficulties inherent in definition, coverage and techniques of data collection and reporting make it hazardous to chart the course of the streams of migration that constitute this extensive redistribution of population. Inevitably these difficulties become more acute the further back into the nineteenth century we go. But thanks to the diligent and cumulative efforts of some of the world's leading demographers, the nature and direction of these intercontinental population flows can now be indicated with a considerable degree of confidence.

Taking the emigration statistics first, these suggest a total population outflow overseas of some 46 millions during the period 1821–1915. The mass of the migrants, some 44 millions originated in Europe (see Figure 4), the remainder coming chiefly from Asia. The bulk of the European movement took place after 1880, although with every decade the tide of population movement increased in volume, rising from an average of over 110,000 a year in the period 1821–50 to 270,000 in 1851–80, and to over 900,000 in 1881–1915 (see Table 7). In total some 11–12 million Europeans emigrated before 1880 compared with 32 millions after that date. This acceleration in the rate of emigration from Europe after 1880 was coupled with a significant shift of the source of the population outflow. Before 1880 most of the

24.5m.
North-West
Europe
56.2%

16.1m.
British Isles
36.9%

4.9m.
Germany
11.2%

2.1m. Other S-E
Europe 4.8%

3.5m.
Other N-W Europe
8.1%

4.4m.
Austria-
Hungary
10.1%

4.6m.
Spain &
Portugal
10.6%

8.0m.
Italy
18.3%

19.1m.
South-East
Europe
43.8%

Total outflow: 43·6m.

Figure 4 Emigration from Europe, 1821–1915

Source: As for Table 7.

emigrants came from northern and western Europe; after that date the majority were from southern and eastern Europe.

Over the whole period, the British Isles was the principal source of supply of people, accounting for approximately 37 per cent of the total outflow from Europe.

The other major sources, in order of their importance, were Italy, Germany, Austria-Hungary, Spain, Russia (including Poland), and Portugal. Emigration from Britain was heavy throughout the nineteenth century, whereas the outflow from Italy became substantial only after 1880. Then it grew rapidly, and in the first decade of this century it was heavier even than the outflow from Britain (3.6m. compared with 2.8m.). German emigration, which along with the British accounted for the bulk of the European outflow before 1880, became relatively less important after that date, owing chiefly to the alternative domestic employment opportunities afforded by rapid industrialization.

Table 7 Emigration from Europe, 1821–1915

	In millions					
	1821–50		*1851–80*		*1881–1915*	
	No	%	No	%	No	%
N.W. Europe	3.4	100.0	7.4	91.3	13.7	42.7
Britain	2.6	76.5	4.6	56.8	8.9	27.7
Germany	0.6	17.6	2.1	25.9	2.2	6.9
S.E. Europe	neg.	—	0.7	8.7	18.4	57.3
Italy	neg.	—	0.2	2.5	7.8	24.3
Spain & Portugal	neg.	—	0.3	3.7	4.3	13.4
Austro-Hungary	neg.	—	0.2	2.5	4.2	13.1
Total	3.4	100.0	8.1	100.0	32.1	100.0
Annual averages	113,000		270,000		917,000	

Source: I. Ferenczi and W. F. Willcox (eds.), *International Migration,* op. cit., Vol. I.

Note: N.W. Europe comprises the British Isles, France, Germany, Holland, Belgium, Switzerland, Denmark, Norway, Sweden and Finland; S.W. Europe comprises Italy, Spain, Portugal, Austria, Hungary, Russia (including Poland).

The immigration statistics, which probably give a fuller and truer picture of intercontinental population movements during these years, show a gross inflow of just over 51 million (Figure 5 and Table 8). Not all of these immigrants settled permanently in the countries to which they travelled, but owing to lack of adequate information on the numbers returning home, the extent of the net movement is difficult to gauge. Of the total gross immigration recorded between 1821 and 1915, about 62 per cent entered the United States, 9 per cent Argentina, 8 per cent Canada, and approximately 7 per cent Brazil. Taken together, the Americas received more than 85 per cent of the recorded immigration before 1915. The greater part of the remainder consisted of migrant flows to Australasia and the temperate part of Africa. By and large, the British migrants went to the Dominions and to the United States, the Italians to the United States and Latin America, the Spaniards and Portuguese to Latin America, and the Germans to the United States and, in smaller numbers, to Argentina and Brazil. Despite the weakness and deficiencies of the migration statistics, the predominant flow of population—from Europe to the Americas, and to the United States in particular—is so great that no reasonable estimates of error can alter the picture presented above.

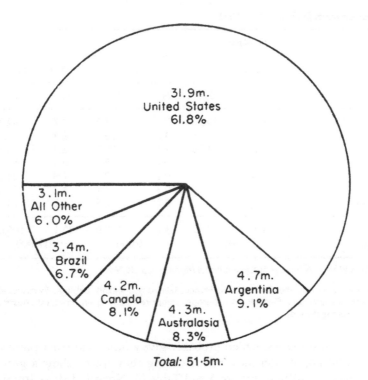

Figure 5 International immigration, 1821–1915

Source: As for Table 8.

MIGRATION AND ITS CAUSES

In discussions of population movements a distinction is often made between push' and 'pull' migration. During the first 60 years of the nineteenth century there is no doubt that the forces operating to generate intercontinental movements of labour were mainly of the 'push' type, in the sense that the migrant was driven from his homeland by adverse economic conditions or other circumstances rather than attracted to his country of destination by the more or less vague expectations of a future improvement in his lot. At the same time the motives for moving were as various as the types of individuals involved. But where a few sought freedom from political or religious principles, judging by the figures alone, most migrants left for reasons which, although social in their implications, were basically economic in origin.[1]

The root causes of the rise of mass emigration from Europe in the years between 1815 and 1870 were the demographic and technical revolutions that were currently transforming the economic and social life of western Europe. Basically it was an outflow of rural population brought about by the classical

Table 8 International immigration, 1821–1915

Country of Immigration	In millions					
	1821–50		*1851–80*		*1881–1915*	
	No	%	No	%	No	%
United States	2.38	67.0	7.73	68.1	21.76	59.4
Canada	0.74	20.8	0.82	7.2	2.59	7.1
British W. Indies	0.08	2.3	0.27	2.4	0.53	1.4
Brazil	0.02	0.6	0.45	4.0	2.97	8.1
Argentina	—	—	0.44	3.9	4.26	11.6
Australia ⎫	0.19	5.4	0.79	7.0	2.77	7.6
New Zealand ⎭			0.25	2.2	0.26	0.7
All others	0.14	3.9	0.60	5.3	1.50	4.1
Total	3.55	100.0	11.35	100.0	36.64	100.0
Annual averages	118,000		378,000		1,046,857	

Source: I. Ferenczi and W. F. Willcox (eds.), *International Migration*, op. cit., Table 6, pp. 236–88; United States Bureau of Census, *Statistical Abstract of the United States*; G. W. Roberts and J. Byrne, 'Summary Statistics on Indenture and Associated Migration affecting the West Indies 1834–1918', *Population Studies* (July, 1966), pp. 125–34.

Malthusian situation of a rapidly growing population pressing on limited means of subsistence. Under the pressure of population increase, the land was subdivided until holdings became too small even in good years to support those who cultivated them. Even when improvements in agricultural methods increased productivity, this tended simply to strengthen the trend towards what List graphically described as a 'dwarf economy (*Zweigwirtschaft*) of tiny marginal holdings.[2] In Ireland and in other countries of the Continent, notably Germany and Scandinavia, the introduction of the potato in particular facilitated the uneconomic subdivision of the land. Where sustenance could be obtained from the potato crop supplemented by the milk of cows or goats, and when no obstacle existed to the minute subdivision of holdings, there was virtually no check to population growth except famine. But if in western Germany the 'push' factor took the form of a truly Malthusian 'over-population', in eastern Germany the people suffered from a social system which produced yields on large estates with a minimum of labour, denying to the peasant farmer not only land ownership and tenancy, but also even regular employment.

Famine finally overwhelmed Ireland in the years 1845–7, and in the space of a few years the country lost about a fifth of its population by emigration, starvation or disease. Even prior to 1847 emigration had drawn off considerable numbers of the Irish population, but now the losses were much higher, reaching an average of 200,000 a year from 1847 to 1854. If, in subsequent years, the outflow was never again as great as it had been during the 1840s and 1850s, it was heavy nevertheless, being 540,000 in the 1870s and 700,000 in the 1880s, and, in the period up to 1890, the Irish continued to contribute to the British emigration to the extent of one-third to one-half of the total annual outflow.

Alternative employment opportunities for displaced rural labour were to be found in urban manufacturing industry or in the construction of railways, but until the last quarter of the nineteenth century the pace of industrialization in most of Europe was decidedly slow. Even when it accelerated, the tendency was for emigration to increase in volume, at least in the short-run, as countries experienced the disrupting effects of industrialization and the introduction of capitalistic forms of agricultural production. Ultimately, however, industrialization in North and West Europe, by increasing employment opportunities and raising relative wages, reduced the 'push' pressures by more than the increase in the American 'pull' which became more pronounced after 1880. Adding to the difficulties of industrial adjustment in Europe in the 1870s and early 1880s was the inflow of cheap American grain which depressed prices and made much of European agriculture unprofitable. Where, as in Britain, the farmer remained unprotected against this competition the result was a partial collapse of agriculture and a massive outflow of rural population overseas. Even here, however, the attraction of empire countries, which often offered subsidized fares, reduced the numbers of migrants going to the United States.

These developments resulted in a significant change in the pattern of European emigration after 1880. It was now the turn of the countries of eastern and southern Europe to experience on a widespread scale the socially-disruptive effects of population growth and economic and technical change. Italy emerged as second only to Britain in importance as a source of emigrants at this time, and after 1900 sent more people overseas than any other European country. There was also heavy emigration from Spain, Portugal, Austria-Hungary, and Russia, and whereas for the latter two countries political oppression provided further stimulus to emigration, the bulk of the population movement that occurred during these years took place because of the pressures of rural overcrowding. In short, whatever the diversity of their places of origin, most European migrants during the nineteenth century were rural workers. Either they were peasants displaced from the soil by the great transformation of European agriculture of these years, or they were artisans similarly displaced by the conversion of handicraft work to factory production.

AIDS TO MASS EMIGRATION

Financial assistance

The willingness to emigrate under pressure of adverse economic circumstances was not in itself sufficient to bring about a mass outflow of population from Europe. Willingness to move had to be backed by ability to do so. This latter problem, which involved basically the cost of movement, became apparent quite early in the nineteenth century, when the poor and destitute came to constitute a growing proportion of the total emigration from Europe. The high peak in this outflow of pauper labour came with the Irish famine of the late 1840s, which had the effect of removing from the land the poorest inhabitants or those who had been living on the margin of subsistence.

During these early years the growing outflow of peoples from Europe was made possible partly because the climate of public and official opinion became more favourable to the emigration of the poor. This was shown not only by the removal of restrictions on emigration in countries such as Britain, Germany and Sweden, but also by the fact that the state and other interested bodies, such as philanthropic organizations, emigration and colonization societies, trade unions, and even individuals, appropriated money to pay the costs of emigration of poor people. In Britain, particular importance attaches to the Colonial Land and Emigration Department, which was established in 1840 for the purpose of organizing the sale of land in Australia and New Zealand as a means of raising money to assist emigration to these colonies. As a result of its efforts some 339,339 emigrants went to Australasia between 1847 and 1869 at a cost of £4.9m., of which £532,000 was raised by the emigrants or their friends and the rest came from colonial funds. More limited financial aid was provided by the parishes, which were empowered by the British Parliament in the 1830s to raise money on the security of the local rates to assist the emigration of the locally unemployed. Additional help came from philanthropic individuals and societies, as well as from landlords seeking to escape the excessive burden of the poor rate caused by unemployment, while in the towns the trade unions were also active in supporting the emigration of out-of-work members. On the continent, a somewhat similar system of private and state assistance for emigrants developed in Germany, especially after the uprisings of 1848, when state governments came to look on emigration as a means of getting rid of a potentially dangerous proletariat. Only in Baden, however, was there a serious programme of state subsidization of emigration during these years.

As publicly subsidized emigration declined in importance after the 1850s, financial aid to migrants came increasingly from governments and private persons or groups in the receiving countries. In particular, assisted immigration remained important throughout the rest of the nineteenth century for

Britain's Australasian colonies and for some Latin American countries, all of which suffered under the twin handicaps of distance and North American competition in their quest for migrants. Thus, between 1861 and 1900 the total number of assisted immigrants entering Australia was more than 388,000, compared with a net gain through immigration of some 767,000. In the next decade only 17,700 assisted immigrants reached Australia, but in the following four years (1911–14) they amounted to almost 145,000 out of a total net gain from the United Kingdom of 198,500.

In Brazil, free passage, free land, and sometimes free machinery, seed and livestock, as well as monthly cash allowances to tide immigrants over the initial period of settlement were powerful incentives which eventually attracted a steady stream of migrants to the country. In São Paulo, for example, where the treasury began defraying transportation costs from southern Europe to the Brazilian coffee plantations in 1887, the number of immigrants reached large proportions. Out of almost 1½m. entering the state between 1890 and 1913, 65 per cent were subsidized. Liberal financial assistance to cover the costs of travel and settlement was also provided by the Argentinian government, which further encouraged immigration into that country by offers of exemption from military service and immunity from discriminatory taxes.[3]

Another form of financial help to migrants which originated abroad was the remittances sent home by prosperous and successful settlers which could be used towards paying the fares of relatives and friends who wished to emigrate. The full extent of these remittances is not known, but a few examples of these financial flows between countries are sufficient in themselves to make us aware of the contribution they must have made towards bringing about the large-scale movement of people that took place after 1860. For the United Kingdom, the annual inflow of remittance money from the United States varied considerably, but between 1848 and 1879 the total amounted to over £21m., enough to emigrate comfortably no less than two million people. Towards the end of the nineteenth century it was estimated that 79 per cent of the British migrants going to the United States had their fares paid by friends and relatives already settled there. Equally striking is the estimated two billion dollars remitted to Italy between 1901 and 1923, 80 per cent of which derived from America. Much of this money represented savings repatriated by Italians returning to their homeland, but some of it was undoubtedly used to finance part of the heavy emigration from Italy that took place during the early years of this century.

Thus, while government assistance to migrants was important for some countries, for example, Australia and Brazil, its overall impact on the volume and direction of international migration before 1913 should not be exaggerated. The great bulk of the migrants had to depend on their own resources or those of their families and friends, including people already settled overseas, to finance their movement abroad. At the same time, the fact that so many people were able to emigrate was in no small way due to the availability of cheaper and more accessible transport.

Cheap transport

In the development of cheaper, faster and more accessible transport the operative factors were the unprecedented expansion of commerce that took place in the nineteenth century and, after 1850, the spread of steamship travel. In the early years of the century it was the growth of the Canadian timber trade and the expansion of the trade of the United States with Europe, particularly in cotton, which gave rise to a considerable increase of unused space on return journeys, so that shipowners increasingly looked to emigrants to provide part of the return freight. As this passenger trade grew in size, intensive competition between the shipping companies brought fares tumbling down. At Liverpool the cost of steerage passage to New York fell from £12 in 1816 to just over £3 thirty years later, and comparable reductions occurred at the other ports of north-western Europe with connections in the New World. But cheaper fares were small compensation for the terrors associated with travel in overcrowded, badly-provisioned, and often unseaworthy boats, and it was not until the 1840s that interested governments were able to secure better treatment and more comfortable travelling for the migrants. However, the final solution to this problem came only with the growth of the steamship trade, which reduced travelling time substantially and placed the passenger trade in the hands of the more reputable steamship companies.

The spread of steamship travel was rapid after 1850, and although sailing-ships still handled about one-half of the emigrant trade in the 1860s, by 1873 the proportion had been reduced to less than 4 per cent. Apart from encouraging emigration by speeding up travel, the steamship companies played a direct part in inducing migration, for in their bid to ensure full passenger lists their ticket agents combed Europe for migrants, conducting extensive propaganda campaigns in favour of settlement overseas.[4] Even more important as a source of information available to potential migrants was the knowledge of conditions provided by friends and relatives who had already migrated or who had returned home after a period spent abroad. Moreover, as the stock of migrants grew so the volume of information about the opportunities for improvement overseas increased and became more widespread throughout Europe. At the same time, government regulations and competition between steamship companies resulted in continuous improvements in passenger facilities. Despite the better facilities and the long-run decline in the purchasing power of money, the cost of steerage passage varied very little after 1850. Thus, in 1913 steerage rates were £5 10s and £6 15s, compared with an average cost of emigrating Irishmen in 1855 of £5 10s per head.

ECONOMIC CONSEQUENCES OF MIGRATION

Immigrant countries

The essential economic function of international migration in the nineteenth century was to redistribute some of Europe's agricultural population to new primary producing regions overseas, where physical and social conditions enabled it to produce more per man than it would have done had it remained at home. Sometimes this result was achieved directly, but not always. Many immigrants, although drawn from largely agricultural economies, contributed to the development of new countries by taking non-agricultural jobs in them, thus releasing more of the native population to expand agriculture. A minority of migrants possessed industrial skills and were responsible for the introduction of new manufacturing techniques. But the chief contribution of immigrants to industrial development in these countries was to be found in the numerical addition to a country's population they made, first as new-comers, and later, through the high birth-rates they sustained, as parents. These growing numbers provided both the labour force and the large and expanding market so essential to industrialization and large-scale production.

Whatever the occupational destinations of the migrants, there was a direct connection between immigration and economic growth in the receiving countries. Each inflow of population acted as a powerful force in pushing up the rate of growth of investment, income and employment. Whether these upsurges in economic growth caused the inflow of foreign population or whether immigration stimulated economic expansion—and there is evidence that both causal sequences operated during the nineteenth century—the contribution of the immigrants to economic growth was obvious. As entrepreneurs, they brought to the recipient countries the capital and knowledge that formed the basis of a wide variety of new manufacturing industries, including, amongst others, textiles, furniture, chemicals, glass-making, and brewing, and as artisans, they supplied the technical skills necessary to make these new industries an initial success. A more characteristic contribution, however, was of another order. Often lacking even the minimum of skills, the bulk of the immigrants fed the construction industries with the manpower needed to build railways and other transport facilities, and to erect cities and equip them with public utilities, sanitation, and other urban requirements. In addition, where, as in the United States, mechanized production was introduced on a large scale, immigrants provided the factory workforce necessary for rapid and sustained industrial growth.

European agricultural skills could not always be put to use overseas. Only rarely, therefore, did immigrants become frontiersmen or pioneer farmers. In more settled areas, however, many European agricultural techniques proved immensely valuable. The introduction of sugar beet and 'everlasting' clover, the growth of wine production, and the diffusion of novel methods of wheat growing are only a few instances of the contributions made by immigrants to the growth of overseas agriculture during the nineteenth century. Moreover, in the neighbourhood of the growing cities, the immigrants often became involved in various types of market-gardening and small-scale intensive agriculture to which native farmers were not accustomed, thus developing a pattern of agriculture that was of genuine importance in the economy, and one that was responsible for bringing about subsequent changes in local consumption habits.

However, immigration involves costs as well as benefits to the receiving country, and the heavy pressures exerted on a country's existing supplies of housing, educational, and transport facilities during periods of heavy immigration are characteristic of these. Furthermore, since the majority of immigrants are wage earners, the likely impact of immigration on the wage system of the receiving country must assume considerable importance in any discussion of the economic consequences of migration. Indeed, the threat, real or otherwise, to the living standards of the indigenous population posed by immigrant labour was the occasion for violent anti-immigration demonstrations in many countries during the nineteenth century. Examination of the available evidence suggests that there was no marked tendency for wages *in general* to fall in the pre-1913 period. But since it is practically impossible to eliminate the effect on the wage level of all the other interacting and continually changing forces, such as technological progress and rising productivity, the spread of industry, and the growth of new employment opportunities, it remains a matter of conjecture whether in particular countries immigration did in the long run have an unfavourable effect on the general wage level in receiving countries. On the other hand, if we concentrate on the wages earned in specific occupations, there is some evidence to suggest that heavy immigration did adversely affect wage levels in certain occupations. Thus, in America, the real wages of unskilled workers remained relatively constant in the periods of heavy immigration after 1880, whereas other incomes increased steadily in real terms. Indeed, the 'pick and shovel' man received only slightly more in the United States than in Europe, compared with the wide differentials between American and European earnings in other occupations and skills, a fact which was put down by contemporary American observers to the enormous influx of immigrants. On the other hand, as Eichengreen and Gemery have shown, 'over time, initially unskilled immigrants managed to close much of the earnings gap between themselves and their skilled counterparts. Thus, while immigrants who had acquired training prior to arrival in the United States initially had the advantage of access to a range of relatively high-paid positions, immigrants who acquired their training after arrival had the advantage of superior opportunities for advancement and earnings growth.'[5] We also find evidence in Argentina and Brazil of heavy immigration retarding the growth of real incomes in certain occupations. But this tendency was not due solely to the increased supply of labour in the market because of immigration. Difficulties are also apparent on the demand side, where the *latifundia* system, which placed the ownership of the land in a few hands, and the slow growth of industry limited the expansion of employment opportunities in both agriculture and manufacturing.

Emigrant Countries

Economic benefits and losses were also experienced by the countries losing population. They suffered a money loss in the capital or property which emigrants took with them as well as the loss of human capital represented by the money expended in rearing, educating and training the emigrant. But the extent of the losses should not be exaggerated. Many of the emigrants were desperately poor, and the majority of them had little or no marketable skills. Even when they possessed skills they were often unsuitable to their new environment. On the other hand, the losing country also benefited from its emigrants in a number of ways. There was the money gain in remittances and in the savings brought back to the country by repatriates, and they sometimes returned with new knowledge and new ideas which could be put to profitable use in the home country. Furthermore, where, as in Ireland, the loss of population was heavy and sustained, there is evidence that emigration did contribute in part to raising real wages and, perhaps more importantly, to increasing the degree of regularity in employment. For the most part, however, emigration operated largely as a safety valve for people stranded in declining occupations and places. It did little to raise the real incomes of growing populations or to expand employment opportunities in losing countries, for these improvements depended more on the spread of industrialization, technical progress, and the growth of productivity than on a simple loss of population. In other words, emigration remained throughout the nineteenth century a palliative rather than a solution for the problems of social and economic change.

INTRACONTINENTAL MIGRATION

The large-scale movement of population was not confined to exchanges between continents. Within the new continents opened up by the migration of largely European people, substantial shifts of population brought about the occupation of extensive areas of new land. Whereas at the beginning of the nineteenth century the European outposts overseas consisted largely of islands and tide-water settlements, in the following century whole continents were conquered in the Americas and Australasia, as the local populations, supported by a growing influx of migrants, turned inland and developed the natural wealth of these largely unoccupied lands. The existence of unoccupied lands in parts of Eastern Europe also brought substantial internal migration within Europe during these years. Much of this movement of population was directed towards Russia, where 4.2m. foreigners settled between 1828 and 1915. Two-thirds of these came from Europe, mainly from Germany and Austria. The remainder came from Asian countries bordering on Russia, especially China, Japan, Persia and Turkey. There was also a significant eastward movement of Russians into Asia. Of the 7m. involved in this long-distance internal migration roughly three-quarters were peasant settlers, the rest, numbering 1.3m., were prisoners and exiles. These migrants settled mainly in Siberia, others went southwards into the steppe country, others to eastern Asia and Turkestan. The bulk of the movement took place after 1890. This movement of population into Asiatic Russia forms part of the general redistribution of Asian population that took place during these years, the nature and direction of which is the subject of the following section.

ASIATIC MIGRATION AND TROPICAL DEVELOPMENT

The Demand for Asian Labour

As the free movement of European people across the Atlantic grew in volume, the centuries old forcible transfer of Africans to the tropical regions of the New World finally came to an end. Despite its legal abolition in a number of countries, the African slave trade was growing rapidly in the early decades of the nineteenth century and, by 1840, it was estimated to have been almost double what it had been in 1807.[6] During the next decade however, Britain's efforts to suppress the trade achieved considerable success, and by 1850 the traffic to Brazil was virtually finished and nearly half of the West African coastline was closed to the slave trade. There was some revival of slaving in the 1850s, due mainly to the expansion of cotton production in the United States during these years, but the outbreak of the American Civil War quickly put an end to the illegal trade there, as well as in numerous other countries, such as Cuba, where it had been carried on under the protection of the American flag.

The abolition of slavery in the period before 1870 resulted in a serious shortage of labour in the tropical plantation economies, and this was partly responsible for the growing volume of Asiatic migration during the nineteenth century. But while some of these migrants (which included mainly people from India and China, and, after 1870, Japan) went to other continents, the bulk of the population movement was confined to Asia and its adjacent islands. Indian migrants, largely indentured labourers, went to the West Indies, Mauritius, South Africa, and South America, and still larger numbers were imported into the plantation and mining economies of Ceylon, Malaya and the East Indies. Chinese intercontinental migration, which was

on a considerable scale between 1848 and 1873, was broadly similar in direction and character to that of Indian emigration during these years, but with a
somewhat larger number of 'free' Chinese emigrating to countries such as the
United States and Australia. Nearer home, the Chinese went chiefly to south-
east Asia, including Burma, Siam, Indo-China and Malaya, and to the East
Indies, the Philippine Islands, and Formosa. The bulk of the Japanese indentured labour went to Hawaii. Large numbers of Japanese also emigrated to
Asiatic Russia, America and Korea.

Under the system of indenture, the labourer undertook to work for a fixed
period of anything up to five years in return for the cost of his passage, a fixed
wage, and certain other amenities such as free housing and medical care. On
expiration of his contract the labourer could renew it or settle permanently in
the receiving country by taking up alternative employment. After 1857,
Indian indentured labourers, who were employed largely in other colonies
of the British Empire, could also return home at the expense of the colony
which had imported them. From the start the system of indentured
labour was subject to grave abuse, and in extreme cases work on the plantations was little better than slavery. The governments of the countries
involved in this exchange of labour endeavoured to control the worst of the
abuses, and from time to time the emigration of indentured labour was
suspended. Even so, the problem of ensuring fair treatment for indentured
labour continued to exercise the minds of government officials well into the
twentieth century.

The Volume and Direction of Asian Migration

Adequate statistical records exist for only some of the intercontinental flows
of Asian migrants. One well-documented movement was that directed to the
West Indies, where the freeing of the slaves in 1833 left the sugar plantations
with a severe labour shortage. Of the 536,000 mainly indentured labourers
introduced into the colony in the period 1834 to 1918, some four-fifths
(430,000) came from India. Other British colonies outside Asia to which
Indians migrated in any numbers during these years were South Africa and
Mauritius. Although the full extent of the population inflow into the colonies
is not known, a total of 161,000 Indians was recorded in the South African
census of 1921. Within Asia, Indian migrants went chiefly to Ceylon and
Malaya. In Ceylon, the immigrant labour worked mainly in the coffee and tea
plantations, and, although for the majority of them their stay was only temporary, the net inflow of Indians into Ceylon between 1839 and 1913
amounted to over 1.8m. persons. In total some 15.8m. people left India
between 1871 and 1915, and 11.7m. returned, leaving 4.1m. as net
migrants. The heavy return flow is explained largely by the indenture system
which, as we have seen, bound a migrant to work for a plantation employer
for a fixed number of years.

Like the Indian emigration, the bulk of the Chinese migrants went to other parts of Asia. The Straits Settlements received 5.7m. Chinese between 1881 and 1915, and large numbers of Chinese also went to Siam after 1885 so that by 1922 their numbers in that country totalled 1½m. A further quarter of a million Chinese emigrated to the Philippine Islands before the American take-over of the islands from Spain in 1898 resulted in the application to the Philippines of the Chinese Exclusion Act already in force in the United States. Next to Asia, the Americas attracted the most Chinese. Thus, some 18,000 Chinese entered the West Indies under contract between 1852 and 1884, and by 1862 there were over 60,000 Chinese in Cuba. In Peru, where as a result of an immigration law passed in 1849 large numbers of Chinese were brought into the country to work on plantations and on the guano beds, the numbers of Chinese entering the country between 1849 and 1874 have been variously estimated at between 80,000 and 100,000. Gold discoveries in California were responsible for the early flows of Chinese into the United States, and by the end of the century over 300,000 had entered the country, mainly in the years before 1882, when a reaction against the use of Chinese labour in railway construction and other forms of employment led to the passage of an Act of exclusion. Gold also brought an influx of Chinese into Australia in the 1850s, and by 1861 they numbered 38,298. But with the decline in alluvial gold mining, and following the restrictions placed on Chinese immigration by the various Australian colonies, which culminated in the Commonwealth Immigration Restriction Act of 1901, the number had declined to 22,000 by 1911. Overall, the number of Chinese living abroad increased by perhaps 5m., but since large numbers of Chinese were recruited for work abroad under the indenture system, the gross outflow was likely to have been substantially greater than this figure suggests.

Japanese emigration was not legalized until 1885, when an agreement was signed by the Japanese government and certain Hawaiian sugar plantation owners under which Japanese contract labourers were permitted to emigrate to Hawaii. An Imperial edict legalizing emigration of Japanese labourers in general soon followed. Consequently, between 1885 and 1907 approximately 540,000 Japanese emigrated, of whom one-third went to Hawaii and a further 14 per cent each to the United States and Korea. Other countries receiving more than 10 per cent of the outflow included Asiatic Russia and China. In the following period, 1908 to 1924, a further 643,000 emigrants left Japan. Of these, 38 per cent went to Asiatic Russia and about a fifth to the United States. Smaller numbers went to Hawaii, China, Brazil and Peru. After 1907, Japanese immigration into the United States slowed down, following the conclusion of the so-called 'Gentlemen's Agreement', under which the Japanese government undertook to limit the issue of passports valid for continental America to certain selected groups of Japanese migrants. Complete exclusion followed in 1924.

NOTES

1 The chief example of migration because of religious persecution is the flight of 1½m. Jews from Russia to the United States in the 15 years preceding World War I.
2 F. List, *The Land System, Dwarf Economy, and Emigration* (Stuttgart, 1842).
3 Free land or land obtained against a nominal fee was also made available in the United States, following the passage of the Homestead Act of 1862, and in Canada after the Dominions Act of 1872.
4 Steamship companies and railway construction companies in the United States attracted thousands of emigrants by paying much of the prospective emigrant's fares. At one time a single transatlantic steamship company had no fewer than 3,400 agents arranging passages and advancing money from America to emigrants from the British Isles.
5 Eichengreen, B. and Gemery, H. A., 'The Earnings of Skilled and Unskilled Immigrants at the End of the Nineteenth Century', *Journal of Economic History* (June, 1986), p. 442. It must be noted, however, that the above conclusion applies to the 'old' immigrant groups, that is, foreign workers born in England, Wales, Scotland, Germany, and Scandinavia.
6 The increase was from 100,000 to 200,000 a year, of whom 150,000 were carried across the Atlantic and 50,000 went to the Arab world.

SELECTED REFERENCES

Berthoff, R. T., *British Immigrants in Industrial America, 1790–1950* (Cambridge, Mass., 1953).
Davie, M. R., *World Immigration* (New York, 1936).
Engerman, S. L., 'Servants to Slaves to Servants: Contract Labour and European Expansion', in Emmer, F. C. (ed.), *Colonialism and Migration: Indentured Labour Before and After Slavery* (Dordrecht, 1986).
Ferenczi, I., and Willcox, W. F., *International Migration* (2 vols., New York, 1929–31).
Gould, J. D., 'European Inter-Continental Emigration 1815–1914: Patterns and Causes', *Journal of European Economic History* (Winter, 1979), pp. 593–679.
Handlin, O., *The Positive Contribution by Immigrants* (Paris, 1955).
Isaac, J., *Economics of Migration* (London, 1947).
Johnson, C., *A History of Emigration from the U.K. to North America, 1763–1912* (London, 1913).
Latham, A. J. H., *The International Economy and the Underdeveloped World 1865–1914* (London, 1978), Chap. IV.
Richardson, H. W., 'British Emigration and Overseas Investment, 1870–1914', *Economic History Review* (Feb., 1972), pp. 99–113.
Scott, F. D. (ed.), *World Migration in Modern Times* (Englewood Cliffs, 1968).
Taylor, P., *The Distant Magnet: European Migration to the United States* (London, 1971).
Walker, M., *Germany and the Emigration, 1816–85* (Cambridge, Mass., 1964).
Woodruff, W., *Impact of Western Man* (New York, 1966), Chap. III.

Chapter 4

Commercial policy in the nineteenth century

A country's commercial policy determines the nature of its trading relations with the rest of the world. For this reason it is necessary to examine commercial policy in the nineteenth century in some detail before turning to look at the trade flows which, along with the movements of labour and capital, link countries together internationally. Although protectionism was widespread before 1850, and was revived again after 1880, during the intervening period there was a general reduction of restrictions on trade. This movement towards freer trade took place at two levels. At the national level it involved the economic unification of a number of nation states which later came to play a prominent part in international economic affairs. At the international level it involved the widespread adoption of free-trade policies, which reached a peak in the third quarter of the nineteenth century, and which marked the end of the system of privileged trading blocs and restricted commerce characteristic of the growth of the colonial empires of Britain, France, Holland, and Spain in the period before 1800. At both levels the advantages of free trade provided the rationale for the movement towards closer economic and political relations between the areas concerned.

In Britain, France, and the United States economic unification had been completed by the beginning of the nineteenth century. Elsewhere, however, economic fragmentation was the rule. This was particularly so in Europe, where, as a result of the Congress of Vienna (1815), Germany was organized as a loose federation of 39 states each economically independent of the others, and Italy was similarly fragmented into a number of politically and economically independent states. Since national economic unification was an indispensable prerequisite for the economic development of these countries, as well as for the growth of a world economy, the economic integration of Germany through the German *Zollverein* (1834) and the emergence of a unified Italian state in 1861 were important landmarks in the growth of the international economy. They were not the only examples of national economic integration in the nineteenth century, however, for they were preceded and followed by similar movements in many other European and overseas countries.

Equally striking was the movement towards free trade that reached its peak in the 1870s. Adopted initially by Britain, the policy of free trade between nations gained wide acceptance on the Continent in the years after 1860. Even so, universal free trade was not attained at this time despite the favourable circumstances, and only Britain and Holland adopted policies of complete free trade. Nevertheless, for a comparatively brief period in the 1860s and the 1870s the world came close to attaining the ideal trading conditions postulated by classical economic theory.

BRITAIN ADOPTS FREE TRADE

In Britain, the intellectual foundations of the case for free trade were laid down by Adam Smith in his work *The Wealth of Nations* published in 1776. Smith's analysis was not without its weaknesses, however, and it was left to other economists, notably David Ricardo (*Principles of Political Economy and Taxation*, 1817) and John Stuart Mill (*Principles of Political Economy*, 1848) to complete the theoretical system justifying free trade begun by Smith. The theory of international trade developed by the classical economists consisted of an explanation of the bases of the gains from trade and of the way in which these gains would be distributed among the trading nations. According to the theory, nations, like individuals, should specialize in the production of those goods which they can make with relatively greatest efficiency. This would make it possible for them to produce a larger output of goods through a more efficient allocation of resources, with the possibility of exploiting unused economies of scale as an added advantage. In short, the gains from trade consist of the *extra* output generated by international specialization. Moreover, it is the existence of this extra output which makes it possible for each trading country to benefit from the international exchange of commodities. The conclusion of classical trade theory, that every trading nation stood to benefit from international specialization and exchange, explains why the doctrine of free trade exerted such a powerful hold over economic thought in the nineteenth century and why it is still widely advocated today.

The apostles of free trade in Britain had an early success when the Eden Treaty of 1786 relaxed some of the tariff on trade between Britain and France. But this trend towards trade liberalization was reversed during the wars with France, when the need for war finance led to a substantial rise in the British tariff. After the war these trade barriers were only slowly dismantled, despite demands for greater trade liberalization by the supporters of free trade. Two problems made the adoption of complete free trade impracticable at this stage in Britain's political and economic development, however. First, the government lacked an alternative source of revenue to protective duties. More importantly, the full realization of free trade depended upon the repeal of the Corn Laws which, by placing a duty on imports of wheat, protected British farmers from foreign competition. Such legislation, however, was hardly expected from a government which drew its support largely from the agricultural interest. Even so, a start was made in the years of expanding trade after 1823, when budget surpluses temporarily overcame the revenue difficulty, thus enabling Huskisson as President of the Board of Trade to make a cautious beginning at fiscal reform.

However, the crucial moves towards free trade were made in the 1840s. In his budget of 1842, Sir Robert Peel abolished the outstanding export duties on British manufactured goods and reduced the import duties on no fewer than 750 articles in the customs list. To make up the expected loss of revenue the income tax, which had been levied during the Napoleonic Wars and then abandoned, was reintroduced for three years. The next step was taken in 1845 when with the renewal of the income tax for another three years, Peel swept away 520 customs duties and abolished the remaining export duties on raw materials.

With the income tax likely to replace customs duties as a source of government revenue, free trade for Britain now depended on the abolition of the Corn Laws. But the agricultural interest in Britain remained staunchly protectionist, and despite various attempts at reform the Corn Laws remained largely unimpaired at the beginning of the 1840s. Britain's economic circumstances were changing, however. Since the end of the eighteenth century Britain's growing population had made her increasingly dependent on imported wheat and, by the 1840s, she was feeding between 10 and 15 per cent of her population on foreign wheat. Britain was also changing politically, for the growth of manufacturing industry was shifting the balance of political power from a rural to an urban electorate, where industrialization was creating a new economic interest which demanded 'cheap bread' and an end to agricultural protection. In support of these demands the Anti-Corn Law League, first set up in 1838, maintained an unrelenting attack on agricultural protection. Despite the brilliance of its campaign, however, it was not the League but the catastrophic Irish famines of the years 1845–6 which made the repeal of the Corn Laws inevitable. In the face of mass starvation, restrictions on the free import of food could not be tolerated and the Corn Laws were finally abolished in 1846, although a brief respite from foreign competition was afforded to British farmers by not making the Act fully effective until 1849, when, except for a registration fee of one shilling, corn came into Britain free. In that year another pillar of protectionism was removed with the repeal of the Navigation Laws which threw the carrying trade as well as the import of corn open to all nations.

In the course of the next 25 years Gladstone completed the movement towards free trade in Britain. He carried through further tariff reductions in 1853, and equalized the duties on sugar in 1854. For the next few years the necessity of financing the Crimean War (1854–6) delayed further progress. Finally, in 1860, Gladstone introduced the first of the great series of budgets which completely freed Britain's foreign trade. In that year the number of dutiable items was reduced to 48, and most of the remaining food duties were abolished. Only those on sugar and confectionery remained an important source of revenue. All preferential duties admitting imports from British possessions at a favourable rate were also abolished at this time. Subsequent budgets put timber on the free list in 1866, removed the registration fee on corn in 1869, and freed sugar of duties in 1875, but for all practical purposes it was the budget of 1860 that marks Britain's emergence as a free trade nation within the international economy.

THE SPREAD OF FREE TRADE

Inspired by Britain's example, the classical economists believed that the rest of the world would subsequently move towards complete free trade to the mutual benefit of all concerned. For a brief period after 1860 this dream of universal free trade appeared to be approaching reality, as the policy of trade liberalization spread to other countries through the negotiation of commercial treaties and tariff agreements. The manner in which this trend towards free trade was brought about and the extent to which foreign trade was liberalized during these years will be examined shortly. First of all, however, a brief comment on the economic unification of Germany is called for as an example of the operation of the free-trade principle at the national level.

The Zollverein

Prussia played the major role in the economic and political unification of Germany. Beginning in 1819, a series of treaties was signed with other German states which culminated in 1831 in the formation of the Prussian Customs Union, the first common market of any significance. Meantime, a similar union between Bavaria and Württemberg in 1827 led eventually to the establishment of the Bavarian Customs Union. Finally, in 1833, the Prussian and Bavarian Customs Unions decided to unite to form the Zollverein.

The Zollverein, which came into existence on January 1, 1834, included 18 states with a total population of 23.5 million people. The fundamental principles of the union, as with all the previous customs unions, was a common tariff (based in the main on the rates in force in Prussia) against all states outside the Union, and the abolition of all duties on goods passing between the various member states. Complete economic integration was not attempted, and each state kept its own commercial code, patent laws and government monopolies. As for the proceeds of the customs duties, these were divided amongst the states in proportion to population. After its formation new states were admitted to membership of the *Zollverein* so that by 1852 it included all the states that were eventually to constitute the German Reich.

The Cobden–Chevalier Treaty (1860) and its Consequences

The Cobden–Chevalier Act of 1860, which represented the culmination of the trends towards trade liberalization evident in both France and Britain during the 1850s, was the first of a series of commercial treaties which in effect converted the greater part of Europe into low tariff blocs in the 1860s. In Britain, the only duties on manufactures with any perceptible protective quality in the 1850s were on luxuries like lace, cambric handkerchiefs, carpets and shawls, and the long untouched series of silk duties. These protective duties interfered almost exclusively with trade between Britain and France. Hence the importance of the Cobden–Chevalier Treaty. By it, Great Britain agreed to abolish all duties on manufactured goods, to lower the duty on brandy to the colonial level, and to reduce the import duties on wines. These concessions were offered to all countries alike, but would in fact be most beneficial to France. On the other hand, France made concessions only to Great Britain. These included reductions of the duties on British coal and coke, bar and pig iron, steel, tools and machinery, yarns, and manufactured goods of hemp and flax.

A number of important results followed from the Anglo-French treaty of 1860. First, it inaugurated a chain of other tariff treaties negotiated in a free-trade spirit, for France now began to conclude similar commercial treaties with other countries for the reciprocal relaxation of tariffs. These included agreements with Belgium and the *Zollverein* in 1862; with Italy in 1863; with Switzerland in 1864; with Sweden, Norway, the Hanse towns, Spain and Holland in 1865; with Austria in 1866; and with Portugal in 1867. Even Britain, despite her inability to offer tariff concessions once she had completed her free-trade programme, secured treaties with Belgium (1862), Italy (1863), and the *Zollverein* and Austria (1865).

Second, the countries whose economies were linked by low-tariff treaties in the 1860s soon began to co-operate in other matters necessary for the further expansion of international trade. Many conventions were signed during these years to facilitate international communications—railways, canals, telegraphs, postal arrangements and so on. In 1868 the Rhine—a vitally important commercial link in western Europe—was at last declared a freeway for ships of all nations. Other agreements liberalized navigation on the rivers Scheldt, Elbe, Po and Danube. In 1857, Denmark and the principal maritime powers agreed to the abolition of the Sound dues. By establishing the Latin Monetary Union in 1865, France, Italy, Switzerland and Belgium agreed to standardize the value of their coinage, which besides temporarily stabilizing the international bimetallic standard, naturally facilitated commerce between these countries.

Finally, the Anglo-French treaty of 1860 included a most-favoured nation clause, which also became a feature of most of the following series of commercial treaties. Under this clause the reductions granted by Britain in its tariff against particular classes of goods imported from France were extended to goods of those classes imported into Britain from all other countries. The importance of the most-favoured nation clause lies in the encouragement it gave to trade to expand on a multilateral basis. It prevented discrimination because the reduction of duties to one country meant that they were automatically reduced to all other countries enjoying most-favoured nation treatment with the country reducing them. By including the clause, the treaty of 1860 left a permanent mark on commercial policy, and the existence of the treaty clause became a potent means of restraining tariff increases during the latter part of the nineteenth century. Its use demonstrated conclusively that bilateral trade negotiations are the most effective of all methods of tariff reduction, provided they aim at multilateral trade.

If the movement towards free trade was, in part, the outcome of the general removal of mercantilist restrictions on economic activity, which became widespread in Europe after 1850, the reasons why individual European countries adopted free trade were varied. In the Netherlands, it was largely the result of the pressure exerted by the major export interests, merchants, shipowners, and bankers. In France, on the other hand, it was the industrialists interested in cheap raw material and machinery imports rather than exporters who were the prime movers, although the French government, which appreciated the political gain arising out of the commercial policy, also provided strong support for it. In Germany, the Prussian landed aristocracy's domination of the agricultural export trade accounts for the adoption of a liberal trading policy by an ultra-conservative ruling class. The Italian case seems to be one in which the free trade doctrine was imported from abroad by a strong political leadership and imposed on relatively disorganized local political and economic interests.

Outside Europe, the independent states were less affected by free trade. In the United States, for example, the trend towards freer trade begun in the 1830s was reversed in 1861.[1] On the other hand, perhaps the most questionable use to which the most-favoured nation clause was put was in opening up trade with the East. Here, trade concessions granted initially to Britain and the United States by China and Japan respectively were later extended to all other western countries through the use of the principle of most-favoured nation treatment. As a consequence of these trade treaties with the western powers, which amongst other things stipulated the rates of duties to be levied on their imports and exports, both countries were temporarily deprived of their right to determine tariff policy, a loss of sovereignty that for China continued until 1930.

British Colonial Commercial Policy

The adoption of free trade also brought about a change in British colonial commercial policy. Under Huskisson, the British colonial system had been transformed from a monopolist into a preferential system, with British goods receiving preferential treatment in the colonies and colonial produce gaining tariff preference in the British market. In the next 30 years or so, however, the preferential system was gradually dismantled, and the colonies were free to follow their own independent commercial policies. The reactions of the colonial governments to this new situation were varied. The removal of preferential duties on wheat in 1849, and the complete abolition of those on timber in 1860 placed Canada in a difficult position. Unable to withstand European competition in the British market, she now looked to trade with the United States as an answer to her problems. In 1855 a reciprocal trade treaty was signed with the United States and, despite its abrogation in 1866, trade between the two countries grew rapidly. In Australia, the British preferences were swept away in 1851 and the colonies were free to pursue their own commercial policies, with New South Wales favouring free trade, Victoria protectionism, and the others emphasizing the levying of duties for purely revenue purposes. New Zealand's early tariffs were also designed to raise revenue and had little protectionist bias. In South Africa, the abandonment of preferential wine duties in 1860 left the country virtually free to fix its own tariff. In 1866–7 a protective tariff was introduced without any opposition from Britain. In India, throughout the 1860s, there was a general tendency to reduce tariffs, especially on cotton manufactures. Apart from revenue requirements, Indian commercial policy reflected the political pressures on the British government to maintain India as a market for British cotton textiles and to prevent its emergence as an export competitor.

Overall, however, the commercial policies adopted by the colonies were of little immediate economic significance for Britain. As the dominant industrial power in a world moving towards free trade, her colonial monopoly was no longer valuable when a world market lay within her grasp. Only after 1880 when the competition of the newly-industrializing nations became acute, was there a revival in the importance of the imperial market.

THE ECONOMIC CONSEQUENCES OF FREE TRADE

Stimulated by its release from restrictions, international trade grew apace. The available, admittedly rough, estimates suggest that the value of international trade doubled between 1830 and 1850, and at least trebled and may have nearly quadrupled in the next 30 years. In per capita terms, world trade grew at a decennial rate of 33 per cent between 1800 and 1913, and reached a peak rate of growth of 53 per cent per decade in the period 1840–70. The rapid expansion of foreign trade that occurred in the third quarter of the nineteenth century was of course not solely due to the advent of free trade, and it is difficult to disentangle its effects on trade from those of the other important influences at work during these years. Even so, free trade played its part, and in two respects at least the commercial policies adopted during these years continued to influence economic events in the protectionist period that followed.

The first of these long-run effects of free trade relates to the use of the most-favoured nation clause in the commercial treaties and agreements entered into during these years. The unconditional form of the clause, by which each country received without any question of reciprocal concessions whatever tariff reductions were granted by every country with which it had a treaty, was a potent means of restraining tariff increases during the latter part of the nineteenth century. In addition, many important treaties, which ran for long periods, contained provisions binding rated items against an increase. These provisions had the effect of preventing any increase of duties on a large list of imports. Moreover, since every country had many treaties containing such provisions and expiring at different dates, it became difficult for any of them to embark upon wholesale tariff increases. In short, the most-favoured nation clause placed certain limits on the spread of protectionist policies in the period after 1880. The second long-run effect was more general in its influence, and concerns the part played by free-trade policies in generating the atmosphere of freedom in which economic affairs were conducted in the nineteenth century. Despite the restrictions increasingly placed on trade in the period after 1880, this 'atmosphere' of freedom persisted up to 1913. In particular, the setting out of the legal rights of aliens in many of the commercial treaties negotiated during these years enabled trade to expand in a world where the rights of the private traders and of private property were guaranteed by an extensive network of treaties. In short, these treaties created a stable world, in which traders were free to come and go, to organize and invest abroad, almost as freely and safely as in their own countries.

As for the economic impact of free trade on the economic growth of individual countries, McCloskey has argued that, contrary to the conventional wisdom, free trade *lowered* the rate of growth of British national income by shifting the terms of trade against her.[2] While the available economic evidence tends to support McCloskey's conclusion, two general points are worth noting. First, with the spread of free trade after 1850 any reduction in British income growth consequent upon her pioneering espousal of free trade was likely to be moderated. Second, since, under the most-favoured nation clause, tariff reductions were reciprocally related, the choice of a sub-optimal tariff level by Britain must have meant that tariff levels in other free trade countries were lower than they could have been had Britain chosen a higher tariff level more consistent with maximizing its domestic income growth.

THE RETURN TO PROTECTION

For the classical economist, as for many economists today, universal free trade took on the form of an eternal truth, independent of time or place. Yet in a very real sense the doctrine was a product of its time, for it became the creed of a nation confident in its own power to defeat all rivals in the drive for markets and forced by natural circumstances to depend on the rest of the world for a large part of its supply of food and raw materials. But if free trade had an obvious appeal for the industrially successful nation, it was the failure of the doctrine to deal with the problem of economic development and the complicated relations between advanced and backward economies that formed the basis of the criticisms levied against it by nineteenth-century protectionists such as List, Hamilton and Carey. The controversy is by no means settled even today.

The case for Protection

The basis of the protectionist argument is to be found in Alexander Hamilton's famous *Report on Manufactures* (1791), which remains one of the most elaborate general arguments for protection ever written. In his report to the American Congress, Hamilton stressed both the desirability of national self-sufficiency in manufacturing, and the importance of a sizeable non-agricultural consuming class for a stable and prosperous agriculture. Manufacturing industry, he argued, should be encouraged to grow by the use of a system of bounties and subsidies, and behind a protective tariff, which would free domestic manufacturers from foreign competition, and thus enable them to expand the scale of their operations, thereby achieving economies comparable to those enjoyed by foreign competitors. In this way the 'infant industries' would quickly attain maturity, and would then be able to produce at least as cheaply as foreign manufacturers.

Strongly influenced by Hamilton, the German, Friedrich List (*The National System of Political Economy*, 1841) was highly critical of the classical theory of free trade. In particular, he reproached the classical economists with having purposely ignored the differences in economic strength between the nations which they had invited to trade freely with one another on an equal footing. A country's commercial policy, List argued, was related to its level of economic development and it was therefore wrong to advocate one policy as being universally applicable. He concluded that while free trade is beneficial during the early and later (commercial–industrial) stages of development, the transition from an agricultural to an industrial society could be achieved only through a policy of protection. List therefore demanded an 'educational' tariff on the products of infant industries designed to protect them for a limited period of time from the competition of foreign industries not naturally more efficient but simply more advanced in development.

While Hamilton and List advocated protection only as a temporary 'educational' measure, another American, Henry Charles Carey, went beyond both in demanding protection as a permanent feature of economic policy. Like Hamilton, Carey stressed the fundamental community of interest between agriculture and manufacturing by maintaining that all industrial growth is determined and limited by the available surpluses of agricultural products. In the event, it was this combination of agricultural and manufacturing interests that provided the broad support for the protectionist policies adopted by the United States.

Protection in the United States

While the debate on protection was going on in the United States in the 1790s, the wars between France and England, by blocking the accustomed channels of trade and production, provided a practical illustration of the 'benefits of protection'. The wartime shortages gave an enormous stimulus to those branches of American industry, such as cotton, wool and iron manufactures, whose products had previously been imported. But with the end of the war in Europe came the threat of renewed British competition and a demand for protection from the newly expanded industries. The Tariff Act of 1816 provided the required protection, and for the next 20 years the United States followed a continuous policy of protection, moderate at first, but becoming strongly protective after 1824. Protectionist pressures moderated in the 1830s, after the passing of the Compromise Tariff Act of 1833, which provided for a gradual and steady reduction of duties in the years up to 1842, and although tariffs were raised for a while after 1842, liberalization was resumed in the Tariff Act of 1846, and reinforced by that of 1857. Consequently, for a few years, the United States came as near to free trade as it had been since 1816.

Although the trend towards freer trade was reversed in 1861, when the Morrill Act restored the moderately protective tariff level of 1846, it was the substantial rise in duties needed to pay for the Civil War which laid the foundation of the future American system of protection. During these years the average rate on dutiable commodities rose to 37 per cent in 1862, and to 47 per cent in 1864. After the war there was a call for tariff reform, but the war tariff remained the basis of the American protective system until the passage of the Act of 1883, when the general tariff level was lowered some 5 per cent. Thereafter the tariff level was pushed up twice in rapid succession. In 1890 the McKinley Act raised the average level of tariffs to 50 per cent. High duties were placed on textiles, iron, steel, glass, and tin plate, and to appease the farmers, who were facing increased competition from Canadian imports, tariffs were imposed on a number of agricultural products. The Democrats brought about a downward revision of the tariff in 1894, lowering the average level to 40 per cent, but the Republicans speedily reversed the trend with the Dingley Tariff (1897), which not only restored the McKinley rates, but also raised the average level even higher, to 57 per cent. No further change of any significance took place in the American tariff until 1913, when a Democratic administration passed the Underwood–Simmons Tariff Act, which eliminated specific duties, added over 100 items, including sugar and wool, to the free list, reduced tariffs on nearly 1,000 classifications and increased them on a few others, mostly chemicals. The result of these changes was to reduce the rates of duties on dutiable imports to the extremely low average of 16 per cent. Unfortunately, this trend towards free trade in the United States had little opportunity to be tested, for within a year, war had broken out in Europe. The experiment was not to be repeated again until after World War II.

It has been argued by Gary Hawke, on the basis of his investigation of effective tariff protection[3] in the United States during the late nineteenth century, that there was much less increase in the protection given to U.S. industries between 1879 and 1904 than is commonly believed. The development of technology giving value added a larger share in the gross output of many industries and increased tariffs on inputs to many industries offset such increases in tariffs on industrial output as took place. For these reasons, in particular, the major tariff legislation of the 1890s produced a roughly constant level of effective protection. Moreover, the major growth industries in the United States during these years were not those accorded the highest effective tariffs. It is also clear from his study that the cotton goods industry gained greater protection from the nominal tariff on its output between 1879 and 1889, and that wool manufactures were very successful in their efforts to retain high protection for their industry throughout the period under investigation. It is also worth noting that these manufactures figured importantly in the exports of Britain and other European countries.

Protection in Europe

In Europe, a number of economic and political developments combined to bring about a return to protection after 1880. Economically, it was the desire for industrial development and the competition engendered by successful industrialization that was responsible for the growing demand for protection. Backing up the economic case for protection was the revival of nationalism in the late nineteenth century associated with the emergence of new nation states, such as Germany and Italy. In addition to embarrassing foreign industrial competition, increasing tariffs provided the larger revenues needed to meet the rising expenditures on armaments caused by the growing military rivalry between the states of Europe, as well as expenditures on education, public health and social services, which were in part social manifestations of the nationalist feeling. While nationalism and protectionism are not inevitably associated with one another, in nationalism we do have a force providing at least a predisposition toward protection. Taken together, nationalism and the lag in industrialization made protection inevitable.[4]

What actually started the swing to protectionism in Europe, however, was neither of these broad economic and political factors, but two specific economic developments of the 1870s. One was the large inflow of cheap grain into Europe from the United States and Russia; the other was the depression of 1873–9, the longest and deepest period of stagnant trade the world had yet experienced. Farmers and industrialists alike clamoured for relief, and the demands of this coalition of young industry and injured agriculture gave the initial stimulus to protection. Once started, this swing to protectionism was supported and maintained by the deeper forces of nationalism. Over time, pressure groups and vested interests grew in political power, and were often able to influence parliaments into granting greater protection to further their own self-interests. Protection also tended to spread across the board, as concessions to one group of industries made it difficult for governments to refuse similar privileges to others. Furthermore, from the 1890s, rate setting tended to become competitive. This tendency arose out of the two-tiered framework yielded by the commercial treaty system developed during these years. Under this treaty system, high general duties were levied on imports from non-treaty countries, and lower rates were applied to dutiable commodities from countries with which treaties had been concluded. As these treaties were renegotiated periodically, immediately before renegotiation, an extensive upward revision of the general (or maximum) tariff of each treaty country was legislated so as to ensure that negotiations would not result in a 'treaty' (or minimum) tariff detrimental to the country's industries. Such a procedure tended to produce higher all-round protection and, in some cases, tariff warfare, detrimental to all concerned. Taken together these developments produced a swing to protection within Europe that became more pronounced as we approach 1913. Over the whole period 1880–1913, only Britain, Holland and Denmark steadfastly adhered to free trade.

Stimulated by the depressed conditions in industry, the increased competition from imported grain, and the financial needs of the imperial government, protectionist sentiments gained ground in Germany in the late 1870s. Finally, in 1879, moderate tariff protection was extended to both agriculture and manufactures. Raw material imports, however, remained duty-free. Two major upward revisions of duties on grain followed in 1885 and 1888, but the next general revision of the tariff did not come until 1902. By then, the rate increased in the United States, France and Russia, together with the lapse of various treaties in which German duties were fixed by agreement, furnished an additional motive and a suitable opportunity for more protection. The new general tariff introduced much higher rates, particularly on finished manufactures, and was more detailed and specialized than the 1879 tariff. The duties on semi-manufactures were kept low, and raw materials continued to be admitted duty-free. A higher level of protection for agriculture was also provided, with increased duties on grain and livestock. The new system remained in being until it was swept away by the outbreak of war.

Many other countries followed Germany's example. Italy commenced the 1870s with a moderate tariff, but new legislation in 1878 substantially increased protection for manufacturing industry. A year later protection was extended to agriculture. In 1887 rates were raised to a high level and these remained in effect until after the war. The Swiss did not adopt a general tariff until 1884, when duties were imposed which remained only moderately high despite an upward revision in 1891. In 1906, however, new legislation provided high duties on foodstuffs and considerable increases in rates on manufactures. On the other hand, Russia reverted to protection as early as 1868, when manufactured imports were subjected to heavy duties in an effort to promote domestic industrialization. This Act was not superseded until 1891, but in the interim several all-round increases in duties occurred. The 1891 tariff legislation introduced a maximum–minimum rate structure for purposes of tariff bargaining, and placed duties on raw materials and semi-manufactures. The duties on coal, steel, machinery, and chemicals were raised so high that import of these goods practically ceased. Further increases of duties in 1893 and in the early 1900s maintained Russia's position as the most highly protected country in the world.

The demands made by French industrialists for protection were hampered by the persistence of a strong free-trade sentiment and by the existence of long-term commercial treaties which effectively pegged the French tariff at a low level. But in the 1880s, growing dissatisfaction in agriculture brought the farmers into line with the industrial advocates of higher tariffs, and in 1890 the combined protectionist forces gained political power. The Meline Tariff of 1892 meant higher duties all round, including an average increase of 25 per cent on duties on agricultural products, and some substantial increases of rates on manufactures. A two-tier system of maximum and minimum rates was introduced for treaty purposes, with the minimum rates themselves amply protective. A general revision of the new tariff structure did not occur until 1910, and then it was aimed primarily at covering the many new products, such as chemicals and electrical and rubber goods, that had been developed in the intervening years. The Tariff Act of 1910 predominantly favoured manufacturing industry, and only a few increases were granted on agricultural products. There were few reductions, and raw materials generally were exempted from duties.[5]

THE ECONOMIC CONSEQUENCES OF PROTECTION

Given the multitude of influences at work in the international economy during these years, the effect of the return to protection on the character and the volume of foreign trade after 1880 is not easily determined. However, taking into account the many strong 'trade-creating' forces at work in these years, the moderate level of the protective tariff in some countries, and the existence of commercial treaties that lowered them in many others, and remembering that, if tariffs discouraged some forms of international exchange, they also tended to stimulate rivalry in open markets, the conclusion that tariffs probably did not seriously hinder the growth of international trade in the period before 1914 seems a reasonable one. Indeed, world trade grew steadily between 1870 and 1914, averaging some 3.4 per cent annually over the entire period, and was growing faster than total world production which averaged 2.1 per cent per annum.

If world trade did not suffer unduly from the return to protection, the trade of individual countries may well have done so. Britain's export trade, in particular, could be expected to suffer from the protective tariffs imposed by the newly-industrializing nations. Here, woollen exports were the biggest losers, since their best markets were situated in the United States and Europe, where competition and protection were most severe, and since alternative markets were mostly lacking. In contrast, the cotton textile industry overcame its difficulties by exporting finer quality cottons to protected markets and by expanding the sales of cheaper cottons to the newly-developing countries where the protected cotton industries of Europe and America were rarely able to compete. Apart from the possibility of switching exports to unprotected markets, there are other reasons for not exaggerating the impact protection had on the overall level of British exports. Tariffs remained for the most part moderate, and Britain could always depend on the most-favoured nation clause embodied in the commercial treaties of the day to shield her from the worst excesses of her competitors. Moreover, where a long-run decline in British exports did occur it was more often because of a loss of competitiveness than because of protection. Thus, tariffs may have initially lost Britain markets for iron and steel manufactures in the United States and Germany, but later, when American and German producers surpassed the British in efficiency and competitiveness, they became unnecessary to keep British exporters out of these markets. Yet the changes in the composition of British exports due to the tariff were not without their problems for the future, for the shift was towards products which were less profitable and prospectively less capable of expansion. Exports of semi-manufactures grew in importance relative to exports of finished goods, and coal exports expanded rapidly after 1880. The forced specialization on quality products, and semi-manufactured goods, like yarn and pig iron, meant production to satisfy a more volatile demand, thus introducing a greater degree of instability in the British export sector than may formerly have existed. Moreover, the profits of further fabrication, which had previously accrued to Britain, were now passing to those countries which used British semi-manufactures to turn them into finished products. For the time being, however, the shift into new export lines was made without any great difficulty, and British exports continued to grow.

Although agricultural products became more highly protected as time passed, for much of the period between 1880 and 1914 raw materials and foodstuffs, with the exception of grain into Continental Europe, were comparatively free from restrictions, and consequently the 'regions of recent settlement' were not impeded in their growth by prohibitive tariffs. In any case, there was always the British market, the largest in Europe, into which primary producing countries enjoyed freedom of entry for their exports, for Britain's response to the decline in the world price of wheat after 1880 was to complete the liquidation of agriculture as an economic sector of any importance. France, Germany and Italy, as we have seen, responded to the new situation by imposing tariffs in an attempt to maintain the relative price of wheat and to protect grain producers. Denmark, however, did not impose a tariff on wheat. Instead it converted from the growing of grain to animal husbandry and specialization in dairy production. In carrying out this economic transformation, proximity to expanding industrial markets for dairy products in Britain and Germany was particularly helpful. The possibility that other countries, such as France and Germany, could have successfully adopted a similar policy of allowing free imports of grain and transferring domestic agricultural resources out of grain into livestock remains, however, a debatable point. But the failure of the British farmer to adjust quickly to the changed market situation contrasts sharply with the Danish success.

As for manufacturing industry, there is no doubt that the raising of tariff barriers in the United States, Germany and elsewhere initially contributed to its growth in these countries. But by the 1890s the 'infant industry' argument in favour of manufacturing protection was becoming somewhat threadbare, and the case for protection was being based on a variety of other arguments, such as self-sufficiency, maintaining employment levels, industrial diversification, protection of living standards and wage levels and so on, some of which were of dubious economic merit. Indeed, the need for protection at all, even for infant industries, was questioned. Thus, one survey of American protection before 1913 produced the conclusion that the protected industries in the United States had either always had comparative advantage over foreign competitors or they were never able to achieve comparative advantages even with tariff protection. Australian experiences of protection during these years suggest a somewhat similar conclusion, since manufacturing developments in protectionist Victoria do not appear to have been markedly different in rates of growth from those in free-trade New South Wales. Manufacturing industry in both colonies progressed whether tariffs were present or not.

Protection does appear to have had some influence on the structure of industry, however. In both the United States and Germany the big industrial concerns came to dominate manufacturing, and the resulting concentration of economic power contrasted sharply with the diffusion of economic power characteristic of the early stages of the British industrial revolution. As the amount of capital tied up in a particular venture increased, management became less willing to allow the success of the business to be decided by the uncontrolled operation of market forces. Through trusts, holding companies, and business combinations of various kinds, new large business enterprises endeavoured to control the competitive process in an attempt to fix prices and maintain or increase the return on their investment. Protected by tariffs, producers in the United States and Germany were able to eliminate domestic competition and create monopoly markets free from competition. In free-trade Britain, on the other hand, the threat of foreign competition was ever present and attempts at the monopolistic concentration of production were therefore less likely to succeed.

Monopolistic activities also spilled over into the international field in the form of international cartels. At the beginning of the present century it was estimated that at least 40 of these cartels were in existence, and in 1912 the figure was put at 100. They covered industries such as shipping, armaments, steel rails, electric bulbs, aluminium, calcium carbide, plate glass, tobacco, enamelware, and bottles. While international monopolies are not incompatible with free trade, the fact that they appeared in industries dominated by a few large firms suggests that protection, since it played some part in creating national monopolies, also contributed indirectly to creating conditions favourable to the international restriction of competition. Moreover, irrespective of the causes of the growth of these international cartels, their fundamental objectives—the control over prices, markets, supply, and technological change—are deterrents to specialization and trade, not only in products directly under their control, but also in other products manufactured in part from cartelized material. To what extent these cartels did restrict world trade in the period before 1913 is difficult to estimate, and therefore their significance should not be exaggerated. Mere numbers tell us little about their economic significance, which can be gauged only by estimating the proportion of total world trade formed by the commodities under their control, a calculation which has not yet been made. Moreover, the fact that Britain was not a member of most international cartels greatly limited their economic power, because the exercise of their monopoly powers was always subject to the threat of competition from Britain.

One final economic by-product of protection may be touched on briefly. This is the tendency for the existence of tariff barriers to stimulate direct foreign investment in protectionist countries. Since the aim of protection is to exclude foreign products from the domestic market of the country imposing the tariff, foreign firms can overcome these trade barriers by setting up branch factories in the markets concerned. Although not widespread before 1913, there were occasions when this kind of direct investment was undertaken. For example, the American tariff of 1883 hit certain cheaper cotton exports from Britain severely. As a result, several Lancashire cotton firms set up branches in the United States. Part of the American direct investment in Canada during the pre-1913 period was also due to the existence of the Canadian tariff.

While these examples could be multiplied, this type of investment remained comparatively rare before 1913, and direct investment, motivated partly by protection, was not undertaken on a large scale until after World War I.

NOTES

1 See later, pp. 70–1.
2 D. N. McCloskey, 'Magnanimous Albion: Free Trade and British National Income, 1841–81', *Explorations in Economic History* (July, 1980). See also his debate with P. J. Cain, *Explorations in Economic History* (Apr., 1982), pp. 201–10.
3 The rate of effective protection is measured by the percentage increase in domestic value added in the production of a commodity as a result of a tariff. Nominal tariff is a tariff calculated on the price of a final commodity.
4 See also P. T. Ellsworth, *The International Economy*, 1st edn. (New York, 1950), pp. 360–3.
5 Inter-country comparisons of tariff severity are difficult to make, but one estimate for the early years of this century puts the average tariff in Russia at 28 per cent, in the United States at 18.5 per cent, in France and Germany at 9.8 per cent, and in Austria at 7.5 per cent. See C. F. Bastable, *The Commerce of Nations* (London, 1923), p. 106.

SELECTED REFERENCES

Ashley, P., *Modern Tariff History* (London, 1910).
Condliffe, J. B., *The Commerce of Nations* (London, 1951), especially Chaps. VI–IX.
Drummond, I. M., 'The Russian Gold Standard, 1897–1914', *Journal of Economic History* (Sept., 1976), pp. 663–688.
Ellsworth, P. T., *The International Economy*, 3rd edn. (New York, 1964), Chap. XII.
Hawke, G. R., 'The United States Tariff and Industrial Protection in the Late Nineteenth Century', *Economic History Review* (Feb., 1975).
Hilton, B., *Corn, Cash, Commerce. The Economic Policies of the Tory Governments 1815–1830* (Oxford, 1977).
Isaacs, A., *International Trade: Tariff and Commercial Policies* (Chicago, 1948).
Kindleberger, C. P., 'The Rise of Free Trade in Western Europe, 1820 to 1875', *Journal of Economic History* (Mar., 1975).
McCloskey, D. N., 'Magnanimous Albion: Free Trade and British National Income, 1841–81', *Explorations in Economic History* (July, 1980), pp. 303–320.
Saul, S. B., *Studies in British Overseas Trade, 1870–1914* (Liverpool, 1960), especially Chap. VI.
Taussig, F. W., *Tariff History of the United States*, 8th edn. (New York, 1931).
Tracy, M., *Agriculture in Western Europe* (New York, 1964).

Chapter 5

Foreign trade in the nineteenth century

The task of charting the growth and changing nature of world trade during the period 1820 to 1913 has been helped enormously by Professor Kuznets' pioneering work in assembling and analysing the available statistical material, and the following discussion of foreign trade developments in the nineteenth century owes much to his latest work in the field.[1] The discussion itself will be limited to a consideration of commodity trade, since long-term data on the international flows of services (freight earnings, insurance and banking, tourism, etc) are scarce. An analysis of the available services data suggests, however, that earnings on services tend to rise proportionately to commodity trade. Moreover, the average proportion of services to commodity trade is, for all but the smallest of countries, limited to between a tenth and one-sixth. Even so, it should be kept in mind that, for some countries, for example Britain, services income played an important part in covering deficits on commodity trade, and that for others an export surplus on commodity trade could quickly disappear once payments for services are taken into account.

THE GROWTH OF WORLD TRADE BEFORE 1913

Two broad conclusions are suggested by the trends in the foreign trade statistics available for the period 1800 to 1913: first, that the period was characterized by high rates of growth in foreign trade, and second, that world trade grew at much higher rates than world output during these years. For long sub-periods, of 30 years or more, total foreign trade grew at rates ranging from 29 to 64 per cent per decade, and, on a per capita basis, from 23 to 53 per cent per decade. The highest decadal growth rates, whether measured in total or per capita terms, were registered in the sub-period 1840–70, with growth rates tending to rise throughout earlier decades and to decline thereafter. At the same time, world output per head appears to have grown at an average rate of 7.3 per cent per decade between 1800 to 1913, whereas per capita world trade averaged 33 per cent per decade over the same period.

The net result of these changes was a marked rise in the proportion of world trade to world product. By 1913, the volume of foreign trade per capita had grown to over 25 times what it had been in 1800, whereas world output per head had grown only 2.2 times over the same period. This means that during the period 1800–1913 the foreign trade proportion, that is, the ratio of world trade to world product, rose to over 11 times its initial level.[2] Moreover, if, as seems likely, the world proportion of foreign trade to product was about 33 per cent in 1913, it must have been barely 3 per cent in 1800. What brought about this marked rise in the world foreign trade proportion? Partly responsible for this development was the introduction of new nations into the network of world trade during the nineteenth century. More important were the growing propensity to trade displayed by countries during these years, particularly the older and more developed nations of the world, and the emergence of major technological and institutional forces, discussed earlier, which tended to foster a faster rate of growth of trade between countries than growth of output within them.

This marked rise in foreign trade proportions was characteristic of groups of countries and of countries taken individually. These proportions rose markedly in both the developed and underdeveloped parts of the world, with the relative rise in the foreign trade proportion greater for the latter than for the former group of countries, which is not surprising seeing that many of these countries were integrated into the world trading network for the first time during the nineteenth century.[3] Looking at individual countries, the foreign trade proportions of the industrial European countries and Japan rose substantially between 1800 and 1913, while they declined slightly for the younger overseas countries, such as the United States and Australia, which already had high foreign trade proportions at the beginning of our period. In the circumstances, these 'new' regions could hardly be expected to become even more dependent on foreign trade once their domestic economies became more broadly based. This was particularly so with the United States with its abundant natural resources while, in both Australia and America, transport developments seem to have encouraged higher rates of growth of domestic output than of foreign trade. In Europe, on the other hand, limited raw material supplies and a rapidly growing population appear to have increased the continent's dependence on foreign trade throughout the century, so that the foreign trade proportions of European countries grew rather than declined or remained stable.

THE DIRECTION OF WORLD TRADE BEFORE 1913

The distribution of world trade by geographic region over the period 1876 to 1913 is shown in Table 9, while Figure 6 illustrates the position in 1913. As can be seen from the table and figure, Europe dominated world trade in the

Table 9 Regional distribution of world trade, 1876–1913

Region	%					
	1876–80			*1913*		
	Exports	*Imports*	*Total trade*	*Exports*	*Imports*	*Total trade*
Europe [1]	64.2	69.6	66.9	58.9	65.1	62.0
N. America	11.7	7.4	9.5	14.8	11.5	13.2
Latin America [2]	6.2	4.6	5.4	8.3	7.0	7.6
Asia	12.4	13.4	12.9	11.8	10.4	11.1
Africa	2.2	1.5	1.9	3.7	3.6	3.7
Oceania	3.3	3.5	3.4	2.5	2.4	2.4
World	100.0	100.0	100.0	100.0	100.0	100.0

Source: P. Lamartine Yates, *Forty years of Foreign Trade* (London, 1959), Tables 6 and 7, pp. 32–3.

Notes: 1. Including Russia. 2. Central and South America, including all colonial territories in the Western hemisphere.

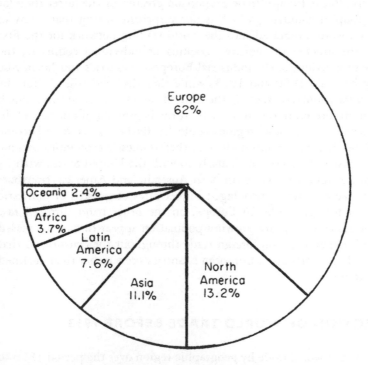

Figure 6 Regional distribution of total world trade, 1913

Source: As for Table 9.

nineteenth century, when it consisted largely of intra-European trade and Europe's trade with overseas areas, especially those settled by Europeans. This predominance was maintained throughout the period up to 1913, despite the continuous growth of the North American share of world trade, and the tendency for the European, and particularly for the United Kingdom, share to fall. In 1913 Europe (including Russia) took some 65 per cent of the world's imports and accounted for 59 per cent of its exports, whereas the North American shares were 12 and 15 per cent respectively.[4]

Because of the spread of industrialization, and the emergence of new centres of primary production overseas, significant changes in the pattern of trade between countries and between regions occurred at this time. For European countries other than Britain, dependence on Europe for imports and for export markets was initially very marked, with the degree of dependence tending to grow as the size of the country concerned diminished. After 1870, however, as the demand for foodstuffs and raw materials drawn from overseas suppliers rose in response to industrial development and population growth, there was some decline in the degree of dependence of European countries on the continental market. At the same time, there were associated changes in the demand for primary products which had important consequences for the different trading countries. Thus, from the 1820s to the mid-1890s, purchases of tropical products grew more slowly than imports of foodstuffs and raw materials coming from temperate regions. Thereafter, however, imports of tropical products from Latin America, Asia, and Africa rose significantly.

The tendency for European countries, including Britain, to draw their imports increasingly from continents other than Europe as the nineteenth century proceeded reflected the heavy dependence of overseas countries on Europe as a market for their exports. The United States was no exception to this rule. By the 1880s, over four-fifths of its exports were going to Europe, and despite a rapid expansion of American exports to Canada, Latin America, and Asia after 1895, the European share was still 60 per cent in 1913. Moreover, two-thirds of United States imports came from Europe in the 1850s, and although Europe's share declined thereafter, it remained around 50 per cent of the total after the 1870s. At the same time, significant changes in the relative importance of the different European countries supplying the American market took place. Britain's share of total imports fell from a peak of 46 per cent in the early 1850s to 17 per cent in the years 1911–13. On the other hand, the share of imports coming from continental European countries, and especially Germany, continued to grow throughout the period and accounted for one-third of the total by 1913.

Two-thirds of Latin America's trade was with Europe, with Britain, Germany, France and Spain by far the most important of the countries concerned. If the United States is included, the share rises to 90 per cent in the years 1901–5. The trade of Africa and of Oceania was even more dependent on the European market than was that of Latin America, with Britain in particular a major source of exports to and by far the biggest importer of merchandise from these two continents. Canadian trade, on the other hand, was dominated by Britain and the United States. Whereas Britain remained the more important market for Canadian exports throughout the century before 1913, over the years Canadian imports from the United States grew at the expense of those from Britain until, late in the nineteenth century, she lost first place in the Canadian market to the United States.

India, China and Britain constituted a tightly-knit trading bloc in Asia in the period before 1880. After the 1870s, however, the picture begins to change. The closing down of the opium trade in the 1880s, the rise of Japan as the first Asian industrial power, and the economic penetration of China by European powers other than Britain were developments that significantly altered the pattern of international trade in the Far East. As Japan industrialized, the structure of its foreign trade was completely reversed, from one in which raw materials were exported and finished manufactures imported to one in which manufactures were exported and raw materials imported. The direction of Japan's foreign trade changed in sympathy with these developments. Asia replaced Europe and the United States as the main source of Japanese imports, supplying almost one-half of these needs by 1913. By that date Asia had also become Japan's leading regional export market.

Despite the growing industrial importance of the United States and Japan in the late nineteenth century, the direction of world trade in the period before 1913 was dominated by Europe's ever-growing demand for foodstuffs and raw materials. Before World War I, Europe absorbed more than 80 per cent of the exports of Belgium, Holland, Argentina, South Africa and New Zealand; 75–80 per cent of those of Germany and Australia; over 60 per cent of those of France, Italy and the United States; and more than half of Canada's and India's. The foreign trade of Britain was distributed almost equally among the Empire, continental Europe and the rest of the world. Europe's share in the imports of these and other countries was somewhat less than its share in their exports. Considering both imports and exports, it appears that Britain carried on an extensive trade with all parts of the world; Canada belonged to the American economic community; China and Japan had the strongest commercial ties with Asia; and almost all other nations gravitated towards European markets.

The extent to which Europe dominated world trade before World War I is seen even more clearly if we consider the percentage distribution of the flow of merchandise trade in 1913. Two-fifths of this trade represented intra-European exchange, slightly more than one-fifth of Europe's imports from non-European countries, and 15 per cent exports from Europe to non-European countries. Thus, trade among non-European countries accounted for less than one-quarter of the world trade in merchandise in 1913.[5]

THE COMPOSITION OF WORLD TRADE BEFORE 1913

The longest series of data on the composition of world commodity trade reaches back to the late 1870s, and distinguishes primary products from manufactured articles. The most intriguing feature of the series is the fact that the proportion of primary products to total trade remained remarkably constant in the period up to 1913, and beyond (see Table 10). This stability was maintained despite the spread of industrialization and the consequent decline in the relative share of primary production in total output, and despite significant changes in the composition of the export trade in primary products. Since primary products bulk large in the exports of underdeveloped countries, and since many such economies were newly integrated into the pattern of world trade with the passing of the nineteenth century, the stability in the share of primary products in world trade might possibly be explained in terms of these developments counteracting the growth of trade in manufactures between industrializing countries. But, as Kuznets has shown, the slight rise in the share in world trade of underdeveloped countries—from 27 to 28 per cent of the total—does little in itself to explain the fact of stability. Further explanation must be sought in the details of the foreign trade of the regions and countries concerned.

Table 11 and Figure 7 show the nature of the changes in the regional distribution of trade in primary products and manufactures during the period 1876–1913. In these years the volume of the export trade in primary products more than trebled. With the exception of 'Other Europe', all regions shared in the expansion, with the growth outside Europe and North America being especially strong between 1895 and 1913. The North American share in this trade grew only slightly, whereas Europe, often overlooked as an exporter of primary products, saw its share rise to almost one-half of the world total around 1900, and then drop back to the level of the late 1870s by 1913. Complementing the export of primary products was the import trade in manufactures. The volume of this trade almost trebled between 1876–80 and 1913, with imports into North America more than quadrupling in volume

Table 10 Share of primary products in world trade, 1876–1913

	Based on volume in current prices %	Based on volume in 1913 prices %
1876–80	63.5	61.8
1886–90	62.3	62.2
1896–1900	64.3	67.7
1906–10	63.2	64.0
1913	62.5	62.5

Source: Kuznets, op. cit., Table 6, p. 33.

Table 11a Trade in primary products: regional shares, 1876–1913

Region	%					
	1876–80		*1896–1900*		*1913*	
	Imports	*Exports*	*Imports*	*Exports*	*Imports*	*Exports*
U.K. and Ireland	29.7	3.1	25.8	3.9	19.0	6.2
N.W. Europe[1]	39.3	22.6	45.0	27.6	43.1	25.2
Other Europe	11.2	20.2	10.4	18.1	12.3	14.7
U.S. and Canada	7.2	16.1	8.5	18.7	11.3	17.3
Rest of world	12.6	38.0	10.3	31.7	14.3	36.6
World	100.0	100.0	100.0	100.0	100.0	100.0

Table 11b Trade in manufactures: regional shares, 1876–1913

Region	%					
	1876–80		*1896–1900*		*1913*	
	Imports	*Exports*	*Imports*	*Exports*	*Imports*	*Exports*
U.K. and Ireland	9.1	37.8	10.4	31.5	8.2	25.3
N.W. Europe[1]	18.1	47.1	20.3	45.8	24.4	47.9
Other Europe	13.3	9.2	12.2	10.3	15.4	8.3
U.S. and Canada	7.7	4.4	9.6	7.4	12.1	10.6
Rest of world	51.8	1.5	47.5	5.0	39.9	7.9
World	100.0	100.0	100.0	100.0	100.0	100.0

Source: Yates, op. cit., Tables 19, 21, 23 and 25, pp. 47–51.

Note: 1. Includes Finland, Sweden, Norway, Denmark, Germany, Belgium, the Netherlands, Switzerland and Austria.

during these years, and those of continental Europe more than doubling between 1896–1900 and 1913. With the import trade in manufactures growing so strongly in Europe and North America, the share of the underdeveloped countries in this trade actually fell in the years up to 1913.

Looking at the situation in reverse, and concentrating on those regions which predominantly exported manufactures and imported primary products, we find that the most striking features of the world export trade in manufactures was the growth of the North American share and the decline in the United Kingdom share over the whole of the period 1876–80 to 1913. Continental Europe's share remained stable, and Japan entirely accounts for the high Asian proportion. The rest of the underdeveloped world was a

Figure 7(a) Regional shares of world trade, 1876–1913, trade in primary products

virtual non-starter in manufacturing production and export by 1913. Turning to the import trade in primary products, the United Kingdom's share fell heavily after 1876–80, whereas because of rapid industrialization and rising real incomes, the shares of North America and continental Europe rose. The growing imports of primary products into the rest of the world after 1896 consisted primarily of food and raw materials for Japan.

Table 12 and Figure 8, which give the respective shares of primary products and manufactures in the total trade of the developed and underdeveloped regions of the world, reveal certain other important features in the composition of world trade before 1913. First, and most obviously, the developed countries chiefly exported manufactures and imported primary products, whereas the trade pattern was reversed for the underdeveloped countries, which mainly exported primary products and imported manufactured goods. Moreover, among the developed countries we find, as we would expect, that primary products are a much larger element in the exports of the United States and Canada, on the one hand, than of the United Kingdom and N.W. Europe, on the other. Similar differences are evident in the structure of imports, with primary products a smaller and manufactures a larger element in the import trade of the former than of the latter. Perhaps the most interesting feature of Table 12, however, is the trends in the structure of the trade in

Figure 7(b) Regional shares of world trade, 1876–1913, trade in manufactures

primary products which it reveals. Taking the export trade first, we notice that the shares of primary products rose for the United Kingdom and N.W. Europe, and declined for all other regions, both developed and underdeveloped. The trends in the structure of the import trade in primary products show declining shares for the United Kingdom and N.W. Europe, a stable share for the United States and Canada, and a fluctuating, if declining, share for Other Europe. It is, however, the trend in the structure of imports of the underdeveloped countries that differs significantly from those of developed countries. In the underdeveloped regions imports shifted toward, not away from, primary products; the share of the latter rising from 31 per cent in 1876–80 to 40 per cent in 1913. As Kuznets points out, it is probably the slight decline in the share of primary products in the trade of developed countries combined with a rise, also slight, in the share of primary products in the trade of underdeveloped countries, plus a shift in the relative weight of different regions, for example, the rise in the weight of the United States and other developed areas overseas and the decline in the weight of the United

Table 12 Shares of primary products and manufactures in total trade of each region, 1876–1913

Region	%					
	1876–80		1896–1900		1913	
	Primary products	Manu-factures	Primary products	Manu-factures	Primary products	Manu-factures
Export trade						
U.K. and Ireland	11.9	88.1	17.2	82.8	30.3	69.7
N.W. Europe	43.8	56.2	50.5	49.5	48.0	52.0
Other Europe	78.1	21.9	74.9	25.1	75.6	24.4
U.S. and Canada	85.7	14.3	81.0	19.0	74.1	25.9
Underdeveloped countries and rest of world	97.6	2.4	91.6	8.4	89.1	10.9
World	61.9	38.1	62.8	37.2	61.8	38.2
Export trade						
U.K. and Ireland	85.8	14.2	82.6	17.4	81.2	18.8
N.W. Europe	60.9	39.1	62.0	38.0	59.9	40.1
U.S. and Canada	63.5	36.5	63.0	37.0	63.4	36.6
Underdeveloped countries and rest of world	30.9	69.1	29.2	70.8	40.2	59.8
World	64.9	35.1	65.6	34.3	65.0	35.0

Source: Kuznets, op. cit., Table 8A, p. 38; see also Yates, op. cit., Table 28, p. 55.

Kingdom, which accounts for the stability in the share of primary products in world trade between 1876 and 1913.

However, this stability in shares hides significant variations in the composition of the trade in primary products and manufactures. Within the manufactures component for the developed countries, a decline in the share of textile manufactures occurred along with a rise in the share of metal manufactures, and a fairly general rise in the share of other manufactures (chemicals, paper and wood products, clay and glass products). These changes in the composition of the exports of the developed countries were partly due to industrialization and the consequent changes in the structure of domestic output that accompanied it—involving a move away from primary production towards manufacturing, and within the latter a move away from textiles to metal manufactures, chemicals, and engineering products. They were also partly caused by the extension of the international economy and the consequently greater international division of labour, which applied within manufacturing activity as well as between manufacturing and primary

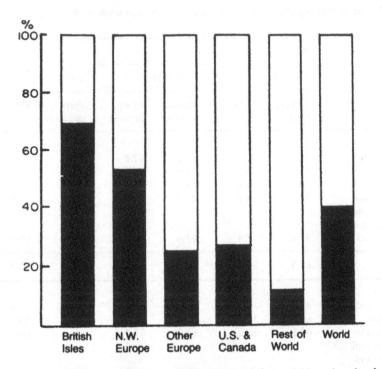

Figure 8(a) Shares of primary products and manufactures in total trade of each region, 1913, exports

Note: The shaded area represents manufactures.

production. In the changed situation the developed countries found themselves at a growing comparative disadvantage in the production of foodstuffs and raw materials at the same time as their efficiency in manufacturing production was increasing.

Given the rapid expansion of metal manufacturing after 1870 and the consequent increase in the demand for ores and concentrates, the changes in the composition of the world trade in primary products are much what we would expect. The shares of foodstuffs and agricultural raw materials in the total trade declined, while that of minerals increased. Detailed inter-country comparisons based on the level and trend in the shares of the different commodities in imports and exports are out of the question here, but the broad trends—the prevalent rise in the share of manufactures in both exports and imports, the particularly marked decline in the shares of food and agricultural raw materials and of textile manufactures in both exports and imports, the equally general rise in the shares of metal product manufactures and of other manufactures—all are clearly characteristic of most developed countries within the periods covered by the available statistical material.

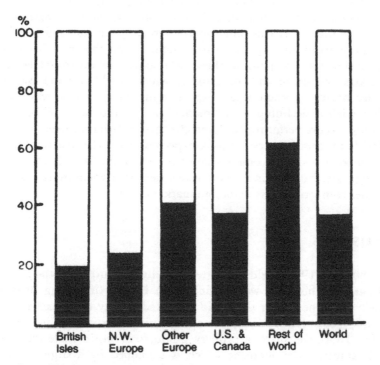

Figure 8(b) Shares of primary products and manufactures in total trade of each region, 1913, imports

Source: As for Table 11.

Note: The shaded area represents manufactures.

One other aspect of these general trends in the structure of world trade calls for comment. It concerns the relative decline of Britain in world trade after 1870. Despite the sharp fall in Britain's relative share of world trade in primary products, from about 30 per cent in 1876–80 to 19 per cent in 1913 (Table 11a and Figure 7(a)), there was a marked increase in Britain's dependence on overseas sources of supply. This was only to be expected, given Britain's limited supplies of natural raw materials and her free trade policy. By 1913, seven-eighths of Britain's raw materials (excluding coal) and just over half of her food came from overseas. As for manufactured exports, almost all of the decline in Britain's share of this world market appears to have taken place after 1890. Whereas Britain seems to have held her own in textiles, chemicals and non-metalliferous materials, and raised her share of the world export trade in miscellaneous finished goods (furniture, leather, rubber manufactures and so forth) and drink and tobacco products, the losses arose in iron and steel, in metal manufactures, and in transport equipment. When Britain's export performance is examined in terms of the distribution of her exports between expanding, stable, and contracting commodity groups, a further weakness is uncovered. Britain was losing ground in commodity groups, such as machinery (including motor vehicles) and iron and steel, for which world demand was expanding most rapidly. On the other hand, her export expansion was occurring in those commodity groups (miscellaneous finished goods and drink and tobacco) for which world demand was declining. Her most important single export item, cotton goods, was also a commodity with a declining world market. As to the cause of Britain's disappointing export performance, some changes in Britain's overall shares of world trade in manufactures was to be expected, given the structural shifts in the commodity and area composition of trade noted earlier. Even so, the evidence suggests that Britain's export losses were overwhelmingly due to a decline in her competitiveness in foreign markets.

CONCLUSIONS

Between 1800 and 1913 world trade grew rapidly, far outpacing the growth of world output. This trade was dominated by Europe (including Britain), whose trade with the rest of the world consisted largely of an exchange of manufactured goods for primary products. Despite the spread of industrialization after 1850, the share of primary products in world trade remained remarkably stable, a development which is explained by a slight relative decline in demand for primary products by developed countries being offset by a moderate increase in the exchange of primary products between the underdeveloped countries. Throughout the period after the late 1870s, the share of foodstuffs and agricultural raw materials in world trade in primary products tended to decline, whereas that of non-agricultural raw materials rose. A change in the composition of world trade in manufactures is also apparent, with the textiles share declining and that of metal products and other manufactures rising.

This rapid growth of trade during the second half of the nineteenth century and the associated changes in its commodity composition and direction created a new and increasingly more complex network of economic activity and trade embracing whole continents or sub-continents. The earlier pattern of largely disconnected trading arrangements mainly centred on Britain gave way after 1860 to a new multilateral trading system based on a worldwide pattern of economic specialization. The general nature of the new pattern of world trade is clear enough. It involved an exchange of manufactured goods for raw materials and foodstuffs between the rapidly industrializing countries of Europe and North America and primary producing countries situated for the most part in the rest of the world. With the exception of Britain, the industrializing countries ran up heavy balance of payments deficits with the primary producers. Britain, on the other hand, largely because of her free trade policy, became a heavy importer of both manufactures and primary produce. She was also the most important exporter of manufactured goods to non-European primary producers, as well as the world's largest foreign lender. Consequently, Britain had a trade surplus with the primary producing countries. This surplus, plus Britain's invisible earnings (payments for services, such as banking, insurance and shipping, rendered to foreigners and earnings on foreign investments), provided the foreign exchange she needed to cover her excess of imports from industrializing countries, thus providing these countries in turn with the means with which to finance their deficits with primary producers overseas. This, broadly, was the character of the multilateral system of trade settlement that had emerged by 1913. In the next chapter the growth and development of this system during the nineteenth century is examined in greater detail.

NOTES

1 S. Kuznets, 'Quantitative Aspects of the Economic Growth of Nations: X-Levels and Structure of Foreign Trade: Long-term Trends', *Economic Development and Cultural Change*, Part II (Jan., 1967).
2 The foreign trade proportion is given by the ratio 25:2.2.
3 Kuznets, op. cit., p. 15. Kuznets includes in the developed countries Canada, the U.S., Europe, Australia, New Zealand, and, after 1880, Japan and the Union of South Africa. The underdeveloped countries cover Africa (excluding South Africa after 1880), Asia (excluding Japan after 1880) and Latin America.
4 For a detailed study of European trade in the nineteenth century, see Paul Bairoch, 'Geographical Structure and Trade Balance of European Foreign Trade from 1800 to 1970', *Journal of European Economic History* (Winter, 1974), pp. 557–608.
5 W. S. *and* E. S. Woytinsky, *World Commerce and Governments* (New York, 1955), p. 71.

SELECTED REFERENCES

Cairncross, A. K., 'World Trade in Manufactures since 1900', *Economia Internazionale* (Dec., 1955). Reprinted in Cairncross, *Factors in Economic Development* (London, 1962), Chap. XIV.
Green, A., and Urquhart, M. C., 'Factor and Commodity Flows in the International Economy, 1870–1914', *Journal of Economic History* (Mar., 1976), pp. 217–252.
Hanson, J. R., *Trade in Transition: Exports from the Third World, 1840–1900* (New York, 1980).
Kuznets, S., 'Quantitative Aspects of the Economic Growth of Nations: X-Levels and Structure of Foreign Trade: Long-term Trends', *Economic Development and Cultural Change*, Part II (Jan., 1967).
Lamartine Yates, P., *Forty Years Trade* (London, 1959).
Latham, A. J. H., *The International Economy and the Underdeveloped World, 1865–1914* (London, 1978).

Saul, S. B., 'The Export Economy, 1870–1914', *Yorkshire Bulletin of Economic and Social Research*, Special Number (May, 1965), pp. 5–18.
Woodruff, W., *Impact of Western Man* (New York, 1966), Chap. VII.
Woytinsky, W. S., and E. S., *World Commerce and Governments* (New York, 1955).

Chapter 6

The growth of a multilateral payments network

INTRODUCTION

An important development associated with the growth of the international economy between 1870 and 1913 was the emergence of a complex multilateral payments network, which facilitated the movements of goods, services, capital and income payments to such a degree that the braking forces of certain impediments to the growth of international commercial relations after 1870 were minimized. Before embarking upon a description of the growth and development of this network of trade and payments, however, it is necessary to define certain concepts of vital significance to the subsequent discussion.

The balance of payments of a country is a systematic record of all economic transactions between the residents of that country and residents of foreign countries during a given period of time. However, in order to simplify the following analysis, we shall assume that only commodities are traded between countries and that only gold is used to settle any outstanding trade balances. The fact that services and other 'invisible' items also enter into a country's foreign trading account, and that capital flows from country to country, does not in any way invalidate the conclusions we draw from an analysis of our highly simplified trading system, and it is always possible to extend the argument to cover all types of foreign transactions.[1]

Trade and payments patterns between countries may develop along a number of lines. A *Bilateral* trade and payments system arises when the payments for commodity imports received by country A from country B are offset by payments for exports from A to B. If, under gold standard conditions, these two flows of payments do not entirely offset one another over a certain period, usually one year, then a balancing movement of gold will occur from the debtor to the creditor country.

A *Triangular* payments system introduces a third country, C, into the international trading network. Such a system is illustrated in Figure 9, where each country in which an arrow originates has a payments surplus with the country at which the arrow is pointed. Consequently, for each country in

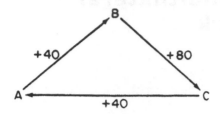

Figure 9 A triangular payments system

the system a deficit in one direction may be partly, wholly, or more than offset by its surplus in another direction. Thus, A's deficit with C is just offset by its surplus with B; B's deficit with A is more than offset by its surplus with C; and C's deficit with B is partly offset by its surplus with A. It is essential to note that in the triangular payments system a large proportion of the international payments between countries will still be settled bilaterally and that it is only each country's remaining payments surpluses and deficits with other countries that will enter into the triangular system. The significance of such a triangular system is that it overcomes the need for balancing each bilateral surplus or deficit, and thus reduces the extent of international gold flows. For example, in Figure 9, whereas bilateral balancing would produce gold flows of 160, because of triangular settlement, a gold flow of only 40 (from C to B) would occur.

Finally, a *Multilateral* payments system is defined as one including more than three countries or regions (A, B, C, D, etc). In this situation, which is illustrated in a highly simplified form in Figure 10, an extension of the 'roundaboutness' of trade settlements occurs. Once again, the fact that a country's payments surpluses in one direction can offset its deficits in another reduces the need for gold movements as a final balancing item in international transactions. Thus, moving around the rim of the diagram (where the largest favourable balances are conventionally recorded) we find that the offsetting of debits and credits leads to a gold flow of only 30 compared with 100 when the outstanding balances are settled bilaterally. But multilateralism

Figure 10 A multilateral payments system

involves more than this, for each country will trade with all the other countries included in the system, that is, A will trade with C (the dotted arrow in the diagram) as well as with B and D. It is probable therefore that a multilateral payments system will include a number of triangular payments networks like ABC and ACD which will also work to reduce gold flows between countries. Thus, if country A has a surplus of 5 with country C in addition to its surplus of 10 with B, a gold flow of only 25 will now be needed to achieve 'worldwide' balance. It follows therefore that the larger the number of countries trading multilaterally the greater the opportunities for offsetting deficits and surpluses and, consequently, the smaller the flow of gold needed to achieve overall balance between the countries concerned. It also follows that the smaller the demands placed on the available stock of gold in the trading countries, the less is the likelihood of a country restricting its trade with other countries in order to protect its gold holdings. In other words, the existence of a multilateral payments system is a powerful support to the growth of trade between countries.

This is the sort of payments system which Hilgerdt discovered emerging from his estimates of international trade for the period after 1870. By arranging countries according to the order and direction of their trade balances in a chosen year, he found that each country had an import balance with practically every country or group of countries which preceded it in a circular flow system and an export balance with countries succeeding it. A definite pattern of trade and payments emerged even when countries with similar economic structures were grouped together.[2] Hilgerdt concluded from his study that the servicing of unfavourable trade balances in the late nineteenth century entailed an extensive 'roundaboutness' of payments of various kinds. He also noted that, despite the existence of a pattern of multilateral settlements, a substantial part of merchandise trade continued to be settled on a bilateral basis, in the sense that the value of exports from (say) B to A was offset to some extent by B's imports from A. Hilgerdt estimated that about 70 per cent of all trade was bilateral during the late nineteenth century, and that probably a rather small proportion of the remainder was offset by foreign investment and other non-trade money flows. This meant that from 20 to 25 per cent of total world trade was multilateral in nature by World War I.

DEVELOPMENT OF THE SYSTEM

The multilateral settlement of international transactions was no new phenomenon restricted to the late nineteenth century. Multilateralism, at least of a primitive type, had been a major feature of international economic relations for centuries. Thus, the triangular system comprising the United Kingdom, Western Europe and the Baltic countries had dominated Northern Europe's trade for many years, and the 'slave' triangle, linking Britain, Africa and the

West Indies provided another example of this type of trading pattern. Other triangular trading systems developed during the first half of the nineteenth century. By the 1860s, for example, Britain's trade deficits with the United States were largely covered by her surpluses with Latin America, and a British deficit with China was offset by a surplus with India. But the new payments network that began to emerge after 1870 was essentially different from these earlier trading systems. Whereas the latter consisted of disconnected triangular networks centred on Britain, with each triangle arising out of an entirely different set of trading circumstances, the post-1870 variety was more complicated in nature and wider in scope. It arose partly out of the merging of some of the previously disconnected triangular systems, and partly out of the growing importance in world trade of countries and regions other than Britain. Thus, by 1914, in contrast to the disconnected pattern of trading activities centred on Britain characteristic of the period before 1870, there existed a complicated system of international exchange based on a network of economic activities embracing most parts of the world. Britain still played a central role in the new system, but her trading relations with the rest of the world had undergone a profound change.

Within the new system, which is described in a simplified form in Figure 11,[3] the United States emerged as a separate link in the chain of international trade and payments in the years after the 1880s. At the beginning of that decade the bulk of American exports, which consisted predominantly of primary products, was shipped to Europe, from which region the United States also received more than half of its imports. In this way, the country experienced export surpluses with Europe (including Britain) and trade deficits with the rest of the world. As substantial domestic capital accumulation occurred, however, rapid industrialization got under way, and by the mid-1890s the United States had become a net exporter of manufactures. In consequence, by 1910–14 the early pattern of American trade had altered dramatically. Even when capital flows, interest and dividend payments and other 'invisibles' are taken into account, the United States still had a large surplus with the United Kingdom, but compared with the 1880s its deficit with continental Europe was smaller. On the other hand, America's import surplus with the Tropics, chiefly India and Brazil, had enlarged considerably, mainly because of its increased demand for raw materials and foodstuffs. Most

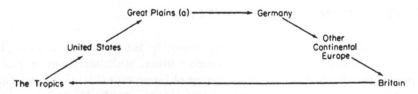

Figure 11 The multilateral trade system after 1900

Note: (a) Canada, Australia, Argentina, etc.

important of all, however, was the emergence of an American export surplus with the Great Plains countries, especially Canada, which came about largely because of their increased demand for American manufactures. It was this large and growing export surplus with the Great Plains region, rather than the credit balance with Britain or the large reductions in deficit balances with continental Europe, which financed the United States' growing deficit with the Tropics.

As the United States became less dependent on the European market for its trade, the Great Plains region was drawn close to Europe by improvements in land and sea transport and by the growth of the European market for agricultural and other land-intensive commodities. As a result it quickly opened up favourable trade balances with the continent. On the other hand, despite an expansion of exports to Britain, these land-intensive countries became large debtors of Britain and tended to rely more and more on their favourable trade balances with continental Europe to finance their growing imports of British goods and the servicing of their accumulated capital debts and other 'invisibles' payments due to Britain. As the period progressed, however, it was with America that these countries came to record their largest import deficits.

After the early 1880s, Germany also emerged as another link in the network of trade. Because of the rapid growth of its manufacturing industries and a relative decline in its agriculture, Germany's demand for raw materials and foodstuffs grew rapidly, and import surpluses with the Great Plains countries developed when they began to replace the United States as the German source of supply of these commodities. During the 1890s, moreover, German trade deficits with other major continental countries turned into surpluses when Germany found in these countries a ready market for its increasing exports of manufactures. These other European countries in turn increased their export surpluses with the United Kingdom, at least until 1900. Although these surpluses declined thereafter, because of heavy imports of British coal and colonial produce, they nevertheless remained fairly substantial, and produced a partial offset to the deficits which these countries had developed with Germany and the Great Plains region.

At the centre of the new multilateral trading network stood Britain, whose major contributions to its development during the period 1880 to 1914 included her growing import surplus, which declined somewhat after 1910; her free trade policy, which greatly facilitated the growth of the exports of other countries by providing a readily accessible market (partly at the expense of British agriculture); and the expansion of her international lending, which produced a favourable effect on Britain's balance of payments as income receipts from these foreign investments continuously increased.

In 1880, when foreign lending was relatively small, Britain's large deficits with continental Europe and the United States, and her smaller deficits with Australia, Canada, Egypt, and several other countries, were largely offset by favourable balances with India, South America, Turkey and Japan, with approximately one-third of British deficits with the United States and the continent being settled through India. By 1910, however, certain major changes had occurred in the British trade and payments pattern. Total negative balances with the United States had risen, Canada, the Straits Settlements, and South Africa (all recipients of large British investment) had by now become creditors of Britain, and South America was no longer a major debtor to Britain. In 1910, therefore, the settlement of British debit balances tended to flow to a large extent through the Far East and Australia. In particular, India, which offset approximately 40 per cent of Britain's total deficits, continued to provide the key to the United Kingdom's payments system by maintaining heavy export surpluses with continental Europe, the rest of the Empire, China and Hong Kong, and to a lesser extent, Japan and the United States—in other words, with many of Britain's creditors at the time. The importance of India to Britain became even more marked in the period from 1910 to 1914. The balance of payments of Australia, Brazil, Argentina, and Canada all moved sharply against Britain, but fortunately for Britain the surplus with India expanded still further. While the Indian market continued to absorb large quantities of British manufactures, the entry of which into many other countries was impeded by tariff protection, Indian products exported to the continent, the United States and elsewhere attracted little tariff attention. As a result, Britain was able to absorb large quantities of foodstuffs, raw materials and manufactures from highly protected countries without having to increase her exports to these countries. Had the United Kingdom also moved towards protection during the period, international trade would undoubtedly have expanded at a slower rate, for industrial Europe and the United States would have been compelled to find other markets for their exports or to adjust their industrial structures.

An attempt to estimate the pattern of settlement for the year 1910 has been made by S. B. Saul. Figure 12 is adapted from his 'highly approximate' estimates of the overall trade balances between various pairs of countries or regions for that year so as to make the resulting system of multilateral trade comparable to that shown later for the year 1928 (see Figure 17, page 222). The arrows in the figure indicate the balances of merchandise trade, in millions of pounds sterling or of dollars (in brackets) pointing from net exporting to net importing countries or region. For example, in 1910 the United Kingdom had an export surplus with the Tropics (India), but import surpluses with the United States, Continental Europe and the Great Plains of £50 million, $45 million and £12 million respectively. On the other hand, the United States had export surpluses with the United Kingdom and the Great Plains, but imported more from the Tropics and from Continental Europe than it exported to these regions.[4]

When all these trends are taken into account the complexity of the multi-lateral payments network can be appreciated. Not only did it provide a

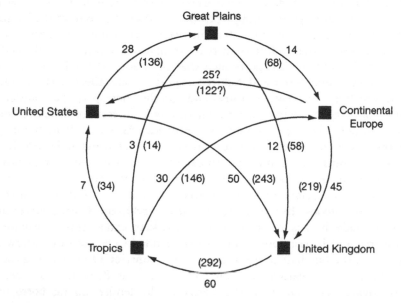

Figure 12 The system of multilateral trade in 1910

Source: S. B. Saul, *Studies in British Overseas Trade 1870–1914*, Fig. 2, p. 58.

Note: The size of the export surplus between Continental Europe and the United States is subject to reservation.

substantial supplement to the bilateral balancing of payments, it also tended to reduce to a minimum the movement of gold for balancing purposes. It therefore facilitated the smooth working of the international monetary system, and promoted a much larger expansion of world trade than would have been possible had this trade been more dependent on the use of gold as the sole means of settling international debts. As a result, numerous countries in the network were able to attain relatively high rates of growth in production and incomes through the consequent increased opportunities for trade.

FOREIGN INVESTMENT AND THE MULTILATERAL SETTLEMENTS NETWORK

The growth of the multilateral payments network also facilitated the massive flows of capital and investment income which passed between countries after 1870. Although at first sight these flows appear to add strictly monetary factors to a system alleged to concentrate on 'real' flows of goods and services, it is important to note that the settlements network was to a very large extent concerned with 'real' transfers of such capital and investment income from one country to another.

When foreign capital flows from one country to another, its transfer may be effected in several ways, for example, through a shift of gold from the lending to the borrowing country, through an increase in the capital receiving country's imports from the lending country (or from other countries), or through a decline in the borrower's exports such that the trade balance becomes more unfavourable. Gold flows and reduced exports rarely effected the transfer during the late nineteenth century, and for the most part the transfer of capital from lending to borrowing countries took the form of increased commodity imports by capital-receiving countries. As far as British foreign investment was concerned, there were no 'tied' arrangements under which the borrowing country was committed to use the funds acquired for purchasing only British-made commodities. Nevertheless, for some borrowing countries, such as Australia before 1890, the British market was the major source of manufactured goods. But progressively after 1880, the United States and Germany made inroads into British export markets, and a continuously higher proportion of British foreign investment tended to be used by borrowing countries in the purchase of goods from these countries. Other lending countries probably experienced the same sort of trend as Britain, to a lesser or greater degree depending on the status of the lender among borrowing countries as a producer of manufactures.

Thus, increasingly towards the end of the period, the international transfer of foreign investments tended to be brought about in an indirect manner, and formed an integral part of the entire multilateral payments network. The importance of the network in providing a mechanism supporting the smooth flow of capital during the period is exemplified by the fact that had India not been able to absorb large amounts of British manufactures, the United Kingdom could not have invested in Canada to the extent possible after 1904, since much of the large British investments in that country was used to purchase commodities in the United States. It was only because America was experiencing a payments deficit with India, and India one with the United Kingdom, that the indirect transfer of capital to Canada operated with a minimum of friction. As for the 'real' transfer of the interest and dividends payable on British (and other) foreign investments, whenever this investment income increased and began to exceed new British capital outflows, payments, especially from the Tropics and the Great Plains countries, began to be transferred to Britain partly by way of the trade surpluses these regions had with the United States and continental Europe respectively.

CONCLUDING REMARKS

What was the significance of the multilateral settlements system for the international economy as a whole? First, it allowed countries to obtain international means of payment which could be used to acquire additional goods and services probably not available on a strictly bilateral basis; second, it permitted debt servicing to be transferred in a circuitous route from borrower to lender not possible under a bilateral system without impediments to the free flow of goods; third, it promoted the real transfer of foreign investment on a multilateral basis; and finally, it minimized gold flows for settlement purposes. One result was an enlarged volume of foreign trade. Moreover, because a country was able to finance deficits in one direction through surpluses in another, it was possible for those countries which were neither large debtors nor large creditors to aid debtor countries to pay, and creditor countries to receive, financial payments due. The world economy could thus achieve maximum benefits from trade and investment, especially when barriers to trade and capital flows were minimal, that is, under a system of free trade and convertible currencies.[5] During this period, the convertibility of currencies was generally maintained, but from the early 1880s protective tariffs became widespread in the world economy and tended to slow down the rate of growth of world trade somewhat and altered its direction considerably. In a multilateral trading network, the introduction of such restrictive measures on the trade between any two links in the network was likely to affect the trade of all other regions in the system, as well as the financial relations between debtor and creditor countries at opposite ends of the network. In addition, such artificial trade barriers could affect the functioning of world commodity markets and thus the prices of staple products sold in those markets. But the fact that Britain adhered to free trade, while possessing a safety valve in India when it came to a settlement of her own foreign payments, helped to minimize the restrictive effects of greater protection in the world economy after 1870. Britain's policy, even if followed unconsciously, allowed the multilateral system to grow rapidly with the minimum disruption from tariffs.

Thus, while bilateral settlements between countries continued to predominate in international transactions, the growth of multilateralism, especially after 1870, provided the world economy with an additional mechanism for facilitating trade and payments between countries, and partly for this reason, international monetary crises were comparatively rare during these years, despite tremendous changes in the size and structure of both world production and trade. Yet the most successful years in the functioning of the multilateral trade and payments network also mark the period during which the first seeds of its future destruction were planted. For it was then that there appeared signs of a narrowing of the British payments surplus, upon the size of which the efficient functioning of the system so heavily depended. Although multilateralism was to survive after World War I, its destruction followed quickly in the early 1930s in the face of a worldwide depression and the continued decline in Britain's international economic position.

One other feature of the functioning of multilateralism in the period before 1913 is worthy of comment. This is the extent to which foreign capital relied on the multilateral payments network for its effective transfer between countries. In the absence of such a network, capital exports would almost certainly have been lower than they were, and interest and capital repayments more difficult to effect. As we have already noted, the emergence of a multilateral payments network led to economies in the use of gold in international commercial transactions, and this fact partly explains the successful functioning of the gold standard in the period from 1880 to 1913. Nevertheless, any international payments balances outstanding after bilateral and multilateral settlements had been effected, had to be settled through the use of gold. This is a convenient point, therefore, to consider the nature and functioning of the international gold standard in the period before 1913.

NOTES

1 A country's balance of payments is simply a statement of its commercial and financial transactions with the rest of the world in the course of a year. This account must balance for much the same reason that the debits and credits in ordinary double-entry bookkeeping balance. It contains what are called autonomous items and financing items.

Autonomous items are classified into current account (goods and services) and capital account. The current account includes the value of commodity exports and imports, the difference between which represents the balance of trade (favourable when exports exceed imports and unfavourable when an import surplus occurs), and receipts and payments for 'invisible' items such as transportation, investment income, travellers' expenditure, and other services. The current account is favourable (in surplus) when monetary receipts for exports and invisibles exceed monetary payments for imports and invisibles. The capital account includes all autonomous capital flows into and out of the country. The balance of payments is said to be in surplus when, for autonomous items, all monetary receipts exceed all payments, and in deficit when payments are greater than receipts. The financing items offset the autonomous balance and ensure that the whole statement balances, that is, they indicate what happens to the surplus monetary receipts when the autonomous items are in surplus, and how an autonomous deficit is financed. Under the pure gold standard, the financing items normally comprised changes in the gold stocks of each country.

2 For figures demonstrating the nineteenth-century trade and payments systems in chosen years, see Folke Hilgerdt, 'The Case for Multilateral Trade', *American Economic Review*, Vol. XXXIII, No. 2 (Mar., 1943), p. 395; and S. B. Saul, *Studies in British Overseas Trade 1870–1914* (Liverpool, 1960), p. 58.

3 The diagram is similar to that in Hilgerdt, op. cit., p. 395. Saul's diagram is slightly different. But it is possible to construct a number of diagrams of the network depending on the degree of generalization of regions. All would serve the same purpose, however, namely, to give a description of the multilateralism which existed at the time.

4 Saul, op. cit., p. 58, Figure 2. Figure 12 does not cover all triangular and multilateral settlement patterns that arose in the period before 1913. As Saul has shown, a more detailed breakdown of each region included in the figure would reveal a much more complicated system of trade and payments than the one outlined in Figure 12.

5 Carl Major Wright in 'Convertibility and Triangular Trade as Safeguards against Economic Depression', *Economic Journal* (Sept., 1955), asserts that multilateral trade and currency convertibility are two aspects of the same phenomenon, each a necessary condition for the other.

SELECTED REFERENCES

Ellsworth, P. T., *The International Economy*, 3rd edn. (New York, 1958), pp. 148–55.

Hanson, K.-E., 'A General Theory of the System of Multilateral Trade', *American Economic Review* (Mar., 1952), pp. 59–68.

Hilgerdt, F., *The Network of World Trade* (Geneva, 1942).

Hilgerdt, F., 'The Case for Multilateral Trade', *American Economic Review* (Mar., 1943), pp. 393–407.

Latham, A. J. H., *The International Economy and the Underdeveloped World, 1865–1914* (London, 1978).

Saul, S. B., *Studies in British Overseas Trade, 1870–1914* (Liverpool, 1960), especially Chaps. III and IV.

Wright, C. M., 'Convertibility and Triangular Trade as Safeguards against Economic Depression', *Economic Journal* (Sept., 1955), pp. 422–35.

Chapter 7

The growth of an international monetary system

The gold standard before 1913

Whereas trade within a country is made easy by the existence of a single currency common to all its regions, international transactions require a monetary system capable of handling trade involving the use of a variety of national currencies. Of course, this multicurrency barrier to trade can be overcome by conducting the international exchange of commodities on a barter basis, and in ancient and medieval times this type of international transaction often occurred. But bartering obviously places severe limitations on the growth of trade at any level, and so during quite early times foreign exchange markets, in which different currencies could be exchanged for one another, made their appearance thus placing foreign trade on a monetary basis. Precious metals, notably gold and silver, also came to be used to finance international trade, although their use had certain drawbacks, particularly in the high cost of transporting metals from country to country and the risks involved in such transfers. For this reason the expansion of foreign trade and commerce came to depend very much on improvements in the operation of foreign exchange markets and on the perfecting of devices to reduce the risks attached to fluctuations in the rate of exchange of one currency in terms of another.

With the growth of foreign commerce, financial innovations were quick to appear. The bill of exchange was introduced early, and by the fourteenth century a simple multilateral clearing system had been established. Much later, during the seventeenth and eighteenth centuries, the first 'forward' exchange markets were developed to overcome the uncertainty of future movements in the 'spot' rate of exchange, so reducing the risks inherent in fluctuating exchange rates. By this time Amsterdam had become the most important foreign exchange market in the world, closely followed by London, which was fast assuming a major role in world finance in the eighteenth century. At the beginning of the nineteenth century, therefore, foreign exchange markets were quite sophisticated in their operations and the financing of foreign trade and other international dealings had become quite complex. Throughout its history, the international financial system had adapted itself to meet the needs of an expanding foreign commerce and the process of adaptation continued during the nineteenth century, when a new international monetary system—the gold standard—evolved in response to the demands of a growing foreign trade and an expanding international flow of capital.

BIMETALLIC AND MONOMETALLIC STANDARDS

At the beginning of our period, only Britain was on a gold standard for both domestic and international dealings. Most other major trading nations at this time were operating either a bimetallic standard, for example, France and the United States, or a silver standard, as were most other European countries.

For a country to be wholly committed to a full gold standard five basic requirements had to be met. First, the unit of account had to be tied to a certain weight of gold; second, gold coins had to circulate domestically and any bank notes in circulation had to be convertible into gold on demand; third, other coins in use had to be subordinate to gold; fourth, no legal restrictions were to be imposed on the melting down of gold coin into bullion; and finally, there had to be no impediment to the export of gold coin and bullion. Bimetallism, on the other hand, involved the employment of both silver and gold coins as standard money or legal tender under conditions similar to those just outlined for gold. Compared with the gold standard, however, a bimetallic standard had one major drawback: it worked smoothly only as long as the ratio between the values at which the two metals could be freely minted into coins approximated to their values in international bullion markets. If divergence of these values did occur, then the metal with the higher international market value would tend to be sent abroad and be replaced by the other, leaving the country with a monometallic rather than a bimetallic standard.[1] Hence, the instability of the system, and the periodic, but not always successful, efforts to achieve international agreement to fix the ratio of the price of gold and silver. Despite its drawbacks, however, the fear that one metal alone would fail to satisfy the world demand for money and so produce general deflation led to the widespread adoption of the bimetallic standard in the nineteenth century. In fact, for most of the time Britain alone adhered to the gold standard. It was not until the 1870s that other major trading countries began to move gradually in the same direction as that taken by Britain at the end of the Napoleonic Wars.

BRITAIN ADOPTS THE GOLD STANDARD

By the late eighteenth century Britain had moved to a *de facto* gold standard, after a long period during which silver had continuously disappeared from domestic circulation. The predominance of gold over silver had begun as early as 1717, when the gold guinea was given a value of 21s. Silver was so undervalued in terms of gold thereafter that it soon came to perform the function of a subsidiary coinage, the silver coins remaining in circulation having become so worn that it was unprofitable to withdraw them from circulation and melt them down for export. Silver's importance as a monetary unit was reduced still further in 1774, when the legal tender status of silver coins was restricted to payments up to £25. The supremacy of gold as a unit of account in Britain was assured from that year.

The movement towards the adoption of a gold standard in Britain was halted during the war years, when, as a wartime measure, cash payments were suspended in 1797 and the Bank of England freed from its obligation to convert its notes into gold. Immediately after the end of the war, however, the *de facto* gold standard of the late eighteenth century was made *de jure* by the passing of a number of Acts of Parliament. The Coinage Act of 1816 allowed for the minting of a Gold Sovereign, a 20s gold piece, the first of which was issued in the following year. The gold content of the sovereign was fixed in accordance with the mint price of gold, which had been maintained throughout the eighteenth century at £3 17s 10½d an ounce. Silver coins were legally subordinated to gold and were further restricted by being made legal tender for payments of up to only £2. In 1819 the convertibility of bank notes was restored, when an Act of Parliament committed the Bank of England to resume cash payments in gold bullion and, after 1823, in gold coin. This Act also repealed the law prohibiting the melting down of coin into bullion, and the trade in bullion was declared free. With the resumption of cash payments in 1821, Britain was legally on the full gold standard.

INTERNATIONAL MONETARY STANDARDS UP TO 1870

The task of maintaining stability within the bimetallic system, through exercising control over the world prices of gold and silver, fell to France. The performance of this function imposed few problems in the years between 1815 and 1850, when demand and supply conditions for both metals were fairly stable. There was some withdrawal of silver from circulation, as gold production steadily declined and its value appreciated relative to that of silver, but France possessed relatively large reserves of both metals and was easily able to absorb silver at the expense of gold without actually moving to a silver standard. The United States was also legally on a bimetallic standard for most of the nineteenth century. Until the 1830s, however, the country really operated on a silver standard, because at 15 to 1 the American mint ratio of silver to gold undervalued gold and led to its disappearance from circulation. But a *de facto* silver standard was inconvenient for a country which traded primarily with another, Britain, which was on a gold standard. It was probably for this reason that the Coinage Acts of 1834 and 1837 reduced the gold content of the dollar and established a new mint ratio of 16 to 1. Since this ratio was above the free market ratio, which generally settled around the French mint ratio of 15½ to 1, the previous trend towards a silver standard was replaced by a movement to a *de facto* gold standard similar to that found in Britain during the eighteenth century.

The pressures on the bimetallic standard mounted after 1850, when the discovery of substantial gold deposits in California and Australia produced dramatic changes in currency dealings and metal markets. The relative price of gold fell and the French mint ratio of 15½ to 1 proved to be inappropriate to the new world market situation for it overvalued gold. As silver appreciated relative to gold, France absorbed large quantities of gold and the French franc became a gold unit as Gresham's Law became operable. In an effort to stabilize the situation and promote an international bimetallic system, France summoned a meeting of the franc-using nations in 1865. As a result of this meeting, France, Belgium, Switzerland and Italy (often referred to as the Latin Monetary Union) agreed to regulate their currencies jointly. The agreement, however, did little to alleviate the monetary pressures exerted on the bimetallic countries.

As for the other European countries, by 1870 they were either on a silver standard—the Germanic States, Holland and Scandinavia—or, like Russia, Austria-Hungary, Italy, Greece, and more recently France, had been forced by wars and revolutions to issue inconvertible paper money, which, with the exception of the French issues, were depreciated paper.[2] Outside Europe, the Orient and Latin America were on silver, and the United States had inconvertible and depreciated notes, issued during the Civil War, still in circulation. By 1870, therefore, the gold standard was far from being internationally adopted. Britain alone operated on a legal gold standard. Bimetallism existed legally in the United States and the Latin Monetary Union, and Germany, Holland, Scandinavia, Latin America and the Orient adhered to the silver standard.

THE SPREAD OF THE GOLD STANDARD

During the 1870s the movement towards gold accelerated, and silver declined rapidly in importance as an international standard. This sudden change in the international monetary situation was brought about by two developments, each of which drastically affected the relative prices of the two main monetary metals. First, Germany transferred from a silver to a gold standard. It did this for a number of reasons. To begin with, several east European countries with which Germany had important trading relations had abandoned a silver standard for inconvertible paper so that Germany no longer derived any advantage from adherence to the silver standard in its commercial relations with these countries. Moreover, most of Germany's commercial relations with non-European countries tended to be financed through Britain where a gold standard operated. Finally, delegates from a number of European countries to an international monetary congress held in Paris in 1867 had overwhelmingly favoured the adoption of a universal gold standard. Given these arguments in favour of a changeover to gold, the large war indemnity extracted from France by Germany in 1871–2 provided the means for bringing it about. In 1872 a new currency unit, the mark, was adopted to replace the silver thaler and silver was relegated to subsidiary coins of limited legal tender. Surplus silver bullion and coins of large denominations were used to buy gold in the bullion markets to overcome the domestic shortage of gold for coinage purposes. In two years Germany acquired £50m. ($243m.) of gold, and so great were the pressures exerted on the markets that the price of silver in terms of gold commenced to decline dramatically.

The fall in the price of silver, and hence its demise as an international monetary standard, was also brought about by the sharp increase in the world output of silver that followed the discovery of large deposits of the metal in Nevada and elsewhere. In the face of the glut of silver in the world market, which was aggravated by the suspension of the minting of silver coins in the United States in 1873, the price of silver in terms of gold dropped below 16 to 1, and countries on a silver or bimetallic standard faced the possibility of substantial monetary inflation. As a result, the demonetization of silver became general after the mid-1870s. Holland, crushed in between a gold-using Britain and a gold-using Germany, was the first to go. In 1874 it ceased coining silver and not longer afterwards adopted gold as its unit of account. Norway, Sweden and Denmark quickly followed suit. The Latin Monetary Union, under pressure from its inception, encountered extreme difficulties in the early 1870s and its members were compelled in January 1874, to limit their coinage of five-franc pieces. In 1878 they suspended the minting of silver coins altogether, and from that time onwards France and her colleagues operated on the so-called 'limping' (or 'lame') gold standard. Silver was still legal tender, but it was neither coined nor used to any significant extent in commercial transactions, though banks continued to hold large quantities of the metal. Effectively, however, these countries adhered in all other ways to the gold standard. By 1878, therefore, Britain, Belgium, Holland, France, Germany, Switzerland and the Scandinavian countries were operating on gold, and, since most other continental countries were using irredeemable depreciated paper money, silver was no longer an international standard of value in Europe.

The movement to gold was completed by the end of the century. In the United States bimetallism was not legally abandoned until 1900, but the country was effectively operating on the gold standard once convertibility of paper notes was restored in 1879. Austria moved to gold in 1892, and Russia and Japan in 1897, the year in which India adopted a gold exchange standard by pegging the rupee to sterling. A year later the Philippine peso likewise became tied to the American dollar. After 1900, other countries, including Siam and Ceylon in Asia, and Argentina, Mexico, Peru and Uruguay in Latin America, eventually adopted the gold standard, while others were, by the outbreak of World War I, proceeding in that direction. By 1914 China was alone among major countries in still clinging to a silver standard.

This brief description of the pre-1914 gold standard brings out one of its most striking features, namely, its relatively short duration as an international monetary system. Whereas it is not possible to date precisely its beginnings—it did not exist in 1870, but it did in 1900—World War I certainly marks its end, for, as we shall see, the postwar restoration of the system was short-lived. In short, the international gold standard was in full sway only from perhaps 1897 (some would argue 1880) to 1914, less than 20 (or just over 30) years.

THE ROLE OF STERLING AS AN INTERNATIONAL CURRENCY AND THE IMPORTANCE OF THE LONDON CAPITAL MARKET

In the institutional field, the developments in the London capital market were of paramount importance for the efficient functioning of the international gold standard. With Britain's increasing importance in world trade, organized markets were established in London for many types of commodities, a move which was greatly enhanced in the early years by the continued growth of the British re-export trade and later by the adoption of free trade. These markets in turn acted as a stimulus to British shipping and created a growing need for insurance facilities to cover transport risks. As a result of these developments, London grew in importance as a centre of international commerce and finance, and various institutions, such as discount houses, merchant banks, insurance companies, and other specialist financial organizations, which were later to provide the essential services for a rapidly expanding international economy, began to increase in numbers. From the beginning of the nineteenth century, therefore, London forged ahead of Amsterdam, Hamburg and Paris as the leading financial centre of Europe and thus of the world.

While these developments were taking place, a growing proportion of world trade was being financed by short-term credit in the form of foreign bills of exchange. Under these arrangements, by accepting a bill an importer guaranteed payment within (say) three months of acceptance. The foreign exporter, on the other hand, if he required ready cash before the bill matured, could discount it with a bank (or other financial institution willing to do so) for something less than the face value of the bill, thus allowing interest to the discounter for holding the bill between the date of discounting and maturity and for accepting the risk against default. It was not until the early nineteenth century that these financial arrangements were perfected in Britain by the merchant banks and bill brokers, each of which came to perform a specialized function. The merchant banks, which were well known and respected for their integrity, then began to accept bills on behalf of reliable businessmen and firms whose names were less familiar than theirs. In other words, for the payment of a small commission, the merchant banks, by endorsing a bill of exchange, would guarantee that it would not be dishonoured on maturity. In this way the merchant banks ensured that a large number of bills would be available for discounting. The discounting function was performed initially by the bill-broker—a financial go-between who accumulated bills of exchange and sought out banks with surplus funds, with a view to persuading them to invest in the bills in his care. For his trouble and his knowledge, he charged a small commission. Some years later, the bill-broker began to give way to the dealer, who was himself a principal and not merely a commission agent. Supplementing his own sizeable funds with money borrowed on call or short notice from the large London banks, he used the money to discount bills on his own account. Still later came the discount houses, which were little more than large-scale dealers. They had more capital to invest; they took deposits from the public and paid interest on them; and they did a much greater volume of business.

The acceptance houses did not restrict their business activities to the market for short-term credit. With the growth of British investment abroad after 1820, they came to specialize in foreign security issues as well, and before 1850 they were also important dealers in foreign exchange and bullion. Later, however, the various merchant houses came to specialize either in the acceptance business or in the issue of securities, and foreign exchange dealings came to be concentrated in the hands of the branches of foreign banks in London. These branches increased rapidly in number after 1870, when the growth of the London capital market and the extent of Britain's foreign trade made it essential for many foreign banks to establish branches in the centre. Increasingly, in the years up to 1914, the operations of these foreign branch banks presented a growing challenge to the supremacy of the bill on London as an instrument of international payments. For, through the use of the telegraphic process, the accumulated sterling reserves in these foreign branches tended to replace the bill on London as a method of payment across the exchanges.

The growing importance of the London capital market, especially after 1870, was associated with the increasing use of sterling as an international currency. Throughout the nineteenth century Britain, on the whole, maintained a continuous surplus on current account in its dealings with the rest of the world. But she did not amass large gold reserves chiefly because of her willingness to invest the surplus abroad. Yet, from experience over a number of decades, foreign institutions and traders confidently accepted the ability of Britain to maintain the convertibility of sterling into gold. The stability of sterling was unrivalled, and the possibility of its devaluation never even considered. Sterling was as good as gold, and in some respects even better, because it was more convenient, in the sense that British exporters and importers, who dominated world trade, preferred to draw and to be drawn on in pounds sterling, and because it brought in an income, for holders of sterling received interest payments, whereas gold holdings earned nothing.

Given the general acceptability of sterling throughout the international economy, it is not surprising to find that gold played only a minor role in settling international debts. The vast majority of payments were made either by the transfer of bills payable in sterling, or by the purchase and sale of bills payable in foreign currencies, or simply by the transfer of credits in the books of banks, although the volume of business conducted under the latter two heads was never large before 1914. Hence sterling bills of exchange were used not only to finance the exports and imports of Britain, but also those of a large part of the rest of the world. The reasons for this worldwide preference for the pound sterling as a medium of international payments were numerous. It came about partly because Britain was the world's largest trader, the dominant carrier in world trade, and the largest single source of foreign capital. In part also, it was because the value of the pound sterling was kept stable throughout the period 1821 to 1914 by rigorous adherence to the gold standard. But equally important was the high standing of the British acceptance houses and the assurance that any bill receiving their endorsement could be readily discounted, at the world's most favourable rates, in the London discount market. Combined together, these forces turned London into the financial centre of the world, and the pound sterling into an internationally acceptable currency.

THE WORKING OF THE GOLD STANDARD

Whereas sterling was used to finance the bulk of international financial transactions in the nineteenth century, gold remained the ultimate means of settling balances which could not be adjusted in any other way. Moreover, the international acceptability of sterling in settlement of debts depended in the final analysis on its ready convertibility into gold. For these reasons, it is necessary to examine in some detail the working of the gold standard in the period before 1914.

Under the gold standard, because the basic monetary unit of each country on the gold standard had a fixed gold content, the value of each country's currency was fixed in terms of all other currencies at the 'mint parity' or 'par' value. But if the par rate of exchange between two currencies, say the pound sterling and the dollar, was fixed by the gold content of each currency, the market rate of exchange was determined by the forces of demand and supply. In the market, if the demand for dollars rose relative to their supply, the market rate of the dollar in terms of sterling would rise; if the demand declined, the market rate would fall. Under the gold standard, however, the fact that residents in member countries could export or import gold freely placed limits on the extent to which the market rate could rise above or fall below the par rate. If the demand for dollars in London increased so much relative to the supply that the market rate of exchange (dollars per pound sterling) rose above the mint parity rate by more than the cost of exporting gold, it would have been profitable for those demanding dollars to buy gold in London, ship it to New York, and sell it for dollars in that market. Similarly, if the demand for dollars had fallen relative to the supply forthcoming so that the market rate of the dollar had declined below the mint parity by more than the cost of shipping gold, those willing to supply dollars (and thus demanding sterling) would have profited by shipping gold from the United States to London and selling it for sterling.

The cost of shifting gold from one financial centre to another allowed a certain degree of flexibility in foreign exchange rates. Consequently, the market rate could fluctuate according to the forces of supply and demand between two values, termed the 'gold export' and 'gold import' points. These limiting rates of exchange were established at values above and below the par value determined by the cost of transporting gold. The distance between the gold points could change over a time if transport and other costs altered. Similarly, the distance between the two points was relatively large or small depending on the distance between the two countries whose currencies were linked together. In general, the spot rate of the dollar in London would move towards the gold export point when Britain experienced a deficit in its balance of payments with the United States (an excess demand for dollars and an excess supply of sterling in the exchange market). Similarly, a British surplus with the United States would produce an excess supply of dollars (demand for sterling) and a decline in the market rate of the dollar towards the gold import point.

Normally, most transactions would have been conducted in foreign exchange, and only large and persistent imbalances between the two countries would have produced gold flows. But while gold flows produced short-run balancing of the supply of and demand for foreign exchange, they obviously could not be continued indefinitely, for a country could not sustain gold exports forever without running out of the metal. Gold imports could go on somewhat longer perhaps, but eventually the importing country's trading partners would exhaust their supplies of gold. What then was the nature of the longer-run mechanism of adjustment under the gold standard which prevented these situations from arising?

One answer to the question was given by the classical economists, such as David Hume, Adam Smith, and J. S. Mill, who worked out the 'price-specie-flow' mechanism. According to this explanation, price changes induced by gold flows were supposed to bring about the adjustment. Suppose a country develops a balance of payments deficit because of excessive imports and proceeds to export gold to cover this excess. This loss of gold will reduce the domestic money supply, since either gold circulates as money in the country or the banking system keeps the country's internal supply of money adjusted to the quantity of its gold reserves. A decrease in the domestic money supply will lead to a decline in commodity prices, since less spending with output unchanged means lower prices. Lower prices for goods will, in turn, increase exports, as foreigners find the country a cheaper place in which to buy. Lower domestic prices will also reduce imports, since domestic substitutes for foreign goods become cheaper relative to foreign supplies. In the gold-receiving country the process is reversed. The inflow of gold increases the domestic money supply and raises commodity prices, which makes exporting more difficult and the importing of cheaper foreign supplies more attractive. These changes in the export and import capacities of the two countries will alter the supply and demand conditions in the foreign exchange market and bring about adjustments in exchange rates until a new equilibrium is established.

Late in the nineteenth century this price-specie-flow mechanism was elaborated in a number of ways, the most important of which concerned the effects of gold movements on the monetary policy of the central banks. In Britain, in particular, it was argued that gold flows led to changes in Bank Rate—the Bank of England's discount rate—which were in themselves automatic and which formed part of the adjustment mechanism. Thus, it was argued that, as gold exporters obtained gold from the Bank of England, the Bank's ratio of reserves to liabilities would decline. If this decline persisted, the Bank would eventually raise its discount rate (Bank Rate) automatically to prevent further depletion of its gold reserves. Such action would produce increased interest rates generally and a restriction of credit. This would have an adverse effect on business activity and employment and lead to a fall in prices and wages, which would reinforce the direct effects of the price-specie-flow mechanism. On the other hand, when a gold inflow took place, the increased money supply would mean an abundance of credit and interest rates would fall. Declining interest rates would stimulate domestic activity and generate an upward pressure on wages and prices. If interest rate policy was, in this way, a 'rule of the game' requiring strict observance by monetary authorities, the gold standard mechanism would truly have been an automatic system. The combination of specie flows and interest rate changes would have produced an era of stable exchange rates, and, given a moderately large stock of monetary gold in each country, although its size was subject to fluctuation, it would not be in danger of permanent depletion, since a loss of gold would be automatically corrected by the operation of the adjustment mechanism.

DIVERGENCE BETWEEN CLASSICAL THEORY AND EMPIRICAL EVIDENCE

The weakness of the price-specie-flow theory of adjustment is that it fails to conform to the available empirical evidence on the functioning of the pre-1913 gold standard. Thus, contrary to the classical theory's prediction of divergences between the movements of exports and imports both within countries and between countries on the gold standard, we find a high degree of parallelism of movements in these trade flows.[3] Second, export prices in a number of countries moved together over time, although the classical theory would have called for more frequent divergences. Third, there is evidence to suggest that prices and especially wages were rather more inflexible in a downward direction than was implied in the classical theory and thus other forces would have been required to supplement any downward pressures which may have occurred when efforts were being made to restore a country's balance of payments to equilibrium. Fourth, major central banks often ignored the rules of the game and neutralized the foreign payments imbalance by refraining from using discount rate policy when such use would adversely affect the domestic economy. If, for example, it became necessary to increase interest rates to reinforce the deflationary tendencies required to improve the competitiveness of domestic industries and thus ensure that the trade balance became more favourable, central banks often allowed interest rates to decline in an endeavour to avoid the deflationary situation created by the outflow of gold. Fifth, the importance of capital movements was entirely neglected in the price-specie-flow theory, despite the fact that the current account of the lending countries remained for many years in continuous surplus, and the recipient countries continuously experienced an unfavourable balance on current account. In short, classical theory tended to be too preoccupied with the trade account and industrial competitiveness.

Since international capital flows depended to a large degree on economic conditions in the lending countries, it was the recipient countries which suffered most from changes in the level of foreign lending, particularly by way of instability in their exchange rates and their external balances. Finally, the discount rates of the major central banks in surplus and deficit countries tended to move together as the automatic adjustment mechanism came into action, and not, as one would expect from classical theory, in a divergent manner.[4]

As a result of the development of the monetarist approach to balance of payments adjustment, the gold standard mechanism has received considerable attention in recent years.[5] This approach ignores the distinction between current and capital accounts by viewing the balance of payments as a whole and, in its simple form, stresses that money (including gold) flows into and out of a country depended upon the stock concepts of demand for, and supply of, money within a country at any point in time. Money supply consisted of the supply of domestic credit and international monetary reserves. If the supply of domestic credit was fixed, any change in the demand for money would have been accompanied by a change in international monetary reserves, that is, by an inflow or outflow of money (including gold). On the other hand, if the supply of domestic credit rose (say) so that the money supply increased relative to the demand for money, reserves would be run down, and vice versa. Flows of international money therefore depended upon relative changes in the demand for money and the supply of domestic credit. Extending the reasoning to central bank activity, if the international money reserves were decreasing, changes in the discount rate could not only change the relations between the demand for money and the supply of domestic credit but also influence movements in such reserves.

OTHER FEATURES OF THE ADJUSTMENT MECHANISM

As noted above, the classical theory was over-simplified to the extent that it concentrated on the current account balance and neglected capital movements, the existence of which allowed the current account to remain unbalanced for a number of years. Later theorists supplemented classical theory by including capital movements, but early in the twentieth century economists were still at a loss to explain the rapidity with which the gold standard adjustment mechanism had in many cases produced external balance. The answer was eventually found in the changes in incomes which accompanied the price movements. Thus, a fall in a country's exports reduces the income of its export industry and through multiplier effects brings about a reduction in spending on wages, salaries, raw materials, consumption goods, and savings. There will also be a decline in the country's demand for imports, which, by offsetting the fall in its exports, will tend to bring about balance in the country's external payments position. On the other hand, a rise in exports, by increasing domestic incomes will tend to work in the opposite direction, reducing the payments surplus generated by expanding exports by encouraging a greater volume of imports. As Scammell points out: 'the potency of income adjustment can be judged from the fact that, on certain occasions, balance of payments adjustment has taken place in spite of simultaneous neutralising action by the central bank to offset the effects of gold flows.'[6] In other words, there is a strong case for arguing that the major burden of adjustment in the gold standard was carried by changes in income.

Another feature of the adjustment mechanism overlooked by the classical economists was the role played by international flows of short-term capital, which grew in importance as communications between nations were improved. Thus, a deficit country experiencing downward pressure on its exchange rate was likely to receive an inflow of foreign short-term capital.

This would come about for two reasons: first, because foreign speculators would be attracted by the profits to be made from purchasing a currency whose price (in terms of other foreign currencies) was likely to rise once the central bank adopted monetary policies aimed at correcting the balance of payments deficit; and second, because the higher interest rates associated with these monetary policies provided an added incentive to capital inflow, by offering it a higher return than could be obtained in its country of origin. By providing a partial cover for the receiving country's balance of payments deficit, the inflow of short-term capital would tend to reverse the downward movement of the exchange rate, help to minimize gold outflows, and speed up the adjustment process. One must be careful, however, not to exaggerate the importance of these capital flows, for, despite the unlikelihood of a devaluation, some short-term capital outflow may have occurred. Moreover, other countries may have responded to the new situation by increasing their interest rates in order to minimize the outflow of short-term capital from their money markets.[7]

In one respect at least the classical theory was correct—it predicted few international monetary problems. Once cannot help being impressed by the relatively smooth functioning of the nineteenth-century gold standard, more especially when we contemplate the difficulties experienced in the international monetary sphere during the present century. Despite the relatively rudimentary state of economic knowledge concerning internal and external balance and the relative ineffectiveness of government fiscal policy as a weapon for maintaining such a balance, the external adjustment mechanism of the gold standard worked with a higher degree of efficiency than that of any subsequent international monetary system. Trade and capital movements proceeded smoothly over the gold standard period (1880–1913), exchange rates, especially among major trading countries, remained comparatively stable and quantitative restrictions on trade and other payments were remarkably absent. What made this efficient functioning possible? Perhaps the chief reasons accounting for the successful working of the gold standard are to be found in the position of the United Kingdom in the international economy, the growth and strength of sterling as an international currency, and the working of the multilateral settlements network. Britain remained the major trading country throughout the century and the most important source of investible funds. Although it acquired and maintained a persistent trade deficit, it experienced a continuous current account surplus through its large 'invisibles' earnings from shipping and foreign investments. Nevertheless, Britain's gold reserves remained relatively low throughout most of the period, for the current account surplus tended to be offset to a large extent by the capital outflow which occurred during the period. To a more limited extent, other western European countries tended to follow this pattern when they, too, became major lenders. Moreover, there was complete confidence in sterling as an international currency. Sterling balances tended rarely to become too small or too large, chiefly because of the structure of the British balance of payments. 'Britain's inelastic demand for imports and the elastic nature of the demand for her exports ensured that in times of depression Britain ran a deficit in her balance of payments. Thus, if during a slump British capital exports declined, the deficit on current account compensated for this; while in times of boom the situation was reversed.'[8]

The gold standard period was an era of rapid industrial growth in the world economy, and in the circumstances it was possible to achieve adjustment without the appearance of deflationary tendencies. Changes in demand could readily be met by alterations in industrial structures, and if the adjustment process demanded price changes, these could be accomplished without widespread unemployment and reduced profits. In other words, the international economy was, to a large extent, dynamic and flexible in its operation. Often, too, an adverse payments situation did not lead to large reductions in international reserves because of the cushioning effect provided by the longer-term credit facilities which increasingly became available during these years. Furthermore, there was a greater degree of discretion exercised by central banks in the implementation of their policy than the classical theory admitted. This was true even of the Bank of England, for adjustments of Bank Rate were never completely 'automatic'. While protection of its gold reserves remained of paramount importance in determining the Bank of England's monetary policy, it nevertheless exercised considerable discretion in the choice and timing of its actions and was always aware of the need to achieve external balance with a minimum of interference with the level of domestic business activity. Finally, the growth of a complex multilateral settlements network by providing a variety of ways of offsetting payments between countries considerably reduced the need for gold flows to balance international accounts. This reduced the need for countries to hold large stocks of gold for balancing purposes and thus helped to prevent a shortage of gold from developing as more and more countries came to adopt the gold standard in the years after 1870.

CONCLUSIONS

During its relatively brief existence, the gold standard was not the standardized or automatic international monetary system it was widely believed to be in the 1930s. There were various versions of the gold standard, including the gold exchange standard, and the discretionary monetary policies of governments exerted some influence on the automatic functioning of the mechanism. Even so, the system worked smoothly, without large and frequent lapses of confidence in the parities of major currencies. This success was due in part to the growth of a multilateral settlements network, and in part to the predominance of Britain in the international economy, which led to the increasing use of sterling as a supplement to gold in the settlement of international commercial transactions. Indeed it is the growing use of sterling as an international currency and the declining use of gold in domestic money supply which give support to Triffin's argument that 'the nineteenth century could be far more accurately described as the century of an emerging and growing credit-money standard, and of the euthanasia of gold and silver moneys, rather than as the century of the gold standard'.[9]

NOTES

1 Once the mint ratio and the world market ratio diverged, it paid those who could do so to engage in arbitrage at the various exchanges. Suppose, for example, that the Paris exchange is offering 15½ ounces of silver for one ounce of gold and that an American merchant holds 1,000 ounces of gold. If the United States mint ratio is 15 to 1, he can obtain 15,000 ounces of silver for his 1,000 ounces of gold at an American mint. But if the gold is sent to Paris, he can get an extra 500 ounces of silver for it. It will pay him, therefore, to convert his gold into silver in Paris and to reconvert all his Parisian silver into gold in Washington. The final result of this process is, of course, that all gold leaves the United States and silver becomes the circulating medium. Gold was 'undervalued' and, according to the workings of Gresham's Law, that 'bad' money drives out 'good', the gold coinage does not circulate.

2 'Irredeemable' or 'inconvertible' legal tender notes cannot be converted into gold on demand, but only when the government is willing to allow it. Normally, of course, in a gold standard country, bank notes are convertible into gold on demand. An inconvertible currency may depreciate in value relative to gold, if the quantity issued tends to be excessive, and relative to convertible currencies if the excessive issue leads to, or is accompanied by, inflation.

3 The price-specie-flow theory predicts that a deficit country's exports would rise and its imports fall during the adjustment period. Conversely, a surplus country would experience opposite changes in the volume of its import and export trade.

4 See R. Triffin, *Our International Monetary System: Yesterday, Today, and Tomorrow* (New York, 1968), and W. M. Scammell, 'The Working of the Gold Standard', *Yorkshire Bulletin of Economic and Social Research* (May, 1965). This section and the one that follows lean heavily on these two sources.

5 For a review of this and other approaches during the last 20 years, see B. Eichengreen, *The Gold Standard since Alex Ford*, Working Paper No. 3122 (National Bureau of Economic Research, Cambridge, Mass.), Sept., 1989.

6 Scammell, op. cit., p. 43.

7 Barry Eichengreen (loc. cit., pp. 31–2) has noted that recognition of the fact that the Bank of England would act to preserve its gold reserves and the likelihood of it receiving some co-operation from foreign central banks in pursuing this policy tended to ensure that financial markets acted as if they anticipated central bank action and so no destabilizing capital movements occurred. As a result, the need for actual intervention was minimized.

8 Scammell, op. cit., pp. 44–5.

9 Triffin, op. cit., p. 21. Gold was becoming less important as a domestic currency towards the end of the nineteenth century due to the increasing use of credit

money (paper currency and bank deposits), which perhaps accounted for over 90 per cent of the total expansion of money from the 1870s to 1913.

SELECTED REFERENCES

Beach, W. E., *British International Gold Movements and Banking Policy, 1881–1913* (Cambridge, Mass., 1935).

Bloomfield, A. I., *Monetary Policy under the International Gold Standard 1880–1914* (New York, 1959).

Bloomfield, A. I., *Short-term Capital Movements under the Pre-1914 Gold Standard* (Princeton, 1963).

Bordo, M. and Schwartz, A. (eds.), *A Retrospective on the Classical Gold Standard, 1821–1931* (Chicago, 1984).

Eichengreen, B. (ed.), *The Gold Standard in Theory and History* (New York, 1985).

Feavearyar, Sir Albert, *The Pound Sterling*, revised by E. Victor Morgan (Oxford, 1963).

Haberler, G., *The Theory of International Trade* (London, 1936).

Hawtrey, R. G., *The Gold Standard in Theory and Practice* (London, 1927).

Morgan, E. V., *A History of Money* (Harmondsworth, 1965).

Nurkse, R., *International Currency Experience* (Princeton, 1944).

Rostow, W. W., *British Economy of the Nineteenth Century* (Oxford, 1948).

Scammell, W. M., 'The Working of the Gold Standard', *Yorkshire Bulletin of Economic and Social Research*, Vol. XVII, No. 1 (May, 1965).

Triffin, R., *Our International Monetary System: Yesterday, Today and Tomorrow* (New York, 1968).

Viner, J., *Studies in the Theory of International Trade* (New York, 1937).

Yeager, L. B., *International Monetary Relations* (New York, 1966).

Chapter 8

International aspects of economic growth in the nineteenth century

The spread of industrialization

INTRODUCTION

The international economy played a major role in promoting the spread of economic growth in the nineteenth century. The flows of trade, capital and labour, which linked countries together economically, not only provided the means whereby the benefits of economic growth, in the form of higher real incomes, could be transmitted from country to country, but they were also the mechanism through which the technological and social innovations that are the essence of modern economic growth could be diffused. As a result, the economic growth of most countries came to depend as much on their ability to take advantage of the opportunities for trade and for the acquisition of new knowledge and additional factors of production presented by the international economy as on the quantity and quality of the economic resources domestically available to them. It is for this reason that any discussion of the nineteenth century international economy must include an examination of its function as an 'engine of growth'.

Obviously the international diffusion of modern technology and the stimulation of economic growth through an expansion of foreign trade are economic processes that are not independent of each other, if only because export-led growth implies some measure of technological and social change. Nevertheless, it does simplify our discussion of the international economy as a mechanism for transmitting economic growth and technical change between countries in the nineteenth century if we treat the two processes separately. Separate treatment is further justified by the fact that the spread of industrialization throughout Europe and North America, and the export-led growth characteristic of primary producing countries, represented significantly different responses to the economic opportunities presented by the emergence of an international economy in the century or so before 1913. Although a great deal of detailed work remains to be done in this relatively neglected field of historical research before a satisfactory account of the functioning of the international economy as a growth mechanism is possible, the general nature of its operation in the period before 1913 is readily apparent.

The nineteenth century world economy is best viewed as being composed of a centre and a periphery, with growth at the centre building up economic pressures tending to diffuse the development process to the periphery. Initially, Britain stood at the centre of this growth process, but as the century progressed, Europe, and in particular north-west Europe, came to play a larger part in fostering the spread of economic development overseas. Britain's central role in the world economy during these years rested on a technological revolution that began in the second half of the eighteenth century, and continued between 1820 and 1880 to transform a predominantly agrarian economy into the world's first industrial nation. But imitators were not lacking and, partly through a flow of capital and skilled labour from Britain, the new industrial technology spread first to Europe and then to the United States, so that by the 1870s, when Britain's rate of industrial growth began to slow down, these other countries began to play their part in the process of transmitting growth to the less developed regions of the world.[1]

The peripheral regions were incorporated in this international growth process through a steady and persistent increase in the demand for primary products, which many of these areas were well able to produce. Industrialization in Britain soon exposed her limited range of natural resources and her growing inability to feed a rapidly growing population. Increasingly Britain was forced to rely on other countries to supply her mounting needs for foodstuffs and industrial raw materials. To a lesser extent the other industrializing countries of Europe also came to depend on overseas sources of supply of primary products. The growing pressure of industrial demand on the centre's natural resources and supplies of foodstuffs and raw materials, and the resulting tendency towards rising prices, prompted a search for cheaper supplies in the periphery and an outflow of capital and skilled labour to develop peripheral sources of supply. In this way a cumulative process of growth was initiated in a number of countries overseas by the relation between the export demand for primary products and the inflow of foreign capital and labour that was associated with the expansion of the export sector. Particularly favoured by these developments were the United States and, later, the regions of recent settlement, including Canada, Argentina, Uruguay, South Africa, Australia and New Zealand, each of which, at different times and to varying degrees, came to depend on growth through primary product exports and the inflows of foreign capital and labour associated with it. At the other end of the spectrum were those peripheral countries which remained largely unaffected by these revolutionary changes, or those which became 'enclave economies', that is, countries in which foreign demand and the new technology serves to revolutionize the export sector while leaving the rest of the economy virtually unchanged.

The failure of the expansion and modernization of the export sector of the enclave economy to spark off growth in the rest of the economy is only one of the problems arising out of the international record of economic growth in the nineteenth century. There are many others. Why, for example, did economic growth spread to only a limited proportion of the total world population? What accounts for the slow spread of industrialization? For even in Europe and the United States, rapid industrialization occurred only after 1870, more than a century after the new technology had emerged in Britain. More pertinent to the present discussion is the question whether these 'failures' in the diffusion of economic growth reflected weaknesses in the functioning of the international economy or whether they were the result of the existence of other obstacles to the spread of economic development. These questions, and many others like them, are the subject of a continuing and lively debate, for they are matters of enormous importance to the study of the economic problem of under-development, and to cover adequately the issues they raise would require another and much longer book than this. All that is possible here is for us to offer a few general observations on these issues so that the broad nature of the problems they raise and their relevance to the functioning of the international economy are more easily appreciated.

THE SPREAD OF INDUSTRIALIZATION

It is a matter of general observation that the diffusion of technology is closely related to the problem of mobility—of goods, people, ideas and behaviour. It is also apparent from what has been said so far in this book, that mobility in this sense was greatly enhanced during the nineteenth century by innovations in transportation and communications and in the field of international finance which greatly facilitated the large-scale movement of goods, men and capital between countries. These flows of economic resources were, in turn, important channels for the diffusion of the new industrial technology, since physical capital embodied it, immigrant artisans and entrepreneurs possessed the required technical skills, and imported goods provided opportunities for adaptive imitation.

Given the opportunity for adopting new methods of production presented by the international economy, the spread of technical innovation also required an economic incentive. Probably the most effective stimulus to innovation is the market to be supplied: both its size and the rate at which it is growing. A large and rapidly expanding market creates an environment that is highly conducive to technological advance and to all forms of innovation, including the adoption and adaptation of foreign techniques.

THE CONTRIBUTION OF THE INTERNATIONAL ECONOMY

The emerging international economy was itself an important form of market expansion in the nineteenth century. Foreign trade is simply an extension of domestic trade, and expanding opportunities for the international exchange of commodities did encourage the spread of industrialization. In Britain, industrialization was initially based on a rapidly expanding export of cotton textiles, and later it came to depend increasingly on exports of iron manufactures and coal. In the United States before 1860 raw cotton exports played a part in supporting early industrial development in the country, and industrialization in Germany late in the nineteenth century was also closely tied up with an expansion of manufactured exports. Even in Russia and Japan, where governments created domestic markets for industrial goods through their own demands for military and railway equipment, the ability to develop an export trade, in wheat for Russia, and in cotton textiles for Japan, was necessary to provide the foreign exchange needed to service the inflow of foreign capital or to purchase the foreign machinery essential to industrialization. Whether the demand for industrial goods was satisfied directly through an expansion of manufactured exports, or whether it was created indirectly, through the growth of primary products exports leading to a rise in domestic real incomes, expanding foreign markets created an environment highly favourable to technological diffusion.

The growth of markets, both at home and abroad, is closely related to improvements in transportation, since poor transport facilities automatically restrict the size of the market thus limiting the scope for the use of modern technology. For this reason, good transport is perhaps the most powerful single weapon for accelerating the importation of modern industrial techniques. In this respect, foreign investment was often of vital significance, since much of it in the nineteenth century went into railway building on the Continent and in North and South America and Australasia. Some of this capital also went into the development of shipping lines, the construction of docks and harbours, improvements in communications, and the provision of other ancillary services necessary for an expanding foreign trade.

The size of the domestic markets of some countries was also increased by immigration, which allowed population to grow faster than it would have done if dependent only on natural increase. Moreover, where the immigrant population could be used in combination with unexploited or unused economic resources, per capita real incomes often rose (thus further increasing market size) because a larger workforce permitted greater specialization and the use of more productive techniques. Furthermore, as in the United States and elsewhere, part of the immigrant workforce could be utilized in constructing the transport network so important for the growth and exploitation of domestic and foreign markets.

Finally, for a number of countries within Europe the movement towards larger domestic markets was aided by the gradual reduction of internal barriers to trade, by such trade liberalizing measures as the freeing of the Rhine to all shipping, and by the setting up of customs unions, such as the German *Zollverein*. At the same time the spread of free trade policies after 1850 provided most countries with expanding opportunities for the international exchange of goods and services. Later in the nineteenth century, however, the widespread adoption of protectionist policies, while reducing the size of foreign markets, encouraged industrialization in some countries by preserving the domestic market for local producers.

On the supply side, a country's rate of capital accumulation is obviously a major determinant of its capacity to absorb new ideas and new methods of production. Where, for example, technical change is embodied in capital equipment, a country's rate of capital investment is all important, since, in general, the more investment the greater the degree of technological progress. Capital shortage therefore may hinder technological diffusion in a number of ways. For example, it will place limits on a country's stock of social overhead capital, especially transport facilities, with all that that implies for the growth of the market. The need for relatively abundant supplies of capital is also stressed where innovations in techniques cannot be made singly but require simultaneous development in a number of industries. Moreover, the fact that techniques can rarely be borrowed without adaptation further adds to the capital cost of introducing the new methods of production. Finally, the fact that industrialization in the nineteenth century was accompanied by population growth and urban development meant that there were heavy demands on capital in the form of housing, public utilities and the additional tools and machines needed to equip an expanding workforce. While in most countries the bulk of their capital needs were satisfied out of domestic savings, the availability of foreign funds to finance the construction of social overhead capital, especially transport facilities, communications and public utilities (the demand for which was particularly heavy in the new countries overseas), meant that domestic savings could be used largely to finance the growth of primary production and manufacturing industry in borrowing countries without this expansion being threatened by inadequate transport or the lack of other ancillary services.

For many countries foreign trade and immigration flows also partly overcame the obstacles to industrialization caused by lack of natural resources, skilled labour and enterprise. In so far as the adoption of modern industrial techniques is dependent on natural resources, geographical location or some other unequally distributed endowment, growth opportunities are not likely to be equally available to all countries. Limited natural resources was probably an important factor restricting industrialization in many of the smaller countries of Europe. French economic development, it has been argued, suffered from a shortage of coal. But, whatever the relevance of scarcity of natural resources as an obstacle to technological diffusion, it must have become less important with time as progress during the nineteenth century began to make alternative processes possible, or to make imported resources effective substitutes for inefficient, highly-priced domestic supplies. Moreover, if the raw materials necessary for industrial development could be imported from abroad, so too could the necessary skills and entrepreneurial ability. Historically, the trader from abroad and the immigrant artisan have long been the main channel for the importation of foreign techniques; where the nineteenth century differed from earlier times was in the scale on which these movements of labour occurred and in the wider range of skills that people carried with them when they moved from country to country.

International Transfer Mechanisms

What prompted the greater part of the flow of labour, capital and trade between countries were differences in the relative prices of these resources in different countries. In the case of both labour and capital, non-economic considerations exerted some influence on their movement internationally, but for the most part it was differences in wage rates and the rates of return on investment that prompted the flow of factors of production from regions where earnings were low to those where they were higher. With commodity trade too, the exchange was prompted by differences in the relative prices of the goods traded, which reflected in turn differences in the costs of production in the various countries engaged in foreign trade. In so far as the flows of goods, capital and labour took place in response to differential economic advantages of this kind, they acted as spontaneous or 'natural' carriers of modern technology and ideas. On the other hand, specific and direct attempts were often made by governments and other interested bodies to transfer technologies internationally. In addition to sending students abroad to study the new techniques, governments also encouraged the inflow of foreign skills and capital through the use of subventions to immigrant entrepreneurs and guarantees of dividends on foreign loans. Implicit in such policies was the assumption that the diffusion of the new knowledge, either nationally or internationally, was likely to be slow in the absence of conscious efforts to encourage technological change.[2]

CAUSES OF THE LIMITED SPREAD OF INDUSTRIALIZATION

International

Yet despite the existence of these natural carriers of technology on a scale previously unmatched in history, and despite the efforts made by some governments to reinforce the market influences determining the volume of direction of these trade and factor flows, the rate at which the new technology was diffused was slow, and the spread of modern industry limited. Thus, by 1913 the spread of industrialization was limited largely to western Europe, North America and Japan. While questions concerning the slow spread of industrialization in the period before 1913 can be answered only by a more detailed analysis of the problem than can be attempted here, a question more pertinent to the present discussion is whether 'failure' in the diffusion of modern industrial growth reflected weaknesses in the functioning of the international economy as a mechanism for transmitting growth between countries, or whether it was largely the result of the existence of other obstacles to the spread of modern technology. Unfortunately we are still far from fully understanding the detailed working of the international economy as an 'engine of growth' in the nineteenth century, and much research remains to be done to fill the gaps in our knowledge. We are, for example, still limited in our knowledge concerning the extent to which the economic growth of individual countries was dependent on the existence of the international economy, or how a country's dependence on the international economy may have changed over time, answers to which questions are obviously needed if we are to be able to weigh the relative importance of domestic and international obstacles to the spread of industrialization. Because of our lack of knowledge in these matters, comment on the problem just raised is necessarily limited, but nevertheless a few general observations on it can be offered.

To begin with, if the diffusion of modern industrial technology was limited before 1913, it was partly because the supply of capital and labour available for international transfer was limited, and because not all of the countries desiring to import these productive resources were equally well-placed to attract them. For a number of reasons North America, and especially the United States, was particularly attractive for foreign investors and migrant labour, and western Europe, because of its compactness and its proximity to Britain, the seat of the industrial revolution, was also conveniently placed to take advantage of the new technology. The fact that these two regions received the lion's share of the economic resources that did shift internationally during these years meant simply that there were fewer of these resources available for other capital and labour-importing countries, and their prospects for industrial development suffered correspondingly.

Moreover, in some countries primary production continued to be more profitable than manufacturing activities, in the sense that these countries' real income could be increased more rapidly by their specializing in agricultural and mining production and exchanging their surpluses of primary products for manufactures produced elsewhere. As long as the real incomes of primary producers were sustained by the mounting demand for foodstuffs and raw materials of the industrializing regions at the centre of the international economy, the spread of industrialization to peripheral countries was limited by the economic advantages accruing to them from the growing territorial division of labour which formed the basis of the expanding international economy of the nineteenth century. When, however, changing demand and supply conditions in the post-World War I period resulted in a downward pressure on primary product prices, which reduced the real incomes of countries supplying these commodities, industrialization programmes became a feature of many of these countries, as their governments endeavoured to diversify domestic economic activity by encouraging the production of manufactured goods previously purchased out of the export earnings of primary producers.

National

While the international economy may have functioned in such a way as to limit the spread of industrialization in the nineteenth century, for the most part the major obstacles to the diffusion of modern technology were to be found within countries rather than between them. The available evidence for this period suggests that the diffusion of modern industrial technology between countries was much faster than its diffusion within countries. Thus, Watt's steam engine, first brought out in England in 1776, was introduced into France in 1779, into Germany in 1788, and into Italy in 1816. On the other hand, within Britain the steam engine did not come into general use until after 1850. In the other European countries, however, the lag was even greater, and in Italy the steam engine was still far from widely used even in 1913. A similar situation developed in the United States where the steam engine was introduced towards the end of the eighteenth century and quickly adopted for use in river boats. But it was not widely used in American industry until after the Civil War. Another example is to be found in the spread of the idea of interchangeable parts and standardized production. Developed in the United States well before 1850, and introduced into the British government's arms factory at Enfield in the 1850s, these innovations were adopted only very slowly by British manufacturers. While further evidence of disparate rates of technological diffusion between and within countries exists, for example, in the spread of new textile machinery and modern metallurgical processes during the nineteenth century, what obviously needs explanation is the cause of this disparity. In particular we need to know why, with easy international movement of inventions, a country's capacity to adopt new techniques on a wide scale should be so difficult to foster or to impart.

As we have already indicated, the adoption of modern technology is partly dependent on the availability of markets, capital, natural resources, and the necessary labour skills and entrepreneurial ability. But while limited markets and shortages of productive resources could be partially overcome with the help of foreign trade, capital and labour, in the final analysis the available domestic supplies of capital and entrepreneurship were often crucial in bringing about successful industrialization. Moreover, non-economic influences, particularly social attitudes, customs and beliefs are important determinants of the rate at which new techniques are diffused throughout an economy. The incompatibility of the new industrial technology with existing institutional arrangements, the reactions of merchants and businessmen to the uncertainty and risks attached to new ways of doing things, and the concern for social and political stability are only a few examples of the forces generating the social rigidities and resistance to change likely to be encountered in an industrializing society. The existence of such forces serves to remind us that technological change is a cultural, social, psychological, and political process, as well as imitation and adoption of techniques. Yet on the question of whether major structural shifts in the socio political fabric must precede or accompany the adoption of industrial technology, the facts, such as they are, are not unambiguous. In France, for example, a very strong concern for continuity in the social and cultural sphere meant that technical change was relatively slow and that the government did not play a major role in promoting economic development. Germany, on the other hand, achieved rapid industrialization despite the fact that the old order retained much of its force. Denmark and Sweden also appear to have created expansionary economies as much by changing the direction of their economic efforts as by altering the structure of their institutions or the habits of their peoples. In South and East Europe, however, the existence of an essentially feudal system, and the rigid social stratification which accompanied it, as well as the low social value attached to industry and profit in the culture of some of these countries, constituted insurmountable barriers to the adoption of the new industrial technology, backed up as they were by deficiencies of resources, scale of markets, and education. Only Russia, in this part of the continent, succeeded in industrializing to any significant extent, and then only after the resistance of the government and other conservative forces had been overcome, largely by outside events.

Outside Europe the spread of industrialization to the United States, Canada, and, to a lesser extent, the other regions of European settlement overseas was helped by a level of receptivity to the new technology that was at least as high as that in Britain and the more industrially advanced countries in Europe, with which countries they shared a common social, economic and cultural background. These ties were also useful in fostering periodic inflows of European capital and labour, which considerably assisted the diffusion of industrial techniques within the countries concerned.

High receptivity to the new technology was not confined to European countries or their offshoots overseas however. In Asia, Japan began industrializing rapidly towards the end of the nineteenth century and in this respect it is interesting to contrast the experiences of Japan and China before 1914 when confronted by Western technology and economic intervention. Displaying a common policy of exclusiveness and virtual absence of contracts with foreign countries, as well as a social structure and system of land ownership that acted as a barrier to industrialization, their responses to Western intervention in their affairs were totally different. Whereas Japan adopted Western industrial techniques rapidly and succeeded in achieving economic 'take-off' seemingly without any major social or cultural changes, the Chinese government remained contemptuous of Western civilization and opposed to all forms of social and economic change.

Some idea of the extent of the spread of modern industrialization by 1913 is given in Table 13, which contains indices of output of manufactures per head of the population for a wide range of countries. These output indices are based on the average proportionate share of manufacturing output for the period 1925–9 allocated to each country and taken back to 1913 by the use of industrial production indices. The measure of industrial output for each country was then divided by its population and the result expressed as a proportion of United States output per head. Given the manner of their construction the indices contained in Table 13 obviously should be treated as orders of magnitude, with wide margins of error, especially at the bottom end of the table.

What the table reveals is the relatively limited spread of the new industrial technology by 1913. The United States, Britain, and most of western Europe were relatively well industrialized by this time, as were Canada, Australia and New Zealand, whose highly productive agriculture provided, as in the other industrially advanced countries, a strong domestic demand for manufactured goods. Elsewhere, however, in eastern and southern Europe, in much of Latin

Table 13 Index of output of manufactures per head of population, 1913

USA	100	Poland	13
		Russia	9
Europe		Yugoslavia	6
UK	90	Romania	6
Belgium	73	Greece	4
Germany	64		
Switzerland	64	Other	
Sweden	50	Canada	84
France	46	Australia	75
Denmark	46	New Zealand	66
Netherlands	44	Argentina	23
Norway	39	Chile	17
Austria	31	Japan	6
Czechoslovakia	28	Mexico	5
Finland	27	South Africa	5
Italy	20	Brazil	2
Hungary	19	India	1
Spain	15		

Source: W. A. Lewis, *Growth and Fluctuations 1870–1913* (London, 1978), Table 7.1, p. 163. For a more detailed explanation of the construction of the Table, see Lewis, op. cit., fn 9, p. 313.

America, and in most of Asia and Africa, the process of modern industrial developments had barely begun by the outbreak of World War I.

CONCLUSIONS

The spread of industrialization from Britain to the continents of Europe and North America was assisted by the functioning of the international economy. The flows of capital, labour and trade, which linked together the countries of the world, provided the channels through which modern industrial technology could be diffused between nations. If the extent of this technological diffusion was limited in the nineteenth century, it was partly because the stock of capital and labour available for international transfer was limited and partly because not all of the countries desiring to import these extra productive resources were equally well-placed to attract them. But what was an even greater obstacle to the spread of industrialization was the fact that many countries, even when they received inflows of foreign labour and capital, lacked the internal flexibility necessary for them to take advantage of the changing technological opportunities that presented themselves. It was this weakness rather than any fundamental deficiency in the functioning of the international economy as an 'engine of growth' that accounts for the limited industrialization before 1914. To industrialize successfully, there had to be capital formation, technical change, reallocation of resources, as well as changes in social, political and cultural attitudes to economic activity. Since in most countries the forces of inertia were strong and deeply entrenched, the spread of industrialization was necessarily a slow process.

NOTES

1 But, as Rondo Cameron has recently stressed, 'it is necessary to distinguish between the mere diffusion of technology and the distinctive pattern of industrialization that occurred on the continent [and in the United States] as a result of this diffusion'. ('A New View of European Industrialization', *Economic History Review* (Feb., 1985), p. 10). Cameron goes on to argue (pp. 22–3) that, besides the British model of industrialization, there were several others in which such factors as the availability of coal and the needed human resources formed two basic ingredients with international investment and financial institutions performing subordinate roles.

2 These two methods of transmitting technical knowledge enable us to draw a distinction between technological diffusion on the one hand and technological transfer on the other. Whereas the former term can be used to describe a natural spontaneous process of knowledge transmission, technological transfer incorporates 'an additional specific element, namely, planned and purposive type of action. It implies a conscious, predeterminate effort and commitment of resources to transplant technology from one country to another, and from one use to another.'

(D. L. Spencer and A. Woroniak (eds.), *The Transfer of Technology to Developing Countries* (New York, 1967), p. 186.) Both mechanisms played their part in the process of economic development in the nineteenth century.

SELECTED REFERENCES

Cameron, R., 'A New View of European Industrialization', *Economic History Review* (Feb., 1985), pp. 1–23.

Landes, D. S., *The Unbound Prometheus* (Cambridge, 1969).

Mathias, P., and Postan, M. M., *The Cambridge Economic History of Europe*, Vol. II (Cambridge, 1978).

Milward, A., and Saul, S. B., *The Economic Development of Continental Europe, 1780–1870* (London, 1973).

Milward, A., and Saul, S. B., *The Development of the Economies of Continental Europe, 1850–1914* (London, 1977).

Pollard, S., *Peaceful Conquest: the Industrialization of Europe 1760–1970* (Oxford, 1981).

Rostow, W. W., *The World Economy: History and Prospect* (London, 1978).

Supple, B. E., *The Experience of Economic Growth* (New York, 1963).

Chapter 9

International aspects of economic growth in the nineteenth century

The export economies

INTRODUCTION

Outside the industrializing countries, economic growth was primarily a reflex action to the steady and persistent rise in the world demand for primary products. In these peripheral countries, economic growth took place for two reasons. First, trade was the means whereby the benefits of technological progress in Europe could be passed on to the rest of the world, mainly through the exchange of manufactured goods for foodstuffs and raw materials. At the same time, specialization in the production of those primary products most suited to the economic resources of these countries tended to raise the general level of their skills and productivity. Moreover, this increased productivity, along with the continued growth of exports and the accompanying rise in real incomes, provided an incentive to the establishment and expansion of other forms of economic activity and paved the way for further economic development. In this way an expansion of primary product exports could induce growth in the rest of the economy.

Faith in the transmission of development through trade was not too difficult to justify in the light of what was happening during the nineteenth century. Great Britain, for example, was developing successfully, first on the basis of textile exports, and later by expanding her exports of coal and iron. More relevant for primary producing countries, however, was the experience of the United States, which grew impressively before 1860, largely as a result of a rapid expansion in her raw cotton exports. Other nineteenth century examples of successful development based on primary product exports include Denmark, Sweden, Australia, Canada, New Zealand, South Africa and, to a lesser extent, Argentina and Brazil. In certain other countries, the export trade, if not a leading sector, was still a most valuable support to economic development. In Russia, for example, wheat exports provided the foreign exchange needed to service the inflow of foreign capital essential to industrialization, whereas in Japan, where the creation of a domestic mass market was precluded by the low income condition of the peasants and workers, the expansion of foreign markets was imperative as an outlet for the products of the country's new manufacturing industries.

Yet, if, during the nineteenth century, there were many countries in which exports played an important part in inducing growth in the rest of the domestic economy, there were many others, accounting between them for the bulk of the world's population, in which foreign trade failed to generate conditions conducive to self-sustaining growth. Broadly speaking, two explanations have been advanced to account for this breakdown in the transmission of growth through trade. The first explanation emphasizes the drawbacks and disadvantages of dependence on exports of primary products for promoting economic growth, while the second attempts to explain why growth in the export sector fails to carry over to the other sectors of the economy and cause a general expansion of the economy. The first approach concentrates on the drawbacks to a country's specializing in primary production. In particular, the disadvantages arising out of a country's dependence on a single export product are stressed, with all that this means for the country's future development should the world demand for the product fall, or should superior sources of supply be discovered elsewhere. Other disadvantages to primary production include the excessive price fluctuations displayed in the markets for primary products and their influence, through a country's foreign exchange earnings, on its financing of economic development. Finally, there is the declining terms of trade argument which runs to the effect that specialization in primary production is an undesirable policy in the long-run, since it condemns primary producers to ever-declining terms of trade.[1] While each of these arguments has some relevance in explaining the growth experiences of the export economies during the past hundred years or so, what is of immediate interest is the second explanation of the phenomenon, which concentrates attention on the factors limiting the carry-over of growth from the export sector to the rest of the economy. It is this carry-over problem which lies at the centre of the successful or unsuccessful transmission of growth through trade.[2]

REGIONS OF RECENT SETTLEMENT

In discussing the carry-over problem it is useful to draw the distinction between those countries in which, despite immigration, labour was scarce but land abundant, and the overcrowded countries of Asia. The former group of countries, often described collectively as the regions of recent settlement, include Canada, the United States, Australia, New Zealand, South Africa and Argentina, and they constitute for the nineteenth century the outstanding example of growth through trade in primary products. In them, a large inflow of European labour and capital supplied the factors needed for export industry production, with the immigrant workers and entrepreneurs making up a rapidly integrated and largely homogeneous society, conversant with European needs and markets and receptive to the forces of innovation and change. In some of these countries, such as the United States and, to a lesser extent, Canada and Australia, the large size of the country could give rise to internal economic development independent of any significant impetus from the export sector, while in all of them, abundant and readily accessible natural resources attracted foreign capital with the profits to be made from their exploitation.

Moreover, with the exception of Argentina, these were high-wage economies. Generally speaking, we should expect to find higher wage levels in sparsely populated countries than in densely populated ones, as well as a tendency for wage levels to show a rising trend over periods of rapid expansion of output requiring more (scarce) labour. These expectations are broadly borne out by experience in the newly settled regions of North America and Australasia. What is even more important, however, is that high wages assisted economic development in two ways. First, they provided buoyant markets, even in countries with relatively small populations. Second, through the efforts of entrepreneurs to counteract high wage costs and overcome labour scarcity they generated technical progress, which in turn supported and enhanced the high productivity which came in time to provide the basis upon which these high wages were paid. This interaction between rising productivity, high wage levels and expanding domestic markets was not experienced by all labour-scarce countries. In the Argentine, for reasons shortly to be discussed, the high-wage/low-rent economy never materialized in the nineteenth century, and the opportunities for the further development of the economy were correspondingly reduced despite very high rates of growth in the country's export sector. It is for this reason that we include the Argentine in the following discussion of those countries in which export expansion was unsuccessful or only partially successful in generating self-sustaining growth.

THE EXPORT ECONOMIES

Owing to the steady growth in the world demand for primary products characteristic of the period, the demand side can be neglected in attempting to explain the breakdown in the transmission of growth through trade that occurred in a large number of countries during the nineteenth century. To explain the phenomenon we have to concentrate on the supply side, where two major problems presented themselves to peripheral countries desiring to benefit from the growth forces generated by European industrialization. First, these countries had to integrate themselves into the expanding lines of trade created by the rising European demand for foodstuffs and raw materials. When this was achieved, the expansionary forces generated within the export sector of these integrating economies had then to be diffused throughout the rest of the economy. In other words, the lack of successful economic growth in underdeveloped countries during the nineteenth century can be explained either by inadequate or late integration into the world economy, or by the obstacles which prevented the growth forces originating in the export sector from transmitting themselves to the rest of the economy.

Late integration into the world economy partly explains the relative backwardness of many African economies. Although there was a rapid expansion of African exports in the late nineteenth century, the extent of the continent's integration into the international economy was seriously limited by transport difficulties. In a continent with few navigable rivers, where the ravages of the tsetse fly restricted the use of animal power, and where, as a result, porterage was the chief means of transport, the transition from an economic system based on slave labour to one based on wage labour tended to have a paralysing effect on transport and through it on internal trade. Apart from gold and ivory, there were few commodities that could bear the high cost of porterage from the interior. When it arrived, even the railway could provide only a limited system of communications in the absence of animal-drawn wheeled transport and feeder roads. As far as low-value bulky commodities were concerned, a radius of 30–40 miles from a railway, or a navigable river for that matter, was the extreme limit of profitable production for export under conditions of porterage. This transport deficiency blunted the impact of world demand on the African economy and accounts for the persistence of a substantial African subsistence economy which, through its low productivity and lack of monetization, slowed down the overall economic growth of the continent.

In those regions and countries which did achieve relatively early and successful integration into the world economy, the problem is one of explaining the lack of successful export-led growth. Here, two broad categories of explanations have been put forward, the one economic, the other political and socio-cultural. The economic explanations tend to concentrate on the differential effects on economic growth of the various export commodities according to their production characteristics. In particular, this approach singles out for attention the export sector's demand for inputs, its effects on income distribution and the creation of markets, and the opportunities it provides for the diffusion of technical, organizational and administrative skills. The second approach stresses such factors as land tenure systems, the basic values and attitudes of the indigenous population, political conditions, including the effects of colonialism, and other largely non-economic considerations. In actual fact, neither set of explanations is completely independent of the other and, in discussing the failure of export-led growth to materialize in any given country, both must be taken into account, although the weights to be allocated to each will obviously vary from one country to another.

The economic explanations centre on the different types of productive activity to be found in the primary producing countries and their differential effects on income distribution and the opportunities for long-term development. In particular, the distinction is drawn between peasant export economies, on the one hand, and those economies primarily dependent on exporting the products of mines and plantations on the other. These basically different patterns of productive activity are important because they generate different export-income distributions between foreign and domestic producers, and because they provide differing opportunities for improving the skills and productivity of the indigenous population.

Peasant exports, which include such commodities as rice, palm-oil, cocoa, cotton, rubber and copra and other coconut products, are important in Africa and a number of Asian countries. Apart from land, peasant production typically requires very little durable capital equipment, since it amounts to little more than an extension of the traditional economic organization and technology of the subsistence sector. It is also a form of production which has little need of outside capital and labour. In fact, where the peasant combines the growing of cash crops with other crops intended for his own personal consumption, export production is largely self-financing. Typically, too, peasant production draws little or no labour from outside the household. Two links, outside the peasant's control, are needed, however, to connect him to the world markets for which he produces. Improvements in transport and communications can help open up new areas of production, and a middleman is often necessary to collect, process and convey the peasant's produce to foreign buyers as well as supply the imported goods that act as an inducement to increased export production, since by stimulating new wants among the peasants, the expansion of imports can act as a major dynamic force encouraging the expansion of exports.

In the last quarter of the nineteenth century the output of many peasant economies increased substantially in response to a growing world demand for their products. Between 1870 and 1913 peasant rice exports from Burma and Thailand grew some 10 to 13 times. Egyptian cotton production rose from 500,000 kantars in 1860 to 3.1m. in 1879 and 7.7 m. in 1913. On the west coast of Africa palm oil and oil-seed accounted for over three-quarters of the total value of Nigerian exports in 1913, and cocoa contributed 80 per cent to the value of the Gold Coast's total exports in the same year.

Despite these impressive export performances, in most countries their impact on the rest of the economy was either limited or insignificant. There were a number of reasons why this should be so. The partial commitment to export production implicit in an economic set-up where the peasant household continued to produce all its own subsistence requirements in addition to growing cash crops, limited the spread of a money economy. If, in addition, market transactions were restricted largely to an exchange of exports for imports, then the monetized sector obviously had little impact on the rest of the economy. On the other hand, complete export specialization, while more conducive to the development of the domestic market—since peasant

families producing for export would set up a cash demand for locally produced foodstuffs and other locally-produced goods and services—was not
without its drawbacks.[3] The peasant was now completely at the mercy of an
often unstable export market. More important, his activities ceased to be self-
financing so that in the event of drought, plant disease, or a fall in world
prices, he might be forced to fall back on outside sources of credit, including
money-lenders who charged high rates of interest. In these circumstances,
partial specialization often represented a rational response to the prevailing
set of economic conditions under which the peasant operated.

The spread of a money economy was also restricted by lack of transport
which, as we have already seen, accounted for the persistence of a subsistence
sector in large areas of Africa. Limited technical knowledge, primitive
methods of production, and poor-quality produce also reduced the level of
peasant income, either by keeping productivity low or by influencing the
prices received for peasant produce on world markets. In some countries the
increase in production and exports achieved during these years was absorbed
partly by an increase in population and partly by a rise in the level of living of
the upper and middle classes and by a much smaller rise in that of the mass of
the population. This appears to have been the case in Egypt in the half
century before 1913.[4] There was also the possibility of a part, and often a
substantial part, of the peasant's income passing into the hands of some
person or group in the export sector, especially in those situations where the
middleman handling the peasant's crops could exercise monopoly power.
Thus, a few foreign import-export firms could combine to purchase the
peasant's output at low prices while selling him imports at highly inflated
prices. Alternatively, this monopoly power could be exercised by a government agency, such as the Nederlandse Handel Maatschappy, which was set
up in the Dutch East Indies in the 1820s to purchase peasant produce at low
fixed prices or to acquire it as taxes in kind. Exploitation of the peasant could
also occur when the peasant's crops had to be processed at a company factory
possessing a local monopoly. This appears to have happened in Cuba, where
improvements in sugar technology and an influx of foreign capital led to a
reduction in the number of sugar mills and an increase in the manufacturing
capacity of those that survived. At first competition between the mills
worked in favour of the sugar farmers. But later, when, in order to ensure
adequate supplies of sugar cane, the mill companies created territorial monopolies by purchasing plantations and by building private railways to transport the cane to the mill, the surviving farmers found themselves completely
at the mercy of one or other of the large companies.[5]

While peasant export economies have certain features that are potentially
highly favourable to the spread of economic growth, from its very beginnings
plantation-type production displayed characteristics highly inimical to successful economic development. This type of agriculture predominated in
Latin America and the Central American and Caribbean regions where sugar,

bananas, coffee and cotton were the major plantation crops grown. It was also to be found in Ceylon, parts of India and in south-east Asia, where the emphasis was on tea, coffee, and rubber. In 'Africa, plantations developed relatively late. By the 1890s cocoa, coffee, and tobacco plantations had been established in the German Cameroons, and sisal was first introduced into Tanganyika in 1892. Banana plantations in the Cameroons, tea plantations in Nyasaland and East Africa, and oil-palm plantations in the Belgian Congo, were not established until the start of this century

Originally based on the use of slave labour, in the nineteenth century, plantation production was characterized by a high degree of foreign owner-ship and control; the provision of finance by foreign banks and agency houses; large scale, factory style operation of the plantations using large amounts of labour specially imported from abroad for these purposes; control of the import–export trade by foreigners; and virtually complete reliance on imported supplies of capital equipment, estate supplies and, often, even food for the workforce. These key characteristics of plantation production had important consequences for the working of the export sector and its capacity to transmit growth to the rest of the economy.

Where the export sector consisted almost wholly of foreign-owned plan-tations employing foreign capital and imported labour, it constituted an enclave economy which, because the income it generated was largely remitted abroad, contributed little to the formation of the domestic market and the promotion of local economic growth. Low wages with no rising trend (despite rapid growth of output) was also characteristic of those export economies where use was made of indigenous labour. In some countries, such as the Central American republics, where the coffee and banana plantations have to depend on the local population for their workforce, money wages, plus a variety of devices designed to cut off the peasant from free access to land, were used to force the local population into employment at low wages. When these methods proved insufficient, the governments often resorted to more direct, coercive measures in an effort to meet the labour requirements of the rapidly growing export sector. Similar policies, including the imposition of money taxes on the indigenous population, were used in Africa to drive the natives into paid employment in the mines and plantations. In other plantation economies, the relatively abundant supply of cheap labour imported from India and China tended to depress wages in the export sector as well as in the economy generally. In so far as the local population was deterred from entering employment in the export sector by the prevailing low level of wages, they tended to crowd into alternative paid occupations, thus depressing wages in those industries as well. Alternatively, the local popula-tion was forced to fall back on the subsistence sector, with its associated low productivity and lack of market contact.

The outcome of this situation was a high concentration of a country's income and wealth in the hands of a small group of people, whether of local or foreign origin, and, as a consequence, an underdeveloped domestic market. Foreign ownership also meant leakage of export income overseas, but even when the plantation owners were local entrepreneurs employing local capital, their contribution to local economic growth, either through their consumption or their investment expenditures, was often minimal. In some economies the local entrepreneurs formed too small a group to permit economic production for their domestic demand; in others, contact with Western culture and consumption patterns turned them into large-scale importers of foreign goods and services. In both situations the end result was the same, the creation of a group of 'luxury importers' who contributed little to the promotion of a domestic market, either by way of consumption or of investment. Indeed, it was much more profitable to invest in export production, and where the concentration of income generated substantial local saving, it was channelled almost wholly into the further expansion of the export sector.

If the market contribution of the export sector to domestic economic growth was small, so too was the technological contribution, in the sense of improvement in the quality of the workforce. Since there was little pressure from labour for higher wages, the entrepreneur had no interest in replacing his labour by capital or in improving the skills of his workforce. The same arguments applied to land where it was in abundant supply. Lacking any incentive for improvements in methods of cultivation or of labour skills, the tendency for the entrepreneur to invest new capital in the simple extension of his plantation was reinforced. Given the prevailing pattern of resource availability, with capital scarce and land and labour abundant, the method of production used and the form of investment taken were rational ones, although their capacity for promoting growth in the rest of the economy was limited. Potentially, mining was the most effective form of production for diffusing technical skills and raising the level of labour productivity. In fact, its potential was rarely ever realized. Initially, the use of modern mining techniques inevitably meant that foreign skills had to be imported as well, and the indigenous workers could find employment only as unskilled labourers. Over time the structure of the mining labour force changed very little, either because of discrimination against local workers, which prevented them from gaining promotion and the opportunity to acquire new skills, or because the nature of the local workforce gave the employer no incentive to impart new skills to it.[6] The outcome of all this was a tendency for the low wages paid to the local workforce to persist, along with relatively little improvement in its average level of skill.

Whether in plantation or mining economies, these low wages eventually became institutionalized in a cheap labour policy which was justified on a number of grounds, including the low productivity of the workforce, its customarily low material standard of living, its lack of response to the incentive of high wages, and the belief that, in general, indigenous labour not only had low productivity but that it also had limited capacity for improvement.

Since low wages meant low productivity, the cheap labour policy became self-justifying, and through the vicious circle of low wages and low productivity, the productivity of the indigenous workforce even in thinly populated countries was fossilized at its very low initial level. It was the pattern of low wages and productivity perpetuated by the cheap labour policy of the mines and plantations, rather than primary production as such, which accounted for the failure of exports in underdeveloped countries to be a leading sector initiating growth in the rest of the economy.

The other set of factors relevant to this discussion is comprised of the social, political, cultural and legal constraints on the propagation of export-led growth. These constraints largely reflected the psychological and ideological attitudes generated by the export economy's one-sided orientation, wherein agricultural production for export was what really counted. Change in the existing socio-political system, in so far as it occurred, was effected only to the extent required for the realization of this objective. This fact is seen all too clearly in the land tenure system that developed in the plantation economies. Where property in land became economically meaningful only when coupled with technical and commercial know-how and easy access to finance, the resulting system of land ownership was rapidly structured around the plantation as the central type of organization in agricultural export sectors. This structuring of the export sector was often brought about by deliberate government policy. In the Central American republics, for example, the inability of the respective governments to raise capital on international markets made them dependent upon foreign firms, particularly banana producers, for the building of railways and the improvement of port facilities. In return these plantation companies received generous land grants and other government incentives, including exemption from taxes. In other countries, what government policy failed to do in the way of discriminating between those who could and those who could not own land, the market did through unequal access to financial and commercial processes and institutions and through differences in technical knowledge. Whatever the forces at work, be they government or free market inspired, the outcome was almost always the same, a bimodal property distribution, with a few enormous plantations at one end of the scale and many very small farms at the other.

Although it was not a plantation export economy, a similar state of affairs developed in the Argentine. Here, the early growth of an export economy based on cattle-raising led to the fertile areas of the Pampas passing into the hands of a few large cattle ranchers. Later, when new export lines were developed, particularly wheat, the lack of readily accessible land for occupation by immigrant farmers seriously impeded the growth of output and employment in the rural sector.

The tendency toward concentration of land ownership affected the development of agriculture and of the economy as a whole in a number of different ways. First, it restricted the growth of rural output and employment as well as the growth of domestic markets. The lack of available agricultural land held back rural output by discouraging immigration, since the immigrant was obliged to work as a tenant farmer or as a low paid field hand. Alternatively, immigrants were forced into the towns, thus swelling the supply of manpower for urban employment and forcing down wages in these labour markets. Second, the concentration of land ownership led to a stratified society in which the bulk of the country's income and wealth went to a few people, while the mass of the population lived on incomes barely above the subsistence level. With income concentrated in a few hands, there was a disproportionate demand for luxury consumption and investment, usually met out of imports, whereas the low income level of the mass of the population restricted the latter's demand for manufactured goods and was therefore an obstacle to industrial development. Industrial growth was also limited by the free trade policy adopted by nearly all of these countries. The landowning class constituted the ruling political group and, mindful of its own interests and those of foreign circles to which it was linked in a variety of ways, it advocated a free trade policy which, by allowing the unrestricted entry of foreign manufactures, limited the development of the basic industries needed to integrate the whole economy.

Looking at the overall performance of the export economies during the period before 1900, Hanson argues that most less-developed countries (LDCs) had entered the world trade network by 1860, at a time when the demand for their exports was expanding particularly rapidly. After 1860, however, conditions were rather different from what they had been in the immediately preceding decades in three important respects. The rate of growth of LDC exports declined; Great Britain's share in the exports of the LDCs began to fall; and, most significantly, the LDCs faced increasing competition in many of their specialties, for example, sugar, copper and artificial dyes, from the now developed countries.[7] What these developments suggest is that the capacity of individual third-world countries to promote economic growth in their economies through export expansion was much more limited after 1860.

On the other hand, in his survey of the economic development of 41 LDCs, Lloyd Reynolds concludes that 'politics apart, the main factor determining the turning point [at which a country's "extensive growth" turned into "intensive growth"] has been [its] ability to participate effectively in the trade opportunities opened up by the expansion of the world economy'.[8] A country's export capacity, in turn, was influenced by its natural resource supplies, the diversity of its resources and products, and the capacity of government to provide a framework of policies conducive to export expansion. If we accept Reynolds's definition of the turning point and his chronology of turning points for individual LDCs, which no doubt would be the subject of dispute by some economists and economic historians, then 18 such countries achieved economic 'take-off' after 1860 compared with only five in the period before

1860. Of course many of the countries which achieved the transition to 'intensive growth' after 1860 had been incorporated into the international economy, often to a limited extent, before that year, for example, Peru, Nigeria, and Sri Lanka (Ceylon). But others, many of them in Africa, had to wait on the coming of the railway and the steamship for effective integration into the world economy on anything like a meaningful scale.

The two studies referred to above are, of course, not incompatible with each other. Even if the rate of growth of world demand for the exports of the LDCs did slow down after 1860, it may still have been high enough to promote the economic transformation of a growing number of these countries. Abundant and very rich natural resources, resource and commodity diversity, which allowed switching from less-profitable to more-profitable commodity production in response to changing world demand, as well as the benefits of colonial rule, particularly in the form of increased access to metropolitan markets, must have played a part in allowing export expansion to continue to influence significantly economic development in a number of LDCs. During the period after 1860, the substitution of colonial produce for produce previously imported from independent countries may also have occurred to an increasing extent in metropolitan markets, especially after 1880. The 'backwash effects' of colonialism were not limited only to the colonial economy. As Hanson admits, a fuller understanding of the complex relationship between export expansion and economic growth in the LDCs will come only with more detailed studies of the economic growth experience of individual export economies and a greater knowledge of the pattern and changing world demand for, and supply of, those commodities that played such an important role in the early economic development of these countries.

ECONOMIC IMPERIALISM AND COLONIALISM

Economic development was also hindered for various reasons in those territories which became colonized following the burst of imperialist expansion that occurred in the late nineteenth century. Beginning in the 1880s, a wave of 'colony grabbing' began that continued until the outbreak of war in 1914. Africa was divided among the European powers, British control was extended over Burma and Malaya. France consolidated its Indo-Chinese empire. Even the United States was not free from this desire for political and economic expansion. The Philippine Islands were seized during a war with Spain, a republic was established in Hawaii, and political intervention occurred in Mexico, Costa Rica, Dominica, Colombia and Nicaragua.

The root causes of this burst of imperialism in the late nineteenth century are extremely complex, as the numerous theories put forward to explain the phenomenon indicate. Some explain the acquisition of colonies in these years in purely political terms, seeing the colonies either in strategic terms or as political bargaining counters for use in the game of international diplomacy. Still others see the new imperialism as a manifestation of a popular and emotional concern for national prestige and power. Economic explanations of the phenomenon abound. The commercial needs of Europe, in particular, are stressed, including the growing need for new markets fostered by the spread of protection and the growth of industry; the desire to gain control over supplies of raw material, particularly tropical products; and the need to find alternative outlets for surplus capital for which domestic investment opportunities did not exist. Providing an additional pretext for intervention in the affairs of other countries and possibly leading to their eventual acquisition as colonies, were the missionaries, planters, labour recruiters and traders of the colonizing countries. These people, who through their activities (usually quite unwittingly) undermined the established order in the foreign territory, often forced their country's government to step in to protect their lives and property and to restore political stability.

The need for colonies has often been argued in purely economic terms, yet the available evidence suggests that the colonial annexations of the late nineteenth century were of limited economic benefit to the colonizing powers. Most of these tropical colonies were too poor to provide valuable markets for manufactured exports, and while some of them were suppliers of important industrial raw materials, for example metals and crude rubber, the combined share of the colonies in the raw material markets of the world was relatively small. Consequently, with the exception of Britain, whose empire was by far the largest and provided uniquely favourable markets and a wide variety of raw materials, trade with the tropical dependencies was only a small fraction of the total trade of their owners. Moreover, even when the trend towards protectionism became intense, the fact that up to World War I and beyond, Britain, Holland, Belgium and Germany retained liberal commercial policies in their dealings with their colonies meant that non-colonial nations generally had easy access to the colonial markets of these states.

If tropical colonies were not acquired to provide exclusive markets and sources of raw materials and foodstuffs for the metropolitan country, neither were they an important outlet for the surplus capital of that country. Indeed there is very little geographical correlation between capital exports and the acquisition of new colonies after 1880, and compared with foreign investment in Europe and the regions of recent settlement, the funds invested in Africa and south-east Asia were relatively insignificant. Thus, whereas by 1914 almost $11,000m. of British investments were to be found in the United States and the British Dominions, only some $600m. was invested in West Africa, the Straits Settlements and the rest of Britain's recent overseas acquisitions. Furthermore, many imperialist powers—notably Russia, Italy, Portugal and Spain—far from having an embarrassing surplus of capital, were net importers of capital and must therefore have had other motives for making annexations. Nor, when it was undertaken, was investment in the tropics always highly profitable. Studies of the type of loans issued in the heyday of colonial expansion reveal that the greater part was in fixed interest government securities; that the profitability of this investment was only marginally higher than that of domestic investment; and that in the end some European investors lost their money through defaults. On the other hand, the return on some risk capital (equities) was often high, and probably higher than could be obtained at most times on industrial investments in Europe or America. Yet the high profits earned on colonial equity investments were more the result of the heavy industrial demand for particular products, for example metals and rubber, the scarcity of local capital, and the superior bargaining position of Western countries in their dealings with politically and economically weaker societies, than the outcome of the exercise of formal imperial power as such.

In fact, to assume that political control is necessary if one country is to exercise economic domination over another is to forget that this end can be achieved just as well through the use of diplomatic and economic advantage as through direct colonial rule. Some historians argue, for example, that Europeans by using their easy access to the financial and technical resources of the West were able to skim the most readily available profit opportunities in the underdeveloped continents, thus making the job of indigenous economic development extremely difficult. This is the thesis of 'informal imperialism', whose nature and functioning have been amply illustrated in the earlier pages of this chapter.

Whatever the nature and extent of the benefits accruing to the metropolitan powers from the possession of colonies, however, there can be little doubt that colonization placed severe limits on the economic development of the annexed territories. In these countries the indigenous population could not resist penetration by Westerners into the heart of their economy, or the reorganization of their laws and institutions according to the interests of Western entrepreneurs and governments. Changes in the system of land tenure, the conditions of labour supply and the nature of the economic activities of large populations were introduced by colonizing governments. At the same time, the setting up of an orderly framework of government administration and the introduction of sanitation and other public health measures caused a rapid growth of population in many colonies. The result was a disruption of the traditional balance between population, natural resources and technology.

The case of India may be cited by way of illustration. Here, the British need of an efficient and simple method of raising land revenues resulted in two systems of land tenure being introduced. In the Presidency of Bengal, the land was concentrated in the hands of a group of great landlords who were expected to remain strongly pro-British, since their income and security depended, in the last analysis, upon the strength of the British regime. Elsewhere in India, the British made land settlements on a field-by-field basis with the individual cultivating peasants, as in southern Madras, or on an estate basis with groups of leading families in the villages, as in the central parts of India. Where peasant farming predominated, the nature of the revenue and land tenure systems—annual payment of taxes in money and in full, plus the private property structure of landholding which permitted mortgaging, transference, alienation—meant that in time of drought or other financial difficulty, the peasant was forced to turn to the moneylender and merchant for credit. Whichever land tenure system operated, however, it afforded to the landlord and moneylender a means for drawing away from the peasant everything but the mere minimum required to keep cultivation going.

Another result of British rule which served to undermine the position of the peasantry was the increase in population. Political stability and improvements in sanitation and other public health measures served to reduce the death rate while leaving the birth rate unchanged. The population rose, exerting pressure on the available supply of land. Industrialization could have provided the answer to the population pressure in rural areas by taking up the surplus labour, but so long as India remained a major market for British manufactures, a full-blooded industrial policy was out of the question. When industrialization did get under way in India towards the end of the nineteenth century, its scale was inadequate to deal with the emerging population problem. The net effect of population increase, therefore, was rural overcrowding which, in the absence of any attempt to improve agricultural techniques, placed severe limits upon the ability of the agricultural sector to generate surpluses of crops for sale and for export. In short, the overall nature of the economic situation in India was much the same as that described earlier for the plantation economy: a concentration of income and wealth in a few hands; the vast mass of the indigenous population subsisting at a low level; and a commercial policy which hindered the spread of industrialization within the economy.

It is not possible in the compass of one short chapter to deal adequately with all aspects of the economic impact of nineteenth century European industrialization and imperial expansion on the underdeveloped regions of the world. Rather, what we have endeavoured to show here is how the characteristic features of export production in these countries, along with the existence of certain legal, political and cultural institutions and processes, hindered the spread of growth throughout their economies even when export expansion did occur. In doing this, we are not arguing that the integration of these countries into the international economy was not beneficial to them. Living standards did rise in these countries, even if, for the bulk of the population, the improvement was small. Moreover, in many underdeveloped countries the choice was not between foreign-inspired development and indigenously stimulated growth, but rather between what happened and nothing. In short, European economic expansion in the nineteenth century, despite its various destructive elements, was a powerful agent of modernization, and colonial status was often the price that had to be paid to gain admission to the industrial age. Whether, for the countries colonized, the benefits of colonialism and imperialism outweighed the costs of political and economic subservience to another country, however, is still an open question.

NOTES

1 According to this argument, while the gains of technological progress in industrial countries are distributed to producers in the form of higher incomes—because of the existence of industrial monopolies and upward pressures exerted on wages by well organized trade unions—in the primary producing countries competitive pressures ensure that the gains from technical improvements in agriculture and mining are passed on in the form of lower prices. Consequently, it has been claimed that in the long run the prices of manufactured goods (the imports of primary producers) have tended to rise relative to the prices of primary products (the exports of these countries). This, in turn, has meant that primary producing countries were able to purchase fewer and fewer manufactured goods with a given quantity of primary product exports.

2 A country's ability to overcome the difficulties inherent in monoculture and unstable primary product prices depends very much on the flexibility of its economic structure. This question of flexibility is closely connected with the problem of the carry-over in export-led growth.

3 The extreme situation was reached in Malaya during the rubber boom at the start of this century, when so much rubber was planted by Malayans and to a lesser extent by Chinese and Indian smallholders that the country came to depend upon imports for much of its staple food supply.

4 C. Issawi, 'Egypt since 1800: a study in lop-sided development', *Journal of Economic History* (March, 1961), p. 11.

5 Ramiro Guerray Sanchez, *Sugar and Society in the Caribbean, An Economic History of Cuban Agriculture* (London, 1964).

6 For example, the unskilled workforce in African mining consisted largely of migrant African workers who spent only a limited time in paid employment before returning to their tribal areas.

7 J. R. Hanson, *Trade in Transition. Exports from the Third World 1840–1900* (New York, 1980).

8 Lloyd G. Reynolds, 'The Spread of Economic Growth to the Third World: 1850–1980', *Journal of Economic Literature* (Sept., 1983), p. 964. He defines 'extensive growth' as an increase in productive capacity absorbed by population growth; and 'intensive growth' as a situation in which productive capacity rises appreciably faster than population so that there is a sustained rise in per capita income (p. 943).

SELECTED REFERENCES

Albert, B., *South America and the World Economy from Independence to 1930* (London, 1983).

Cairncross, A. K., *Factors in Economic Development* (London, 1962), especially Chaps. XI and XII.

Falkus, M. E., *Readings in the History of Economic Growth* (London, 1968).

Hanson, J. R., *Trade in Transition. Exports from the Third World 1840–1900* (New York, 1980).

Headrick, D. R., *The Tools of Empire. Technology and European Imperialism in the Nineteenth Century* (Oxford, 1981).

Headrick, D. R., *The Tentacles of Progress. Technology Transfer in the Age of Imperialism, 1850–1940* (Oxford, 1988).

Latham, A. J. H., *The International Economy and the Underdeveloped World 1865–1914* (London, 1978).

Lewis, Sir W. A., *Tropical Development, 1880–1913. Studies in Economic Progress* (London, 1970).

Munro, J. F., *Africa and the International Economy 1800–1960* (London, 1976).

Myint, H., *The Economics of Developing Countries* (London, 1964), esp. Chaps. III, IV, and IX.

Nurkse, R., 'Patterns of Trade and Development' (Wicksell Lecture, Apr., 1959). Reprinted in *International Trade and Finance. A Collected Volume of Lectures, 1958–1964* (Stockholm, 1965).

Owen, R., *The Middle East and the World Economy 1800–1914* (London, 1981).

Reynolds, L. G., *Economic Growth in the Third World 1850–1980* (London, 1985).

Spender, D. L., and Woroniak, A., *The Transfer of Technology to Developing Countries* (New York, 1968).

Chapter 10

Trends and fluctuations in the international economy before 1913

Along with economic growth, fluctuations in economic activity may be transmitted from country to country through the operation of the international economy. Since economic fluctuations appear to be a characteristic feature of industrial economies, and since the nineteenth century saw the emergence of a number of these economies closely linked with each other through trade, labour and capital flows, it is not surprising to find evidence of a tendency for economic expansion and contraction in one industrial country to spill over into other industrial countries. But the spill-over effects of these fluctuations did not stop there. They also spread to primary producing countries, producing excessive fluctuations in the prices and volume of their exports which, through their influence on these countries' foreign exchange earnings, placed severe constraints on their capacity to generate sustained economic growth. Potentially more damaging to the long-term prospects of growth in these countries, however, is the claim that the spread of modern technology has been associated with a secular tendency for primary product prices to decline relative to the prices of manufactured goods. If true, this movement of the terms of trade against primary producers meant that they were, and are, faced with the possibility of a long-run decline in their export real incomes.

THE INTERNATIONAL TRANSMISSION OF BUSINESS CYCLES

The available historical evidence suggests that in the past there has been a substantial degree of business cycle conformity between countries, especially when the fluctuations have been violent ones. The international impact of the great financial crises of the nineteenth century has long been recognized and is amply borne out by an examination of the business annals of numerous countries for the period.[1] But while it is true that the importing of an erratic shock, such as a financial panic, by one country from another represents one type of transmission of economic fluctuations, studies of such phenomena are only the first step in a full-scale investigation into the possibility that complete cycles are transmitted between countries. Even when countries are found to conform over the full cyclical expansion and contraction, this is not sufficient in itself to justify the conclusion that business cycles are regularly and immediately transmitted from country to country. Indeed, as some economists have noted, the conspectus of trade cycles to be found in the business annals may point only to the necessity of fluctuations in capitalist economies rather than to the existence of the international transmission of business cycles. Moreover, even if transmission did take place in the nineteenth century, the annals tell us little about the mechanism by which it was affected or the predominant direction of these effects.

An important hypothesis concerning the functioning of the international economy in the nineteenth century has served only to emphasize the need for more detailed investigations of the nature of cycle propagation during these years. S. B. Saul has argued that whereas before 1890 Britain was able, through the export of capital, to lessen the impact of slumps on the international economy, after that date, because of the spread of industrialization and the growth of a more closely integrated system of multilateral trade, she was less able to perform this 'buffer' function. In the earlier period the international economy consisted of a number of self-contained trading networks, with little economic contact between the countries in each network, except through Britain, which stood at the centre linking them together. Thus, a slump in the United States would affect, say, Australia only indirectly through its impact on the British economy, where the consequent fall in the American demand for British exports, by reducing the level of economic activity in Britain, would lead eventually to a decline in the British demand for Australian exports. This decline in Australian export income, however, could be offset to some degree by the export of British capital to Australia, so that that country was able to maintain or even raise its level of imports and economic activity despite the American recession. But after 1890, because of the spread of industry and the accompanying growth in the world demand for industrial raw materials and foodstuffs, direct trading relations between continental Europe and the United States and the primary producing countries overseas, especially those in the British Empire, became more common. The system of separate trading blocs gradually coalesced into a single network of world trade and the possibility of fluctuations being transmitted directly from one part of the international economy to another became more and more real. In this new situation, British capital exports were called upon to nullify not only the decline in the British demand for colonial produce brought about by a slump, but also the equally great, if not greater, direct fall of demand for these goods from other countries as well. In so far as economic expansion in one region offsets economic decline in another, the British task of acting as a stabilizer of the world economy was made that much easier. When, however, decline was general, her efforts to act as a buffer were largely inadequate. Indeed, the generally depressed economic conditions then existing could constitute a major deterrent to the international flow of capital.[2]

It should be noted that Saul implicitly assumes the transmission of cyclical influences, although the statistical data he uses in support of his hypothesis do not in themselves tell us much about the workings of the mechanism of transmission. Moreover, no attempt has yet been made to test the relationship between cyclical activity in the various trading countries for conformity with Saul's hypothesis. Much more research is obviously necessary before the validity of this hypothesis concerning the changing structure of world trade and its impact on the international transmission of business cycles in the nineteenth century is fully established. In the meantime, his work remains an outstanding contribution in this largely neglected field of historical research.

LONG SWINGS AND THE INTERNATIONAL ECONOMY

While a greater knowledge of the nature of international business cycle transmission will obviously help us better to understand the functioning of the international economy as a mechanism of growth during the nineteenth century, what is perhaps of even greater relevance in this connection are the longer fluctuations in economic activity to be observed in both North American and European economies after 1870, and probably before, for it has been argued that these fluctuations exhibit an inverse relationship which is suggestive of a pattern of alternating growth between the different parts of what has come to be called the Atlantic economy.

The existence of long swings in economic activity, averaging between 15 and 25 years' duration is now an undisputed fact. Investigations have revealed such fluctuations in building activity, where the phenomenon has long been recognized, railway construction, public utilities, and migration. They are also evident in the merchandise imports and exports of a number of countries, as well as in the flows of capital between countries. Given the existence of these long swings in economic activity in a number of countries, two questions immediately pose themselves. The first concerns the nature and internal logic of the long swing in economic activity. This matter is currently under investigation, and much more work, both of a theoretical and an empirical nature, needs to be done before a clear understanding of the mechanism of the long swing is possible.[3] More immediately relevant, however, is the second question, which is concerned with the nature of the international relationship between the long fluctuations in economic activity in different countries. Of particular importance in this context is the evidence of long-term inverse movements in British home and foreign investment and the related tendency, at least in the period after 1870, for general long swing movements in economic activity in the United States and Canada to vary inversely with swings in British building and domestic investment generally.

Table 14 illustrates the nature of this inversion. The figures in columns 1 and 2 describe the opposing movements in Britain's home and foreign investment. Domestic investment rose in the 1870s and 1890s and early years of the present century, and declined in the 1880s and in the years after 1906. Foreign investment, on the other hand, moved in the opposite direction, falling in the 1870s and 1890s and rising in the 1880s and 1900s. Outflows of population from Britain[4] move parallel to the outflow of capital. Since a large part of both flows of men and money went to the United States and Canada after 1870, these countries received substantial injections of population and capital from Britain, as well as from other European countries, in the 1880s and 1900s. These were periods when domestic investment and economic activity were running at high levels in the North American economy. In other words, in those periods when domestic investment and business activity were depressed in Britain, the United States and Canadian economies were growing rapidly, and this economic growth was sustained partly by the outflow of population and capital from Britain to these countries. On the other hand, in those periods when the British economy was growing rapidly, the outflow of capital and population slowed up, and the growth of the North American economy was correspondingly reduced.

It is, however, the explanation of this pattern of fluctuations rather than the existence of the phenomena, which is presently the subject of argument. According to Cairncross, for example, the explanation is to be found in the behaviour of the terms of trade, since British foreign investment generally varied with Britain's terms of trade, increasing when the terms of trade worsened and decreasing when they improved. Since a worsening in Britain's terms of trade meant a rise in import prices relative to export prices, investment opportunities in those countries supplying Britain's imports—mainly primary producers—became more attractive. Moreover, changes in the terms of trade would also affect real wages, with a movement unfavourable to Britain lowering British real wages, since the cost of living of the working classes was highly dependent on import prices, especially of foodstuffs. Consequently, as well as stimulating an outflow of British capital, a deterioration in the terms of trade would also exert some push on emigration. Moreover, a pull on emigration would develop in overseas countries, as the inflow of capital made settlement in them more attractive through the employment opportunities that it created. Thus, there was a close and consistent interrelationship between a deterioration in Britain's terms of trade, falling real wages, rising emigration and rising foreign investment. Finally, given the existence of certain types of population-sensitive capital formation, emigration resulted in a decline of domestic investment in Britain for emigration left houses empty, and this depressed house building and investment in public utility services and other public works which are closely dependent

Table 14 Great Britain, the United States and Canada: inverse long swings in economic activity, 1871–1913

Period	Britain			United States		Canada		
	Net domestic fixed capital formation £m.	Capital outflow £m.	British immigration (000s)	Net capital inflow $m.	Net capital expenditures railways $m.	Immigrant arrivals (000s)	Net capital inflow* $m.	Total fixed capital formation $m.
	(1)	(2)	(3)	(4)	(5)	(6)	(7)	(8)
1871–75	358	373	370	896	940	181	166	n.a.
1876–80	382	124	178	−348	383	162	93	n.a.
1881–85	297	309	385	258	996	477	167	n.a.
1886–90	174	438	423	1,045	642	409	242	n.a.
1891–95	289	260	195	392	726	182	202	n.a.
1896–1900	540	202	76	−807	−130	157	124	n.a.
1901–05	686	245	201	−730	328	556	317	1,061
1906–10	446	729	325	238	1,808	1,088	830	2,025
1911–13	267	618	191	−66	1,216	1,108	1,156	2,919†

Sources: Col. 1: B. R. Mitchell and P. Deane, Abstract of British Historical Statistics (Cambridge, 1962), Table, pp. 373–4. Col. 2: A. H. Imlah, Economic Elements in the Pax Britannica (Cambridge, 1958), pp. 72–5. Col. 3: U.S. Bureau of Census and Statistics, Historical Statistics of the U.S. Colonial Times to 1957 (Washington, 1960), Table, pp. 56–7. Col. 4: J. G. Williamson, American Growth and the Balance of Payments 1820–1913 (Chapel Hill, 1964), Table B–19, pp. 280–1. Col. 5: M. J. Ulmer, Capital in Transportation, Communications and Public Utilities: Its Formation and Financing (Princeton, 1960), Table C–1, pp. 256–7. Cols. 6 and 8: M. C. Urquhart and K. A. H. Buckley, Historical Statistics of Canada (Cambridge, 1965), Tables, pp. 23, 138. Col. 7: A. I. Bloomfield, Patterns of Fluctuation in International Investment Before 1914 (Princeton, 1968), Appendix 1, pp. 42–4.

Notes

* Excluding net short-term capital flows.
† For the years 1911–15.
n.a. not available.

upon the rate of growth of population and urbanization. This, in turn, led to a general fall in home investment, a rise in unemployment, and therefore increased pressure to emigrate.[5]

When the terms of trade moved in Britain's favour, the opposite sequence of events took place. Import prices fell relative to the prices of British exports, discouraging foreign investment and resulting in a rise in British real wages, which served to reduce the desire to migrate overseas. The decline in the level of economic activity overseas, which was partly the result of the cessation of British capital exports, also served to deter emigration from Britain. The increased availability of capital in the home market, along with a fall in interest rates, and a rising demand for new houses to accommodate a relatively faster growing population, served, on the other hand, to bring about an upsurge in domestic investment.

While broadly accepting the Cairncross position, Brinley Thomas prefers to give much greater weight to the causal role of migration. He sees these population movements as the main influence producing the cycles in building activity which he considers to lie at the core of the inverse movements in British home and foreign investment. He also argues that up to the 1860s the pace of economic activity in the United States was conditioned by the inflow of migrants and capital from Britain and Europe. After that decade, however, the immigration waves were largely determined by the course of American domestic investment in producer durables, with American building activity continuing to lag behind immigration.[6]

Whereas Thomas favours a shift over time in the locus of the economic stimulus generating long cycle interactions, other economists and economic historians have tended to argue in favour of one centre to the exclusion of all others. Thus, some economic historians have emphasized the central role of the United States in this interactionary process, while others have reacted to the American pull hypothesis by directing attention to changes in Britain's willingness to lend abroad or to the domestic ingredients in Britain's bursts of home investment as important determinants of these alternating fluctuations in economic activity. One weakness of this debate is that it is centred almost exclusively on economic interactions within a region often referred to as the Atlantic economy. It is true that Brinley Thomas has claimed that the inverse cyclical relationship to be found within the Atlantic economy before 1914 can also be extended to take in the remaining countries comprising the regions of recent settlement. Such an extension appears questionable, however, especially as the experiences of some of these other countries fit rather uneasily into the framework of inverse cycles. The Australian experience, for example, does not seem to fall within the Atlantic economy hypothesis, since the Australian long swings appear to be longer (some 30 years in duration) and consequently fewer in number than those recorded in other countries. As a result, the Australian long swing pattern differs in many notable respects from that of the United States and Canada on the one hand, and that of

Britain on the other. The part played by continental Europe in the international long swing mechanism also remains obscure. Thus, long swings are not apparent in French net capital exports, and some economists have also argued that, in contrast to the British experience, high rates of French capital exports tended to coincide with high rates of domestic growth, although this conclusion is not based on a long swing analysis. Furthermore, since a not inconsiderable part of the capital exports of European countries went to tropical regions and since the export trade of these regions was highly dependent on the demand for tropical products in industrial countries, the role of the tropics in the interactionary process needs to be examined. Preliminary investigations reveal that long swings in American demand appear to have been of some significance in accounting for secular fluctuations in the growth of rubber exports and for those found in the series of sugar exports from Hawaii and Puerto Rico. On the other hand, Cuban sugar exports and world sugar exports moved in response to world demand and long swings are not apparent in these series.

More recently, Solomou, after a detailed analysis of Kuznets cycles during the period 1850 to 1913, concluded that inverse long swings between home and overseas investment are to be observed in all the major capital exporters—Britain, France and Germany—and that the variation of overseas investment correlates with changes in the terms of trade for these three countries. This suggests that the investment swings were profitability induced swings. In turn, international variations in the terms of trade were the result of simultaneous domestic influences and structural changes in the world economy. Thus Solomou's analysis supports the Cairncross explanation of international inverse long swings in economic activity rather than that of Thomas.[7]

The conflicting opinions on the causes of the inverse long swing mechanism and its centre of origin, and the gaps in our knowledge concerning the part played by countries and regions outside the Atlantic economy in the interactionary process, serve only to underline the considerable amount of research still needed in this field. What is already apparent, however, is that the long-cycle mechanism offers an attractive framework within which to study the growth process associated with the functioning of the international economy in the years before 1913. That these long fluctuations are to be observed in the international flows of capital, population and trade emphasizes this fact, for these flows represented some of the real forces at work influencing changes in the level of economic activity in different parts of the world at this time. It should also be obvious from our brief review of the subject, that the economic phenomenon under investigation is too complicated and far-reaching for it to be encompassed by uni-causal explanations or for it to be viewed as an economic stimulus to growth continuously located in any one country or region. Whatever the true nature of the mechanism generating these inverse long swings in economic activity, its functioning obviously depended on the complicated interplay of many variables, including immigration, the terms of trade, lenders' preferences, and so on, as well as on numerous other factors whose importance have yet to be assessed.[8]

LONG-RUN TRENDS IN THE TERMS OF TRADE

Before commencing a description of trends in the terms of trade for a number of countries during the nineteenth century it is necessary to consider briefly the nature and significance of the terms of trade concept. The commodity (or net barter) terms of trade compare the changing relationship between export and import prices for a particular country over a number of years. A weighted index is usually constructed for both export and import prices in terms of base year prices and from these two indexes the terms of trade index is derived by calculating the export price index as a percentage of the import price index. The main use of the terms of trade index is to determine (purely on the basis of relative price changes), whether over a number of years a country gains additional real income (or loses it). If for instance, a particular country's export volume remains unchanged in two successive years, but export prices increase by 10 per cent on the average, the money incomes of exporters will increase by 10 per cent despite the fact that total production remains unchanged. If, at the same time import prices are constant, the country is able to obtain a greater volume of imports for the same volume of exports. In other words, the country experiences a gain in terms of real income. On the other hand, if export prices declined by 10 per cent, other things remaining the same, a reduction in real income would eventuate. To summarize: a net gain will always accrue to a country so long as its import prices increase at a slower rate, or decline faster, than its export prices. On the other hand, if import prices increase faster, or decline more slowly, than export prices, the country will tend to lose real income purely from changes in international prices.[9] On the production side, increased export prices, especially if the trend is sustained for a period of several years, would tend to produce a transfer of factors from other sectors into export industries, thus altering the country's distribution of productive factors. In this way, long-run trends in the terms of trade can have an important effect on the economic growth path of a country whose development is highly dependent on its export income.

When we come to examine the long-run trends in the terms of trade during the nineteenth century we find that reasonably accurate information exists for only a handful of countries, and that for most of them the data relate only to the period after 1870. The longest terms of trade series available are those for the United Kingdom and the United States, both of which cover the period 1800–1913. Taking the British estimates first, these reveal a general long-run decline in the commodity terms of trade during the period from 1802 until the mid-1850s, followed by a sustained upward trend over the rest of the period. The tendency for the United Kingdom terms of trade to deteriorate over the first half of the nineteenth century arose because British cotton export prices fell faster than raw cotton import prices. Between 1814 and 1843 the prices of raw cotton imports fell by almost 80 per cent, while cotton textile prices declined even more sharply, partly because of the fall in raw cotton prices, and partly because of the technological advances occurring in the production of cotton textiles. The heavy weighting of cotton textiles in British exports and the precipitate fall in cotton textile prices led to a decline in the weighted average of British export prices that was greater than that of import prices with a consequent deterioration in the British commodity terms of trade. Indeed, if textile manufactures in general are removed from the terms of trade series, the residual series exhibits a fluctuating pattern with no long-run tendency to deteriorate.

Between 1857 and 1873 there was a decided improvement in Britain's commodity terms of trade as export prices rose while import prices fell. Thereafter, up to 1881, a deterioration set in, caused by a heavy fall in export prices. From 1882 to 1913 both export and import prices moved together, declining in the years up to the mid-1890s and rising in the remainder of the period up to 1913. As a result of the relative movements of the two series, the British terms of trade tended to become progressively more favourable, initially because import prices were falling generally faster than export prices, and later because export prices tended on the whole to rise faster than import prices. Thus, except for the trough in the series between 1873 and 1884, the terms of trade index moved in such a way as to allow Britain to experience considerable gains from trade as the result of price changes for more than half a century.

The American terms of trade improved substantially during the second half of the 1790s, and then deteriorated sharply in the years up to the end of the Napoleonic Wars, when wartime shortages brought about a sharp rise in import prices. This was followed by a period of generally improving terms of trade between 1815 and 1860, the most favourable periods being 1816–19, the mid-1830s, and 1849–60. Import prices followed a general downward trend until the late 1840s after which they tended to rise. On the other hand, export prices fluctuated more widely with the most favourable improvements occurring during the 1830s. Over the 20 years after 1860 the American commodity terms of trade appear to have continued an upward trend, although there was some deterioration in the early 1870s. In the remaining years up to 1913 there is little apparent upward or downward trend in the United States terms of trade. Thus from the end of the Napoleonic Wars until World War I, movements in international prices tended on the whole to benefit the United States economy, with perhaps the most unfavourable effects of price movements occurring during the late 1880s and the 1890s.

Terms of trade estimates are available for a few European countries after 1870. What is most striking about the German series, especially after 1880, is its exceptional stability, for even during the one period of marked change—the years of deteriorating terms of trade between 1901 and 1913—the index fell only 12 per cent. It is therefore highly unlikely that Germany either lost or gained real income during these years as a result of changes in international trade prices. The French experience was very similar to that of Germany. Like Germany, with the possible exception of the last decade before World War I, when a deterioration of approximately 20 per cent is apparent in the French terms of trade, the French economy tended not to be too greatly disturbed by movements in the relative prices of its imports or exports.

The only other countries for which reasonably acceptable statistical series have been constructed for periods of 30 or more years before 1914 are India, Japan, New Zealand and Australia. Despite the violent fluctuations exhibited by the Indian series, it has a definite upward trend over the period 1861 to the mid-1890s, followed by a general levelling out during the remainder of the period. On the other hand, the Japanese terms of trade rose in the years up to 1900 and then displayed a tendency to fall thereafter. Despite the deterioration in the Japanese terms of trade in the 1900s, however, the available evidence suggests that neither Japan nor India experienced any significant loss of real income because of relative movements in international trade prices. The New Zealand data suggest that the terms of trade deteriorated throughout the 1860s, recovered in the early 1870s and followed a sustained upward movement over the remainder of the period. Contrary to expectations, the Australian data exhibit different characteristics from those of New Zealand. There appear to have been favourable terms of trade for Australia during the 1870s, an adverse movement during the 1880s and the first half of the 1890s, and then a sustained improvement over the remainder of the period. Although it can be reasonably concluded that New Zealand received fairly substantial increases in real income from international price movements, such a conclusion is harder to sustain in the case of Australia, given the economic difficulties experienced by that country during the 1880s and the early 1890s.

Thus, an analysis of the available data on the terms of trade suggests that only in a relatively few periods did any country experience a long-run loss of real income because of sustained adverse movements in world prices, for example, Britain between 1800 and 1850, the United States in the 1820s and in the 1890s, and Australia between 1880 and 1895. Generally speaking, however, these losses in real income resulting from deteriorating commodity terms of trade were offset by other changes, such as increased productivity reducing costs of production in export industries, so that any net loss of real income, if it occurred, was unlikely to have been very large. Even more interesting is the conclusion that primary producing countries, such as Australia, New Zealand and India, all of which traded extensively with the United Kingdom, could experience improving terms of trade at the same time as Britain did. This could happen because of the effect of falling freight rates on the prices of internationally-traded goods. Thus, the price of a primary product could fall in the country importing it despite increased production costs in the exporting country, if a reduction in transport costs more than offset the rise in production costs. It could also come about because of the different production mixes of the exports and imports of the different countries involved in trade with each other. It is noticeable, for instance, that because of the similar commodity composition of the two indexes, the Australian import price index follows fairly closely the trend in the British export price index from 1870 to 1913. On the other hand, great divergences exist between the Australian export price index, which was heavily influenced by the prices of a few products of major importance, such as wool, and the British import price index which incorporated a much wider range of commodities. Given the different commodity composition of imports and exports and variations in the movement of the prices of individual commodities, the possibility of the import and export price indexes of different countries, and consequently their commodity terms of trade, moving together are greatly enhanced. It therefore does not follow that an improvement in the terms of trade of an industrial country must lead inevitably to a deterioration in the terms of trade of the primary producing country.

Long-run fluctuations in the prices of agricultural products play a significant role in the explanation of world economic growth during the modern era, as put forward by W. W. Rostow and Sir Arthur Lewis. According to Rostow, for example, the process of world economic growth involves basically the interaction of three forces: the adjustment of food and raw material production to the growth of population and industrial production; the impact on total production and prices of the classic sequence of leading sector 'complexes' (cotton textiles; railways and iron, steel, chemicals and electricity; and the motor-car); and a housing cycle responding to population growth and migration. Technological change clusters around the opening up of new areas of primary production and the leading sector complexes with their associated backward and forward linkages. Although Rostow argues that the existence of Kondratieff long waves[10] is not an essential element in his dynamic theory of world growth, he believes nevertheless that the international economy has experienced four marked, if irregular, Kondratieffs between 1790 and 1972 in the relative scarcity and abundance of foodstuffs and raw materials. Kondratieff expansions are marked by high or rising prices of primary products and of interest rates; and an income shift towards a rapidly expanding agriculture, towards 'profits' and away from the urban wage share. Kondratieff contractions exhibit opposite changes in these variables.[11] In his study of economic growth and fluctuations in the world economy, Lewis also gives a central role to long waves in prices and the terms of trade, which, he argues, are related to changes in the rate of growth of supplies of agricultural products.[12] Not all economists and economic historians are agreed on the validity of Kondratieff long waves; critics arguing that such secular fluctuations are neither self-generating nor justified on theoretical grounds. Nevertheless, since the onset of the world recession in the mid-1970s, increasing attention has been paid to the possibility that 'long waves' of approximately 50 years' duration have been a feature of the growth of the world economy since the late eighteenth century.

PHASES OF GROWTH

The long-run growth of the international economy has figured importantly in the recent work of two economists: Angus Maddison and Solomos Solomou.[13] While Maddison concedes that major changes in the growth momentum during the capitalist epoch have occurred, it is his view that their explanation can be sought not in systematic long waves, such as the Kondratieff thesis, but in specific disturbances of an *ad hoc* character. Major system shocks, such as the depression of the 1930s, change the momentum of capitalist development at certain points. Thus, Maddison believes that, for a better understanding of the evolution of the international economic system, it is worthwhile to divide the period since 1820 into separate phases of growth which have a meaningful internal coherence in spite of wide variations in individual country performance within each of them. Since his analysis is based on the aggregate economic performance of 16 major economies over the period 1871 to 1981, his phases of growth refer essentially to the functioning of the international economic system. Moreover, while Maddison's statistical analysis covers only the period from 1871 to 1981, he suggests, on the basis of the more limited statistical data available for the period between 1820 and 1870, that in most respects experience during these years was similar to that in 1871–1913.

Over the period 1820 to date, Maddison believes that there have been four distinct and important phases of development. These were the liberal, market-oriented order which ended with World War I; the period of conflict and autarky from 1914 to 1950; the golden age of fast growth to 1973; and the phase of slower growth and accelerated inflation since then. These successive phases of growth were not initiated by collective planning decisions, innovative ideas, or changes in the ideology of domestic and international policy. Rather, the transition from one phase to another has in practice been determined by some kind of exogenous system shock, such as war, a deep depression, or the collapse of a long-standing international payments mechanism. The phases do not represent 'stages of growth' in the international capitalist system, nor, because the length of the phases vary, are they cyclical in the Kondratieff long wave sense.

In Solomou's account of the long-run growth of the international economy the relative backwardness of countries and the differential growth rates across nations that this gives rise to, play a central role. Like Maddison, Solomou rejects a Kondratieff wave phasing of post-1850 economic growth, preferring to view the era between 1856 and 1937 as one complete 'catching-up wave', with the accelerating trajectory of 1856 to 1913—or 1856 to 1929, if the break in the war years is allowed for—ended by the world depression of the 1930s. Accordingly, the world economy has not grown along a steady and balanced path but has experienced a series of transitions from one steady-state growth path to another due to the effects of world wars and changes in the international economic structure. Solomou's 'catching-up' waves are waves of irregular length and amplitude, and do not fall in the Kondratieff periodicity. Finally, Solomou emphasizes the fact that since a degree of backwardness and therefore a desire to catch up still exists in the world economy this is a sufficient condition for a catching-up wave growth path continuing into the future once rapid economic growth is resumed.

Maddison's and Solomou's explanations of the long-run growth path of the international economy are similar in many respects even if their phasings differ. What both studies serve to do, however, is to draw our attention away from the cyclical fluctuations that have characterized developments within the international economy and to focus it on the underlying growth paths along which the international economic system has moved over the past 170 years.

NOTES

1 See W. L. Thorp, *Business Annals* (New York, 1926); especially useful is Section VI of the Introduction which deals with international relationships between business cycles.

2 S. B. Saul, *Studies in British Overseas Trade 1870–1914* (Liverpool, 1960), Chap. V., esp. pp. 111–16.

3 For a discussion of this problem see M. Abramovitz, 'The Nature and Significance of Kuznets Cycles', *Economic Development and Cultural Change* (Apr., 1961), pp. 225–48.

4 The immigration figures in col. 3 of Table 14 refer only to British immigration into the United States, but total British migration to all countries during these years followed a similar pattern—falling in the 1870s and 1890s, and rising in the 1880s and 1900s.

5 A. K. Cairncross, *Home and Foreign Investment 1870–1913* (Cambridge, 1953).

6 B. Thomas, *Migration and Economic Growth* 2nd edn (Cambridge, 1973).

7 S. Solomou, *Phases of Economic Growth. 1850–1913: Kondratieff Waves and Kuznets Swings* (Cambridge, 1988).

8 For a fuller discussion of some of the problems raised in this section see A. R. Hall, *The Export of Capital from Britain 1870–1914* (London, 1968).

9 The terms of trade argument should not be restricted to changes in prices alone, since other factors are also important in determining the gains from trade over time. For example, improvements in productivity in export industries may reduce the costs of producing exports faster than the fall in their prices, thus nullifying the loss of real income implied in a deterioration of a country's

commodity terms of trade. To take these factors into account, a number of other terms of trade concepts have been developed, some of which can, and some of which cannot, be measured statistically. For practical purposes, however, the commodity terms of trade provide the easiest way in which to use the available data, despite the difficulties that inevitably arise in constructing such an index.

10 Belief in the existence of long waves in economic activity of 40 to 60 years' length is largely the result of the work of a Russian economist, N. D. Kondratieff, who published his results during the 1920s: see N. D. Kondratieff, 'The Long Waves in Economic Life', *Review of Economic Statistics* (Nov., 1935). For a critique of the Kondratieff hypothesis, see G. Garvy, 'Kondratieff's Theory of Long Cycles', *Review of Economic Statistics* (Nov., 1943).

11 W. W. Rostow, *The World Economy: History and Prospect* (London, 1978). According to Rostow, the four long waves in price movements cover the periods: 1790–1848, 1848–96, 1896–1936, and 1936–72: see pp. 299–304.

12 Sir W. A. Lewis, *Growth and Fluctuations, 1870–1913* (London, 1978).

13 A. Maddison, *Phases of Capitalist Development* (Oxford, 1982); S. Solomou, *Phases of Economic Growth, 1850–1973: Kondratieff Waves and Kuznets Swings* (Cambridge, 1988).

SELECTED REFERENCES

Beckford, G. L. F., 'Secular Fluctuations in the Growth of Tropical Agricultural Trade', *Economic Development and Cultural Change* (Oct., 1964).

Bloomfield, A. I., *Patterns of Fluctuation in International Investment Before 1914* (Princeton, 1968).

Cairncross, A. K., *Home and Foreign Investment, 1870–1913* (Cambridge, 1953).

Hall, A. R., *The Export of Capital from Britain, 1870–1914* (London, 1968).

Imlah, A. H., *Economic Elements in the Pax Britannica* (Cambridge, Mass., 1958).

Kindleberger, C. P., *The Terms of Trade: A European Case Study* (New York, 1956).

Lewis, Sir W. A., *Growth and Fluctuations, 1870–1913* (London, 1978).

Morgan, T., 'The Long-Run Terms of Trade between Agriculture and Manufacturing', *Economic Development and Cultural Change* (Oct., 1959).

North, D. C., *The Economic Growth of the United States, 1790–1860* (Englewood Cliffs, 1961).

Rostow, W. W., *The World Economy: History and Prospect* (London, 1978).

Saul, S. B., *Studies in British Overseas Trade, 1870–1914* (Liverpool, 1960), cop. Chap. V.

Solomou, S., *Phases of Economic Growth, 1850–1913: Kondratieff Waves and Kuznets Swings* (Cambridge, 1988).

Thomas, B., *Migration and Economic Growth*. 2nd edn (Cambridge, 1973).

Thorp, W. L., *Business Annals* (New York, 1926), esp. Section VI of the Introduction.

van Duijn, J. J., *The Long Wave in Economic Life* (London, 1983).

Part II

The interwar years

Chapter 11

The international economy in the interwar years

The international economy which had grown up during the nineteenth century came to an end with the outbreak of war in 1914. Four years of armed conflict involving all the great industrial nations left a legacy of problems to the international economy that were never completely solved in the economic reconstruction that followed the end of the war. Consequently, the postwar international economic system was ill-prepared to withstand the shock of a worldwide depression in the early 1930s, and a rapid break-up of the world economy inevitably followed. Five more years of war were to elapse before another attempt at restoring the international economy could be undertaken.

World War I affected the whole structure of the international economy. Trade patterns altered significantly, as the diversion of productive resources in Europe from manufacturing for export to turning out war materials led to the emergence of alternative sources of supply overseas. With the coming of peace, most of this trade returned to its normal channels, but some of the changes persisted, creating difficult problems of economic adjustment for a number of countries, including Britain. The gold standard was another casualty of the war years, when most countries went off gold. Although restored in a modified form by the late 1920s, it never again functioned as effectively as it had done before 1913, and by the early 1930s it had been reduced to a state of near collapse by a series of financial crises. In only one important respect did pre-war trends continue into the interwar period. In the field of commercial policy the movement towards protectionism became more marked, as international considerations were increasingly subordinated to national monetary and employment policies made necessary by postwar reconstruction and, later, by the onset of a world depression.

Associated with these monetary and trade problems was a tendency for the rate of growth of the world supply of primary products and manufactures to outstrip the rate of growth of demand for these commodities. This came about largely because of technological progress and the continued spread of industrialization, which, along with population changes and rising real incomes, led to significant adjustments in the structure of world output and demand. How these real changes affected the orderly functioning of the international economy is the subject of this chapter, while the international monetary problems created by World War I are discussed in the chapter that follows.

PRIMARY PRODUCTION

Technological progress was particularly rapid in agriculture during the interwar years. In temperate latitudes improvements continued to be made in the breeding of plants and animals, and the use of artificial fertilizers became widespread. Mechanized agriculture was also spreading, with improvements in the efficiency of tractors and the introduction of a growing range of ancillary equipment. Many new developments were also evident in tropical and sub-tropical agriculture. Particularly important were the selective breeding of plants, the increased use of fertilizers, the greater attention paid to the control of plant diseases and pests, and the growing use of selective weed-killers. There was also considerable progress in mining operations and in the initial processing of minerals during these years. The mechanization of mining proceeded rapidly in many countries. There was even more rapid progress in the processing of metallic ores, where flotation techniques developed in the early years of the twentieth century made possible the exploitation of low grade ores and complex ores containing several metals. Their use in working the low grade ores of Chile, for example, made that country one of the world's largest producers of copper. Even more striking has been the rapid development of the world's petroleum resources during this century. Along with the opening up of the oilfields and the advances made in drilling and refining techniques went the growth and spread of the world's oil-refining industry. Activity was particularly marked in the Middle East, where oil-refineries were established in Bahrain and Saudi Arabia by American engineers, and in Iraq and Lebanon by British and joint European enterprises.

The widespread adoption of new techniques in agriculture and mining during the 1920s led to a substantial rise in the output of primary products that was added to by the appearance of new sources of supply, many of which had been brought into being by wartime demand and postwar shortages. Consequently, there appeared in the late 1920s a rather general tendency for supply to outrun demand, and there was an appreciable fall in prices as a result. While there were considerable differences in commodity price movements, some rising and others falling or remaining stationary, when it occurred, the fall in prices was mainly in raw materials, though the prices of certain foodstuffs, particularly sugar and wheat, also declined heavily. Even when substantial price falls occurred, however, they did not always reflect the true extent of the changes in market forces, since the sale of some primary products was subject to monopolistic influences with the result that their prices were often higher than they would have been had competitive conditions prevailed. Thus, commodity control schemes existed for varying periods in the 1920s for products such as rubber, coffee, sugar, wheat and copper, and during 1927 and 1928 attempts were made to establish partial restriction of output schemes for petroleum, lead and zinc, although without any really significant effect on prices.

The downward pressure on primary product prices was not due solely to increased productivity and the opening up of new areas of production. Other forces were also at work. The speedy revival of Europe's sugar-beet industry was certainly a more important cause of excessive world sugar supplies than the rapid technical progress achieved in Cuba and Java during these years. Weaknesses in the management of the industry's commodity control scheme, which by holding prices at too attractive levels tended to induce further plantings, were as much a cause of the overproduction of coffee in Brazil as the opening up within the country of new, rich coffee lands. In explaining the overproduction of wheat during these years, the decline in per capita consumption, due to a shift to more expensive foods as living standards rose, needs to be taken into account, along with the increased acreage under cultivation, greater mechanization, and the increased yields due to the application of scientific methods in the selection of seeds and plants. Indeed, as real incomes grew, changes in demand pervaded the world economy. Thus, there was a relative decline in the world consumption of cereals and a substantial growth in that of fruit, dairy products and certain tropical foodstuffs. Canned products, ready-cooked meats and vegetables were eaten far more than in the pre-war period. The consumption of cigarettes increased enormously all over the world, while the demand for cigars and pipe tobacco in general declined. Cotton and wool gave place to silk and artificial silk, as lighter and finer clothing increased in demand. Overall, however, rising incomes were associated with a declining percentage spent on food and an increasing proportion spent on other commodities, especially manufactures. Of course, these shifts in demand were not universal, but where they did occur they were strong enough to call for marginal adjustments in production which became more difficult to bring about as economic conditions deteriorated.

Despite the growing difficulties faced by the primary producing countries, the evidence suggests that the incomes and foreign exchange earnings of these countries *as a whole* were reasonably well maintained until the late 1920s. The economic benefits that flowed from the expansion of trade and output in primary products during these years were not evenly shared, however. The recovery of primary production in Europe in particular was slow, whereas it was in Oceania, South America and Africa, with their specialization in meat, dairy products, wheat, sugar, coffee, and vegetable oils, where the really substantial gains were achieved. The same was true of mineral production, where oil and rubber producers were the main beneficiaries.

POPULATION GROWTH AND MIGRATION

The difficulties facing primary producers may also have been due partly to the slowing up of the rate of growth of Europe's population, which reached its peak during the 1920s. Thereafter it declined, largely because of a fall in the birth rate that had begun in north-western Europe and then spread gradually to the east and south. Even more striking was the decline in North America where, under the influence of the depression, the annual rate of growth of population per 1,000 persons fell from 14.4 in the 1920s to 7.9 in the 1930s. In Asia and Africa, on the other hand, population began to increase more rapidly than in Europe. In India, for example, the first clear signs of a rise in the expectations of life appeared in 1921–31, when a significant fall in the death rate took place. The result of all these demographic changes was a slight decline in the relative importance of European populations. If the combined populations of Africa and Asia are taken as a rough measure of the world population of non-European stock, it accounted for 75 per cent of the world total in 1800, had fallen to 61 per cent in the 1920s, but then recovered slightly to 62 per cent of the total by 1940.

Despite the slowing up in the rate of growth of Europe's population, the pressure to migrate continued to be high. But with few great fertile and readily accessible areas of the world remaining unoccupied, and with the United States in particular showing less willingness to absorb immigrants than it had done in the past, the outflow of population from Europe fell heavily. It declined even further with the onset of the depression, and for a short time in the 1930s Europe became an area of immigration rather than of emigration. Thus, compared with an annual outflow of 1½m. between 1909 and 1914, European emigration declined to around 700,000 annually in the 1920s, and to 130,000 in the 1930s. Britain remained the most important single source of migrants, and southern and eastern Europe continued to provide well over half of the total outflow of population from Europe (Table 15b and Figure 13).

Even though direct restriction of immigration into America was inaugurated by the Quota Act of 1921, which set an upper limit on the number allowed into the country during one year, the United States still took the largest share of gross immigration during the interwar years. Compared with the pre-war period, however, there was a substantial drop in American immigration in the 1920s and 1930s, when the annual average intake fell to less than a quarter of a million compared with an annual average of nearly one million in the nine years before 1914 (see Table 15c and Figure 14).

Of the other countries of immigration, Canada and Australia continued to absorb large numbers of British migrants, as well as a smaller number of migrants from other European countries. Much of Canada's ability to attract and absorb immigrants came from the rapid expansion of its manufacturing and construction industries, and from the 1920s onwards the country showed

Table 15a Growth and percentage distribution of world population, 1920–40

Region	Number (m.)		Distribution (%)	
	1920	1940	1920	1940
Europe (including U.S.S.R.)	487	573	26.9	25.5
North America	117	146	6.5	6.5
Latin America	91	131	5.0	5.8
Asia	966	1,213	53.4	54.0
Africa	140	172	7.7	7.7
Oceania	9	11	0.5	0.5
Total	1,810	2,246	100.0	100.0

Table 15b European emigration, 1921–40

Country/Region	Number (000s)		Distribution (%)	
	1921–30	1931–40	1921–30	1931–40
N.W. Europe	3.11	0.53	45.4	43.1
Britain	2.15	0.26	31.3	21.1
Germany	0.56	0.12	8.2	9.8
S.E. Europe	3.76	0.70	54.6	56.9
Spain and Portugal	1.56	0.24	22.7	19.5
Italy	1.37	0.24	19.9	19.5
Poland	0.63	0.16	9.2	13.0
Total	6.87	1.23	100.0	100.0

Table 15c Gross immigration into selected countries, 1921–40

Country	Number (000s)		Distribution (%)	
	1921–30	1931–40	1921–30	1931–40
United States	2.72	0.44	37.5	31.9
Canada	0.99	0.08	13.7	5.8
Argentina	1.40	0.31	19.3	22.5
Brazil	0.84	0.24	11.6	17.4
Australia	0.95	0.14	13.1	10.1
Others	0.35	0.17	4.8	12.3
Total	7.25	1.38	100.0	100.0

Sources: U.S. Demographic Yearbook (various); Woytinsky, W. S. and Woytinsky, E. S., World Population and Production (New York, 1953); Woodruff, W., Impact of Western Man (New York, 1966), Tables III/4 and 5.

Figure 13 Emigration from Europe, 1921–40

Source: See Table 15.

a preference for the skilled industrial workers essential to its industrial progress. In Australia, where rapid industrialization also set up a growing demand for labour, the Empire Settlement Act of 1922 and the '£34 million agreement' reached between Great Britain and the Australian government in 1925 provided for government loans to assist migration to Australia. Planning for some 500,000 migrants in ten years, the project proved to be over-ambitious. All the same, there was a net inflow of over 300,000 migrants in the 1920s, of whom two-thirds were assisted.

Large numbers of European migrants also went to Brazil and Argentina during these years. In Brazil, where World War I had provided the initial stimulus for industrialization, the immigrants came mainly from Italy and Germany in the 1920s, and there was also a record inflow of Japanese in the 1930s. In Argentina, the immigrants came overwhelmingly from Latin Europe, mainly Spain and Italy. As with all other countries of immigration,

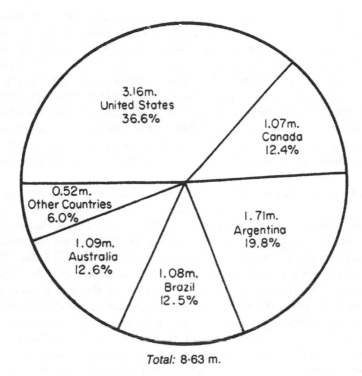

3.16m.
United States
36.6%

1.07m.
Canada
12.4%

0.52m.
Other Countries
6.0%

1.71m.
Argentina
19.8%

1.09m.
Australia
12.6%

1.08m.
Brazil
12.5%

Total: 8·63 m.

Figure 14 International immigration, 1921–40

Source: See Table 15.

the Argentinian population inflow, which was substantial in the 1920s, fell
heavily in the 1930s, when a catastrophic fall in agricultural prices and land
values reduced the flow of immigration and encouraged the Argentinian
government to introduce restrictive legislation.

MANUFACTURING PRODUCTION

The continued spread of industrialization was stimulated by both the war and
the depression. Cut off from European sources of supply during the war years,
manufacturing industry developed rapidly in a number of countries overseas,
and although the return of normal peacetime production saw the collapse of
some of these nascent industries, tariff protection ensured the survival of
many others. After the war, industrialization was rapid in America, Canada
and Australia in the 1920s, and high rates of industrial growth were also
achieved during these years in Brazil, Finland, India, New Zealand, South
Africa and Japan. Relative to the newly industrializing countries, the older

industrial nations experienced declining rates of industrial growth, and even the United States failed to achieve industrial growth rates comparable to those of the newly developing nations during the 1920s, while in the depressed 1930s, industrial activity in the country stagnated. On the other hand, the deterioration in the terms of trade of primary producing countries and the network of restrictions on trade in primary products which grew up in the 1930s forced the governments in a large number of non-industrial countries to foster secondary industry behind tariff protection to safeguard living standards and to keep down unemployment. As a result, industrialization in these countries proceeded with undiminished vigour despite the depression.

Taking 1913 as 100, the world index of manufacturing activity averaged 185 in the years 1936–8, whereas the index for the United States stood at 167, Germany 138, Britain 122 and France 118, all well below the world average. In contrast, many new countries had industrialized at an enormous pace: the Soviet Union's index rose to 774, Japan 529, Finland 289, India 230 and Sweden 223. Over the whole period, therefore, the slower growth of the old countries was largely offset by the rapid progress of the new industrial nations and, as Table 16 clearly shows, significant changes in the distribution of the world's manufacturing production occurred as a result. The notable features of this table include the dominant position of the United States in world manufacturing during the late 1920s and its subsequent decline during the depression years; the increased shares in world manufacturing activity of the Soviet Union and Japan; and the decline in the relative shares of the old-established European industrial powers, Britain, France and Germany.

Too much should not be read into these production figures, however. To begin with, the statistics themselves are open to some questioning, especially those for Russia. More important still, the figures tell us nothing about the significant differences in the nature of the industrial growth being experienced by the various countries concerned. In the new countries, growth took the form of the expansion of textile manufactures and other types of fabrication typical of a country in the early stages of industrialization. On the other hand, in the United States, and to a lesser extent in some of the old industrial countries, industrialization during these years involved the rapid growth of new industries, such as motor-cars, household appliances, and chemicals, as well as the increasing use of new methods of production, such as the assembly line. These new industrial techniques involved a considerable increase in the use of capital and of power. They also brought about significant changes in the composition of world manufacturing output.

As the American experience suggests, the interwar period was marked not so much by startling new inventions as by remarkable advances in the efficiency of already familiar techniques. Fuel economies were achieved in iron and steel production and in the generation of electricity, with the best power stations halving fuel consumption between 1918 and 1939. The variety of

Table 16 Percentage distribution of the world's manufacturing production, 1913–38

Period	U.S.	Germany	U.K.	France	Soviet Union	Sweden	Japan	India	Rest of world	World
1913	35.8	14.3	14.1	7.0	4.4	1.0	1.2	1.1	21.1	100.0
1926–29	42.2	11.6	9.4	6.6	4.3	1.0	2.5	1.2	21.2	100.0
1936–38	32.3	10.7	9.2	4.5	18.5	1.3	3.5	1.4	18.7	100.0

Source: League of Nations, Industrialization and Foreign Trade (Geneva, 1945), Table 1, p. 13.

Note: The 1913 percentages represent the distribution according to the frontier established after the 1914–18 war.

materials available for engineering was greatly extended with the introduction after the war of new alloys, especially the light alloys based on
aluminium. There was also an increasing use of plastics. Few radical
improvements were made in machine tools, although the use of tungsten
carbide as a tool material after 1926 was a significant advance. Refrigeration
techniques improved greatly, and substantial increases in the efficiency of gas
engines, petrol and oil engines, including diesel, and steam turbines were also
achieved during these years. But with the exception of the gas turbine, which
passed through the critical stages of development shortly before the outbreak
of World War II, the 20 years between the two wars were not remarkable for
the invention of prime movers.

By far the most important development in production methods during
these years was the widespread adoption of the assembly line. Initially
developed by Henry Ford as the key to the efficient, large-scale, and therefore
cheap, production of motor-cars, the assembly line system was widely used in
the United States after World War I to mass-produce such items as washing
machines, radios and refrigerators. In addition, many other products, including shoes, stockings, glassware and chinaware, were passed through factories
from operation in a continuous process from raw material to finished product.
By enormously increasing the volume of output, and thereby reducing costs,
the assembly line led to a marked rise in productivity and a consequent
increase in real incomes, which was partly used to purchase the growing
output of consumer goods made possible by the new industrial techniques.

Indeed this emphasis on durable consumption goods is only one of a number of ways in which the new industrial technology was marked off from that
of the nineteenth century, for the new industries were as much concerned
with mechanizing the home as they were with mechanizing production. This
trend, which began around 1900 with the introduction of the telephone, the
gramophone, the bicycle and the motor-car, was continued after the war
when, with the development of the vacuum-cleaner, the washing-machine,
the refrigerator and the radio, machines became familiar in the home. Moreover, the growing range of household electrical appliances and the increasing
use of electricity for domestic lighting and cooking, along with the rising
industrial consumption of electrical power, enormously increased investment
in electrical generating capacity during these years and created a growing
demand for electrical plant and equipment of all kinds.

Apart from the rapid development of the aeroplane, the interwar years did
not witness many new revolutionary changes in the means of transportation.
Railway mileage continued to grow, particularly in less-developed continents, where the railway mileage increased from 156,000 miles in 1920 to
184,000 in 1940. Railway construction was especially heavy in the Soviet
Union where the railway mileage increased by one-half between the wars. On
the railways, locomotive performance continued to improve, and the first
diesel-electric locomotive appeared in the United States in 1924. Other

railway improvements introduced during these years related to traffic control systems, the air-conditioning of trains, and better communication systems for trains. Many of these innovations were the result of efforts to increase railway efficiency in the face of the growing competition of motor transport. This competition was most apparent in the United States where, despite the efforts of the railway companies to counter road competition, the railway mileage in operation in the country declined by almost 19,000 miles between 1920 and 1940. At sea, oil-burning ships were gradually replacing the coal-burner, while improvements in the design of ships led to substantial reductions in fuel consumption. Here, too, competition was beginning to make itself felt, at least for the ocean passenger trade, as air travel became faster, safer, and more regular.

Rapid technological change and the spread of industrialization to new regions brought with them the problem of economic adjustment in established industrial economies. In no country was this more important during these years than in Britain, where the coal and cotton industries declined absolutely in the face of competition from new producers and the development of substitutes for their products. Other British industries in trouble during these years included shipbuilding, which lost ground because of the worldwide excess capacity created by the war, the failure of foreign trade to grow as rapidly as industrial production, and the continuous growth of overseas shipbuilding. While the great staple industries of Britain stagnated and their trade declined, her iron and steel and engineering industries continued to expand, and new industries, notably motor-cars, electrical goods, chemicals, rayon, and various other manufactures underwent a vigorous expansion. Even so, the growth of these industries and the support they gave to British exports failed to offset the decline in Britain's traditional industries. The consequent stagnation of the British economy and the associated decline in Britain's international commercial and financial position goes a long way towards explaining the failure of the international economy to function as smoothly during the 1920s as it had before 1914.

GROWTH OF WORLD INCOMES

Between the wars, the rate of growth of world incomes slowed down appreciably as a result of the economic problems thrown up by the war and the onset of the depression in the early 1930s. Table 17 compares the annual rates of growth of national income, income per capita, and population for selected regions during the two periods 1860–1913 and 1913–29. Whereas growth was by no means negligible after 1913, both total income and income per head slowed down considerably between 1913 and 1929. The rate of growth of world income declined by just under a quarter in the period 1913–29, but with world population continuing to grow at about the same rate as that of

Table 17 Annual compound growth rates of national income, income per head and population for selected regions, 1860–1929

Region	1860–1913			1913–1929		
	Income	Population	Income per capita	Income	Population	Income per capita
North America	3.8	2.1	1.7	2.8	1.6	1.2
Oceania	4.0	3.1	0.9	1.7	1.7	0.0
North West Europe	2.1	0.8	1.3	0.9	0.2	0.7
Soviet Union	2.2	1.2	1.0	1.1	0.5	0.6
South East Europe	1.9	0.8	1.1	1.6	1.3	0.3
Latin America	2.3	1.4	0.9	2.8	1.9	0.9
Japan	2.4	0.9	1.5	4.0	1.2	2.8
Far East	2.8	1.6	1.2	2.4	1.6	0.8
South East Asia	1.1	0.5	0.6	0.9	0.6	0.3
China	0.4	0.3	0.1	0.5	0.3	0.2

Source: D. H. Aldcroft, *From Versailles to Wall Street, 1915–1929* (Harmondsworth, 1987), Table 11, p. 288.

the pre-war period, income per head fell by about a third. The per capita income growth rate in North West Europe was almost halved, while that of the even more economically and politically troubled areas of southern and eastern Europe fell even more heavily. More striking still is the stagnation of per capita income growth in Oceania, where it was Australia that was responsible for the poor result. Australian per capita income experienced some growth in the 1920s, but it failed to offset the contraction of real incomes during the war years, so that by the end of the 1920s Australia's income per head was some 10 per cent down on that of 1913–14.

The main beneficiary of the war years was Japan whose economy grew even more strongly—almost twice as fast—after 1913 than before it. Somewhat surprisingly, growth in North America also slowed down after 1913 despite the fact that this area, like Japan, stood to benefit from the war.

Estimates of income growth rates comparable to those in Table 17 are not available for the period 1929–39, but Maddison has calculated annual compounded rates of growth of GNP for the world's more important trading nations covering the period 1890–1938. These estimates are given in Table 18. Although the sub-periods chosen by Maddison differ from those of Table 17, the general picture that emerges is the same. With few exceptions, the countries listed in the table all experienced declining income growth rates during the interwar years.

Although Germany, Norway and the United Kingdom recorded income growth rates in the period 1925–38 that compared more than favourably with their growth rates in the pre-1913 period, most of Europe was merely making up ground lost during the war and immediate postwar years, in the

Table 18 Annual compounded rates of growth of GNP for selected countries, 1890–1938

	% per annum		
	1890–1913	*1913–25*	*1925–38*
Belgium	3.1 [a]	−0.9 [b]	2.3 [c]
Denmark	3.5	1.8	2.4
France	1.4	1.4	−0.2
Germany	2.9	−1.7	4.1
Italy	2.1	2.0	1.8
Netherlands	2.2 [d]	3.1	1.3
Norway	2.6 [e]	2.3	3.4
Sweden	3.6	1.6	3.1
Switzerland	2.4	2.1	1.9
United Kingdom	1.7	0.2	2.5
Europe	2.1	−0.3	2.2
Canada	4.3	1.0	1.8
United States	3.9	3.0	1.0
Japan	2.3	3.5	3.8

Source: A. Maddison, 'Growth and Fluctuation in the World Economy, 1870–1960', *Banca Nazionale del Lavoro Quarterly Review* (June, 1962), Table 5, p. 141.

Notes
a 1895–1913
b 1913–24
c 1924–38
d 1900–13
e 1887–1913

period after 1925. Both the United States and Canada suffered an appreciable decline in the rates of growth of their real incomes after 1913, with the decline being most marked for the United States in the years after 1925. Of the major trading nations, only Japan appears to have experienced sustained and substantial economic growth throughout the interwar years.

THE INTENSIFICATION OF PROTECTIONISM

Within the world markets for primary products and manufactures, adjustments in supply and demand to take into account the changed economic conditions of the interwar years were made difficult by the spread of restrictions on foreign trade. The war itself was responsible in a number of ways for the intensification of protectionism. In Japan, India, Australia and some Latin American countries, the disappearance of European competition in many lines of manufacturing for four years called forth considerable local production. Some of these 'war babies' died a natural death with the return of peacetime trading conditions, but many others, inspired by motives of self-interest and national security, clamoured for and obtained the support of tariffs. In Australia, iron and steel, machinery, railway materials and chemicals were given protection; in India, iron and steel, cotton textiles, paper, and chemicals; in Argentina, pharmaceutical manufactures.

Protection also flourished in Europe, where the postwar creation of entirely new nations in central and eastern Europe lengthened Europe's tariff frontiers by some 12,000 miles. Behind these barriers, new governments, faced with economic dislocation and production shortages of all kinds, endeavoured to achieve some measure of economic stability. Currency disorders were an added problem in many countries encouraging the use of tariffs and the introduction of many direct restrictions on trade, such as import and export licensing, quotas, prohibitions and exchange controls. France, Germany (after 1925), Italy, Spain, Belgium, and the Netherlands were among the many European countries that introduced tariffs for the first time or revised existing tariffs upwards during the 1920s. These tariffs were not restricted to manufacturing industry or to the control of balance of payments problems created by currency disorders and production difficulties. Agricultural protection also became more widespread and severe in Europe. It played its greatest role in Italy, where, behind high protection, the 'Battle for Wheat' was launched in 1925, to reduce the country's heavy dependence on outside sources of supply. But the movement towards agricultural self-sufficiency was general throughout Europe at this time, and its consequences for the growth of world trade in primary products were grave.

In Britain, the McKenna Act of 1915, which imposed duties of 33⅓ per cent on cars, motor-cycles and certain other manufactures in an effort to save wartime shipping space and foreign exchange, laid the foundations for a return to protection after the war, when the Act remained in force and was extended to commercial vehicles and tyres. Further protection to British industry was afforded by the Safe-guarding of Industries Act and the Dye-stuffs Importation Act, both passed in 1921, which placed duties on the products of a number of key industries, including optical glass and instruments, considered to be vital for national security, and prohibited the importation of all synthetic dyestuffs and intermediate products. Even more crucial for the well-being of the international economy was the introduction by the United States of the Fordney–McCumber Tariff of 1922. This Act, which raised American tariffs to the highest level in the country's history up to that time, was utterly inconsistent with the new-found role of the United States as the world's most important creditor nation. Since high tariffs made it difficult for the debtor nations to earn dollars with which to make interest payments on American loans and to repay war debts, and since gold was in short supply, the difficulties of America's debtors were prevented from becoming glaringly obvious only by the willingness of the Americans to lend capital abroad.

Protection also became a feature of many primary producing countries, where the desire to support war-induced manufacturing industries was supplemented by the need to reduce dependence on foreign manufactures in the face of deteriorating terms of trade. Whatever the reason for introducing protection in these countries, however, one feature of the international economic situation in the 1920s is perfectly clear: the growing range of restrictions placed on trade between nations reflected an enlargement of the objectives of protectionist policy. In particular, the use of commercial policy during these years came to be extended from the protection of certain industries to the protection of a country's balance of payments against declining export prices and the effects of the prevailing currency disorders of the 1920s. Later, during the depression years, commercial policy developed another function, that of creating employment through the setting up of domestic manufacturing industries to cater for demands formerly satisfied by imports which were denied access to the domestic market by the use of tariffs or other restrictive measures.

The spread of protection, the frequent adoption of deliberately high duties for bargaining purposes, and the introduction of quantitative restrictions on trade imposed a severe handicap on the recovery of world commerce in the 1920s, and in an attempt to remedy the situation, the League of Nations called a World Economic Conference in 1927 which had an immediate, though short-lived, effect on trade relations. Through autonomous measures and bilateral agreements, such as the Franco-German Commercial Treaty of August, 1927, which laid the basis for an integrated European treaty system, the rising trend in tariffs was temporarily checked. Another conference summoned in the same year tried to deal with the problem of quantitative restrictions on trade, but it dragged on until 1930 without achieving anything of real value. What finally defeated the efforts of both conferences, however, was the onset of depression and the threat of even higher tariffs in the United States.

This failure of international policy making highlights a fundamental weakness in the international economy during the interwar years. Whereas the major economic problems of the day demanded solution at the international level, the authorities through which existing regulation was exercised were, with few and partial exceptions, national. International attempts to produce solutions to the world's economic problems were made, but they were rare and largely unsuccessful. The League of Nations, which played a useful constructive role in the early 1920s, particularly in negotiating international loans for countries wishing to stabilize their currencies, had a less active role in the 1930s. It produced a large number of reports and inquiries on both international and national affairs, but their effect on policy appears to have been minimal.

This lack of determined international policy making is, of course, easily explained. It was difficult to convince people who remembered the free operation of the international economy during the pre-war years of the necessity for a greater degree of international control in the changed conditions of the interwar period. The postwar difficulties would soon be overcome, it was felt, once the pre-war international monetary mechanism had been restored to full working order. Even more of an obstacle to international co-operation was the decline of economic liberalism which became such a marked feature of the interwar years. If the exigencies of war forced most governments to become more involved in economic affairs, the political changes and economic difficulties of the interwar period ensured that this involvement would continue and even intensify. The spread of new political faiths, such as communism and fascism, the powerful stimulus given to economic nationalism by the war, the economic and financial difficulties of the 1920s, and the depression of the 1930s made it inevitable that the government would play a larger role in the economic life of the nation than formerly. This increasing dependence on purely national solutions to economic problems made international co-operation difficult, if not impossible.

This economic nationalism even spread to the field of monetary policy, where, despite the professed reverence for the gold standard mechanism, the independent national control of the domestic supply of money came to supplant the pre-war principle of the international gold standard, according to which any nation's stock of money was dependent upon the ebb and flow of gold. By giving to the central bank the power to influence strongly the supply of money inside the country, the government tended to insulate the national monetary system from international forces and in doing so it impaired the very mechanism upon which so much faith in future economic progress rested.

SELECTED REFERENCES

Aldcroft, D. H., *From Versailles to Wall Street, 1919–1929* (Harmondsworth, 1987).
Bairoch, P., *The Economic Development of the Third World Since 1900* (London, 1975).
Ellsworth, P. T., *The International Economy*, 3rd edn. (New York, 1964).
International Institute of Agriculture, *World Trade in Agriculture* (Rome, 1940).
Kahn, A. E., *Great Britain in the World Economy* (London, 1946).
Latham, A. J. H., *The Depression and the Developing World, 1914–1939* (London, 1981).
League of Nations, *Quantitative Trade Controls. Their Causes and Nature* (Geneva, 1943).
League of Nations, *International Currency Experience* (Geneva, 1944), esp. Chap. VIII.
League of Nations, *Industrialization and Foreign Trade* (Geneva, 1945).
Lewis, Sir W. A., *Economic Survey, 1919–1939* (London, 1949), esp. Part III.
Lilley, S., *Men, Machines and History* (revised edn., London, 1965).
Tracy, M., *Agriculture in Western Europe* (New York, 1964).
Woytinsky, W. S., and Woytinsky, F. S., *World Production and Population* (New York, 1953).

Chapter 12

The restoration of the gold standard and the economic recovery of the 1920s

The war years saw the end of the gold standard when its two basic requirements, interconvertibility between paper money and gold and the free export of gold, were suspended. Initially, most of the belligerent countries were able to maintain adequate gold reserves and familiar exchange rates, chiefly by taking gold coins out of domestic circulation and concentrating them in official hands. As the years passed, however, it became increasingly difficult for the warring nations to support the pre-war pattern of exchange rates. For Britain and France the difficulty was overcome finally by the receipt of American loans, following that country's entry into the war early in 1917. Lacking such support, the German and Austrian exchanges were in a state of collapse by 1918. But for most countries, including the United States, Britain and the Empire, France, Italy, the Netherlands, Spain, Sweden, Japan, Argentina and Brazil, exchange rates at the end of the war diverged remarkably little from the pre-war pattern despite the upheaval of the previous four years.

POSTWAR INFLATION AND THE RESTORATION OF THE GOLD STANDARD

This apparent normalcy in the pattern of exchange rates cloaked the profound changes that war had brought. In particular, the war economies had all experienced varying degrees of price inflation, the true extent of which had been disguised by price controls and rationing. In the immediate postwar years, a reconstruction boom plus the widespread dislocation of trade and production in central Europe caused a further inflationary rise in prices, which reached a peak in most countries in 1920, and then gave way to a couple of years of business depression and heavy price declines. In Germany, France, and central and eastern Europe, however, inflation continued for several more years, and in the process the old money units of Austria, Hungary, Poland, Germany and Russia were practically destroyed.[1]

In an effort to achieve monetary stability, international financial conferences were held in Brussels (1920) and Genoa (1922). Shortly afterwards, with the help of large international loans from the United States and Britain, financial reorganizations were carried out in Austria (1922) and Hungary (1924). In 1925 further loans for stabilization purposes were made to Poland and Czechoslovakia, followed by similar arrangements with Bulgaria, Italy and Romania. The outstanding event in postwar financial progress, however, was the stabilization of the German mark in 1923–4, which was accompanied by the drawing up of the Dawes Plan for the settlement of the German war debt.

The postwar inflation in Germany was due mainly to the government's refusal to balance its budget. The resulting government deficits were financed initially by borrowing, but when the deficits persisted and even increased in size because of rising prices, the German public refused to take up more government securities and the government was forced to issue treasury bills to cover its excess expenditure. These only added to the quantity of money in circulation and led to a further rise in prices. Eventually, the expanding money supply and rising prices by depreciating the value of the mark caused it to be spent more rapidly. From the combined force of large quantities of money being spent faster and faster runaway inflation inevitably developed.

In the final stages of this hyper-inflation the rise in domestic prices left the increase in the quantity of money far behind, and it was the consequent acute shortage of money which eventually provided the government with the opportunity to bring the inflation under control. A new Rentenmark introduced late in 1923 was quickly taken up by a public long inconvenienced by the lack of a stable currency. This enabled the government to cover its expenditures with new issues of money while taking steps to balance its budget through spending cuts and tax increases. A decline in the velocity of circulation of money as inflationary pressures abated sufficed to offset any further monetary expansion. Stabilization of the mark was completed with the receipt of an international loan of 800 million marks (£40m.) under the Dawes Plan of 1924.

The Dawes Plan was the outcome of a reconsideration of the whole German reparations problems that had inevitably followed the financial collapse of the mark. The Treaty of Versailles (1919) had established the principle that Germany should indemnify the Allies for their war losses, and had created a Reparations Commission to assess the amount. In 1921 the Commission assessed the war damage at 132 billion gold marks (equal to £6,600m.) and laid down a time schedule of payments. It soon became obvious, however, that Germany, already in the grip of inflation, was in no position to meet her obligations. Under the Dawes arrangements, Germany was required to make reparations payments, rising in five years from £50m. to £125m. per annum, the number of years of payments being left undetermined. The first payment was made possible by the floating of an international loan (the Dawes loan), which also enabled Germany to return to the gold standard in 1924 with the introduction of a new currency, the Reichsmark, at the old pre-war gold parity of 23.8 cents. Foreign countries now became interested in the reconstruction of Germany, and for the rest of the 1920s both the government and private firms were able to borrow large sums abroad. The German economic situation was stabilized.

This massive foreign borrowing, however, led to the emergence of a precarious financial situation in Germany in the late 1920s when one last attempt was made to solve the reparations problem. Under the Young Plan of 1929 the reparations figure and period of payment were revised, the annual payments being scaled down to £100m. and the payments terminating in 1987–8. The new agreement took effect in April 1930, supported by a $300m. loan. But with the onset of the depression, Germany was quickly engulfed in a financial crisis which led to a moratorium on reparations payments in June 1931 and, in the following year, their complete abandonment.

Linked with the problem of German reparations was the question of the repayment of inter-allied war debts. Italy, France, and Belgium had emerged from the war in debt to one another and to Britain, while all of them, together with several other countries, had received loans totalling $7,700m. from the United States by the end of 1918. Postwar lending for relief and reconstruction added to these debts, until by the end of 1922, the debt owing to America stood at $9,400m., of which the share of Britain was $4,100m., France $2,900m., Italy $1,600m., with the remainder divided among Belgium, Cuba, Czechoslovakia, Greece, Romania, Russia and Yugoslavia.[2] Since many of the allied countries came to regard German reparations payments as a means of liquidating their American debts, there developed a chain of debt payments commencing in Germany and ending in the United States.

For these debt repayments to proceed smoothly, two requirements had to be met: large sums of marks had to be extracted annually from the German people, and these sums had to be transferred regularly into other currencies— ultimately a large proportion into dollars. These requirements could be met by increasing German taxes sufficiently to release a flow of goods and services for export large enough to earn the foreign exchange needed for reparations payments. But because the German government lacked the gold and foreign exchange necessary to make the initial reparations payment and was also never able to achieve a budget surplus, and because the creditor countries were opposed to accepting the large inflow of German goods needed if the country was to earn the foreign exchange with which to make reparations payments, the transfer process was never able to function effectively. In the event, the problem of reparations and inter-allied war debts was not settled until the mid-1920s, when Germany began receiving large loans of foreign capital, mainly from the United States. Then the chain of debt repayments began to function smoothly, but when this foreign lending to Germany ceased in the late 1920s, the transfer of reparations also stopped, and with it the repayment of the related war debts.[3]

Germany's return to the gold standard, following the floating of the Dawes loan in 1924, was the start of a general return to the gold standard in the next few years. In Britain, the wartime peg of the pound/dollar rate had been abandoned in March 1919 so that a temporarily fluctuating rate could be used to measure progress in deflating British prices enough relative to American prices to make pre-war parity workable again. It was not until April 1925, however, that the pound rose near enough to parity with the dollar for a return to gold to be announced. This decision was made legal shortly afterwards by the Gold Standard Act passed on 13 May 1925. The French inflation, on the other hand, continued until mid-1926 and went far enough to prevent a return to pre-war parity. When, at the end of 1926, the franc was eventually stabilized *de facto* by official dealings on the foreign exchange market, it stood at about one-fifth of its pre-war parity. *De jure* ratification of this 80 per cent depreciation followed in June, 1928, when a law was passed re-defining the gold content of the franc in line with the prevailing exchange rate.

Between 1925 and 1928, the reconstruction of the international monetary mechanism was substantially completed. By early 1926 some 39 countries had returned to gold, either at their pre-war parity or at a devalued level, or had displayed exchange rate stability for a full year. This list included Great Britain, the Netherlands, Sweden, Denmark, Switzerland, Germany, Austria, Hungary, Finland, Czechoslovakia, Yugoslavia, Bulgaria, Russia, the British Dominions, 12 Latin American countries, and the United States, which had returned with ease to the full gold standard in 1919, and thereafter had been the guidepost for the realignment of other currencies. During the next two years most of the countries which had not already done so returned to gold, the most notable being France, Italy and Argentina.

WEAKNESSES IN THE POSTWAR GOLD STANDARD: INTERNATIONAL INVESTMENT

With the restoration of the gold standard it was widely assumed that the most essential aspect of postwar economic reconstruction had been achieved. As it turned out, these hopes were largely illusory. The belief that a familiar and highly efficient international monetary mechanism had been restored to full working order overlooked the fact that, to function successfully, the pre-war gold standard had required a special kind of environment which no longer existed, and that the pre-war machinery was in many essential respects quite different from that which had now replaced it.

Nowhere were the changes so marked, compared with the pre-war period, than in the field of international investment, for the war had brought about shifts of unprecedented magnitude in the structure of international debt. As we have already seen, the war created a whole series of new international debts in the form of reparations and Allied war loans. Moreover, America had emerged from the war as the principal creditor on private account, whereas Germany had been transformed from a major creditor country to a debtor. The war had also weakened Britain's international lending position, by forcing her to liquidate part of her long-term assets, while further losses arose because of the confiscation of British assets in enemy countries and in Russia. French and German losses on these accounts were relatively greater even than those of Britain. On the other hand, the United States had not only repatriated American securities held by British and French investors during the war years, but she had also invested heavily in foreign securities, while granting considerable war credits to the allies.

Britain's efforts to re-establish her international financial position in the postwar years were complicated by her poor export performance. Her problem of expanding exports in the 1920s on the basis of a stagnant economy and in the face of growing foreign competition meant that with imports growing faster than exports, the resulting trade gap absorbed a steadily increasing proportion of Britain's invisible earnings.[4] The result was small current account surpluses, seldom reaching one-third or one-half of the pre-war real size (allowing for price rises), which failed to cover the long-term foreign security issues floated in the highly developed London capital market.

In these changed circumstances, the United States became the chief source of international loans, followed by Britain and France. American lending was concentrated largely in the 1920s, when the total of all American foreign investments grew from $7,000m. in 1919 to $17,000m. in 1930.[5] Just over one-half of the long-term investments were direct investments, almost one-half of which went to underdeveloped countries, mostly in Latin America. Of the portfolio investment, some 40 per cent went to Europe, 29 per cent to Canada, 22 per cent to Latin America, and the other 9 per cent to Asia. In the London capital market new overseas issues averaged £125m. per annum from 1921 to 1930, or about £80m. to £90m. ($390–440m.) after allowing for loan repayments and foreign participation in the new issues. Loans were extended to a number of European countries, including Germany, Austria and Belgium, and to government and public authorities in the Empire. There was also much investment in primary production, including rubber, coffee and oil. Other fields of direct investment included railways, public utilities, finance, mines, and metal smelting. By the end of 1930, British long-term investment showed a slight preponderance of direct over portfolio investment, and a geographical distribution in favour of the Empire, which accounted for 59 per cent of the total invested at that date. Within the Empire, Australia, India, Canada, and South Africa were large borrowers in the 1920s; elsewhere, Argentina and Brazil.

Apart from the emergence of the United States as the world's principal creditor, the other striking feature of international investment activity during the interwar years was the large-scale borrowing of foreign capital by continental European countries in the years after 1924. Germany was the chief capital-importer, absorbing close to $4,000m. from 1924 to 1929, inclusive. Other European borrowers during these years included Austria, Bulgaria, Czechoslovakia, Greece, Hungary, Poland and Romania. Elsewhere, Argentina and Australia, after having exported capital during certain of the early postwar years, returned to their traditional roles of heavy borrowers in the 1920s. The Union of South Africa also raised loans during the middle and late 1920s. Canada, on the other hand, only began to borrow from 1929 onward, when the capital exports from the chief creditor countries were declining. Broadly speaking, London contributed relatively little to the European investments, but supplied a very large share of the money invested in the Empire, including a number of Asian and African countries. On the other hand, investments in Europe and Canada, and those in Latin American countries, were raised chiefly in the United States.

The pattern of foreign investment activity that emerged in the 1920s had a number of weaknesses which acted as powerful destabilizers during the early stages of the worldwide depression that developed after 1929. To begin with, in contrast to pre-1913, when European capital had gone to countries that supplied the foodstuffs and raw materials demanded by Europe's expanding markets, much of the American investment in the 1920s went to nations, particularly those in Europe, whose exports were competitive with, rather than complementary to, those of the United States. Moreover, trading relations between America and Europe had changed significantly. Largely as a result of American industrialization, Europe never regained its pre-war position as a supplier of American imports, averaging only about 30 per cent of the total in the 1920s compared with over 50 per cent before 1913. The United States, however, had become an important market for raw materials and foodstuffs, and since several of these commodities were supplied by countries with whom European nations had export surpluses, America's growing export surplus with Europe depended in considerable measure upon the volume of American imports from these third-party countries. Thus, the world pattern of settlements in the 1920s and, in particular, the growing American trade surplus with Europe depended upon American foreign investments in Europe and elsewhere, a high and stable American demand for the products of third countries, and the existence of a European surplus on current account with these latter areas which was settled in gold and dollars. When, therefore, along with a drastic decline in its imports of raw materials and foodstuffs, American international investment practically dried up in the early 1930s, a world payments crisis was inevitable.

Another source of weakness was to be found in the debtor countries, especially those primary producers faced with declining world prices for their exports. Apart from the possibility that some of the foreign lending of the period, by financing the further expansion of primary production, may have contributed indirectly to bringing about these price falls, the heavy demand for foreign capital in the 1920s was accompanied by a rise in the percentage return on the outstanding investments. Thus, the annual net outward payments of interest and dividends by debtor countries (excluding regular amortization payments and reparations payments) rose from $1,400m. annually around 1920 to about $2,500m. in 1928. This increase in net payments of interest and dividends was not evenly distributed among debtor countries, however. Whereas Canada's net outward payments during these years remained stable, others, such as Australia and Argentina, rose by between 50 and 100 per cent. But the heaviest increases occurred in central and eastern Europe. These rising debt charges came at a time when falling export prices made it increasingly difficult for some of these debtor countries to earn the foreign exchange necessary to finance needed imports and to meet the debt payments on heavy borrowings at high rates of interest. The effect on a country's balance of payments of these developments could be concealed only as long as creditor countries were prepared to fill the gap with new loans and thus give at least an appearance of equilibrium to a situation fraught with instability and danger.

One further threat to international economic stability came from the heavy and frequently unpredictable movements of short-term capital which became a feature of the interwar period. French foreign investment in the 1920s, particularly after 1924, was largely of the short-term kind, involving temporary investment on short-term account or in securities bought on foreign stock exchanges. Some of it also took the form of a flight of French capital for investment in stable foreign currencies, more especially the dollar and sterling, brought about by the instability of the French franc in the mid-1920s. However beneficial these capital inflows were to the receiving countries, they represented de-stabilizing capital flows, since their rapid withdrawal could easily bring about a major financial crisis in the centre experiencing the loss of funds. A difficult situation was made even worse by the practice that grew up of British and American financial institutions using these funds to lend, in their turn, on long and short-term. For this meant that a cessation of French lending, involving possibly the repatriation of French capital, could bring about a chain reaction in the sphere of international finance involving the whole community of international borrowers and lenders.

INSTITUTIONAL WEAKNESSES OF THE RESTORED GOLD STANDARD

The emergence of New York as a major international financial centre had important consequences for the functioning of the restored gold standard. In particular, it involved the decentralization of the international clearing function. Whereas pre-war international transactions had been centralized in London, with payments typically being made in a relatively simple way, by transfer of bank balances held in London, the postwar system became decentralized, with New York and Paris taking over a large part of the function hitherto performed by London. The existence of more than one major financial centre made international clearning more complex and less efficient, for the various centres now had to arrange for offsetting claims among themselves and to hold balances with one another for this purpose. Moreover, the existence of a number of financial centres created the conditions under which foreign-owned funds were liable to move erratically from one financial centre to another in response to changing interest rates, changes in confidence or distrust in currencies, and other developments besides deep-seated balance of payments disequilibrium. This 'hot-money' danger had been far less serious before 1914, when no centre rivalled London as a place where short-term funds might move and be profitably held.

These difficulties were added to by the institutional shortcomings of the new financial centres. New York not only lacked the experience of London in the role of distributing international securities to investors, but its money market was also less responsive to changes in the balance of payments, which tended to make international investment attractive. The overwhelming importance of the financial requirements of the domestic market in American economic life (exemplified by the stock exchange boom of 1928–9), the small fraction that foreign trade constituted in gross national product, together with the slow development of international investment banking in the United States, prevented the establishment of any close connection between a surplus in the American balance of payments and its level of long-term international lending. Moreover, even when capital was lent abroad, American commercial policy placed major obstacles in the way of debt repayment, since the high tariff policy adopted by the United States during these years made it difficult for foreigners to earn dollars in the American market. Borrowers were thus able to make these payments temporarily only by further borrowing rather than by export expansion based on increased productivity associated with the investment of foreign capital and shifts in world production.

The functioning of the international monetary system was also hindered by a shortage of gold, and the rather uneven distribution of the existing gold stocks brought about by the war. The American holdings, as a proportion of the world's gold stock, had grown from 24 per cent in 1913 to 44 per cent at the end of 1923, while those of Britain had risen from 3 to 9 per cent. On the other hand, certain other countries, including Germany, Italy, Russia, India and Brazil, had suffered not only a relative but also an absolute loss of gold during these years. Given this shortage of world gold reserves, some other acceptable means of international payment had to be found to supplement gold. This was the significance of the widespread adoption of the gold exchange standard during the 1920s, which was officially recommended by the 1922 Geneva Conference as a means of alleviating the world shortage of gold. Under this system, assets in the form of foreign currencies could be counted as part of a country's international monetary reserves. In other words, a country was allowed to stabilize its currency in terms of a foreign currency that was convertible into gold and to hold its reserves in the form of that currency. This system was not new. Before 1913 it had been adopted by Russia and Austro-Hungary, among others, in Europe, and overseas by India, Japan and Argentina, which tied their currencies to sterling, and by the Philippine Islands, which linked its currency to the dollar. During the 1920s, however, the spread of the gold exchange standard was largely a European phenomenon.

As it operated in the 1920s, the gold exchange standard had a number of glaring weaknesses. The first concerned the manner in which some countries built up their reserves of convertible currencies. In the absence of a current account surplus in their balance of payments or of access to long-term borrowing, many countries acquired reserves by borrowing on short-term. Such reserves, however, were highly mobile and particularly vulnerable to changes in confidence. Faced with a foreign exchange crisis, a country was thus likely to find that its foreign reserves tended to disappear at the very moment they were most needed. The weakness of London as an international financial centre was another flaw in the system. Since exchange standard countries kept claims on sterling and dollars as reserves, both London and New York had to hold larger stocks of gold than were necessary simply to back their own trading transactions. New York had adequate gold reserves for this purpose, but London had not, and adequate stocks were never acquired. Indeed, London had difficulty preventing a loss of gold in the 1920s, largely because it was lending abroad more than its balance of payments permitted. One answer to the difficulty would have been to place a temporary ban on capital exports, but such a policy would have been inconsistent with London's claim to be a centre of international finance.

One further drawback to the gold exchange standard (and the one which eventually brought the system to an end) was that the most important countries on the exchange standard regarded their use of the system as a temporary expedient. Since the holding of foreign exchange instead of gold was considered by some of these countries as damaging to national prestige, transfer to the gold standard was for them only a matter of time. Of the countries on the exchange standard, France alone accounted for more than one-half of the total central bank foreign exchange holdings at the end of 1928.[6] When, in that year, France decided to take nothing but gold in settlement of the large surpluses accruing to her from the repatriation of French capital that followed the advent of financial stability at home and from the favourable trade balance generated by an undervalued franc, the end of the gold exchange standard was in sight.

Finally, because many central banks adopted policies of offsetting or neutralizing the domestic monetary effects of gold inflows and outflows, the traditional correctives to balance of payments disequilibria did not occur promptly and actively under the restored gold standard of the 1920s. While offsetting was not entirely absent from the pre-1913 system, it may often have been automatic rather than the result of deliberate official policy, as was frequently the case in the 1920s. Thus, the United States pursued a policy of 'gold sterilization' during these years—the Federal Reserve Banks deliberately offsetting some of the country's gold receipts by reducing their holdings of government securities. A similar policy was followed by the Bank of England in the six years after the country's return to gold in 1925. In France, where postwar inflationary experiences may have influenced government policy, gold movements were also not allowed to have their traditional influence on domestic money supplies.

In summary, the gold standard of the late 1920s was little more than a facade. Gold disappeared from active domestic circulation, and the adoption of the gold bullion or gold exchange standards, with all their drawbacks, represented further attempts to economize on gold. Neutralization or offsetting of international influences on domestic money, incomes and prices was widespread so that gold standard methods of balance of payments equilibration were largely destroyed, but without being replaced by any alternative mechanism. Exchange rate adjustments had been carried out by many countries to take account of changed economic conditions, but some rates were clearly pegged at wrong levels. With both the prices and incomes and the exchange rate mechanisms of balance of payments adjustment inoperative, it was only the large injections of American capital into the world economy that prevented the system from collapsing.

THE ECONOMIC BOOM OF THE LATE 1920s

Despite its weaknesses, the restoration of the gold standard marked the beginning of a major industrial boom centred on Europe. After the economic collapse of 1920–1 and up to 1925, Europe suffered a relative decline in its economic standing in the world. Whereas European production did not regain pre-war levels until 1925, it increased by 20 per cent between 1913 and 1925 in Asia and Oceania, by 25 per cent in North America, and by even more in Latin America and Africa. But with the general improvements in economic and political conditions on the continent following the stabilization of inflated currencies and the settlement of the war debts, the stage was set for rapid economic development. Over the next five years the world experienced a construction boom based largely on the need for re-equipping the European countries. In the period after 1925, therefore, growth was much more vigorous in Europe than in the other continents.

The expansion of production that took place in the first postwar decade affected all sectors of the world economy. Food production increased by 10 per cent between 1913 and 1925, and grew by another 5 per cent by 1929 when compared with 1925. Over the same two periods, the production of raw materials grew by 25 per cent and 20 per cent, respectively, the much higher rate of growth in the latter period as compared with that for foodstuffs being the result of the high level of demand for raw materials generated by the European boom. In manufacturing, there was rapid growth in iron and steel production, engineering, and motor-car manufacture during these years. Shipbuilding was running at a high level, with motor-ships increasing as a proportion of total output from 14 per cent in 1923 to 44 per cent in 1929. The output of heavy chemicals grew by a third. Textile production expanded rapidly in Japan and certain other newly industrializing countries, but stagnated in Europe, although the output of artificial silk rose by 133 per cent between 1925 and 1929. By the end of 1929, however, there was much evidence that the boom had passed its peak. Stocks were accumulating and there was considerable surplus capacity evident in manufacturing production. The spread of commodity control schemes indicated the growing difficulties of primary producers. Indeed, in North and South America and in Oceania the peak of productive activity had been reached in 1928. To the effect of accumulating surpluses was added another adverse element—a tendency for imports of capital into these countries to decline. But it was when the outflow of gold from the United States reversed its direction as a result of the Wall Street boom that the true nature of the flaws in the international economy stood fully revealed.

NOTES

1 By the end of their respective inflations, pre-war price levels had been multiplied by roughly 14,000 in Austria, 23,000 in Hungary, 2½ million in Poland, 4,000 million in Russia, and a million million in Germany. (W. A. Lewis, *Economic Survey 1919–1939* [London, 1940], p. 23.)

2 Cleona Lewis, *America's Stake in International Investments* (Washington, 1938), p. 362.

3 The repayment of the Allies' war debts also created difficulties but the several attempts to solve these all foundered on the United States' insistence that they be paid in full. When, however, the Allies were forced to give up their claims on German reparations in 1931, war debts too were soon abandoned. Between 1918 and 1931 the United States received $2.6 billion of the original $12 billion in repayments from the Allies.

4 The claim that Britain's return to the gold standard in 1925 resulted in an overvaluation of sterling relative to the American dollar has been challenged in recent years (K. C. P. Matthews, 'Was Sterling Overvalued in 1925?', *Economic History Review* (Nov., 1986), pp. 572–87). A case for sterling's overvaluation against other currencies, e.g. the French franc, has also been made (J. Redmond, 'The Sterling Overvaluation of 1925: a Multilateral Approach', *Economic History Review* (Nov., 1984), pp. 520–32). To the extent that sterling was overvalued relative to other foreign currencies after 1925, Britain's efforts to expand exports and curb imports would have been made that much more difficult.

5 Including $2,000m. invested on short-term.
6 In 1926 and 1927 the Bank of France acquired the largest stock of foreign currencies—mainly sterling and dollars—of any central bank in the world. Its motive for doing this was to prevent an unwanted appreciation of the franc rather than to adopt the gold exchange standard. An undervalued franc was desired because it assisted French exports.

SELECTED REFERENCES

Aldcroft, D. H., *From Versailles to Wall Street, 1919–1929* (Harmondsworth, 1987).

Bayoumi, T., Eichengreen, B., and Taylor, M. P., *Modern Perspectives on the Gold Standard* (Cambridge: Cambridge University Press, 1996).

Brown, W. A., Jr, *The International Gold Standard Re-interpreted* (New York, 1940).

Drummond, I. M., *The Gold Standard and the International Monetary System, 1900–1939* (London, 1987).

Ellsworth, P. T., *The International Economy*, 3rd edn. (New York, 1964).

Kindleberger, C. P., *The World in Depression, 1929–1939* (Harmondsworth, 1987).

League of Nations, *The Course and Phases of the World Economic Depression* (Geneva, 1931).

League of Nations, *International Currency Experience* (Geneva, 1944).

Lewis, W. A., *Economic Survey, 1919–1939* (London, 1949).

Moggridge, D. E., *The Return to Gold 1925* (Cambridge, 1969).

Royal Institute of International Affairs, *The Problem of International Investment* (London, 1937).

Triffin, R., *Our International Monetary System: Yesterday, Today, and Tomorrow* (New York, 1968).

United Nations, *International Capital Movements During the Inter-War Period* (New York, 1949).

Yeager, L. B., *International Monetary Relations* (New York, 1966).

Chapter 13

The collapse of the gold standard and the disintegration of the international economy

The great depression of the 1930s had its origin in the United States. It is true that signs of declining production had already appeared at various times between late 1927 and mid-1929 in a number of countries, including Australia, Germany, Canada and Argentina, and that commodity prices in the world as a whole began to fall in the second half of 1928. But the economic crisis did not become widespread and severe until after the industrial downturn in the United States in mid-1929 and the collapse of the security market in the October of that year. It is usual therefore to date the beginning of the world depression from the American stock market crash, for the subsequent collapse of the American economy not only intensified the economic difficulties of those countries already suffering from depression, but also brought about a rapid economic decline in most other parts of the world.

CRISIS IN AGRICULTURE

By the middle of 1929, many primary producers were experiencing financial stringency as falling export prices and declining capital inflows gave rise to acute balance of payments problems. Partly responsible for the decline in foreign lending, particularly by the United States, was the rise in interest rates in America during 1928 and 1929, as the stock market speculation intensified. Both the rise in interest rates and the prospect of earning speculative profits kept American funds at home and attracted substantial funds from abroad. This difficult international lending situation was further aggravated by the repatriation of French capital that followed the stabilization of the franc in 1928. The British money market, under pressure from these and other developments, was in no position to fill the gap created by the withdrawal of France and the United States from foreign lending. The result was a general tightening of credit everywhere, and a lack of finance at the very time when the pressure of falling primary product prices was worsening the balance of payments position of the agricultural debtor countries.

When the American stock market crash finally came, it was followed by a virtual end to American lending abroad and a repatriation of American funds. As a result, the economic difficulties in the agricultural debtor countries rapidly approached crisis proportions. In a desperate effort to balance their international accounts and obtain the foreign exchange needed to service their external debt these countries endeavoured to expand exports still further, which only added to the heavy surpluses of primary products thrown on the market. At the same time, the commodity control schemes, which had operated in the 1920s to maintain relatively high prices for some primary products, collapsed because of the lack of foreign capital to finance the with-holding of stocks from the market, releasing a flood of accumulated stocks on to an already depressed market. The dominant feature in the deepening eco-nomic depression of 1930–1 therefore was the collapse of agricultural and raw materials prices, which strengthened the already existing depression in pri-mary producing countries. In this rapidly deteriorating situation any improvement in the balance of payments of the debtor countries could only be temporary, since successful export expansion only depressed commodity prices further, thus making even greater export volume increases necessary in the future if the improved trade position was to be maintained. Furthermore, the restrictions on imports of manufactures imposed by some primary produ-cers tended to spread the depression to industrial countries, which reduced their ability to import foodstuffs and raw materials. Moreover, the policy of expanding exports and restricting imports created a dangerous tariff situa-tion. Thus, a number of European governments reacted to the flood of cheap primary products from overseas by protecting peasant producers at home. Even more damaging for the debtor countries, however, was the Smoot–Hawley Act of June 1930, which substantially increased the American tariff level. Coming on top of the rapid decline in income and production in the United States, the tariff increase only served to reduce further American purchases of foreign goods.

The greatest number of the heavier duties included in the Smoot–Hawley Act was imposed upon manufactured articles, so that exports of European countries, and particularly of Germany, to the United States, were most affected. Europe was, on balance, a large debtor to the United States, and in default of new loans being available or of ready access to the American market for its exports, Europe had to seek to mobilize dollar resources by exporting to third countries earning dollar surpluses. But in 1929 and 1930 these raw material producing countries were in serious trouble, and it was not feasible to increase exports of manufactured goods to them. In any case, indirectly the American tariff made matters even worse for European countries, since many of the third countries retaliated by raising their duties markedly on products of particular importance to the United States, chiefly manufactures, which were also their main imports from Europe.

The deepening of the economic crisis throughout the latter months of 1930, therefore, was due largely to the growing difficulties of the debtor countries, especially those among them which relied mainly upon exports of raw materials and foodstuffs. There were many other complications, perhaps the most important being the steady repatriation of French short-term balances and the imposition of the Smoot–Hawley tariff. The former was accompanied by a persistent drain of gold to France, which not only weakened the financial standing of sterling and the dollar, but also hindered the revival of large-scale long-term capital exports from the United States and Britain. The latter still further hampered the free exchange of commodities which alone could make possible the heavy payments on account of debt services.

FINANCIAL CRISIS IN EUROPE

Until the late spring of 1931, the depression in many respects appeared to be following the course of ordinary business slumps of the past. A number of primary producing countries had gone off gold, but no major international trading country had been involved, and the gold standard was still intact in western Europe and America. Moreover, there were some signs of a definite easing of the economic situation. Although the debtor countries continued to experience financial difficulties, all the changes in official bank rates were downward suggesting conditions of monetary ease in the chief creditor countries, and the accumulation of liquid capital funds. Steadiness or slight rises in seasonally adjusted figures of industrial production in Germany and the United States during the early months of the year even afforded some hope that the revival was not very far away.

This hesitant optimism was soon shattered by the outbreak of an international financial panic. It began in Austria, where a revaluation of the assets of the Credit-Anstalt of Vienna revealed the bank as insolvent. Despite quick action by the Austrian government to guarantee all deposits of the bank, this flaw in Austria's financial structure led to a heavy withdrawal of foreign short-term credits. This was stemmed only when loans by the Bank for International Settlements and the Bank of England to the Austrian government enabled it to guarantee the Credit-Anstalt's existing liabilities to foreign creditors, while, for their part, the foreign creditors of the bank undertook not to withdraw their advances for a period of two years.

Meanwhile the panic had spread to Germany, which had come under suspicion mainly because of its close commercial ties with Austria. A run on the Reichsbank developed, and attempts were made to end it by raising an international loan in support of the bank and by the announcement of a year's moratorium on reparations and war-debt payments. Withdrawals continued, however, and were accelerated when the disclosure of enormous losses by the North-German Wool Company, involving the shutdown of the Danat (Darmstädter und National Bank), converted a run mainly of Germany's foreign creditors into a flight from the mark into foreign exchange by

Germans as well. The German government reacted to this new crisis by temporarily closing the banks and stock exchanges and by raising the discount rate from 7 to 10 per cent. Steps were also taken to introduce exchange controls and to place restrictions on bank payments. The international loan granted earlier was renewed, and, with the panic subsiding, the signing of a standstill agreement, immobilizing for six months the funds owed by Germans to foreign banks, consolidated the movement towards more normal conditions.

Britain, too, was now suffering a steady loss of gold and, throughout the summer months, the Bank Rate rose steadily until it reached 4½ per cent at the end of July. Her difficulties were closely linked with those of Germany and Austria, for British bankers had advanced them a large amount of short-term credit which was rapidly becoming 'frozen' by the inability of the debtors to meet their foreign obligations. In Germany alone, British short-term holdings amounting to $70m. were locked up under the standstill agreement. Unwanted attention was drawn to the volume of short-term claims in London by the publication on 13 July of the report of the Macmillan Committee, which revealed that London's short-term claims on foreigners, including those 'frozen' on the continent, amounted to only about £153m. whereas deposits and sterling bills held in London by foreigners amounted to some £407m. While there is nothing unusual about a banker having demand liabilities far in excess of immediately liquid assets, knowledge of the fact is inconvenient in time of crisis. Almost as damaging to Britain's international financial standing was the publication on 31 July of the May Committee report on the country's public finances. This revealed an impending deficit in the government budget and recommended cuts in government expenditure, as well as tax increases. In an age when the first canon of orthodox finance was a balanced budget, this report served only to convince foreigners of the waywardness of Britain.

With the withdrawal of short-term balances and the sale of British securities intensifying the strain on Britain's gold reserves, the Bank of England secured on 1 August a credit of £50m. from French and American banks. The run continued, however, despite the resignation of a Labour government unwilling to implement the May Committee recommendations on cuts in government expenditure, and the election of a coalition government pledged to put the economies into effect. On 29 August a further credit of £80m. was arranged, but the drain continued. The introduction by the government of a supplementary budget (10 September) designed to balance the government's accounts failed to halt the run, which developed panic proportions following reports of an alleged naval mutiny at Invergordon on 15 September caused by proposed naval pay cuts. During the following three days, over £43m. was withdrawn from the London money market, making a total withdrawal of over £200m. in the preceding two months. On 21 September, therefore, legislation was passed suspending the Bank of England's obligation to sell gold. Bank Rate was raised to 6 per cent, and the Stock Exchange was closed for two days. Temporary restrictions were also imposed on all foreign exchange dealings.

Immediately after Britain suspended gold payments the pound sterling fell heavily in relation to currencies still on the gold standard.[1] In order not to be put at a trading disadvantage, many other countries quickly followed Britain off the gold standard. By the end of 1932, when 32 countries had suspended gold payments, Scandinavia, Portugal, Egypt, Latvia, most of Latin America, Japan, and all British territories and dominions except South Africa were also off gold. Only France and the United States among the big nations, and Belgium, the Netherlands and Switzerland among the smaller states remained on gold for the time being.

Britain's abandonment of gold in 1931 marks the beginning of the sterling area. A number of factors, both non-economic and economic in character, serve to explain why some countries sought to tie their currencies to the pound sterling. One non-economic consideration was the sentimental ties which existed between Great Britain and the other members of the British Commonwealth of Nations. Sentimentality, although important, was definitely not the major reason for adherence to sterling however, since a number of countries not members of the British Commonwealth joined the sterling area, and one of the more important British dominion countries, Canada, did not (Canada's economic ties being much stronger with the United States than with Great Britain). Fundamentally, three economic factors accounted for the willingness, and desire, of some countries to enter the sterling area. First, sterling was an important currency in the world, it was widely used, and its prestige was relatively high. As gold ceased to be an international standard of value, certain countries sought to tie their currencies to another standard of value, in this case the pound sterling. Second, Britain constituted the major market for the exports of many countries. These countries sought to promote a close currency link between Britain and themselves to protect this commercial relationship. In tying their currencies to sterling, the exporting countries were able to protect commodity prices and the competitive position of those producers dependent upon the British market. Third, a number of countries were debtors of Britain, and they accordingly fixed exchange rates between their currencies and the pound sterling in order to preserve a constancy of cost in servicing their debt obligations.

THE END OF THE GOLD STANDARD

After Britain left gold in September 1931, the international panic centred on the United States, and nearly $2,000m. in gold left the country in the fiscal year ending June 1932. To stop the drain the American monetary authorities were forced to adopt a savage deflationary policy to the accompaniment of rising unemployment and still deeper depression. When therefore the United States came to leave the gold standard, it was because of a deliberate act of policy aimed at relieving the desperate financial and economic conditions existing in the country rather than because of any external balance of payments difficulties as such. In its search for a policy of combating the depression, the newly elected Roosevelt administration believed that a revival of the American economy could only follow from a general rise of domestic prices, and for this reason a number of government policies were initiated and aimed at bringing this about. Finally, on 20 April 1933, the United States suspended gold payments in the belief that if the price of gold was raised commodity prices would automatically rise in direct proportion, thus encouraging business expansion.

The abandonment of gold by America marked the virtual end of the gold standard. The next year or so saw the gradual polarization of countries around a few major industrial powers and the eventual emergence of a number of regional currency systems. At its peak this decentralized currency mechanism consisted of the sterling area, centred on Britain, the dollar area, headed by the United States and composed chiefly of Latin American countries, the exchange control area of central and south-east Europe in which Germany played a leading role, the yen area dominated by Japan in the Far East, and the gold bloc in western Europe.[2] Although it was not formally constituted until after the collapse of the World Economic Conference in mid-1933, the gold bloc began to take shape when the central banks of Belgium, France and the Netherlands began to suffer foreign exchange losses following the depreciation of sterling in 1931. The remnant of the gold standard was not long in existence, however. As the depression continued, and balance of payments pressure mounted, doubts were entertained about the ability of the gold countries to resist devaluation. Consequently a speculative flight of capital developed in these countries, reinforced later by growing fears of war. Belgium was the first to go, devaluing its currency by 28 per cent in March 1935. The other members of the gold bloc followed at the end of September 1936. France devalued by 30 per cent and Switzerland by approximately the same amount. No definite margin of devaluation was set by the Dutch, but a newly established equalization fund kept the exchange rate against the dollar in the vicinity of 20 per cent below the old parity.

GROWTH OF RESTRICTIONS ON FINANCE AND TRADE

The widespread exchange and trade regulations which accompanied the collapse of the gold standard, while offering greater resistance to uncontrolled capital movements, prevented any return to a steady capital outflow from creditor to debtor countries during the 1930s. Exchange control hindered the repatriation of capital, while trade regulations eliminated a large portion of the multilateral trade through which returns on foreign direct investments as well as the service of foreign loans had been transferred. Moreover, the volume of lending inevitably declined during these years, and the direction of the loans became even more circumscribed than formerly because of the development of regional currency blocs. The loans floated in London were thus, with few exceptions, confined to members of the British Commonwealth and certain other countries within the sterling area. Countries with overseas territories confined themselves chiefly to supplying these territories with funds, and Japan invested largely in Manchuria. Other loans, based on geographical proximity or close economic relations, included those by the United States to Canada, by Sweden to other Scandinavian countries, and by Belgium, the Netherlands and Switzerland to France. France and the other members of the gold bloc also recorded heavy capital exports during the middle and late 1930s. But only a small part of this capital went to debtor countries. The bulk represented capital seeking refuge in other creditor countries, particularly the United States, because of the menacing monetary instability in Europe and, after 1936, because of increasing political instability and the growing threat of war.

The depression of the 1930s and the financial difficulties associated with it also had a profound influence on commercial policy during these years. Confronted by a worldwide depression, no country escaped untouched, and there was consequently a reaction against international economic interdependence. Each nation fell back on its own resources and pursued a policy of fostering internal recovery first and foremost. In such an atmosphere, the regulation of foreign trade and financial transactions was a natural and inevitable development. Broadly speaking, these controls took two main forms: those aimed directly at controlling the making of payments between countries, and those affecting in the first instance the movements of individual commodities between countries. The former group included exchange controls and all the various blends of clearing and payments agreements associated with it; the latter, tariffs, import quotas, prohibitions, and the like. While the distinction between the two types of trade controls is not completely clear cut, for in operation they overlapped at every stage, it does provide us with convenient headings under which to discuss the developments in commercial policy during the 1930s.

Exchange Control

Although any form of government intervention that affects the level of foreign exchange rates is, in a broad sense, exchange control, the narrower and more common interpretation of the term refers to various forms of official restrictions upon private transactions in foreign exchange. Where such restrictions were introduced during our period, governments, often through central banks, assumed control of foreign exchange by requiring exporters to surrender the foreign money received from sales abroad and by requiring importers to purchase foreign exchange from authorized sources, with both the buying and selling of foreign exchange taking place at official rates fixed arbitrarily by the government. Whereas few countries succeeded in passing through the depression without resort to some exchange restrictions, if only for a short period, severe and thorough-going systems of control were necessary in debtor countries faced with difficult payments problems and, sometimes, the danger of a simultaneous flight of both domestic and foreign capital. In these countries, of which Germany is a leading example, the government attempted to control all transactions that affected the demand for and supply of foreign exchange. Inevitably the system of control grew more complex, as it became necessary to implement the overall regulations with a host of detailed provisions designed to eliminate evasion.

The increasing severity and persistence of exchange control policies in the 1930s was partly the result of a broadening in the objectives supporting its introduction and retention in the countries concerned. While the original object of exchange control was to curb the outflow of capital associated with the financial crises of the early 1930s, with the deepening of the depression the objectives of such a policy soon multiplied. Thus, the insulation given to an economy by exchange control afforded an opportunity to introduce domestic expansionary measures to raise incomes and increase employment. Exchange control was also necessary if a country wished to maintain an official rate of exchange higher than that dictated by the free interplay of market forces, either because it feared exchange depreciation would lead to inflation, or because depreciation would lead to subsequent increases in the burden of debt service.[3] It could also be used to protect domestic industries, since such a policy enabled a country to allocate foreign exchange for imports on a product by product basis, so that the exclusion, or carefully controlled admission, of particular imports brought about by the lack of foreign exchange also served to protect the home market for domestic producers. Finally, exchange control was used to acquire revenue for the government. By setting a higher rate (or rates) for selling than for buying foreign exchange, the difference accrued to the government as profit. A number of countries (e.g. Argentina and Chile) employed exchange control for this purpose, amongst others.

Bilateral Trading Agreements

As a matter of historical fact, however, the main change of emphasis that occurred in the use of exchange control during these years related to the control of trade. The shortage of foreign currency which made exchange control necessary was not merely general, but tended to be relatively greater for some currencies than for others. Moreover, the fact that some currencies were relatively more scarce than others led to bilateralism, that is, to a deliberate balancing of accounts between pairs of trading countries. Bilateral arrangements had advantages other than just that of overcoming the trading difficulties associated with shortages of foreign currencies. They were attractive in situations where the opportunities for trade discrimination afforded by exchange control enabled one country to gain from its monopoly control of the trade of other, often smaller, countries. Germany in particular was able to take advantage of this sort of situation in its trade with eastern and central European countries in the 1930s. These arrangements could also be used to settle the problem of blocked balances held by exchange control countries. These bilateral arrangements, however, included one significant new element. Whereas the bilateral trading arrangements for dealing with problems other than those of blocked balances almost invariably involved only exchange control countries, the problem of blocked balances often involved free exchange market countries as well.

What all these bilateral arrangements had in common was that they were agreements between pairs of trading countries designed to keep trade at a relatively high volume, but to do so without the accumulation of soft currencies, which could not be used to settle hard currency deficits, and without incurring deficits payable in hard currencies. In other words, these agreements sought to reduce the need for settlement in gold or scarce foreign exchange. Such agreements took three major forms: (a) private compensation agreements, (b) clearing agreements, and (c) payments agreements.

Compensation agreements, the simplest of the new trading devices, were merely a modern form of the age-old principle of barter. Obviously, no currency transactions were necessary when two countries could agree to an exchange of goods of equal value. Where governments were involved in such barter deals, the arrangements were described as a compensation agreement. More often, however, the negotiations were conducted by private individuals or firms, in which case the term private compensation was used to describe the transaction. A considerable volume of German trade came under these compensation deals in 1932 and 1933, including the exchange of some 9 million marks worth of German coal for Brazilian coffee, and the exchange of German fertilizer for Egyptian cotton. In some countries the growth of these trading practices was encouraged by the setting up of organizations to act as middlemen in these barter deals. The Polish Company for Compensation Trade, which began operations in November, 1932, was one of the more important of these organizations. In Germany, on the other hand, chambers of commerce established clearing information bureaux for this purpose, and in Copenhagen five importing firms organized, in 1934, the Association for Commodity Exchange to arrange private compensation transactions with foreign firms.

Private compensation agreements, even when assisted by barter agencies, involved enormous difficulties, since they required the offsetting of individual exports and imports in each transaction. Clearing agreements, which were also entered into during these years, avoided these difficulties by providing a broader and more general procedure for offsetting claims. Under such arrangements each country agreed to establish, usually in its central bank, an account through which all payments for imports and exports were to be cleared. For example, under the German clearing arrangement with Yugoslavia, German importers of Yugoslavian goods would pay marks into an account at the Reichsbank, where they were credited to the account of the Yugoslav clearing agency. German exporters to Yugoslavia were then paid marks from this fund, debited to the Yugoslav account. In Belgrade, the opposite process took place. Yugoslav importers made payments into the clearing account in dinars and exporters received dinars from the account.

As with many developments in the exchange control field during these years, the Germans led the way with clearing arrangements. The first was signed in 1932 with Hungary, and by 1937 Germany had negotiated clearing agreements with every European country except Britain and Albania, as well as with Argentina, Chile, Uruguay and Colombia. The principal feature of these clearing procedures was that they covered not only payments arising from merchandise trade, but also various other payments, including the transfer of interest and dividends, travel expenditures, shipping services, remittances, and so on. In each case, exchange clearing provided a way of settling individual transactions between two countries in terms of their respective domestic currencies.

The view that, because strict bilateral balancing of accounts was very rare, Germany could use such clearing arrangements to exploit countries largely dependent on it for their export trade appears to be exaggerated. It has been argued that under the conditions of rapid economic recovery which characterized Germany in the mid-1930s it was relatively costless, and often politically rewarding, for Germany to forego the advantages of monopoly exploitation.[4] It is nevertheless true that Germany's monopsony position as an important market for the goods of south-eastern Europe, together with the closing of the British and French markets to those products, meant that these countries were helped by selling their foodstuffs to Germany on clearing account and that they were willing to wait some time to get manufactured goods in exchange. Outside Europe, German clearing arrangements with Latin America succeeded in bringing back its trade with that part of the world almost to the levels of the 1920s.

Payments agreements differed from clearing agreements chiefly in that they covered a wider range of transactions and used the normal method of payment over the foreign exchanges rather than special clearing accounts. In addition, a payments agreement often linked an exchange control country with a free exchange country, whereas clearing agreements were negotiated only between exchange control countries. Consequently, most of the payments agreements in force in the summer of 1939 were between free exchange countries of western Europe, on the one hand, and exchange control countries in central and south-eastern Europe or Latin America on the other.

The chief reason for free exchange countries becoming involved in bilateral agreements during these years was the difficulty of realizing frozen debt and service payments in exchange control countries. A major item of frozen debt arose out of the standstill agreements negotiated during the financial crisis of 1931. Britain had been deeply involved in these developments and it is not surprising therefore to find that the first creditor country to make use of payments agreements in its relations with debtor countries was the United Kingdom. Thus, the Anglo-German Agreement of November 1934 is generally regarded as the model of subsequent payments agreements, although the British government had first employed the payments principle in the Runciman–Roca Agreement of May 1933, with Argentina. The Anglo-German agreement limited Germany's imports from Britain in any month to 55 per cent of the value of its exports to Britain during the last month but one. Apart from a sum earmarked at the beginning to clear existing commercial debts, the surplus 45 per cent was partly used to service the Dawes and Young loans in Britain and to cover other charges, including the payment of freight expenses in sterling, the remainder being placed at the free disposal of the Reichsbank.

Confined to preventing capital movements, exchange control need not result in restrictions in trade, discrimination between countries, or protection of particular producers. Indeed, it was currency overvaluation rather than exchange control as such that was ultimately responsible for the contraction of trade that took place during the 1930s. Once exchange control is applied in support of currency overvaluation, payments made in the currencies of control countries lead inevitably toward the accumulation of blocked balances. Bilateral trading arrangements, which are themselves only instruments of policy, then become necessary to liquidate these frozen claims. In the process, trade is distorted and discrimination against countries inevitably practised. It is then but a short step from this type of discrimination to discrimination with a view to economic domination. Throughout the process, however, exchange control and bilateral trading arrangements are essentially instruments or tools of policy.

Whatever the reason for adopting a policy of exchange control, however, its use led inevitably to a loss of world real income, because by distorting trade from its normal channels into bilateral grooves, the resultant trade represented less gain in welfare terms to its participants than trade carried out under full multilateral conditions. Yet given that the setting of equilibrium exchange rates and the liberalizing of international payments was impossible in the depressed conditions of the 1930s, bilateral trading arrangements did make possible trade in specialized commodities that would not otherwise have taken place. Both partners to clearing payments agreements gained. Exports to other exchange control countries increased, despite the economic difficulties of the early 1930s, and these additional exports made it possible to acquire useful imports. Moreover, exchange clearing made possible the liquidation of frozen balances, and permitted the maintenance of debt service owed to creditor countries.

Tariffs and Other Restrictions on Trade

Despite the spread of exchange control, tariffs remained the greatest single obstacle to the international movement of goods in the 1930s. The upward movement of tariffs, which characterized the early depression years, continued well into the middle 1930s, when there was some relaxation of restrictions from late 1936 onwards. But in 1938 the decline in world trade and a fall in primary product prices led to a resumption of the upward movement. By the end of the 1930s, therefore, close to half the world's trade was restricted by tariffs alone.

Britain's conversion to whole-hearted protectionism represents the outstanding single development in the tariff history of the period. In practice, Britain was still predominantly free trading at the beginning of the 1930s, for out of £1,030m. of imports, £138m. paid revenue duties, and only £13m. were subject to McKenna or Safeguarding Act duties. But the situation changed radically with the passing of the Import Duties Act of March 1932. This Act imposed a general duty of 10 per cent *ad valorem* on all imports into the United Kingdom, except Empire goods and those named on a free list, which included most foodstuffs and raw materials. The Act also set up an Import Duties Advisory Committee to recommend additional duties. In April, a 33⅓ per cent duty was placed on most kinds of steel; the general level of duties on manufactured goods was raised to 20 per cent, on luxury goods to 24–30 per cent, and on a few items (including some chemicals) to 33⅓ per cent. With a few exceptions, British Empire products again received exemption from these charges.

The other significant feature of commercial policy in these years was the spread of import quotas and other forms of quantitative controls over trade. France was the first country to adopt import quotas on a wide scale as a means of combating the depression, and she was quickly followed by a number of other countries. By the end of 1932, eleven countries had fully fledged quota or licensing systems. Despite its further spread, import quotas remained primarily a European instrument of trade control. At the beginning of 1939, twenty-eight countries, nineteen of them European, operated quota or licensing systems applying to a substantial range of commodities.

There were various reasons for adopting quantitative import controls. They could be used to protect domestic manufacturing and, perhaps even more importantly, to protect domestic agriculture from the severe overseas competition that followed the violent fall in primary product prices in the early 1930s. Import quotas were also of vital importance to the gold bloc countries after the abandonment of the gold standard by Britain and the United States. With their currencies becoming overvalued in the face of currency depreciation elsewhere, these countries experienced severe balance of payments pressures. Denied the use of exchange control by their adherence to the gold standard, they imposed severe control on imports to bring their foreign trade into balance. Moreover, import quotas often formed part of national recovery programmes. In 1933, for example, the United Kingdom introduced quotas on agricultural products in support of national marketing schemes aimed at reviving British agriculture and in favour of Empire producers. Import quotas were also used for purposes of retaliation and commercial bargaining.

Import quotas were even more damaging to international trade than tariffs, since a quota directly limits the level of permissible imports and thus operates independently of the price mechanism. Thus while it is always possible for the foreign exporter to beat the tariff by lowering his price sufficiently to make him competitive with domestic producers even when the tariff is added to his price, the quota limits the importation of a commodity to a fixed amount irrespective of supply and demand conditions (or prices) in the domestic or foreign markets. But while appreciating the additional restrictions placed on foreign trade by import quotas as compared with tariffs, the extraordinary difficulties of the 1930s should always be kept in mind when considering the welfare implications of these additional controls on international exchange. In the depression years tariffs proved completely inadequate in protecting domestic industry, whether agriculture or manufacturing, from distress sales of foreign goods induced by serious deflationary pressures abroad. Only import quotas could ensure the strict limitation of these imports, thus reducing the damage they inflicted on domestic production and employment. Moreover, where balance of payments difficulties called for the reduction of a country's imports, import quotas or the licensing of imports provided the only certain way of confining the total value of imports within predetermined limits. It is not surprising, therefore, to find that import licensing and other forms of quantitative restrictions on imports were often used in connection with systems of exchange control.

INTERNATIONAL FINANCIAL CO-OPERATION

The Bank for International Settlements (BIS) had been set up in Basle in Switzerland in 1930 under the Young Plan to facilitate the flows of reparations payments from Germany to the recipient countries. After the reparations moratorium of July 1931, it continued to perform its subsidiary function of promoting central bank co-operation. The monthly meetings of its Board members, mostly central bankers, provided a venue for discussion and attempts at co-operation. As noted above, the BIS arranged loans to the Austrian government after the Credit-Anstalt disaster. Throughout the

1930s, the Bank also provided short-term credit facilities to a number of central banks. Nevertheless, its attempts to encourage central bank co-operation at this time were of minor importance.

By the middle of 1932 the opinion was widespread that international action was necessary to combat the breakdown of international trade and finance and to promote economic recovery. Consequently, a World Economic Conference was held in London in June 1933, to discuss among other things the question of currency stabilization. However, shortly before the meeting was convened, the dollar went off gold and was allowed to fluctuate freely without any immediate hope of stabilization. With the future of the dollar uncertain, international agreement on currency stabilization was impossible, and the Conference was adjourned without having achieved any worthwhile success.

The need for some measure of international financial co-operation arose again in 1936, when the abandonment of the gold standard by the gold bloc countries created problems for those countries operating exchange stabiliza-tion funds. Meanwhile all major obstacles to an agreement between the major financial powers in the world had been removed by the final collapse of the remnants of the gold standard and by the change in the American govern-ment's attitude to international currency stability following the stabilization of the dollar in 1934. The result was the Tripartite Monetary Agreement between France, Britain and the United States, which was concluded just before the French devaluation in September, 1936, and which was later joined by Belgium, Holland and Switzerland. While it would be a mistake to exaggerate the concrete accomplishments of this Agreement, which were largely in the field of technical co-operation, it was important, nevertheless, because it endorsed the principle of managed exchange rates which had come to replace the free exchange rates associated with the gold standard, and because it involved recognition of the need for effective international co-operation in a managed exchange rate system. In this sense the Tripartite Monetary Agreement of 1936 was a forerunner of the International Monetary Fund.

The interwar period witnessed the beginnings of the transfer of inter-national financial hegemony from Britain to the United States which was completed by the end of World War II. Despite increased American involve-ment in European economic affairs in the 1920s, it is going too far to claim that the outcome of this involvement was a new 'American-shaped world order'.[5] In any case, in the 1930s, America's domestic economic difficulties tended to take precedence over her involvement in international economic affairs. On the other hand, Britain's abandonment of the gold standard in September 1931 brought about the total collapse of the international mone-tary standard which she had pioneered in the early nineteenth century. She, nevertheless, remained the head of one of the strongest regional economic entities—the Sterling Area—to emerge from the ruins of that system.[6]

REGIONAL ECONOMIC CO-OPERATION

The failure to achieve international agreement on matters of trade and finance in the early 1930s led many nations to consider the alternative possibility of trade liberalizing agreements on a regional basis. An early example of this type of economic co-operation was that between the Danubian agricultural countries, Hungary, Romania, Yugoslavia and Bulgaria, which in the early 1930s obtained tariff preferences for their chief exports in a number of individually negotiated bilateral agreements with European industrial countries. The regional economic pact between Italy, Austria and Hungary brought about by the Rome Agreements of 1934, and the series of agreements reached in the 1930s between the 'Oslo Group' of nations, comprising Denmark, Sweden, Norway, Finland, the Netherlands, Belgium and Luxembourg, provide further examples of these attempts at regional economic co-operation. In the Americas the Pan American Conference attempted to deal with the problem of trade restrictions in the western hemisphere. The United States concluded a number of reciprocal trade agreements with Latin American countries in the years before 1939, and a number of trade liberalizing agreements were also concluded between pairs of Latin American countries. Owing to their relative importance in Latin American trade, even more such agreements were negotiated with European countries. Although, on balance, these regional agreements were probably trade diverting rather than trade creating in their effect on the international exchange of goods and services, they did help to revive business confidence and reverse the trend towards economic nationalism.

By far the most important regional economic pact of these years was the establishment of a general preferential system within the British Commonwealth as a result of the Ottawa agreements of 1932. Under these arrangements Commonwealth countries agreed to extend to each other increased import preference. As for tariff reductions within the Empire, the results were meagre. What was achieved by way of increased trade within the Commonwealth was achieved not by the reduction of tariffs within the Empire but by raising them to those countries outside it. Moreover, although imperial preference increased Britain's share in the trade of Empire countries, it also deflected foreign competition into other markets where Britain's position was less favourable. The drawbacks to Britain of this changed pattern of trade only became apparent in the period after the end of World War II.

In colonial territories the open door policy formerly favoured by the chief colonial powers was gradually abandoned with the onset of the depression and the growing impact of Japanese competition in colonial areas in the Far East and elsewhere after 1931. Complete tariff assimilation between the mother country and its colonies constituted the policy pursued by France, the United States and Japan in relation to certain of their colonies. On the other hand, within the British, French (non-assimilated colonies), Portuguese, Spanish and Italian empires, tariff preferences were extensively employed. At the same time, import quotas and foreign exchange regulations provided convenient openings for discrimination in favour of intra-imperial trade.

INTERNATIONAL COMMODITY CONTROL SCHEMES

International commodity schemes constituted practically the only significant multilateral economic agreements concluded in the 1930s. These inter-governmental agreements, between leading producing countries, or between the producing and leading importing countries as well, were concerned with matters relating to the production and marketing of certain primary products. Where only producers were involved, the object of these agreements was to control production and exportation so as to stabilize prices, or even to raise them. Some of these international agreements evolved from private cartels set up in the 1920s to control the prices of certain products, such as rubber, tea, and tin, while others grew out of the attempts of individual governments to deal with the problem of surplus production and unstable prices. Cases in which international commodity agreements evolved through government sponsorship included coffee, sugar and wheat.

It was the collapse of these earlier control schemes and the depressed prices of primary products during the early 1930s that led to the establishment of a number of international commodity agreements in the years from 1931 onwards. These included agreements covering tin and sugar (1931), tea and wheat (1933), rubber (1934), and copper (1936). All of these schemes covered 80–90 per cent, or even more, of exportable production, and, with the partial exception of the tin scheme, all relied on quantitative control of production. Pricing policy was largely one of opportunism or expediency. Overall, however, these schemes did not play an important part in the history of primary production during the 1930s. Their influence was decisive only for tea, tin and rubber, and they had some influence on the production and export of sugar and copper. Even if these achievements were confined to a limited field, however, the mere fact that control schemes were set up for so many products, and that their marketing was sufficiently well organized to enable the schemes to operate reasonably efficiently is important as a pointer to what might have been achieved had a more vigorous international economic policy been fostered by the major trading powers.

Because the interwar period with its falling prices and substantial excess capacity in many lines proved especially favourable for their development, private and government sponsored agreements between normally competitive firms located in two or more countries became more frequent in manufacturing industry. Thus, at the outbreak of World War II, an American estimate placed the number of international cartels at 179, of which 133 involved manufactured and semi-manufactured goods, including steel, chemicals, electrical products, oil and aluminium. These cartels had as their central objective the reduction of competition so as to stabilize prices and, where possible, enjoy monopoly profits. They were also used occasionally as instruments of government policy. This happened in Germany in the 1930s, when various cartels dominated by German producers were used by the Nazi government to maintain German exports at the expense of other countries, and to assure the German economy of supplies of foreign currency.

Like all monopolies, cartels tended to restrict the volume of world trade and divert its channels. In particular, international cartellization tended to divide the world into spheres of commercial influence by allocating to the nationals of certain countries exclusive selling rights in certain territories. Thus, in the cartel arrangements of the 1930s, American firms were normally assigned the American market, sometimes the whole of North America and, on occasion, part of Latin America. British firms laid special claim to Empire territory, while the growing strength of German firms in a number of cartels won them increasingly large areas of Europe as their exclusive market. It is perhaps in those situations where markets were allocated amongst the members of the cartel that the reduction of trade was most apparent, for example, where the United States market became the exclusive preserve of American firms, for under these arrangements potential trade is simply stopped at its source.

CONCLUSIONS

The worldwide depression of the 1930s, and the collapse of the gold standard which accompanied its onset in the early years of that decade, were responsible for the spread of financial and trade practices which severely restricted the exchange of goods between countries. Even when devices such as bilateral trading agreements promoted trade flows between countries which might not otherwise have taken place, the benefits derived from this increase in the volume of international trade were offset by the loss of welfare to its participants consequent upon the trade being conducted through bilateral rather than multilateral channels. Distortions of trading patterns and consequent loss of welfare were also characteristic of those regional economic blocs operating preferential trading arrangements. The net outcome of all these developments was a substantial slowing up in the growth of international trade during the interwar years, which is examined in detail in the next chapter.

NOTES

1 Sterling fluctuated freely on the foreign exchange market up to April 1932 when the Exchange Equalization Account was established. Operated by the Bank of

England under Treasury control, the Account's purchases and sales of sterling in the market were supposed to smooth out excessive short-run fluctuations. In particular, the Account operated to protect the domestic credit base from the effects of international short-term capital movements.

2 A number of countries with diverse commercial and financial ties, such as Canada and Argentina, did not fit naturally into any one of these groups, and had to maintain an intermediate and precarious position in this system of group exchanges.

3 Since foreign loans are ordinarily expressed in the currency of the lending country, a rise in the exchange rate for the lender's currency increases the amount of domestic money that the debtor country must pay out to acquire the lender's currency necessary to service the foreign debt.

4 See Larry Neal, 'The Economics and Finance of Bilateral Clearing Agreements: Germany, 1934–8', *Economic History Review* (Aug., 1979), pp. 391–404.

5 See F. Costigliola, *Awkward Dominion. American Political, Economic and Cultural Relations with Europe, 1919–1933* (New York, 1985).

6 For a more detailed discussion of this transfer of leadership see B. Rowland (ed.), *Balance of Power or Hegemony?* (New York, 1976), esp. Chap. VI, 'The Historiography of the Interwar Period: Reconsiderations', by David P. Calleo.

SELECTED REFERENCES

Bordo, M. D. and Rockoff, H., 'The Gold Standard as a Good Housekeeping Seal of Approval', *Journal of Economic History*, 56 (1996), pp. 389–428.

Drummond, I. M., *The Gold Standard and the International Monetary System, 1900–1939* (London, 1987).

Ellsworth, P. T., *The International Economy*, 3rd edn. (New York, 1964).

Gordon, M. S., *Barriers to World Trade* (New York, 1941).

Kindleberger, C. P., *The World in Depression, 1929–1939* (Harmondsworth, 1987).

League of Nations, *International Currency Experience* (Geneva, 1944).

Lewis, Sir W. A., *Economic Survey, 1919–1939* (London, 1949).

Rowe, J. W. F., *Primary Commodities in International Trade* (Cambridge, 1965).

United Nations, Dept. of Economic Affairs, *International Cartels* (New York, 1947).

Yeager, L. B., *International Monetary Relations* (New York, 1966).

Chapter 14

International trade during the interwar period

THE GROWTH OF WORLD TRADE IN THE INTERWAR YEARS

Between the two wars there was a sharp break in the expansion of world trade. Although the volume of foreign trade continued to grow, the rate of growth of total trade per decade declined from an average of almost 40 per cent in the period 1881–1913 to 14 per cent in the period 1913–37. The decline in per capita trade, from a decadal average of 34 per cent in the period 1881–1913 to 3 per cent in 1913–37, was even more striking. Given the economic difficulties of the interwar period, this decline in world trade is not surprising. What was disconcerting about foreign trade developments during these years, however, was that the retardation in the rate of growth of world trade was clearly more marked than that in the rate of growth of world product, whether measured on a total or per capita basis. Thus, over the period 1913–37 the total product of 13 developed countries grew 22 per cent and increased per capita 13 per cent compared with an increase of almost 11 per cent in total trade and a decrease of slightly more than 3 per cent in per capita trade.[1]

This tendency for output to grow faster than trade was not uniformly maintained throughout the interwar years, however. Largely on account of the expansion in the United States, industrial production emerged from the war less battered than trade. In the 1920s, however, trade revived rapidly and was probably growing slightly faster than world output towards the end of the decade. This improvement in trade relative to output was maintained in the early years of the 1930s when the loss in the volume of international trade because of the depression was less than the decline in world industrial output. But with recovery world production revived more rapidly than world trade and, by 1937, industrial production had grown to 104 per cent of the 1929 figure, whereas the quantum of world trade registered only 97 per cent.

These trends in world output and world trade suggest that the foreign trade proportion, that is, the ratio of world trade to world product, declined during the interwar period, despite an increase in the number of trading nations, largely brought about by the postwar political settlement in

Europe. During the war years the world foreign trade proportion probably fell, but it was the depression of the 1930s and World War II that sharply reduced the volume of foreign trade and the world trade proportion, so that by the late 1940s and early 1950s it was probably at its lowest since 1913.

THE DIRECTION OF WORLD TRADE BETWEEN THE WARS

World War I interrupted the customary flow of trade between continents and nations, bringing about a decrease in Europe's trade and an increase in that of the United States. The decline in Europe's share of total world trade continued during the interwar years, despite some recovery in the 1930s when the depression checked the expansion of American trade. Consequently, by 1937, Europe was responsible for just over half of world trade compared with almost two-thirds in 1913 (see Table 19). This decline in Europe's importance in world trade came about for various reasons. It was due partly to the fall in the trade share of the Soviet Union, which accounted for close to 4 per cent of total world trade in 1913, but only some 1.5 per cent in the late 1920s and around 1 per cent in the late 1930s. It also reflected the continued growth in the importance of the North American continent in world trade, whose share in 1937 was larger than it had been in 1913 despite the set-back of the 1930s. An even more important cause of the shift in relative shares over the period was the continuous increase in the proportion of world trade of the largely underdeveloped regions of Asia, Africa and Oceania. In 1913 they accounted for 17 per cent of world trade; by 1937 their combined share had grown to almost a quarter of the total trade.

The same trade picture is examined from a somewhat different angle in Table 20, which shows the changing shares of developed and underdeveloped countries in world trade during the period 1913–37, measured in constant prices and excluding the Soviet Union. Here it can be seen that the decline in Europe's share in world trade during the interwar years is accounted for solely by the decline in the share of Industrial Europe, since Other Europe's share was slightly larger in 1937 than it had been in 1913. The pattern for North America to be found in Table 19 is repeated here, with the region's share in total trade growing in the period up to 1928 and then declining in the 1930s. The trade of Japan and the newly industrializing areas of South Africa and Oceania expanded continuously as a proportion of world trade, as did the share of the rest of the world, although the trade improvement experienced by the latter group of countries was largely concentrated in the period between 1913 and 1928.

Despite the various changes in the direction of world trade that occurred during the interwar years, the trade conducted between non-European nations only rose from just under a quarter to just over a quarter of the total

Table 19 Distribution of world trade by geographic regions, 1913–37

Region	%								
	1913			1928			1937		
	Exports	Imports	Total trade	Exports	Imports	Total trade	Exports	Imports	Total trade
Europe [1]	58.9	65.	62.0	48.0	56.2	52.1	47.0	55.8	51.4
North America [2]	14.8	11.5	13.2	19.8	15.2	17.5	17.1	13.9	15.5
Latin America [3]	8.3	7.0	7.6	9.8	7.6	8.7	10.2	7.2	8.7
Asia	11.8	10.4	11.1	15.5	13.8	14.6	16.9	14.1	15.5
Africa	3.7	3.6	3.7	4.0	4.6	4.3	5.3	6.2	5.7
Oceania	2.5	2.4	2.4	2.9	2.6	2.8	3.5	2.8	3.2
Total	100.0	100.0	100.0	100.0	100.0	100.0	100.0	100.0	100.0

Source: P. Lamartine Yates, Forty Years of Foreign Trade (London, 1955), Tables 6 and 7, pp. 32–3.

Notes:
1 Including Russia.
2 Canada and the United States.
3 Central and South America, including all colonial territories in the Western hemisphere.

Table 20   Shares of developed and underdeveloped countries in world trade, 1913–37

	Constant prices (excluding the U.S.S.R.)					
	Industrial Europe	U.S.A. and Canada	Oceania, South Africa, Japan	Others	Of which	
					Other Europe	Rest of world
1913	54.4	14.5	5.4	25.7	5.7	20.0
1928	43.1	18.8	6.9	31.2	7.9	23.3
1937	43.8	16.5	9.5	30.2	6.3	23.9

Source: Kuznets, op. cit., Table 2, p. 11.

Table 21   Percentage distribution of world trade in imports, 1913–38

	%	
	1913	1938
World trade	100	100
Intra-European trade	40	29
Imports to Europe from Non-European countries	22	27
Imports to Non-European from Europe	15	17
Trade among Non-European countries	23	27

Source: W. S. Woytinsky and E. S. Woytinsky, *World Commerce and Governments* (New York, 1955), pp. 71, 80.

world trade, and Europe still dominated the trade picture in 1938 as it had done before 1913 (see Table 21). Whereas intra-European trade fell substantially from 40 per cent of the total world trade in imports in 1913 to 29 per cent in 1938, this fall was largely offset by an increase in trade between European and non-European countries In other words, the economic difficulties of the interwar years while restricting trade within Europe tended at the same time to sustain and even encourage trade between Europe and the rest of the world.

THE CHANGING COMPOSITION OF WORLD TRADE

The broad nature of the changes in the commodity structure of world trade during the interwar period is illustrated in Table 22 and Figure 15, which describe the trends in the regional shares in world trade in primary products and manufactures. As far as the world trade in primary products is concerned, the most striking development during these years was the rapid growth of the export share of the underdeveloped countries, from just over a third of the total in 1913 to around half in 1937. Taken together, these countries

Table 22a Trade in primary products: regional shares, 1913–37

Region	%					
	1913		1928		1937	
	Imports	Exports	Imports	Exports	Imports	Exports
U.K. and Ireland	19.0	6.2	19.9	4.8	22.9	4.8
N.W. Europe[1]	43.1	25.2	34.2	14.5	33.7	15.6
Other Europe	12.3	14.7	10.5	16.0	8.5	13.7
U.S. and Canada	11.3	17.3	16.7	20.0	15.8	15.5
Underdeveloped and rest of world	14.3	36.6	18.7	44.7	19.1	50.4
World	100.0	100.0	100.0	100.0	100.0	100.0

Table 22b Trade in manufactures: regional shares, 1913–37

Region	%					
	1913		1928		1937	
	Imports	Exports	Imports	Exports	Imports	Exports
U.K. and Ireland	8.2	25.3	9.1	21.8	8.8	19.5
N.W. Europe[1]	24.4	47.9	17.5	40.9	17.5	41.8
Other Europe	15.4	8.3	15.7	4.6	13.3	5.8
U.S. and Canada	12.1	10.6	12.8	19.2	10.6	19.7
Underdeveloped and rest of world	39.9	7.9	44.9	13.5	49.8	13.2
World	100.0	100.0	100.0	100.0	100.0	100.0

Source: Yates, op. cit., Tables 19, 21, 23 and 25.

Note.
1 Includes Finland, Sweden, Norway, Denmark, Germany, Belgium, Netherlands, France, Switzerland and Australia.

exported the whole range of tropical and temperate foodstuffs, as well as all the non-ferrous metals and petroleum, the demand for which was growing rapidly at this time. Even more striking, however, was the heavy decline in Europe's share of the world export trade in manufactures, from over four-fifths of the total trade in 1913 to approximately two-thirds in 1937. Within the total European share, the United Kingdom's share continued the decline which had begun well before 1913, but the decline in that of continental Europe was a completely new trend which became apparent only after 1913. Offsetting the falling European share were increases in the shares of this trade originating in North America and Asia, chiefly Japan. As for the import

Figure 15(a) Regional shares in total world trade, 1913–37, primary products

trade in manufactures, the tendency for the share of the industrialized countries in this trade to decline was associated with an extension of the share
going to the non-industrialized countries of the world.

Despite these changes in the commodity structure of world trade, the
export trade of developed countries continued to be dominated by manufactures, while their import trade consisted largely of primary products. The
reverse, of course, was still the case foᴀ the underdeveloped countries which,
apart from Japan and India, continued to export mainly primary products.
Moreover, within the developed countries, primary products continued to be
a larger proportion of the exports and a smaller fraction of the imports of the
United States and Canada than for the United Kingdom and Ireland and the
other industrial countries of north-west Europe. Finally, the stability in
the share of primary products in world trade noted earlier for the period
before 1913 was maintained throughout the interwar years (see Table 23).

This continued stability of the share of primary products in world trade
was maintained despite significant changes in the composition of the commodity group. As Table 23 shows, the food and agricultural raw materials
shares in primary products exports declined throughout the period 1913 to
1937, while that of minerals rose. This decline in the relative importance of
foodstuffs in foreign trade was associated with a number of significant
changes in the composition of world trade in food during these years. The

Figure 15(b) Regional shares in total world trade, 1913–37, manufactures

Table 23 Shares of commodity groups in world exports, 1913–37 (actual values)

Year	Food	%		Total	Manufactures	Total trade
		Primary products Raw materials				
		Agriculture	Minerals			
1913	27.0	22.7	14.0	63.7	36.3	100.0
1927	24.3	21.5	15.8	61.6	38.4	100.0
1937	23.0	21.0	19.5	63.5	36.5	100.0

Source: Yates, op. cit., Table 16, p. 44.

trade in certain tropical foodstuffs, particularly cocoa, coffee, bananas and citrus fruits, increased substantially in the interwar years, both in volume and value terms. On the other hand, there was the relative stagnation of trade in certain non-tropical foodstuffs, especially cereals, which was partly due to the rising self-sufficiency of western Europe in these lines of primary production.

In the export of dairy products, New Zealand benefited immensely from the growing world trade in butter, which reached a peak of 615,000 tons in 1934–8. By 1937 it supplied a quarter of the world's exports. The volume of the meat trade also expanded during the 1920s, and suffered only a minor fall in the 1930s when, because of imperial preference and the fact that Britain took between three and four-fifths of the world's exports of meat, Australia and New Zealand grew at the expense of Argentina and Uruguay. Finally, Africa emerged as a major supplier of tropical foodstuffs, particularly cocoa, oilseeds and fats, a development which took place at the expense of traditional Latin American exports.

The depressed group of agricultural raw materials during these years included cotton, silk, and hides and skins. Their decline was due partly to competition between the various agricultural products themselves, for example, rubber replaced leather in a number of uses, and wood pulp in the form of rayon competed against cotton and silk. Competition also came from the mineral realm, where petroleum-based compounds made synthetic rubber and, later, nylon, and synthesized chemicals provided dyes and drugs previously obtained from the juices of plants. With the growing production of man-made fibres the European demand for raw cotton declined during the interwar years, being only partly offset by rising Japanese imports. The foreign trade in raw cotton was also reduced by the spread of cotton manufacture to countries, such as Brazil and India, which produced their own raw cotton. Among the raw cotton exporters, the salient changes were the rise of Brazil, the continued expansion of Egypt and India, and the decline of the United States. The growth of rayon production also brought about a heavy fall of raw silk exports from Japan and China. Unlike cotton and silk, the volume of the wool trade continued to grow in the 1920s and held its own in the 1930s, and its greater stability compared to the other textiles may be put down largely to the lack of competition from synthetics. The world consumption of natural rubber also increased throughout the interwar period and was accompanied by a significant shift in the source of supply. Whereas, in 1909–13, 80 per cent of the rubber traded came from the Amazon basin, Central America, and Central Africa, by the end of the 1930s it came almost wholly from south-eastern Asia.

The rise in mineral exports indicated in Table 23 is attributable to petroleum and, to a lesser extent, to non-ferrous metals. Other significant changes in world trade in minerals during these years included the switch of the United States from being an exporter to an importer of copper, lead and zinc; Europe's growing deficiency of minerals; and the rising importance of Africa and Latin America as producers of minerals including copper, lead, zinc, iron ore and petroleum. For the newest of the non-ferrous metals—bauxite and aluminium—demand grew rapidly during the interwar years. Apart from America, mining was located mainly in Europe—Italy, Hungary, Yugoslavia and France. Some supplies were obtained from the Netherlands East Indies, and in the 1930s a start was made in the Gujanas. Among the fuels the growth of petroleum was spectacular. From virtually nothing in 1913 the trade grew to be worth $1,170m. in 1929. Europe was the main importer, with the United States, the Netherlands Antilles, and Venezuela the main exporters. In international trade, coal continued to be important, and as late as 1938 it was surpassed only by cotton. But whereas the combined exports of coal of continental Europe fell very little between the wars, Britain's exports of this product declined substantially.

The interwar years also witnessed significant changes in the commodity composition of world trade in manufactures (see Table 24 and Figure 16). The most striking change was the continued shift away from textiles and towards engineering products. Metals and chemicals showed a slight upward trend, while miscellaneous manufactures, composed largely of consumer goods, showed a downward movement after 1929. Indeed the trends in the various commodity groups included in Table 24 suggest that during the interwar years international trade in manufactures moved away from consumer goods and towards capital goods, with trade in manufactured materials remaining fairly stable. In support of this conclusion, it has been estimated that the combined shares of textiles and other consumer goods in the world export of manufactures fell from 52 per cent to 38 per cent between 1913 and 1937, while that of manufactured materials, including iron and steel, rose from 29 to 33, and of capital goods from 19 per cent to 29 per cent.

These changes in the composition of the export trade in manufactures were associated with a significant change in the direction of this trade. Up to the early 1930s, the greater part of the expansion in manufactured exports went to the non-industrial parts of the world, trade in manufactures within the industrial group of countries accounting for rather less than half the total

Table 24 Commodity pattern of trade in manufactures (exports), 1913–37

	%		
	1913	1929	1937
Engineering products	19.6	27.2	30.2
Non-electrical	9.7	11.4	12.9
Electrical	2.6	4.0	4.9
Transport	7.3	11.8	12.4
Textiles	28.2	23.2	18.2
Metals	13.8	12.7	16.0
Chemicals	8.5	8.1	9.5
All other manufactures	29.9	28.8	26.1
Total	100.0	100.0	100.0

Source: Cairncross, op. cit., p. 244.

Table 25 Shares of leading exporters in world trade in manufactures, 1913–37

		%		
		1913	*1929*	*1937*
U.K.		30.6	23.8	22.4
U.S.		13.0	21.4	20.3
France		12.7	11.1	6.1
Germany		27.5	21.9	23.4
Belgium, Italy, Sweden and Switzerland		13.1	14.3	15.4
Canada		0.7	3.4	5.0
Japan		2.5	4.1	7.5
Total		100.0	100.0	100.0
	£m.	1,292	2,342	1,723

Source: Cairncross, op. cit., Table 4, p. 235.

increase. During the remainder of the 1930s, however, this intra-trade declined much more heavily than did manufactures exported to non-industrial countries, chiefly because the trade restrictions of these years affected the intra-trade far more severely than exports to non-industrial nations. As we have already noted, inter-European trade in manufactures fell precipitately during these years, a development which was partly offset by a rapid expansion of trade in manufactures between the United States and Canada. The overall effect, however, of a net decline in trade in manufactures between industrial countries and an expansion of such trade between industrial and non-industrial countries was that the share of manufactures in total world trade changed very little during the interwar period.

Table 25 and Figure 16 show the changing shares of the leading exporters in world trade in manufactures between 1913 and 1937. The picture they give is a familiar one. The shares of the United Kingdom, France and Germany in this trade declined through the period, their combined share falling from just over 70 per cent of the total world trade in manufactures in 1913 to about 52 per cent in 1937. On the other hand, the American share advanced from 13 per cent to 20 per cent over these years, despite a set-back in the 1930s because of the depression. Even more striking is the rise of Japan, and the equally rapid emergence of Canada as a large industrial exporter. In trying to explain these shifts in the relative positions of the different countries engaged in exporting manufactured goods, the possibility suggests itself that those countries which gained most in relative importance in world trade in manufactures during these years—the United States, Japan and Canada—did so by concentrating on the export of those commodities, for example engineering products, which were growing in relative importance in world trade. This does not appear to have been so, however, since each of these countries

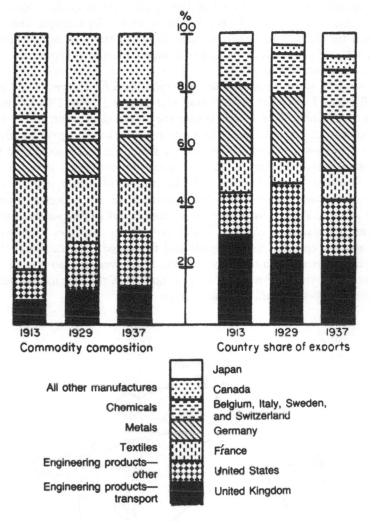

Figure 16 World trade in manufactures, 1913–37 (commodity composition and country share)

Source: As for Tables 24 and 25.

advanced by improving its competitive position in different groups of commodities. The American advance was mainly in the expanding export lines, such as engineering products and transport equipment, Canada's in the stable group of miscellaneous manufactures, and that of Japan chiefly in the declining textile group. In short, the available evidence suggests that changes in the relative position of countries in world trade in manufactures during the interwar years were not so much due to structural shifts in the world demand for these exports as to each country's ability to compete in markets for individual groups of commodities. Thus it has been argued, for example, that the main reason for the fall in Britain's share in world trade in manufactures between 1899 and 1937 was her failure to compete in export markets for iron and steel and engineering products.[2]

The network of world merchandise trade calculated for the year 1928 and shown in Figure 17 describes the situation as it emerged in the 1920s following the end of World War I, and before the world depression led to the disintegration of the international economy into a series of regional trading blocs. The countries included in the trading system in 1928 accounted for nine-tenths of the world's trade, and the arrows in the figure indicate the direction of balances of merchandise trade, in millions of dollars, between the countries and regions in the system by pointing from net exporting to net importing groups. The dominance of the United States in the postwar international trading system is obvious. It enjoyed export surpluses with every region except the tropical raw materials and food-producing countries. On the other hand, Britain's trading position was much weaker than that of the United States. She enjoyed an export surplus only with the Tropics and was a substantial net importer from all other groups.

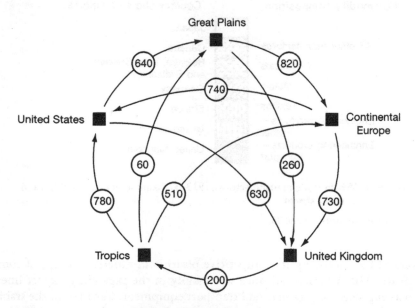

Figure 17 The system of multilateral trade in 1928

Sources: Folke Hilgerdt, *The Network of World Trade*, League of Nations, Geneva, 1942, Table 44, p. 77; Karl-Erik Hansson, 'A General Theory of the System of Multilateral Trade', *American Economic Review*, vol. XLII, 1952, pp. 59–68.

DIMINISHING TRADE HYPOTHESIS

What impressed many economists during the interwar years, however, was not so much the poor export performance of individual countries as the declining importance of foreign trade generally. The slow growth of trade in manufactures between 1913 and 1929, the extreme declines in the volume of this trade in the depression years, and the tendency for the ratio of foreign trade to national income to decline in many countries lent support to the hypothesis of diminishing foreign trade. Stated briefly, this hypothesis implied that technological progress, the spread of industrialization, rising real incomes, and certain other forces at work in the international economy during these years would lead, other things being equal, to a decline in the volume of trade between nations. The technology of advanced industrialization, it was argued, is in part a technology of substitution, which replaces natural materials by synthetics largely produced from local resources. Technological progress also involves economizing in the use of raw materials, reductions in material wastage in production, as well as improvements in retrieving and re-using scrap. All these developments it was felt, would slow down the growth in demand for raw materials, the trade in raw materials, and trade in general, relative to output.

The spread of industrialization was also thought by many economists to be a trade-reducing factor. Although it was agreed that, initially, industrialization would raise the level of trade in capital goods, the diffusion of technological knowledge throughout the world, it was argued, would eventually reduce the existing gaps in comparative cost advantages in such a way as to reduce trade. In particular, the spread of industrialization was expected to lead to considerable import substitution with a consequent dampening of trade in manufactures. Of course, successful industrialization also meant rising living standards in newly industrializing areas, and for this reason other economists argued that, on balance, industrialization would be beneficial to foreign trade. Even so, it was conceded even by these economists that certain kinds of trade including some of the traditional exports of the older industrialized countries, for example simple textile manufactures, would shrink.

Rising real incomes also entered the argument as a factor discouraging trade. Taking Engels' law, that foodstuffs is a declining fraction of rising per capita real incomes, and its corollary, that in advanced industrial countries the service component in the national output tends to rise, a case was made out for a contraction of world trade in foods and agricultural raw materials, and for a declining foreign trade ratio to total output because of a growth in the output of services—such as housing, mass education and government—which are mainly produced and consumed domestically, and which contribute very little to international trade. Another argument, which parallels that of the secular stagnationists of the United States concerning the closing of the American frontier and its impact on domestic economic growth in the 1930s, emphasized the gradual exhaustion of the trade expanding forces generated by the integration into the world economy of previously undeveloped areas. As more and more of these regions were absorbed into the international economy, through expanding world demand and improvements in transport technology, so the trade inducing forces of integration were played out, with a consequent slowing up in the rate of growth of foreign trade relative to total output.

Finally, it was argued that the increasing vulnerability of advanced industrial countries to economic instability would lead to growing political pressure for effective controls over economic activity, which would have a harmful effect on international trade. To achieve economic stability, governments would find themselves compelled to extricate as much as possible of the national economy from a world market which they could not control and thus to expand the domestic economy which they could control at least to some extent. In the absence of effective international means of economic control and stabilization, these defensive actions, along with neo-nationalisms and autarchical postures, were bound to lower the foreign trade ratio and bring about certain of the trends in foreign trade to be observed in the interwar years.

These arguments pointing to a future contraction of world trade were never completely acceptable to all economists, however. For some critics of the diminishing foreign trade hypothesis, industrialization was felt to be beneficial to foreign trade by expanding world demand along new lines. Other economists, while conceding that it was becoming possible to produce almost anything anywhere, were nevertheless prepared to argue that there was little evidence that a significant narrowing of the gap in comparative cost advantages had taken place. The arguments based on Engels' law and the shifting structure of world demand were also thought to be exaggerated. In particular it was felt that the decline in world trade relative to world output was attributable much more to the build-up of barriers to trade and specialization than to any of the other factors advanced by the contractionists. There was also a sneaking suspicion that a rapidly expanding world trade demanded higher rates of economic growth generally than were achieved during the interwar years.

NOTES

1 See S. Kuznets, 'Quantitative Aspects of the Economic Growth of Nations: X-Levels and Structure of Foreign Trade: Long-term Trends', op. cit., Table 1, pp. 4–6. The 13 countries covered by the statistics are the United Kingdom, America, France, Germany, Belgium, Denmark, Norway, Sweden, Canada, Japan, Italy, Switzerland and the Netherlands.

2 H. Tyszynski, 'World Trade in Manufactured Commodities, 1899–1950', *The Manchester School* (Sept., 1951).

SELECTED REFERENCES

Aldcroft, D. H., *From Versailles to Wall Street, 1919–1929* (Harmondsworth, 1987), esp. Chap. 12.

Bairoch, P., *The Economic Development of the Third World Since 1900* (London, 1975).

Baldwin, R. E., 'The Commodity Composition of Trade: Selected Industrial Countries, 1900–1954', *Review of Economics and Statistics* (Feb., 1958), pp. 50–71.

Cairncross, A. K., 'World Trade in Manufactures since 1900', *Economia Internazionale* (Dec., 1955). Reprinted in Cairncross, A. K., *Factors in Economic Development* (London, 1962), Chap. XIV.

Cairncross, A. K., and Faaland, J., 'Long-term Trends in Europe's Trade', *Economic Journal* (Mar., 1952), pp. 25–34.

Hilgerdt, F., *Industrialisation and Foreign Trade* (Geneva, 1945).

Kuznets, S., 'Quantitative Aspects of the Economic Growth of Nations: X-Levels and Structure of Foreign Trade: Long-term Trends', *Economic Development and Cultural Change*, Part II, Jan., 1967.

Latham, A. J. H., *The Depression and the Developing World, 1914–1939* (London, 1981), Chap. III.

Svennilson, I., *Growth and Stagnation in the European Economy* (Geneva, 1954).

Tyszynski, H., 'World Trade in Manufactured Commodities, 1899–1950', *The Manchester School* (Sept., 1951), pp. 272–304.

Woytinsky, W. S., and Woytinsky, E. S., *World Commerce and Governments* (New York, 1955).

Yates, P. L., *Forty Years of Foreign Trade* (London, 1959).

Chapter 15

The Great Depression

An overview

THE UNITED STATES AND THE GREAT DEPRESSION

What were the underlying causes of the Great Depression of the 1930s? Where did it originate, and why was it so widespread, so deep, so long? Was it caused by real or monetary factors? There is no general agreement among economists and economic historians as to the answers to these questions. Practically every feature of the international economy in the 1920s can be argued to have contributed to the great slump, and some economists have, in fact, developed explanations of the depression which take account of such features: for example, the instability of the gold exchange standard,[1] the troubles of primary producers,[2] or the dislocations resulting from World War I, including the trend towards increased protection evident in the post-1918 period.[3] Other economists, however, believe that the origins of the world economic crisis which began in 1929 are to be found in the United States, which, by reducing its capital exports and imports of goods, placed an impossible strain, directly and indirectly, upon the international economy. Indeed, given the sheer economic weight of the United States economy in 1929, representing as it did more than half the industrial world, and the impact it was bound to have because of this on world prices, and through prices on world investment, it is difficult to argue that the depression was somehow forced on the United States by the rest of the world. Consequently, while no one has yet tried systematically to prove that the Great Depression did in fact originate in the United States, even those economists who seek further afield for an explanation of the world slump, concede the overwhelming economic importance of the United States in the world economy at the time.[4]

If the United States was a dominant part of the international economy of the 1920s, what were the underlying causes of its domestic slump? Not surprisingly, given the present worldwide recession, there has been a revival of interest in this question in the United States in recent years. Unfortunately, however, much of the work on the causes of the great slump in the United States has been marred by '[a] polemical and unscientific attempt to demonstrate that a single factor, the behaviour of the money supply and monetary policy, either was solely responsible for the Great Contraction of 1929–33 or played no role at all in the first two years of the contraction'.[5] By using Grainger tests to determine causation, Gordon and Wilcox have attempted to resolve the dispute, and while the use of these more sophisticated econometric techniques do not completely clarify the issues, they conclude from their investigations that the timing of the 1929–30 downturn was partially monetary in origin. In particular they point to the rapid monetary growth in 1928 which came to a halt in 1929, thus aggravating the boom and collapse in both output and the stock market, and to the early bank failures in the United States which, they claim, must have had some contractionary influence through the destruction of money reducing aggregate expenditure. Thus, while they conclude that the majority of the decline in nominal spending in 1929–31 was due to non-monetary factors, monetary influences were 'sufficient to explain one-quarter of the drop of nominal income' in these years.[6]

What combination of deflationary forces, both real and monetary, was present in the United States economy during the years 1929–33? Most important was the decline, from 1925 onwards, in both residential and non-residential construction. The main causes of the decline in housing construction were a catching up with wartime arrears, the falling off in family formations, brought about by a slowing down of population growth in the 1920s, and the shortage of mortgage credit in competition with speculative borrowing in 1928–9. On the other hand, non-residential construction continued at a high rate throughout the decade, but this created actual or latent surplus capacity which any significant curtailment of demand was sure to reveal as serious. A second major source of weakness was to be found in the agricultural sector which was still important enough in the 1920s to exert a powerful influence on the total economy Farm incomes ceased to rise after 1925, as increasing world supplies caused downward pressures on the prices of most agricultural products, and in the great agricultural centres of the United States few manifestations of boom psychology appeared after 1926.

Another development that played a part in the decline of 1929 was the continuing shift to durable consumer goods which had begun around the turn of the century. In the 1920s there was a large expansion of productive capacity in the motor-car, radio, and electrical appliances industries, which was assisted by the introduction during the period of hire purchase, or instalment credit as it is known in the United States, as a means of paying for the more expensive of these items.[7] But the continued growth of sales of these new products required high and expanding levels of consumers' incomes and a high degree of confidence about the future. Towards the end of the 1920s there is evidence that consumer resistance was mounting and that some durable consumer goods markets were becoming saturated. This slowdown in the growth of consumer demand may have been due in part to a tendency for incomes to become progressively maldistributed as growing productivity tended to favour profits at the expense of wages and salaries. According to Kindleberger, 'business was in trouble long before the [Wall Street] crash . . . March [1929] was . . . the peak of automobile production, which fell from 622,000 in that month to 416,000 in September, at the height of the stock market. The industrial production index fell after June, and the decline in industrial production, prices and personal income from August to October was at annual rates of 20, 7½ and 5 per cent'.[8]

The collapse of the stock market quickly revealed the structural weakness of the American banking system. Since the early nineteenth century Americans had insisted upon small, weak banking units that were largely required to provide their own liquidity; as values fell, these banks simply lacked the staying power that a few large banks—their fortunes not tied up with any one locality—would have had.[9] During the depression years, three waves of bank failures shook the economy. The first came at the end of 1930 and the beginning of 1931, just when there were signs of an economic upturn. The second came late in 1931, after the Federal Reserve System had raised the rediscount rate to staunch an outflow of gold. The third, and most disastrous, began in mid-1932 and continued almost to the point of total breakdown of the banking system in the winter of 1932–3. In all, 8,812 banks suspended in the years 1930–3, nearly half the number going under in 1933 alone. The failure of the Federal Reserve Banks to appreciate, let alone use, their money-creating powers, along with the inappropriate monetary policies pursued by them during these years substantially worsened the depression in the United States during the years 1931–3.

OTHER FACTORS IN THE GREAT DEPRESSION

Apart from the collapse of its economy there were a number of other ways in which the United States dealt further blows to the international economy. First, the drying up of American foreign capital flows placed a severe financial strain on a number of debtor countries, with a resultant decline in economic activity in these countries. The primary-producing countries of the periphery were doubly disadvantaged by the decline in American lending, for they not only suffered a direct loss of foreign exchange because of the reduced capital inflow, but they also experienced the indirect effects of the decline in United States lending, which by ensuring tight monetary policies in the major industrial countries of Europe probably contributed to a decline in European long-term lending to the periphery, and to a decline in the growth of demand for the exports of the periphery. Even more damaging for some debtor countries, however, was the Smoot–Hawley Act of June 1930, which substantially increased the American tariff level. Coming on top of the rapid decline in incomes and production in the United States, the tariff increase only served to reduce further American purchases of foreign goods. Indirectly, the American tariff made matters even worse for some European trading nations since in retaliation, other countries, particularly those primary producers whose exports of raw materials had been affected by the tariff, raised their duties markedly on American goods, such as manufactures, which were also their main imports from Europe.

Whatever the relative importance of the effects of the decline in American lending and trade for individual countries, it is likely that their combined effect was more important than any form of 'overproduction' in determining the rapid decline in primary product prices and the export revenues of the periphery during the depression years. For Arthur Lewis, the collapse of primary product prices was decisive in explaining the extent and depth of the depression because its ramifications were so wide. Faced with growing economic difficulties, primary-producing countries were either driven off the gold standard or forced to take other measures to protect their international payments, measures which started a train of restrictions on international trade and payments and harmed industrial producers as well. Thus, Lewis concludes that 'if primary commodity markets had not been so insecure the crisis of 1929 would not have caused a great depression. Prices would not have slumped as violently as they did in 1930, and recovery would have been swifter'.[10] One of the difficulties in the way of accepting Lewis's thesis is the fact that in modern times primary-producing countries have been continuously faced with problems in the marketing of their output, and while it is true that primary producers were in a state of delicate balance in 1929, dependent upon a continuation of the manufacturing boom and upon a continuing flow of international credit, it is not clear in what sense 1929 was so very special.

Apart from structural dislocations in primary product markets, practically every other feature of the international economy in the 1920s can be argued to have contributed to the great depression. The difficulties of postwar adjustment, including the problems of reparations and war debts; the weaknesses of the gold exchange standard, including the possible overvaluation of the pound sterling and the undervaluation of the French franc; the spread of protectionism; and the adoption of more nationalistic economic policies involving a considerable degree of government intervention in the economy, have all been advanced by way of explanation of the origins of the Great Depression, or its length and severity. In assessing the relevance of these factors, however, a number of problems arise. First, empirical verification of economic theories is no guarantee that we can rank elements in the explanation of any particular historical event. Such an observation is particularly relevant in evaluating arguments which explain the depression in terms of war-induced industrial dislocation and primary overproduction. Even though these developments may have operated over a long period of time and may even have been of declining importance in the years immediately preceding the economic collapse of 1930, we cannot legitimately discard them or relegate them to secondary importance until we have determined whether and in what way such changes might have had cumulative effects on the functioning of the international economy. Furthermore, it must be noted that some explanations of the depression deal not so much with origins as such but with changes that might have prevented the depression, reduced its length, or moderated its severity. Thus, Friedman and Schwartz argue that the rigid exchange rates prevailing under the gold standard made the rapid spread of the United States depression to other countries inevitable. They argue further that if, in 1931, other countries had followed Britain and depreciated their currencies promptly in terms of gold instead of waiting for years, international liquidity would have increased quickly and the vicious spiral of deflation, import restrictions, and more deflation, would have been cut short.[11] Arthur Lewis suggests that the maintenance of agricultural prices through the operation of buffer stock schemes would have had a similar dampening effect on the depression.

Kindleberger also explains the severity of the 1929 depression in terms of the malfunctioning of the international economy. He believes that the international economy is basically unstable, and that in the 1920s this instability was aggravated by the financial distortions resulting from the war. This instability, he argues, could have been overcome only by effective international leadership which involved: (a) maintaining a relatively open market for distress goods; (b) providing counter-cyclical long-term lending; and (c) discounting in crisis. In the nineteenth century up to 1913, Britain provided the leadership. After 1918, the British could not and the United States would not play the role of leader. Instead, the United States destroyed the trade mechanism through the Smoot–Hawley Tariff; it was unwilling to serve as a lender of last resort in 1931; and it engaged in aggressive currency depreciation by bidding up the price of gold and silver.[12] The need for some form of effective international leadership during the depression years is not in doubt. Yet at the time there was no overwhelming reason why the United States should adopt such a role. It is certainly true that after World War II, because of America's opposition to the spread of communism and its deepening involvement in international economic affairs, it was prepared to exercise such economic leadership, but between the wars American international economic activity was largely peripheral to a continued and overwhelming commitment to domestic economic expansion. In any case, given the fundamental weaknesses in the American banking system, it is doubtful whether it could have effectively exercised the international leadership necessary. In short, if the United States could not save itself from so severe a depression, how could it be expected to save the rest of the world?

LONG-RUN FACTORS AND THE GREAT DEPRESSION

As the economic crisis deepened in the United States there were some econo-mists who claimed that the depression of 1929–33 marked not merely a cyclical downturn but the start of a period of secular stagnation for the American economy. The leading exponent of the secular stagnation thesis in the United States was Alvin Hansen, who strongly stressed the importance of the interrelation between population growth and aggregate demand. Com-pared with the nineteenth century, he argued, the pace of economic develop-ment in the United States after World War I had begun to tail off. Looking for the causes of this slowdown, Hansen found four principal factors: a declin-ing population growth, the disappearance of the geographical frontier, the growth in the absolute volume of saving, and a tendency for new techniques of production to be capital-saving. Hansen saw the expanding population of nineteenth-century America as one of the mainsprings of its growth. How-ever, as the rate of population growth declined in this century, because of a declining birth rate and rigid immigration restrictions, and as the geo-graphical frontier vanished, the investment outlets for America's ever-growing volume of saving declined. For these reasons, he expected severe depressions like that of the 1930s to become the rule rather than the excep-tion, unless compensatory action was taken by the government through the expansion of public demand.[13] The high level of prosperity enjoyed in the United States after 1945 put the stagnation thesis under a cloud. But if the stagnation was too much coloured by the special circumstances of the 1930s, the recent long boom has likewise proved to have been much influenced by the special circumstances of the post-World War II period. Moreover, with the onset of a worldwide recession in the 1970s, attention has once again focused on the possible existence of long-term periodicities or rhythms in the evolution of the international capitalist system.

We have already had occasion in an earlier chapter in this book to refer to the dynamic theory of world economic growth put forward by W. W. Ros-tow.[14] How does Rostow view the depression of the interwar years in terms of his theory? For him, it was a period of chronic surpluses in primary products, caused in part by the distortions of the war and postwar years, and in part by the chronically depressed state of demand. Primary producers in general suf-fered a relative decline in income, limiting their capacity to purchase indus-trial goods and to invest in new methods and techniques. In particular, their catastrophic loss of income between 1929 and 1933 was one major factor accounting for the depth of the depression throughout the world. Most advanced industrial countries, on the other hand, faced a double structural adjustment after 1920: an adjustment to the potentialities of cheapened sup-plies of foodstuffs and raw materials, and an adjustment to the potentialities of a new leading sector complex in the form of the internal combustion engine, electricity and chemicals. Whereas the United States largely benefited from successful adaptation to both kinds of structural change in the 1920s, Britain took advantage of the favourable terms of trade, but because of chronic unemployment and the depressed state of domestic demand, she failed to make the necessary structural adjustments to her manufacturing industry. In general, the adoption of policies of agricultural protection meant that continental European countries sacrificed to some degree the benefits of the lower world prices of primary products and, like Britain, they failed to make the structural shifts to new leading sectors at a pace sufficient to avoid abnormally high levels of unemployment, even during the best years of the 1920s.[15] Thus, Rostow finds the causes of the Great Depression of the 1930s in the real forces underlying the long-run growth and development of the world economy.

One other explanation of the depth and duration of the depression in the United States sees it as the outgrowth of secular trends in the development process.[16] By the 1920s, the American economy had entered an era characterized by the emergence of dramatically new demand patterns and investment opportunities. The failure to respond to these new opportunities derived from the difficulty of altering technology and labour skills to meet these new demands at a time of severe financial instability. Moreover, recovery was lacking in the 1930s because at the time the long-run potentials for growth were shifting under the influence of a secular transformation to sectors whose presence in the aggregate economy was still relatively insignificant. The growth of these industries was, in turn, a response to the emergence of new demand patterns of an increasingly affluent population.

In Bernstein's own words:

> The Great Depression must be viewed as an event triggered by random historical and institutional circumstances, but prolonged by the timing of the process of long-run industrial development in the United States— in particular, by a transition in thes tructure of consumer and investment demand at the higher levels of income reached by the 1920s. The financial machinery of the American economy, caught in heavy deflation, was not equal to the task of pushing open the doors to the patterns of growth characteristic of the [post World War II] era.[17]

There is enough evidence available to suggest that both long-run and short-run factors were operating to bring about the depression of the 1930s, but as yet we have little understanding of how this complex of forces interacted to produce a worldwide depression. Even Rostow's wide-ranging dynamic theory of world growth is deficient in this respect. Much work still remains to be done in analysing one of the most significant events of this century.

NOTES

1 R. Triffin, *Gold and the Dollar Crisis* (New Haven, 1960).
2 Sir W. A. Lewis, *Economic Survey, 1919–1939* (London, 1949), pp. 174–96.
3 H. W. Arndt, *Economic Lessons of the Nineteen Thirties* (London, 1944).
4 See, for example, Lewis, op. cit., p. 175.
5 R. J. Gordon and J. A. Wilcox, 'Monetarist Interpretations of the Great Depression: an Evaluation and Critique', in K. Brunner (ed.), *The Great Depression Revisited* (Boston, 1981), p. 94. The protagonists in the debate are M. Friedman and A. J. Schwartz, *The Great Contraction, 1929–1933* (Princeton, 1965) and P. Temin, *Did Monetary Forces Cause the Great Depression?* (New York, 1976).
6 R. J. Gordon and I. A. Wilcox, 'Monetarist Interpretation of the Great Depression: a Rejoinder', in Brunner, op. cit., pp. 167–8, 171, 172.
7 By 1925, the volume of instalment credit outstanding in the United States was $1,375m., and by 1929, $3,000m.
8 C. P. Kindleberger, *The World in Depression, 1929–1939* (Berkeley, 1973), p. 117.
9 The problem of bank failures was apparent well before the outset of the depression in 1929. Over the nine-year period 1921–9, 5,411 banks failed. Most of them were small country banks, but some were national banks and among the largest in the country.
10 Lewis, op. cit., p. 196.
11 Friedman and Schwartz, op. cit., p. 636.
12 Kindleberger, op. cit., Chap. XIV.
13 A. H. Hansen, *Full Recovery or Stagnation* (New York, 1938). A more recent explanation of the origins of the Great Depression based on declining population growth is that of C. L. Barber, 'On the Origins of the Great Depression', *Southern Economic Journal* (Jan., 1978). Although his view of the population decline is a general one, he places particular emphasis on the rate of population growth in the United States and Germany, the two countries cited by Lewis as industrial centres from which the Great Depression spread.
14 See Chapter 10.
15 W. W. Rostow, *The World Economy: History and Prospect* (London, 1978), Chap. XV.
16 M. A. Bernstein, *The Great Depression. Ddayed Recovery and Economic Change in America, 1929–1939* (Cambridge, 1987).
17 Bernstein, ibid., p. 40.

SELECTED REFERENCES

Barber, C. L., 'On the Origins of the Great Depression', *Southern Economic Journal* (Jan., 1978).
Bernstein, M. A., *The Great Depression. Delayed Recovery and Economic Change in America, 1929–1939* (Cambridge, 1987).
Brunner, K. (ed.), *The Great Depression Revisited* (Boston, 1981).
Fearon, P., *The Origins and Nature of the Great Slump, 1929–1932* (London, 1979).
Friedman, M., and Schwartz, A. J., *The Great Contraction, 1929–1933* (Princeton, 1965).
Kindleberger, C. P., *The World in Depression, 1929–1939* (Berkeley, 1973).
Lewis, Sir W. A., *Economic Survey, 1919–1939* (London, 1949).
Rostow, W. W., *The World Economy: History and Prospect* (London, 1978).

Temin, P., *Did Monetary Forces Cause the Great Depression?* (New York, 1976).
Van der Wee, H. (ed.), *The Great Depression Revisited. Essays on the Economics of the Thirties* (The Hague, 1972).

Part III

The post-1945 international economy

Chapter 16

Planning the future international economy and the transitional period, 1944–50

The 1930s witnessed the collapse of the multilateral trade and payments system which had emerged in the late nineteenth century. In the field of commercial policy, severe restrictions, often of a discriminatory nature, tended to prevail, while the international payments system degenerated into a multitude of exchange controls. In consequence, international flows of capital and labour were severely retarded, and the future of world trade appeared to be particularly gloomy. With the outbreak of war the financial and commercial restrictions on trade were intensified and trade between nations was further reduced. Even while the war was still in progress, however, it was realized that strenuous efforts to reduce trade and exchange barriers would be needed to ensure the proper functioning of the international economy in the postwar years. Preliminary discussions along these lines followed the signing of the Mutual Aid Agreement between the United States and Britain in 1941, which, although predominantly concerned with lend-lease arrangements, also committed the two countries to co-operate in international economic affairs after the war. Subsequently, numerous discussions were held in Washington and London with a view to producing a set of rules or a code of conduct in international monetary affairs to be implemented after the war. At the beginning of these discussions, two plans submitted by the British negotiators (the Keynes Plan) and the American negotiators (the White Plan) were considered. The first proposed the establishment of a clearing union and the creation of a large amount of credit (bancor) to be allotted among all trading nations. It was envisaged that the $35 billion of bancor to be created would not only be used for financing balance of payments deficits but would also serve to help the financing of postwar reconstruction. This plan was unacceptable to the U.S. negotiators who claimed it had inflationary tendencies and because its operations would be too automatic, and not allow member country governments enough discretion in their balance of payments policies. The White Plan, which concentrated on the setting-up of international institutions under the control of member countries, was then debated and out of the many discussions in which compromises were reached, emerged the International Monetary Fund and the International Bank for Reconstruction and

Development. At an international conference held at Bretton Woods, New Hampshire, in July 1944, the agreements to set up these institutions were finalized by the delegates from 44 nations.

THE INTERNATIONAL MONETARY FUND

The ultimate goal of the Fund's operation was to create the conditions under which the transfer of goods and services from one country to another could take place unfettered by restrictions on trade or controls over international payments. To achieve this end, the Fund has three main objectives, each of which clearly reflected the lessons learnt during the interwar years. First, a multilateral system of payments based on a worldwide convertibility of currencies was to be achieved through the elimination of exchange controls.[1] In addition, reasonable stability of exchange rates was to be maintained, competitive currency devaluations avoided and, where exchange adjustments were necessary, these were to be carried out in an orderly fashion. Finally, to enable member nations to pursue domestic policies of full employment, the Fund undertook the virtually impossible task of combining exchange rate stability with national independence in monetary and fiscal matters.

To eliminate foreign exchange restrictions and thus eventually to restore currency convertibility, members of the Fund were to refrain from imposing new exchange restrictions on current account transactions after the war and to avoid practices that discriminated against any currency. But, realizing that exchange controls might be necessary in the difficult early postwar years, the Fund allowed for a transitional period of readjustment and adaptation ending in 1952, after which members still retaining exchange restrictions were to consult with officers of the IMF about their continuance. Exchange restrictions on capital account transactions were not forbidden but were retained as a guard against the destabilizing effects of flights of capital on a country's balance of payments. Indeed, the Fund expected members to introduce controls to prevent such capital movements. Currency discrimination was also sanctioned by the IMF under certain conditions, particularly where a currency was officially designated a scarce currency. As long as it was so designated, member countries were to be permitted to impose discriminatory exchange controls on the use of that currency.

To achieve stability of exchange rates and an acceptable mechanism of international adjustment, the Fund Agreement borrowed some elements from the gold standard and some from the rival system of flexible exchange rates. Thus, under the provisions of the IMF Agreement, each member country was obliged to establish a par value for its currency fixed either in terms of gold or of the dollar, and to peg the exchange rate of its currency against other currencies within a range of 1 per cent above or below that par value. Within this 2 per cent band, the market rate of exchange could move subject to market forces but, if the market rate approached the lower or higher limits of the band ('support points'), the central bank would be required to prevent the exchange rate from moving outside the band. To deal with pressures on these exchange rates due to short-term disturbances in a country's balance of payments or to the difficulties associated with the early stages of more deep-seated payments problems, the Fund established a pool of currencies upon which members could draw. This was made up of the contributions of members, based on assigned quotas, the individual size of which was determined by the level of the contributing country's gross national product and its importance in world trade. The subscriptions themselves were to consist of two components: 25 per cent of the quota was to be contributed in the form of gold and dollars and 75 per cent in the member's own currency. Apart from determining a country's drawing rights on the Fund, the size of its quota also determined a country's voting rights in the Fund's deliberations. The largest quotas were initially assigned to the United States ($2,750m.), Britain ($1,300m.), China ($550m.), France ($450m.) and India ($400m.).[2] Provision was made for a periodic review of quotas and changes in quotas could be made if the Fund deemed such a step desirable for the proper functioning of the international monetary system.

To deal with short-run balance of payments difficulties, members were to be allowed to draw on the foreign currencies held in the pool so that these drawing rights, in effect, provided a form of reserves supplemental to the members' own international reserves. In making such a drawing, a member country would surrender domestic currency to the Fund equal in value to the foreign currencies drawn. A member drawing from the Fund was also expected to make a future repurchase of the domestic currency thus transferred to the Fund with gold and/or convertible currencies. A drawing within the gold tranche (up to the value of the gold subscribed by a member to the Fund) was to be automatic but, to obtain a larger drawing, a member would be required to gain the consent of the Fund. The repurchase provisions were included to preserve the efficacy of the Fund by ensuring that, in the short run, its stocks of currencies in strong demand would not be rapidly depleted. However, where widespread drawings made a currency scarce in the Fund, additional supplies of it could be obtained from the scarce currency country in exchange for gold or by borrowing the currency from the member country. Alternatively, the Fund could declare the currency scarce as noted above, and the Fund could take steps to ration its meagre supply of the currency.

In order to deal with a fundamental disequilibrium in a country's balance of payments the Fund turned to supervised flexibility of exchange rates. Members were to be allowed to change the initial par value of their currencies (i.e. devalue or revalue) only in order to correct fundamental disequilibria. Such a change was to be approved by the Fund—unless the change altered the exchange rate by no more than 10 per cent of the currency's initial par value.

The new international monetary system was constructed on the supposition that each member country would experience fairly regular fluctuations in its balance of payments, with deficits in some years and surpluses in others. Over a period of several years, however, it was expected that surpluses would tend to offset deficits. When a particular deficit was very severe, and a country's international currency reserves fell to a dangerous level, it could approach the Fund for a drawing to carry it over its difficult period. But if the payments deficit persisted over a period of several years and the country thus had to make frequent use of the Fund's resources, a devaluation of its currency would then become acceptable to the Fund, especially if the country's domestic economic policies were not the most immediate cause of the difficulties. A country with a persistent surplus in its balance of payments, on the other hand, would simply amass reserves and would not be under any monetary pressures to rectify the situation comparable to those faced by the persistent debtor country whose reserves were being depleted. But the Fund's powers under the scarce currency clause were deemed sufficient either to deter the surplus country from continuing to amass reserves or to compel it to eliminate its payments surplus by an upward revaluation of its currency or by some other such measure. When the international monetary system was functioning smoothly, the Fund's operations were expected to be of minor importance. On the other hand, should imbalances and other difficulties arise, the Fund was considered to possess ample reserves and sufficient powers to return the world monetary system quickly to stability.

THE INTERNATIONAL BANK FOR RECONSTRUCTION AND DEVELOPMENT

The other institution set up at Bretton Woods in 1944 was the International Bank for Reconstruction and Development (IBRD), commonly called the World Bank. Originally designed to help finance postwar reconstruction, the Bank was later to help extend aid to the developing nations. At first it was intended that the Bank's loan capital, which was set at $10,000m., would be subscribed by member countries, each of which was asked to provide 20 per cent of its subscription (2 per cent in gold or dollars and 18 per cent in its own currency) when the Bank began operations. The other 80 per cent remained on call to meet the Bank's future obligations. By 1959, however, the Bank's capital had been increased to $21,000m., and the bulk of the Bank's lending resources was derived from borrowing in capital markets through the issue of bonds which were guaranteed by the governments of the countries in whose currencies the particular issues were denominated. Furthermore, the function of the Bank had been extended to cover development loans to member countries for specified projects. Such loans were normally tied to the direct foreign exchange costs of the imports needed for the completion of these projects, and the IBRD was given powers to stipulate the foreign country from which the required imports were to be purchased. These development loans were to be repaid in the currencies originally made available, and borrowers were to be charged rates of interest determined by the prevailing rates in capital markets where the Bank's bonds were sold. The Bank was also allowed to lend to private enterprise in member countries.[3] Finally, in addition to its lending function, the IBRD was given powers to offer technical assistance in the use of the funds it provided and to conduct general surveys to help member countries assess their economic potential and prepare development programmes.

THE GENERAL AGREEMENT ON TARIFFS AND TRADE

The efforts to re-establish multilateralism through the setting up of the IMF would have been defeated if trade controls, over which the Fund had no authority, replaced arbitrary controls over international payments. But experience in the 1930s had underlined the close connection between exchange controls and trade restrictions and consequently, between 1943 and 1945, when the formation of the IMF was under consideration, American, British and Canadian officials were also discussing the possibility of extending the principle of international organization into the field of commercial policy. In 1947 a conference called by the Economic and Social Council of the United Nations (ECOSOC) began working towards the establishment of an International Trade Organization (ITO) with a view to extending to trade the same philosophy underpinning the IMF in the monetary field. At the same time, the United States, under its Trade Agreements Act, began talks with a view to the reduction of worldwide import duties. At Geneva, in 1947, negotiations organized by ECOSOC produced the General Agreement on Tariffs and Trade (GATT), which was to be applied until the full ITO was concluded. The provisions for the latter organization were incorporated in the Havana Charter of 1948. However, the United States and a number of other countries refused to ratify the proposed ITO. These countries objected to the provisions relating to full employment policies, international cartels, and the stabilization of primary product prices. At the same time, the success of the first GATT session in Geneva in 1947 did much to reduce the urgency of the creation of such an organization.

GATT incorporated in it the objective enshrined in the U.S. Trade Agreements Act of 1934 (renewed in 1945) which allowed the U.S. administration to negotiate reciprocal tariff reductions with other countries.[4] Thus, the procedure adopted at the negotiations in Geneva in 1947, in which 23 countries participated, involved bilateral bargaining on a product by product basis to obtain the maximum reductions possible in existing duties. Concessions agreed on in this manner were generalized by being granted to all other countries represented at the conference by the adoption of the most-favoured-nation principle. Altogether 123 sets of negotiations covering 50,000 items were completed and incorporated in the GATT, which was signed on 30 October 1947.

The code of conduct included in GATT involved two major principles: first, a multilateral and non-discriminatory approach to international trade and, second, condemnation of quantitative trade restrictions. The first principle was implemented through the inclusion in the code of the most-favoured-nation clause, under which preferential trade arrangements designed to favour one nation over others were prohibited. Exceptions to the rule were allowed, however, and included those preferential systems that had existed in mid-1939, the formation of customs unions or free trade areas and the use of discrimination for temporary balance of payments purposes or by developing countries to aid their economic growth. As for quantitative restrictions, the code precluded them in principle but allowed exceptions in certain circumstances, namely, for short-term balance of payments purposes and to allow developing countries to protect their infant industries. Finally, an escape clause allowed a contracting party to impose quotas to regulate internal marketing of a product so long as it concurrently restricted domestic production of the commodity to such an extent that imports maintained the same share of total domestic consumption as before the imposition of the restrictions. The first GATT allowed for the setting up of a Secretariat with its headquarters in Geneva and thus the General Agreement became institutionalized. The basic philosophy underlying the GATT code of conduct was that each contracting party should enjoy reasonable access to the markets of its trading partners in return for offering the same sort of access to its domestic markets to foreign exporters. In this way, world trade would expand rapidly with all countries experiencing fair trading relations.

As a result of these arrangements in the monetary and commercial policy fields, the countries which joined these postwar international economic organizations could expect at least to avoid the enormous problems they had encountered in their international economic relations in the 1930s. The architects of these institutions, by establishing codes of conduct in international monetary and commercial dealings acceptable to member countries, expected that a postwar international economy would emerge relatively unimpeded by quantitative restrictions on trade and exchange controls on current account transactions.

POSTWAR RECONSTRUCTION

Many parts of the world experienced difficult times in the early postwar years. A long war had deprived consumers in many countries of basic commodities and semi-luxuries and personal savings had grown as a consequence of these shortages. When peace returned, therefore, consumers were anxious to use these savings to satisfy their unfulfilled desires for all types of goods and services. On the other hand, in other countries, especially in Europe, the war had reduced millions of people to desperate poverty. In addition, much of the productive equipment in the warring nations had been destroyed or replacement and new investment had been delayed, so that whole industrial complexes required rebuilding. As a result, the demand for goods and services for consumption and investment purposes outran the available world supplies, while the problem of increasing output was made all the more difficult by the problems of the change-over from wartime to peacetime production. The consequent excess demand that persisted throughout the immediate postwar years produced tremendous inflationary pressures in many countries, which were only partly contained in some by the continuation of wartime rationing and other physical controls. Other countries were not so fortunately placed, and eventually currency reforms were needed to put a stop to runaway inflation. The shortage of fuel and the inability of the agricultural sector to provide the population with adequate supplies of food added to the extreme economic difficulties which existed in Europe.

For several years after the end of the war, then, the international economy experienced abnormal conditions. The only major country to enter into world trade and commerce without undue stress on its balance of payments was the United States, which had emerged from the war in a highly favourable economic position. For a number of years many of its industrial competitors were barely able to meet domestic requirements for manufactures and were thus unable to compete with American exports in foreign markets. Furthermore, European demand for foodstuffs, raw materials, and capital goods was such that the United States was able to benefit considerably from supplying part of the demand, and consequently recorded a highly favourable balance of trade with Europe.[5] Such a situation led directly to a dollar shortage which became almost universal in the late 1940s.

From 1945 to 1948 world production rose and economic recovery continued, but in Europe generally the rate of growth of industrial output was too slow to catch up with demand or to increase exports sufficiently to produce external equilibrium. In the late 1940s, however, two developments occurred which, perhaps more than any others, were responsible for transforming the economic situation in Europe. These were the European Recovery Programme (ERP), inaugurated in April 1948, and the devaluations of September 1949.

The European Recovery Programme, largely inspired by a fear that any further economic deterioration in Western Europe would make the countries in the region easy prey for a Communist take-over, was proposed by the American Secretary of State, George Marshall, in 1947. This programme, aimed at the economic reconstruction of Europe, called Marshall Aid, was to be implemented through the Economic Co-operation Administration (ECA) in the United States and the Organization for European Economic Co-operation (OEEC), established in Europe in April 1948. The OEEC comprised 16 European nations. From April 1948 to the end of 1951, over $11,000m. was provided through the ECA to Europe, France, Britain, West Germany, the Netherlands and Italy receiving 75 per cent of the total. After 1951, Europe received a further $2,600m., mainly in the period up to mid-1953. The aid offered under the ERP took the form of grants of commodities produced predominantly in the United States, foodstuffs, fertilizers, fodder and fuel initially, but, by 1951, raw materials, semi-processed goods and machinery accounted for more than half the commodities supplied under the Plan.[6]

While Marshall Aid represented only about 5 per cent of the recipient countries' gross national products, because of its strategic importance for industrial construction, its economic impact was quickly noticeable. Total manufacturing output in the OEEC countries rose by 13 per cent in 1949 and by 1952 was 39 per cent above the 1948 level. While many other factors undoubtedly contributed to European recovery during these years, the contribution of Marshall Aid remains a very significant one.

The other major event which helped the European recovery, and which led to an improvement in the balance of payments of several countries, was the widespread use of currency devaluation in September 1949. In that month, 19 countries, accounting for almost two-thirds of total world trade, devalued their currencies relative to the dollar by approximately 30 per cent. The basic reason for the devaluations was the distortions which had developed in the pattern of international payments. Even before the outbreak of World War II, exchange rates had not been sufficiently harmonious to produce high levels of production and employment in all trading countries, while the war and the abnormal conditions after 1945 had created new forces to change the trade and payments patterns in the world economy. For these reasons, the initial par values of many currencies established in 1946–7 were out of line with each other and did not truly reflect the differences in domestic purchasing power of the currencies of the various trading countries. As a result the countries with overvalued currencies were not capable of earning the export receipts needed to buy urgently required foreign imports.

The position in Britain, in particular, is worthy of special mention. During the war she had liquidated a large part of her overseas assets to obtain funds out of which to purchase war materials. War demands also forced her to incur vast debts to other countries in the form of accumulated sterling balances, as well as to borrow heavily from the United States. Late in 1945, for these and other reasons, she was forced to seek further financial assistance from the United States. Under the Anglo-American Financial Agreement of July 1946, the United States undertook to advance $3,750m. to Britain in the next four years, while lend-lease and other debt obligations were consolidated into a lump sum of $650m. In return for this aid, Britain undertook to make sterling freely convertible on and after 15 July 1947. The size of the credit proved to be totally inadequate to Britain's needs, however. Within 12 months, over $2,000m. of the loans had been used up and, when the pound was made convertible in mid-1947, the rest disappeared overnight forcing the suspension of convertibility of the pound by the end of August.

Despite Britain's difficulties, economic recovery was rapid in Europe after 1947 and, confronted by sellers' markets, exporters had few problems with which to contend. By 1949, however, the picture was changing. The increased availability of goods in Europe and North America now favoured the buyer and price considerations once again became decisive in export markets. Overvalued European currencies, not a serious hindrance to exports as long as shortages persisted, now became a major obstacle. A revision of exchange values was inevitable. Britain went first, devaluing the pound by 30.5 per cent on 18 September 1949. Within a few days many other countries followed her example, including all the sterling area (except Pakistan) and 11 West European nations.

The improvement in the balance of payments position of a number of countries that followed devaluation was helped by the outbreak of the Korean War in 1950, which raised the level of world demand considerably. In addition, European production continued to expand, thus reducing the region's dependence on foreign goods, especially those of the United States. At the same time its export capacity was increased. Intra-European trade was also beginning to revive with the return to more normal trading conditions. By 1952 the international economic situation had improved considerably. Perhaps the most significant features of the improvement were the disappearance of the American payments surplus in the second half of the year and the general increase in the gold and dollar holdings of other countries. Although the existing controls over trade and payments were to last in varying degrees of intensity from country to country for the remainder of the decade, by 1952 the extreme pressures of the immediate postwar years had almost disappeared.

NOTES

1 Convertibility of a currency is a term that has undergone a definitional change. Whereas under the nineteenth-century gold standard it signified convertibility into gold on demand, since 1940, at least, it has referred to a situation in which there are no restrictions on the conversion of one currency into another for current account purposes.
2 The Soviet Union was given a quota of $1,200m. but declined membership of the Fund.
3 It has always been the Bank's policy not to offer loans where funds are obtainable in private capital markets on reasonable terms. It aims at promoting private investment, not competing against it.
4 The Americans had embarked on a programme of trade liberalization in the 1930s when, under the Reciprocal Trade Agreements Act of 1934, the President was

authorized to sign commercial agreements with other countries reducing existing American duties by as much as 50 per cent in exchange for parallel concessions. This Act was renewed in 1945 for a further three years to allow the administration to negotiate up to 25 per cent from the rates current at the beginning of that year.
5 Other temperate zone countries also experienced large foreign demands for their primary products.
6 Had the Keynes Plan been chosen instead of the White Plan, the need for Marshall Aid would have been minimized.

SELECTED REFERENCES

Behrman, J. N., and Schmidt, W. E., *International Economics* (New York, 1957), esp. Chaps. XVI–XVIII.
Ellsworth, P. T., *The International Economy*, 3rd edn. (New York, 1964).
Horie, S., *The International Monetary Fund* (London, 1964).
Milward, A., *The Reconstruction of Western Europe 1945–51* (London, 1984).
Scammell, W. M., *International Monetary Policy* (London, 1961).
Tew, B., *International Monetary Co-operation* (London, 1960).
Van der Wee, H., *Prosperity and Upheaval: the World Economy 1945–1980* (Harmondsworth, 1986).
Yeager, L., *International Monetary Relations* (New York, 1966).

Chapter 17

The international economy since 1950

ECONOMIC GROWTH, AN OVERVIEW

The Golden Age, 1950–73

By the early 1950s the first stage in the postwar recovery of the international economy had largely been completed. The European economies had been reconstructed, and normal peacetime production had been resumed in most of them. Inflation had given way to price stability and currency overvaluation had been corrected by the widespread devaluations in 1949. These signs of widespread economic improvement meant that, in contrast to the depressed conditions of the 1930s and the grim austerity of the war and early postwar years, the 1950s and 1960s were decades of rapidly rising living standards for the greater part of the population in Western Europe, North America, and Oceania. From 1950 to 1973, real GDP of the top 16 OECD[1] countries rose at an average annual rate of 4.8 per cent while labour productivity (GDP per man-hour) grew at a high rate of around 4.5 per cent a year on average. This transformation in living standards was epitomized in the new and ever-widening range of consumer durables which quickly became an accepted part of the consumption patterns of the people in these countries. Where income levels did not allow immediate purchase of these goods, greater security of employment increased the attractiveness of living on credit, which permitted a more rapid accumulation of these material goods than would otherwise have occurred. In this age of affluence, advertising took on a new importance and television provided the advertisers with a new medium with which to practise their highly specialized selling techniques. But the increased importance of advertising not only reflected the existence of growing affluence but it was also a necessary adjunct to modern industrial technology.

The new techniques that brought about the increase in industrial productivity which largely supported the rise in living standards that was apparent during these years almost inevitably demanded large-scale operations. In secondary and tertiary industries, 'bigness' became a necessity and oligopoly the predominant form of market structure. Since the size of the competing

firms and the large financial resources over which they had command, plus the
need to guarantee some minimum level of profitability to satisfy shareholders,
ruled out price-cutting, firms resorted increasingly to competitive advertising, the promotion of after-sales service, and other forms of non-price
competition. Innovation was another form of inter-firm competition, since
product improvement and the development of completely new products
quickly gave a firm an advantage over its rivals. The threatened loss of markets and of profits was more than enough to keep most large business enterprises abreast of current technical developments and, in so far as these changes
could be affected by what the firm itself did, particularly by its programme of
research and development, the level of investment in the enterprise was raised
correspondingly. Investment was not only the means of ensuring the short-
run efficiency of the firm's plant and equipment, it also became the means of
promoting the long-run growth of the firm.

The shift of emphasis from short-run to long-run considerations evident in
the investment behaviour of large-scale businesses is also to be found in
contemporary macro-economic policy theorizing, where discussion of the
short-run problem of full employment gave way to considerations of the long-
run problem of economic growth. Having achieved fairly high and stable
levels of employment in most developed countries, attention turned to ways
and means of increasing a country's productive capacity, in the sense of
raising the level of output that can be produced when all factors of production
are fully employed, through varying both the quantity and quality of its
available stock of capital as well as by improving the quality of its human
resources. For reasons of political power or prestige or because of the consequent rise in living standards, securing high rates of economic growth
became an important object of economic policy.

Beneath the welter of affluence there developed a desire to improve the
economic welfare of the poorest countries of the world. This desire was the
outcome of several motives. The threat posed to their affluence by the poverty
and misery that abounded in these underdeveloped regions was keenly felt in
most Western countries, especially as this fear was reinforced by the appeal of
Communism as a political ideology and an economic model for the political,
social and economic development of the underdeveloped world. It was also
felt that, while a few advanced countries with special positions to protect
might be hurt by the changes brought about by successful economic development, the economic benefits to be gained from an all-round rise in living
standards and the greater opportunities for trade between nations that would
arise as countries became richer would more than offset these losses. Furthermore, the granting of independence to former European colonies in other
continents committed the former colonial powers to the granting of favourable treatment to these emerging nations to ease the burdens of adjusting to
their newly-won independence. No doubt part of the interest of people in
developed countries in the fate of their counterparts in the underdeveloped

countries stemmed also from genuine altruism, a fact which is most evident in the succession of voluntary appeals for food, medical supplies, and clothing for the inhabitants of the stricken areas of the world. Whatever the motives, however, the channelling of aid from the developed to the underdeveloped countries of the world represented a major change in the field of international capital flows as compared with the pre-1939 period, while the concerted efforts to overcome the problem of economic underdevelopment remained of immense significance for the future of the international economy.

As a result of this support and of their own effort, the developing market economies as a group experienced high rates of economic growth, averaging around 6 per cent annually between 1960 and 1973. Not all developing countries achieved this average rate, while per capita growth rates were well below those of the advanced countries due to higher rates of population growth. The centrally-planned economies also recorded high annual growth rates between 1950 and 1973, averaging close to 5 per cent increases in GDP.[2]

Limited Growth and Economic Problems, 1973–90

This period of extensive growth came to an end after the boom of 1973. World inflation had risen from 5.9 per cent in 1971 to 9.6 per cent in 1973 and was to exceed 15 per cent in 1974, so that national monetary and fiscal policies were increasingly directed towards controlling price increases. In addition to a commodities boom in 1972–3, an expansionary monetary policy in the United States and the convergence of the trade cycles of most industrial countries for the first time in the post-war era, all contributed to the boom. As it subsided, the consequent decline in industrial production in every major advanced country was worsened by contractionary monetary and fiscal policies increasingly implemented against the inflationary forces stimulated by the boom. Conditions changed in the world economy after 1973, with higher inflation rates and higher unemployment levels. At first, the industrial world moved into recession throughout 1974 and most of 1975 at a time when the trend towards higher prices was exacerbated by the substantial increases in oil prices of late 1974. Recovery commenced late in 1975 but, despite a healthy 5.2 per cent increase in real GDP for the OECD as a whole in 1976, economic growth was uneven and averaged only 2.8 per cent for the period 1974–80, compared with an average of just under 5 per cent for the years from 1950 to 1973. At the same time, productivity declined considerably. To a large extent, the lower growth rate of the 1970s was the result of the restrictive economic policies pursued by national governments in their attempts to deal with the problem of inflation. Indeed, guided by the monetarist approach to economic policy, the long-run growth policy which had been so successful between 1950 and 1973 succumbed to the short-run policy of containing inflation, despite its impact on economic growth and employment. During the period 1973–80, consumer prices rose at an average 10 per cent compared with 4 per cent from 1950 to 1973, while unemployment grew substantially in all OECD countries to exceed 4 per cent by 1975 and 5 per cent by 1979.

A second oil price hike in 1979–80 largely accounted for a second major recession in the world economy between 1981 and 1982. While recovery commenced in 1984, economic performance was patchy during the remainder of the 1980s. Real GDP for the OECD recorded an average annual growth rate below 3 per cent. Inflation rates were reduced from 7.5 per cent in 1982 to 2.7 per cent in 1986, but then crept up to around 4 per cent on average towards the end of the decade, while unemployment remained persistently around 8 per cent. Developing countries were also affected in much the same way as developed countries. The exception was a group of the newly-industrializing countries[3] that were able to maintain high growth rates throughout this difficult period.

Changes in the 1990s and Beyond

Another change in the world economy began in the 1990s as economic globalization accelerated. International economic relations brought economies even closer together, and a new approach to domestic economic policy became evident, under which many of the elements of a *laissez-faire* economy became popular, just at a time when central-planning and Communism became increasingly unacceptable. Worldwide economic policies were concerned with short-run economic objectives, such as the containment of inflation, economic efficiency, increased productivity, and greater profitability. These objectives were associated with others, including small government, privatization of state-owned enterprises, downsizing of the workforce in private industry and the public service, and labour market and other microeconomic reforms. In these changed circumstances, it was argued, the free market mechanism would lead to economic growth and eventual full employment. By the 1990s, however, the new approach has led to high and intractable unemployment rates in some countries and the disappearance of minimum wage thresholds in others, producing a new class of people, the 'working poor'. In addition, a widening of the gap between the rich and the poor became evident.

Other major changes in the 1990s included the intensification of European economic integration, the breakdown of central-planning in the Communist-dominated East European countries, and the emergence of a group of newly-classified 'advanced' countries. Despite the steady increase in the geographic size and economic power of the European Economic Community as its membership grew, it became apparent during the early 1980s that it was not performing as well economically as Japan and the United States. Steps were therefore taken to stimulate technological improvements in the region and to increase productivity and competitiveness through the removal of various economic restrictions within the Community.[4]

Finally, the creation of an Economic and Monetary Union (EMU) was begun in 1992 by the general member acceptance of the Maastricht Treaty, which aimed to create a single currency (the euro) and a common central bank (the European Central Bank—ECB). It was intended that all member countries would meet certain conditions, aimed at creating convergence of the various economies, considered essential for the success of the Monetary Union. By 1997, however, when the members were to meet all the conditions for entry, the slow movement of some of them led to a weakening of these conditions to allow several of them access to the Monetary Union. In 1998, the 11 successful members to form the EMU in 1999 were declared, leaving out only the United Kingdom, Denmark, Sweden and Greece.

The benefits for the EU arising from all the changes made in the 1990s are expected to lead to substantial economic growth in the early 2000s, unless a stringent monetary policy is followed by the European Central Bank, reflecting the previous anti-inflation bias (and thus the lack of employment and GDP generating policies) of some of the national central banks in the mid-1990s.

The shift towards a market economy in central and eastern Europe and the breakup of the U.S.S.R. into the Countries in Transition[5] occurred at the beginning of the decade. Later, in 1997, the IMF reclassified some NICs[6] as 'advanced' economies, namely China–Hong Kong, China–Taipei (Taiwan), Korea, Singapore and Israel. In the same year, however, the Asian members of the group, along with Thailand, Malaysia and Indonesia, went into a financial crisis on a scale rarely experienced anywhere else in the world and which wiped out much of the gains from growth these economies had achieved since the 1970s.

Considering the present situation, one can only conclude that, despite the great economic advances achieved in the second half of the twentieth century, the world economy enters the new century with severe economic problems and with millions of people worse off than they had been a few decades before. Moreover, increasingly towards the end of the century, a greater concern has been expressed about the long-term future of the world economy in terms of the depletion of natural resources, pollution of the air, sea and land environments, the ozone layer, and the greenhouse effect. It is certain that all of these concerns will have to be addressed more widely in the future than they have been in the past and, in doing so, new directions for the world economy in the new century may well occur.

POPULATION GROWTH AND MIGRATION

From 1950 to 1995, the world's population rose from 2,500m. to 5,716m., at an average annual rate of growth of 1.85 per cent, increasing by an average annual rate of 2 per cent until the early 1970s but then slowly declining to average 1.75 per cent by the mid-1990s. During these years, the population of Europe rose at only 0.7 per cent annually—chiefly because of a declining birth rate and because emigration was relatively high in the 1950s—while North America recorded 1.3 per cent. All other regions experienced annual increases at or above the world average, the highest being in Africa (2.7 per cent). For Latin America and South Asia it was 2.3 per cent, and for Oceania 1.8 per cent, but East Asia recorded an annual average increase of only 1.7 per cent, which was below the world average.

Immigration contributed substantially to population growth in Oceania and South America, and in many countries in these two regions the natural increase in the 1950s rose above its pre-war average and served to augment the growth through immigration. In Asia, medical improvements and a public health revolution lowered the death rate drastically and, with hardly a fall in the birth rate, the population grew rapidly. Given the rapid growth of world population during these years, concern was soon expressed about the capacity of the world economy to provide adequate supplies of food and raw materials to support the growth in numbers. Subsequently the population growth rate began to fall, if only slowly, in the first half of the 1980s, but the population problem still remains a matter for concern.

From 1945 to 1960 the major source of migrants was Europe, notably, the British Isles (2.2m.), Germany (1.5m.), and Italy (1.3m.). Altogether, just under five million people emigrated from Europe during the 1950s, much lower than the totals of each decade from 1880 to 1910. The chief countries of destination were the United States, Canada, Australia (each of which absorbed more than a million people), Argentina and Brazil.[7] In this period, there were substantial restrictions on the inflow of people into the United States and other recipient countries. Unlike the European emigrants of the nineteenth century whose efforts overseas expanded the supplies of foodstuffs and raw materials for the European market, the bulk of the immigrants of the 1950s entered manufacturing and tertiary industries in the immigrant countries, some of which were competitive with European export industries.

From 1960 to 1990, intercontinental migration slowed down somewhat. While the traditional flows continued—for example, British emigration to Canada and Oceania—high rates of economic growth in Western European countries increased the demand for labour so rapidly that millions of foreign workers from neighbouring countries were absorbed into the national workforce of these countries. While some immigrants came from other continents, such as those from Turkey to Germany and from Algeria to France, large intracontinental flows emerged and grew, such as the workers who moved from Portugal, Yugoslavia and Greece into the industrial regions of Western Europe. Moreover, the lack of restrictions on the movement of labour within the European Community[8] added to the general shift of workers within Europe. Germany recorded a large net population inflow between 1958 and

1973 and, in some years, absorbed over a million immigrants. Access to foreign workers prevented shortages of labour from developing within the Community and thus reduced the pressures of wage inflation. Moreover, with the slowdown in economic activity in the late 1970s, there was a net outflow of labour from Western Europe as foreign workers returned to their home-lands in large numbers, thus easing the unemployment problems in the host countries. As economic activity in the EC recovered in the 1980s, the inflow of foreign workers was renewed but not on the same scale as before 1973, in which year there were over six million foreign workers in Western Europe. Towards the end of the 1970s another form of intercontinental migration began, that of refugees from Asia, mainly Vietnam. During the 1980s, hundreds of thousands of East Asians were absorbed by several developed countries, including the United States, Canada and Australia.

High unemployment in Europe after the 1970s did little to revitalize immigration into that continent and many of the intercontinental and intra-continental migration flows during the 1980s and 1990s have been the movement of political refugees from war and civil strife areas in many parts of the world. Nevertheless, within Asia, there have been substantial inter-national shifts of labour, largely from the Philippines, Bangladesh and Indo-nesia, into Malaysia, Thailand and the Middle East. From 1975 to 1995, some 12 million Asian workers were employed in other countries, over 60 per cent of them being located in the Middle East or elsewhere outside the Asia region. Other major migration movements in the early 1990s were from Asia and Central America to the United States, and from North Africa and North Asia to Europe.[9]

INTERNATIONAL CAPITAL FLOWS—PRIVATE INVESTMENT

International flows of investment capital in recent decades have accelerated the globalization process. Such flows can be classified in terms of foreign direct investment (FDI), involving the acquisition of ownership and/or con-trol of an organization in the 'host' country by the investing company in the 'home' country, or foreign portfolio investment (FPI), in which the home investor obtains shares in a host country's company, say, on the stock exchange (Foreign Portfolio Equity Investment—FPEI) or part control of other forms of investment in the host country without gaining ownership or majority control. FDI may be 'greenfield' investment, in which the investing company sets up an entirely new firm in the host country, or investment in 'cross-border' mergers or acquisitions. Another type of FDI is 'reinvested earnings', earnings not returned to the home office but held in the host country to finance some future capital project. While a high proportion of FDI in the 1950s and 1960s was greenfield, from the early 1970s to the late

1980s, cross-border equities and acquisitions became much more important, rising to a peak of 70 per cent of all FDI inflows. In the 1990s, however, greenfield FDI regained some of its previous importance.

Foreign Direct Investment (FDI)—in total

The world total FDI, transmitted from home country to host country, rose rapidly to around $US20 billion a year in the early 1970s, much of it the result of the United States' multinational corporations (now often called transnationals—TNCs) investing in Europe to overcome the EEC's common tariff. Thereafter, European transnationals rapidly grew in number, while a feature of the 1980s was the rise of the Japanese TNCs. By 1985, both FDI inflows and outflows recorded around $45 billion annually. But a boom in FDI was to occur after 1985, with annual outflows reaching $280 billion in 1991. After a brief downturn, a further acceleration occurred to a new high of $345–350 billion in 1996. By the mid-1990s, however, many other countries, including Hong Kong, Korea, Singapore, Taiwan, China, Mexico and Brazil, could boast their own TNCs. Altogether, in 1996, there were some 45,000 parent companies, 7,900 of them based in the NICs and other developing countries, that had set up some 280,000 foreign affiliates, and the total FDI stock of which was $3,200 billion. The worldwide assets of these foreign affiliates were valued at $8,400 billion. This value had been increasing faster than the world gross fixed investment during the decade to 1996.[10]

A major cause of this accelerated growth in the 1990s was the liberalization of investment criteria in many countries. In addition, a rapid increase in gross saving in several countries provided funds for greater investment. Another reason was the rapid increase in the number of bilateral investment treaties (BITs) aiming to protect and promote investment. In 1996, there were some 1,330 BITs covering 162 countries, a tripling in numbers since 1991. This growth of TNCs led to a rapid increase in international production (the total output of all foreign affiliates) which was valued in 1995 at $7,000 billion in world sales. The growth of these sales from 1987 to 1995 was greater than the growth of exports of goods and services by from 20 to 30 per cent. The gross product of foreign affiliates rose almost threefold between 1982 and 1995.

Yet another reason for the rapid rise in the world sales of TNCs was the opening up of the domestic markets of many countries to competition from abroad in an effort to improve domestic productive efficiency through increased competition. Safeguards against the possibility of monopolization and other devices to restrict trade and competition were also necessary but action in these areas has so far been limited.

Transnational companies have tended to concentrate on manufacturing (chemicals, pharmaceuticals, electronics, computers and foodstuffs), petroleum, telecommunications, and finance. Their entry into a country confers many benefits on it in terms of increased production, investment and employment, and the introduction of new managerial skills. It can favour export expansion or import replacement, and promote the diffusion of new technology. At the same time, the concentration of a number of these international firms in one country may pose serious problems for its government, especially if they control a large part of the country's exports. These problems include the possible relocation of export orders from the local affiliate to another affiliate elsewhere in the world, or the movement of liquid assets out of a country experiencing balance of payments difficulties, thus compounding them.

FDI: National Features

Table 26 shows that the United States was the major host and home country in 1996, by a substantial margin in both cases. For many years after 1945, the United States, almost alone, was in a position to export capital on a large scale. Between 1938 and 1973, its total FDI rose from $11.7 billion to $107 billion, of which re-invested foreign earnings accounted for $8.1 billion of the total. U.S. FDI expanded much more slowly during the difficult years of the 1970s and the early 1980s, but then grew rapidly after 1984. By 1996, as Table 25 shows, it had risen to an accumulated value of almost $800 billion, and by which year it recorded an outflow of $84.6 billion. Almost half of the FDI outflow in 1996 comprised the reinvested earnings of the foreign affiliates. In the 1990s, the European Union absorbed around 40–45 per cent of the total U.S. FDI outflow, Canada, 8–10 per cent, and developing countries, mainly in Latin America, around 30 per cent.

In these years, manufacturing accounted for some 35 per cent of the non-bank FDI, mainly transport equipment (8 per cent), chemicals and allied products (6 per cent), food (3 per cent), and industrial machinery and equipment (3 per cent). In addition, finance (excluding deposit institutions) claimed 37 per cent, petroleum 8 per cent and communications 5 per cent.

In recent years, the United States has become an important host country. Of the total FDI inflow in 1996 of $85 billion, the European Union contributed around $57 billion, Japan $14 billion, Canada $7 billion, and other developed countries $6 billion.

By 1996, FDI inflows into the EU had risen to just under $100 billion. The United Kingdom claimed the largest share (30 per cent), followed by France (21 per cent) and Belgium (14 per cent). Over half the EU FDI inflow during the years between 1986 to 1997 came from other EU members and the United States. In addition, European FDI outflow rose to $160 billion in 1996, with the United Kingdom (33 per cent), Germany (18 per cent), France (16 per cent) and the Netherlands (12 per cent) supplying most of it.[11] While much of this outflow from EU countries went into other EU countries, between 1992 and 1996 the EU share of new FDI dropped from 72 per cent to 55 per cent because of the poor economic conditions in many EU countries.

Table 26 Foreign direct investment, by home and host country, 1985–95 ($ billion)

Country	Average annual			End stock	
	1985–90	1993	1996	1985	1996
Home country					
WORLD	**155.6**	**239.1**	**346.8**	**690**	**3,178**
United States	21.6	74.8	84.9	251	794
United Kingdom	25.2	25.5	53.5	100	356
Germany	12.9	15.3	28.7	60	288
Hong Kong	2.0	17.7	27.0	37	112
France	14.3	20.6	25.2	2	206
Japan	27.8	13.8	23.4	44	330
Netherlands	8.8	12.3	19.9	48	185
Belgium/Luxembourg	3.6	4.9	9.0	5	73
Canada	4.8	5.9	7.5	41	111
Singapore	0.6	2.0	4.8	6	37
Other	34.0	46.3	62.9	96	686
(EU$_{15}$	80	97	160	286	1,404)
Host country					
WORLD	**141.9**	**218.1**	**349.2**	**745**	**3,233**
United States	48.6	43.5	84.6	184	645
China	2.7	27.5	42.3	3	169
United Kingdom	19.0	15.5	30.1	64	345
France	7.2	20.8	20.8	33	168
Belgium/Luxembourg	4.1	10.7	13.9	9	101
Singapore	3.0	4.7	9.4	13	66
Indonesia	0.6	2.0	8.0	25	59
Canada	5.3	5.0	6.7	65	129
Netherlands	5.6	8.8	6.3	25	119
Germany	2.3	1.8	3.9	37	171
Other	43.5	77.8	123.2	287	1,261
(EU$_{15}$	53	81	99	226	1,219)

Source: UNCTAD, World Investment Report, 1996, Appendix B.

The United States and developing countries also received much of the EU capital outflow. In addition, the amounts going to Eastern European countries, hesitant at first, grew rapidly after 1994, when the transformation of these countries from command economies to free-market economies was well under way. Poland, Hungary, the Czech Republic and Russia received the bulk of these capital flows, mainly from Germany. Much of the EU FDI went into finance, distribution, chemicals and allied products, transport equipment, petroleum, non-ferrous metals and non-electrical machinery. A recent feature of EU inward FDI has been a decline in mergers and acquisitions, seemingly indicating a growing shortage of EU firms to be taken over by outsiders.

As Table 26 shows, the United Kingdom remained the largest home and host country in the EU. At first, in the 1950s, British FDI went mainly to Commonwealth countries but, in the 1960s, the focus shifted towards the Continent, particularly after 1973. By 1980, when the total value of British FDI reached $80 billion, the EC share was 20 per cent of the total and that of the U.S. 33 per cent. During the 1980s and 1990s British FDI rose rapidly and exceeded $350 billion in 1996. Its geographic spread was much the same in the latter year as before, with the EU, United States and Commonwealth countries accounting for the major shares. The annual inflow of FDI into Britain rose to some $30 billion by 1996, most coming from the United States, Japan, and other EU countries. In that year, the total value of FDI stock in the United Kingdom was some $356 billion.

In recent years, German direct foreign investment has concentrated mainly on Europe, east and west, although North America's share had increased to over 20 per cent by 1996. France has continued to invest largely in its former colonies, other EU countries, and the United States. The Netherlands has been the other major foreign investor within the EU, investing mainly in other EU countries and the United States.

Since the 1970s, the importance of Japan as a foreign direct investor increased considerably until the second half of the 1980s, following which its performance deteriorated rapidly. North America was Japan's favourite region for investment. It received just under 50 per cent of the total outflow in 1996. Asia (especially China, Indonesia, Hong Kong and Thailand) accounted for around 25 per cent, and Europe 17 per cent. Of the total Japanese FDI in 1996, 42 per cent went into manufacturing, especially electrical and transport equipment. Banking, insurance, and real estate were also highly favoured. In the early 1990s, the newly advanced countries of Asia, especially Hong Kong, Singapore, Taiwan and Korea began to invest in other Asian countries, especially China and Cambodia. Their total foreign stock in 1996 was valued at $191 billion, of which Hong Kong contributed $112 billion. Their industrial preferences include electronics, trading, transportation, electrical goods, construction and hotels.[12] The financial crises of 1997 and 1998 placed a temporary hold on such investments.

Portfolio Investment

Portfolio investment (in public sector and other bonds and corporate equities) also tended to grow very rapidly from the 1970s as the world's capital markets became more integrated. Although it is difficult to obtain completely reliable figures, it appears that foreign portfolio equity investment (FPEI) rose from around $10 billion in the early 1970s to exceed $150 billion by 1986. The growth of capital markets in emerging countries, especially in East

Asia and East Europe, and the increasing globalization of such markets led to a sharp rise in the flows of FPEI to these areas from around $1 billion dollars in 1988 to a peak of $45 billion in 1993. However, a financial crisis in Mexico near the end of 1994 led to sharp reductions in the annual flows of this type of capital and, although a recovery occurred in 1996, the crises in Asian share markets towards the end of 1997 and in most world markets in 1998 affected this type of foreign investment dramatically.

Japan emerged as a major portfolio investor in the late 1980s and in some years accounted for well over 50 per cent of the total. Japan, Germany, France and the Netherlands were the principal portfolio investors in 1995, while Germany, Japan, Italy and Canada were the main recipients, but the available information is fraught with great volatility over time. In the emerging markets, Europe and central Asia, Latin America, and, to an important extent, East Asia, appear to have been the major recipient areas. Singapore and Hong Kong also became important portfolio investors.[13]

Another form of portfolio investment, commercial bank lending to foreign national governments and private firms, has also become important since the late 1970s. At first, the expansion of international bank lending occurred when the terms of trade of the borrowing countries and their currency reserves were falling while real interest rates were rising, and debt servicing became a major problem. Some large debtor countries such as Mexico, Brazil and Argentina, experienced severe financial difficulties which persisted during the rest of the 1980s and, for some, into the 1990s despite rescheduling and other forms of aid introduced after 1982. In the 1990s, bank lending to both national governments and to private firms abroad was facilitated by the greater freedom of capital movements. Despite large annual changes in the banks' long-term lending in the early 1990s, recording −$300 million (net inflow) in 1993, the net aggregate rose rapidly to reach $34 billion in 1996. Sixty per cent of all bank loans to developing countries went to private companies, large amounts went to Chile, China, Indonesia, Malaysia, South Africa, Thailand and Turkey. The financial problems of East Asia in 1997 were partly attributable to some of these loans. Commercial bank loans to the governments of developing countries are used mainly for large-scale infrastructure projects (especially power).[14]

In the 1980s and 1990s there were other innovations in international capital markets, including derivatives. While the expansion of forward exchange facilities largely fulfilled the desire for risk avoidance in a system of floating exchange rates, other changes emerged which helped to free up the world capital markets. The growth of derivatives (instruments whose values depend on the values of other financial assets)—for example, currency or interest rate futures, call and put options, and swaps on stock exchange indexes, interest rates and currencies—was so rapid that they quickly became central to the operation of financial markets, for they acted as instruments for hedging risky investments and for speculative activity.

Derivatives fall into one of two classes, 'exchange traded' (bought and sold on a market, the price determined by market pressures) or 'over-the-counter' contracts between two parties (prices determined by negotiation between the parties involved). In May 1995, the IMF expressed concern over the growing use of derivatives and the need for improving the regulation and supervision of banks because of the increased activity in derivative markets. There is a suggestion that the rapid growth of derivatives may have transmitted disturbances across markets and institutions. By the end of 1996, the notional amounts of exchange-traded instruments (futures and options) outstanding totalled $9,885 billion, of which interest rate futures ($5,900 billion) and interest rate options ($3,300 billion) were the most popular. Over-the-counter instruments amounted to $24,292 billion and interest rate swaps accounted for over half of this amount.

There is no doubt that the international capital market widened considerably during the 1990s, became more complex and much freer in its activities.

INTERNATIONAL CAPITAL FLOWS: FOREIGN AID AND OTHER RESOURCE FLOWS TO DEVELOPING COUNTRIES

While private capital flows to developing countries rose rapidly during the 1990s, official aid flows tended to stagnate. Generally speaking, the net flow of resources to the developing countries includes the net flow of direct and portfolio investment (outlined above), foreign aid, and other resource flows which include bank loans to national governments. Strictly speaking, foreign aid refers to grants or gifts of money or goods from one country to another for development purposes or for alleviating economic crises, such as famine, flood or drought relief. However, it is conventional to broaden the definition to include long-term development loans offered to one country by another as well as aid provided for military purposes. Foreign aid, thus defined, is provided by individual countries, by regional organizations consisting of a number of countries such as the EU, and by international institutions such as the World Bank and its affiliates. Voluntary private aid, collected by private organizations within a country, is another source of assistance provided for developing countries.

From 1945 to 1960, around $26 billion was granted as Official Development Assistance (ODA) to the poor countries by the Development Assistance Committee (DAC) countries, the United States donating $16 billion of this amount. The centrally-planned economies (CPEs) advanced over $6.5 billion. Some $14 billion of all this aid went to Asia, mainly India. In the 1960s the net foreign aid contribution in the form of ODA from the DAC countries was $61 billion, and other 'official flows' totalled $5 billion. The CPEs provided over $8 billion, of which the U.S.S.R. granted $3.8 billion. A feature of foreign aid in this decade was the recognition of the debt-servicing problem encountered by such high debt countries as India and the need for more concessional terms in bilateral loans.

The foreign aid (ODA) from DAC countries in the 1970s, amounting to $150 billion, was thus provided on more favourable terms than previously. At the same time, over $40 billion flowed from members of the Organization of Petroleum Exporting Countries (OPEC) to the non-oil-exporting developing countries, and Eastern Europe offered in excess of $10 billion. It was during the 1970s that private flows to developing countries began to grow rapidly. FDI rose from $3.7 billion a year in 1970 to over $10 billion in 1980 while portfolio flows, including bank loans, rose from below $700 million to over $17 billion between these years. As a result of all these aid flows to the developing countries, their total net external debt reached $650 billion in 1980. In that year, the ODA of DAC countries represented only 36 per cent of the total resource flow while private investment accounted for 54 per cent. Despite a United Nations target of 0.7 per cent of GNP for each donor country's ODA to be achieved by 1975, few DAC members reached this goal, even by the end of the 1980s—the average for the group remaining persistently below 0.4 per cent. In addition, high inflation rates reduced the real value of the annual fund flows to the recipient countries.

From 1981 to 1990, the ODA from DAC countries amounted to some $434 billion but, in real terms, because of high inflation rates the average annual increase was very small. During the 1980s much attention was also paid to the high interest rates and, at times, the increasing value of the U.S. dollar, both of which accentuated the debt-servicing problems of the recipient countries. The high and rising external debts of some of these countries reached crisis levels. Mexico, for example, recorded a very severe debt crisis in 1982. Even when inflationary pressures abated in the donor countries in the late 1980s and interest rates were somewhat lower, the debt problems remained. At the same time, despite the high cost of borrowing, the total external debt of the developing countries rose from $650 billion in 1980 to $1,500 billion in 1990. Countries such as Mexico, Brazil, Argentina and those in sub-Saharan Africa, were the most severely affected by this problem. Several measures, including debt re-scheduling and debt cancelling, reduced the heavy debt burden for some recipient countries.

During the 1980s, private financial flows to the developing world, especially commercial bank loans, increased considerably. This type of development financing arose from the decline of exchange controls and the evolution of international banking. Initially, it was based on sound banking practices assisted by the presence of a number of credit-worthy developing countries. The debt of these countries to the banks in the industrial countries rose from around $17 billion in 1973 to $391.9 billion in 1989. Largely, the growth of this form of debt arose out of the inadequacy of ODA to meet all the investment requirements of the most successful developing countries, but the debt problems noted above applied to these loans also. In addition to FDI and bank loans, portfolio investment in equities was also growing during this decade.

The foreign debt of the centrally-planned economies increased from $5.2 billion in 1971 to peak at $72.6 billion in 1982. When, at the end of the decade, central planning in these countries gave way to a transition to market economies, their aggregate cumulative debt was over $260 billion and, by 1996, had expanded even further to $450 billion, as finance was required to fund the transition. Needless to say, foreign aid from these countries in this decade has been negligible.

During the first half of the 1990s, ODA from DAC countries reached almost $40 billion. Of this amount, just over 70 per cent was provided by EU members. During these years, there were several major changes in the nature of the financial resource flows from the donors to the recipient countries. Official development assistance peaked in aggregate in 1991 and its relative share fell from 55 per cent of the total resource flows in 1990 to 14 per cent by mid-decade—such a decline representing an even greater fall in real terms. In addition, the traditional role of ODA, the financing of long-term development and faster poverty reduction, gave way substantially to the funding of emergency relief and peacekeeping activities, and in supporting the reforms of the transition economies of eastern Europe and the former U.S.S.R. On the other hand, for the heavily indebted poor countries (HIPCs), a Debt Initiative was introduced to help some of these countries to overcome their debt problems. While Sub-Saharan Africa has absorbed up to 40 per cent of this concessional aid, Europe and Central Asia (the transitional economies) increased their share from $166 million in 1989 to around $9 billion in 1996. Nevertheless, donor countries expressed only a modest interest in granting non-concessional aid to these countries in the early years of their transition.

Altogether, total private capital resource flows to the developing countries rose annually from $44 billion in 1990 to $243.8 billion in 1996. The innovations of the 1980s were continued and enlarged in the 1990s and private commercial resources, such as bank loans, replaced much of the ODA of the DAC countries which had previously been considered crucial to the development of the poor countries. The globalization movement, however, tended to 'privatize' these official ventures. There is likely be a slow-down, however, in the flows of private funds going to the developing countries, following the financial crises experienced late in 1997 in all the high-growth Asian countries, and in the currency and stock markets of the world in 1998.[15]

Regional arrangements for promoting aid to the developing countries began in 1958 when the EC set up its European Development Fund (EDF) to assist the development of its 'associated territories', mostly the former French, Belgian and Italian colonies in Africa. Under the Lomé Convention in 1975, the EDF covered all former EC members' colonies in Africa, the Caribbean and the Pacific regions (the ACP countries). In 1961, the Organization of American States created the Inter-American Development Bank (IDB) to help finance development projects, especially of a social overhead nature, within the Americas. The total cumulative lending by the IDB, to 1995, was $40.5 billion, net of cancellations and exchange adjustments. The Asian Development Bank began to operate in 1968 and, to 1995, had advanced $32.3 billion for over a thousand projects in over 30 countries. The African Development Bank was established in 1963 and the African Development Fund in 1973. The total loans and grants of these two institutions to the end of 1995 was $17.2 billion. These regional development institutions gave priority in their loans to agriculture and agro-industry, public utilities, transportation, and energy, in the form mainly of technical assistance.

Multilateral financial assistance was initially channelled through the World Bank which began operations in 1946. To 1960 it had approved 260 development loans worth a net $5 billion. Its lending rose rapidly after 1960, averaging $1 billion a year by 1970. Further acceleration then occurred as inflation became a major problem in all recipient countries. By 1981, the Bank had lent $68 billion, of which 32 per cent had gone to Latin America, 28 per cent to Europe and the Mediterranean countries, and 23 per cent to Asia and the Pacific. Asia's share began to rise in the 1980s at the expense of that of Europe and the Mediterranean countries. By the 1990s, however, the opening up of the world's capital markets gave the recipient countries of World Bank loans another source of funds and, from 1991 to 1995, the Bank recorded a relatively small decrease in its net disbursements, due to repayments exceeding loans. From 1988 to 1995 the cumulated assistance provided by the Bank rose from $155 billion to $164 billion, all the increase being non-concessional flows. The main sectors attracting World Bank loans by the 1990s were economic infrastructure (over 60 per cent) and social and administrative infrastructure. Apart from financial aid, the Bank also offers technical assistance on a growing scale to an increasing number of developing countries.

The International Development Association (IDA) was established as an affiliate of the World Bank in 1962 to provide developing countries with access to 'softer' loans than those offered by the World Bank. The IDA obtains its funds from donor members of the Bank and these funds have to be replenished from time to time. Eventually, the IDA will become self-financing as loans are repaid, but such loans carry a long period of grace (ten years) and a long maturity of 50 years. Recipients pay a service charge on loans of 0.75 per cent. In 1995, when the cumulated total of IDA concessional flows had reached $79 billion, $31.3 billion had been granted after 1987. Sub-Saharan Africa absorbed around 40 per cent of IDA loans, while the Middle East, North Africa, and Southern Europe took over 20 per cent. It was aimed at improving social, administrative, and economic infrastructure, agriculture, and programme assistance. Because the IDA concentrated its lending on the poorer developing countries, its existence allowed the World Bank to extend its relatively 'harder' loans mainly to the not-so-poor developing countries. The International Finance Corporation (IFC) was another affiliate of the World Bank, created to promote and encourage the growth of private enterprise in member countries by making loans to private firms. While its limited financial resources have prevented the IFC from having any significant economic impact on developing countries, it encourages outside private investors to participate in its investments, thereby often stimulating private investment flows into many projects in developing countries. In the 1990s it advanced an average $1 billion a year in non-concessional loans to developing countries.

The United Nations, through its numerous agencies has initiated considerable flows of concessional funds to the developing world. These flows averaged around $5.6 billion a year between 1990 and 1995. Altogether, between 1991 and 1995, a net disbursemant of $70 billion of concessional aid and $36 billion of non-concessional aid flowed from multilateral organizations.

In the changing world of the 1990s, foreign aid, itself, came under scrutiny. Some commentators argued that it was wasteful in the hands of the recipients and that alternative sources existed for countries to borrow to satisfy their development needs. A further argument was that, if aid was still to be disbursed, it should be given only if it is used properly. Even IDA loans, which are offered only to the least developed, poorer countries, should be granted only to those that are already reforming their economies. On the other hand, it is noted that bilateral aid is not always altruistic, much of it is tied to the donor countries and therefore indirectly aids the donor's exporters.

TECHNOLOGICAL CHANGE AND WORLD TRADE

The increased emphasis placed on trade as a mechanism for promoting economic development leads naturally to a consideration of the ways in which technological change influenced the postwar pattern of world trade. Partly because of the backlog of promising, unused innovations built up during the 1930s, and partly because of the research stimulated during World War II, which had considerable peacetime significance, technical progress was very rapid after the war. In later years, innovative capacity was sustained at a high level by a large increase in the funds, both public and private, devoted to research and development (R&D). In the United States, the amount spent on R&D rose from 1 per cent of GDP in 1950 to 2.8 per cent in 1960 and, in the U.S.S.R., during the same period, it grew from 1.2 per cent to 2.5 per cent. This trend was repeated in most other advanced countries. By 1993, the United States still spent 2.8 per cent of GDP on R&D, while Germany (2.5

per cent), France (2.4 per cent), the United Kingdom (2.15 per cent) and South Korea (2.1 per cent) were other major investors. Thus, billions of dollars were spent annually on R&D and over two million scientists were employed in these fields.[16]

All this innovative activity created an ever-growing range of new raw materials, productive processes, energy resources, and production and consumption goods. The period witnessed the introduction of the transistor, the micro-chip and the various products in which it was used, such as compact disc players, video recorders, and mobile telephones. Other examples include plastics, synthetic resins, man-made fibres, including oil-based synthetics, new metals and metal products of aluminium and alloy steels, and whole ranges of antibiotics and other life-saving drugs. New production processes were installed in most industries and prefabrication became a common method of production. Nuclear energy provided a new form of fuel for possible use in transportation and other industries in the future, while the possibilities of solar and wind power are also being explored. Many types of electronic devices, including television and radar equipment, which are the basis of automation and cybernetic methods, were more widely adopted. The list is far from complete, but it is long enough to show the nature of the far-reaching technological changes that occurred after 1945.

While technological progress in the production of goods provided increased opportunities for trade, transport improvements continued to assist the international movement of commodities and people. Railway construction remained an important form of transport investment in many developing countries after 1945 but, in the highly industrialized nations, the importance of the railway declined in the face of the rising relative efficiency of road transport. The growing use of motor transport and of the aeroplane enormously increased the consumption of petroleum and other oil products, and this was reflected at sea by the rapid enlargement of oil-tanker capacity and by the rapid change-over to motor ships. In addition, from the late 1950s, containerization became a major means of speeding up the handling and transportation of goods. Increasingly, after 1945, air transport of people and goods by domestic and international airlines made substantial inroads on land and sea transport. In particular, air travel made possible the rapid extension of the international company, by providing the necessary face-to-face communication needed to administer complex affairs with appropriate speed and reasonable cost. More recently, domestic and international communications have been improved by satellite transmission, improved telephony, facsimile and electronic mail, with the Internet further encouraging the speed of international economic activity by private companies, and contributing to the vast information revolution that is altering the very nature of many productive and household activities.

In terms of the flow of technology resulting from the build-up of FDI and other means of transfer, technological diffusion has occurred at an accelerating rate. The international flows of royalties and other technologically-related flows give us some idea of the size and direction of technological diffusion and of the success of such ventures. UNCTAD's breakdown of the receipts and payments of the income flows of the five major investing countries shows that the United States dominates in the receipts of royalties and licence fees, its share being over 50 per cent, that a major proportion of these income flows occur within a small group of countries—the United States, the United Kingdom, Japan, Germany, France and the Netherlands—and that while there are only small technology flows to the developing countries, some of them, including Mexico, Brazil, China and India, are important recipients of industrial know-how.[17]

What effects have these changes in production and consumption had on world trade? The answer lies, perhaps, in the extent to which world trade has increased. Trade among the rich nations has been stimulated not only because it provided a channel for the diffusion of the fruits of technological progress between the industrial countries, but also because manufactured products became more sophisticated and consumer tastes varied with respect to the different brands of products being produced in different countries. Thus, for instance, American cars are sold in Europe and European cars are sold in the United States. In some respects, developing countries lost out from the advances made in synthetic products and the economies made in the use of natural materials, for instance through electrolytic tin-plating and the systematic recovery and reprocessing of metals. The demand for such staple exports as crude rubber, wool, silk, indigo, nitrates, jute, hemp, vegetable oils, and hides and skins, certainly declined during the period—in most cases as the outcome of the technological advances made in the chemicals industry—and, as a result, many developing countries lost valuable export markets while, at the same time, rich countries gained new export industries. But this trend has not all been in the one direction for, through direct foreign investment, licensing, joint ventures and other means, a number of developing countries, especially in East Asia, gained enormously by becoming the major producers of many of the new products because of the cheapness of their factors of production, and thus provided reverse trade flows of these technological products back to the rich countries. Indeed, their development strategy has revolved around such production and trade.

CONCLUDING REMARKS

In the second half of the twentieth century, international economic relations became more complex, more extensive, and much closer than in any previous period. The world became divided naturally into three general areas, the advanced industrial nations, the developing countries, and the centrally-planned (later transitional) economies. International co-operation produced large flows of resources, commodities, ideas and technology from country to country and from continent to continent. During the period up to 1973, many countries experienced a long period of unparalleled economic growth. For various reasons, especially the persistence of severe inflationary pressures, the next decade was fraught with economic difficulties which did not completely disappear despite all official attempts to deal with them. Lower levels of inflation in the industrial countries were achieved in the second half of the 1980s but low growth and high unemployment remained major economic and social problems, persisting in many countries up to the end of the 1990s. Given the increasing degree of economic interdependence (or globalization, to use the fashionable word) since the 1950s, most countries were adversely affected by the downturn in the industrial world in 1974 and the relatively poor economic performances generally prevailing thereafter. Within the developing countries, however, the NICs, particularly those of east Asia, were able to achieve high rates of economic growth during the last few decades despite the quantitative restrictions placed on many of their manufactured exports by the industrially advanced countries. Much of their production was the result of the transfer of new technology from the richer countries.

It was also after 1973 that the debt problems of many developing countries increased in intensity and, although the many efforts to curtail the growth of external debt have yielded some success, severe debt problems still persist in several countries, because of the 'Asian crisis' of 1997–8 and the turmoil in world commodity and financial markets in 1998.

NOTES

1 The OECD (Organization for Economic Co-operation and Development) is an institution created out of the OEEC in 1960 and mainly comprises the major advanced countries of Western Europe, North America, Japan and Oceania. Its major function is to advance economic co-operation among its members in such a way as to improve the economic performance of the world as a whole. There are 29 members, including recent entrants, Austria, Czech Republic, Finland, Hungary, Korea, Mexico, Poland and Turkey.
2 The centrally-planned economies, or Communist-dominated countries, included Albania, the Baltic States, Poland, Hungary, Bulgaria, Czechoslovakia, German Democratic Republic, Romania, Yugoslavia, the U.S.S.R., Mongolia, China, North Vietnam, North Korea, Cambodia and Cuba. Many of these countries were grouped under the Council for Mutual Economic Assistance (CMEA or Comecon).
3 At that time, the newly-industrializing countries (NICs) included: Hong Kong, India, Indonesia, Israel, Korea, Singapore, Taiwan, Argentina, Brazil, Mexico, and, in Europe, Greece, Portugal and Spain. The Asian and American NICs receive more attention here than the European countries which are now members of the European Union.
4 See later Chapter 20, p. 299, for a fuller discussion of these points.

5 The CITs included the CEECs (Albania, Belarus, Bosnia and Herzegovina, Bulgaria, Croatia, Czech Republic, Estonia, Hungary, Latvia, Lithuania, Macedonia (former Yugoslav Republic of), Moldova, Poland, Romania, Slovakia, Slovenia, Ukraine and Yugoslavia (Federal Republic of); the Transcaucasus and Central Asian Countries (Armenia, Azerbaijan, Georgia, Kazakstan, Kyrgyz Republic, Mongolia, Tajikistan, Turkmenistan and Uzbekistan). Russia is also classified as a CIT.

6 See IMF *World Economic Outlook*, May, 1997, p. 4, Box 1.

7 See W. Woodruff, *The Impact of Western Man* (New York: Macmillan), 1966, pp. 106–7.

8 The terms EEC (European Economic Community), EC (European Communities), and EU (European Union) will tend to be used when each one was current, all of course referring to the same geographical entity.

9 See 'International Migration: a Global Challenge', *Population Bulletin*, April 1996, vol. 51, no. 1.

10 These figures and some other information in this section come from UNCTAD, *World Investment Report, 1997—Transnational Corporations, Market Structure and Competition Policy*, New York and Geneva, 1997. UNCTAD has calculated that the stock of FDI, which had reached $1,000 billion in 1987, doubled by 1993 and reached $3,200 billion in 1996, op. cit., p. 3.

11 These figures calculated from UNCTAD, op. cit., Annex Tables, especially B1 and B2, pp. 303–12.

12 See op. cit., pp. 46–9.

13 See op. cit., pp. 107–120, and IMF, *Balance of Payments Statistics*, Annual.

14 See World Bank, *Global Development Finance*, 1997, vol. 1, Washington, pp. 3–6.

15 For recent data on this section, see: World Bank, op. cit., pp. 3–39, and 190–200. Also see IMF, *World Economic Outlook*, October 1997, p. 210.

16 See OECD, *Observer* (February, 1988), pp. 22–4 and UNCTAD, *World Investment Report*, 1997, pp. 21–2.

17 UNCTAD, *World Investment Report*, 1997, pp. 21–2.

SELECTED REFERENCES

Anon., 'International Migration: a Global Challenge', *Population Bulletin*, April 1996, vol. 51, no. 1.

Bank for International Settlements, *Annual Report*, various issues.

Boltho, A., *The European Economy: Growth and Crisis* (London: Oxford University Press, 1982).

International Monetary Fund (IMF), *World Economic Outlook*, Washington, various issues.

Maddison, A., *Phases of Capitalist Development* (London: Oxford University Press, 1982).

Maddison, A., *Monitoring the World Economy 1820–1992* (Paris: OECD, 1995).

Organization for Economic Co-operation and Development (OECD), *The Flow of Financial Resources to Developing Countries*, Paris, various issues.

OECD, *Development Co-operation*, Development Assistance Committee, Paris, various issues.

Postan, M.M., *An Economic History of Western Europe* (London: Methuen, 1967).

United Nations, *Demography*, various issues.

UNCTAD, *World Development Report 1997—Transnational Corporations, Market Structure and Competition Policy* (New York: United Nations, 1997).

Woodruff, W., *The Impact of Western Man* (New York: Macmillan, 1966).

World Bank, *Global Development Finance, 1997* (Washington, 1997).

Chapter 18

International monetary relations, 1945–2000

At Bretton Woods it had been expected that postwar reconstruction and the restoration of normal trading and commercial relations between countries would be largely attained by 1952. In fact, it was not until the late 1950s that most of the industrial countries were willing to consider the adoption of currency convertibility, a necessary step for the International Monetary Fund (IMF) system to function smoothly.

THE IMF: 1947–61

The IMF began its operations on 1 March 1947, by which date members had submitted the initial par values of their currencies and had paid their subscriptions into the Fund. Thereafter, despite the pervasiveness of inflationary pressures and other problems of postwar reconstruction, including a worldwide shortage of U.S. dollars, the Fund's currency transactions up to 1952 did not exceed $850 million. The Fund's limited role in international economic affairs during these years came about because of the continuing use of exchange controls, the exclusion of Marshall Aid recipient countries from IMF drawings, the 1949 devaluations, and the need for countries to implement suitable monetary and fiscal policies to contain inflation before IMF aid became available. Yet the Fund endeavoured with moderate success to recreate a multilateral system of trade and payments by attempting to reduce the use of exchange restrictions, quantitative import controls, and multiple exchange rate practices.

Multilateralism, however, could be fully realized only when current account convertibility was widely adopted, and this could not occur until Fund members had amassed adequate reserves of convertible currencies with which to conduct their international monetary transactions and establish realistic exchange rates. Only the U.S. dollar was available as a major convertible currency at the time. The first move to this end, the widespread currency devaluations of September 1949, was aborted in the following year by the resumption of inflationary pressures in most devaluing countries following the outbreak of the Korean War. Moreover, economic recovery had only just begun to restore industrial production in Europe and the basis for expanding trade relations had still to be laid. By 1952, therefore, the transition to a stable world economic environment was still not completed, and the Fund's position in international monetary affairs had still to be asserted.

In the 1950s, despite the continued shortage of the dollar, world trade expanded rapidly and the payments situation improved for many of the non-dollar countries, especially those in Western Europe and the developed primary producers. The European payments improvement resulted not so much from an increased demand for European products as from the increasing worldwide competitiveness of the European export industries as they regained their pre-war position as major exporters. 1958 marked a turning-point in international monetary relations when the United States recorded its first annual payments deficit of the post-war years and a massive outflow of gold and dollars to the rest of the world occurred.[1] It was this large outflow which facilitated the concerted move towards greater currency convertibility. In December 1958, 14 European and 15 other countries announced their adoption of non-resident convertibility, which meant that, in future, the exchange regulations of these countries would allow foreigners, but not residents, to shift funds for current account purposes freely from one country to another. Further improvements in international monetary conditions led, on 15 February 1961, to the adoption of the Fund's current account convertibility requirements (currencies to be convertible into others on demand for current account purposes) by ten member countries; namely, Belgium, France, West Germany, Ireland, Italy, Luxembourg, Netherlands, Peru, Sweden and the United Kingdom.

The Fund began to assume a more positive role in international monetary affairs in 1956 with the appointment of Per Jacobbson as its Managing Director and the granting of the first large drawing, of $562 million, to the United Kingdom, the result of payments problems stemming from the Suez crisis of that year. In 1958, the first review of quotas occurred and a 50 per cent increase was agreed on with larger increases for Canada, West Germany and Japan. The Fund's financial resources rose by $5.1 billion to $14.5 billion. Thus, when the postwar transitional period eventually ended in 1961, the Fund, with larger resources and greater prestige, was in a position to start operating as it was intended at Bretton Woods.

Regional Payments Arrangements

One reason for the failure of the IMF to play a leading role in international monetary affairs before 1956 was that many European countries resorted to regional devices for overcoming their payments problems. One such arrangement was the European Payments Union (EPU), which arose out of the need for greater flexibility in intra-European payments if Marshall Aid was to work effectively. This scheme incorporated automatic clearing of all payments deficits, regardless of size, the automatic settlement of reciprocal deficits, and machinery for correcting intra-European payments disequilibria. The Bank for International Settlements (BIS) acted as the agent of the member countries. The IMF opposed the formation and existence of the EPU, chiefly because it provided a rival mechanism for settling balance of payments difficulties. Although the EPU became redundant in 1958 when most of its members accepted non-resident convertibility, it remained during the 1950s one manifestation of the European desire to achieve financial independence of the United States and of Europe's preoccupation with its own well-being rather than with the international economy as a whole.

Another regional payments arrangement in existence during these years was the Sterling Area, which had contracted sharply with the outbreak of World War II to include the British Commonwealth (other than Canada), the Colonial Territories, Ireland, Egypt, Sudan, Iceland and Iraq. The need to conserve gold and dollars for war purposes led, in 1939, to the introduction of exchange controls which remained in force until the late 1950s. The principle underlying the system was simple. All gold and foreign currency earned was directed into a single pool, the Exchange Equalization Account, and all external payments from the Area were made from that pool. Within the Area itself, there was free movement of currencies, whereas payments into or out of the bloc were subject to regulation. The relevance of the Sterling Area disappeared in 1961 when the United Kingdom adopted IMF convertibility.

An Overview of the 1950s

The long period of currency inconvertibility to 1961 not only prevented the efficient working of the IMF, which depended on the widespread convertibility of member countries' currencies, but it also inevitably produced a situation which ensured the Bretton Woods system would never be implemented in the form originally proposed. To begin with, the economic rivalry between the United States and Western Europe, a major factor in the eventual breakdown of the international monetary system, began to appear early in the 1950s. As we have noted, because the IMF was regarded as largely U.S. dominated and because the Fund refused to play an active role in solving the immense monetary problems being experienced in Europe at the time, the West European countries created a purely European substitute—the EPU. This shift in the direction of economic regionalization was carried even further in 1957 with the formation of the European Economic Community. Second, the IMF architects had not foreseen the large increase in world trade and commerce which began in the mid-1950s and the inadequacy of existing gold stocks and gold production to cope with the large increase in the demand for foreign currency reserves that accompanied it. As a result, most countries turned to 'key' currencies to perform the major role in the accumulation of reserve assets. The U.S. stipulation that only dollars (or gold) would be accepted in payments settlements and the U.S. payments surpluses in the 1950s produced a large increase in the demand for the dollar as a reserve asset, a development which bypassed the Fund system. In short, in the 1950s, the international monetary system moved towards a gold exchange standard similar to that of the 1920s and which collapsed at the end of that decade. The emphasis was on virtually rigid exchange rates and on the accumulation and use of key international currencies as reserves. Even before the acceptance of non-resident convertibility in 1958, the dangers inherent in such trends were being stressed by international monetary experts but, as we shall see later, these dangers were largely ignored. The major role of the IMF under the new gold exchange standard was the provision of short-term liquidity through its drawings mechanism to those countries experiencing balance of payments problems and a consequent rundown of their gold and key currency reserves.

THE IMF IN THE 1960s

Innovations in the Fund

IMF quotas were increased further in 1965 and again in 1970, raising the institution's resources to over $29 billion by the end of 1973. Throughout this period a much greater use was made of the Fund than previously and, between 1960 and 1973, total drawings amounted to $23 billion. European currencies were in much greater demand in the 1960s and the Fund's holdings of EEC currencies were very low at times during the decade. In 1961, 1964 and 1965, the Fund's support of sterling led total drawings to exceed $2 billion in each of these years, while in 1968 and 1969, both France and Germany drew heavily from the Fund.

Several other changes in the Fund's financing arrangements occurred during this period. The shortage of dollars in its stocks in the 1950s led to the sale of gold by the Fund to relieve this shortage. By 1960, dollars to the value of $606 million had been obtained in this way. During the 1960s, the Fund's holding of several European currencies was also threatened with depletion and, from 1961 to 1973, further sales of gold to the value of $3.3 billion were effected to obtain additional stocks of these currencies. At the same time, the Fund's powers to borrow currencies from member countries were formalized in 1962 by the establishment of the General Arrangements to Borrow (GAB) which allowed the Fund access to the currencies of ten of the major trading countries (which became known as the Group of Ten) up to certain specified limits. The total borrowing power of the Fund under the GAB was $6 billion and, by 1973, the Fund had borrowed $2.65 billion, almost exclusively in continental European currencies. Borrowing from Italy and Japan outside the GAB amounted to $500 million.

The First Amendment to the Fund's Articles of Agreement was adopted in 1969 as a result of long discussions concerning the need to increase the availability of reserve assets for member countries to hold. As the world's gold production could not expand enough to meet the growing need for international liquidity induced by a rapidly expanding world trade, member countries could increase their reserve assets only by accumulating certain key currencies such as the U.S. dollar and the pound sterling. For such accumulations of a particular currency to occur, however, the issuing country had to be willing to run deficits in its own balance of payments. Should the key currency countries refuse to tolerate such deficits and attempt to reduce or eliminate them, the major source of international liquidity might well dry up and jeopardize the continued growth of world trade. It was with this latter prospect in mind that the First Amendment was adopted to introduce into the system the Special Drawing Right (SDR, or 'paper gold') as a new international 'money', held as book entries in the Fund,[2] but available to supplement the international reserve assets of member countries. The new facility became effective on 1 January 1970, when the first allocation of SDRs to members on the basis of quotas was made. By the end of 1973, almost 6.2 billion SDRs had been allocated in this way.

Finally, two other innovations of this period included, first, the introduction of a compensatory and contingency financing facility (CCFF) beginning in 1963 to aid members experiencing a sudden shortfall in their export receipts below the medium-term trend (compensatory) or an anticipated shortfall (contingency). This facility eventually allowed such members to draw up to 100 per cent of their quotas in the year in which the shortfall occurred. From 1963 to 1973, 29 countries obtained access to the CCFF, drawing a total of $870 million. Secondly, there was the Buffer Stock Financing Facility (BSFF), set up in 1969 to allow a member to draw as much as 50 per cent of quota to aid the financing of an international buffer stock scheme.

The IMF and the International Monetary System

The gold exchange standard, complete with highly inflexible exchange rates, which emerged in a fully-fledged form during the 1960s, had several implications for the future of the Fund. First, whereas the Bretton Woods agreement allowed for changes in the value of a country's currency whenever it was apparent that a 'fundamental disequilibrium' existed in the country's balance of payments, the new arrangements implicitly placed a currency devaluation in the 'last resort' category. Countries compelled by the seriousness of their payments situation to devalue their currencies (such as the United Kingdom in 1967) were virtually accused of gross financial mismanagement. The prevailing prescription for balance of payments adjustment was internal deflation and, if necessary, substantial borrowing to control the outflow of speculative capital.

Secondly, as the 1960s progressed and the United States continued to run substantial payments deficits in support of the demand for increased international liquidity, another problem emerged—that of confidence in the dollar. This problem was compounded by the growing balance of payments surpluses of the industrial countries of Western Europe, as they improved their international competitiveness relative to the United States. Through these surpluses, countries such as Germany, France, the Netherlands and Italy, increased their foreign exchange assets considerably—from $5 billion in 1960 to $34 billion at the end of 1973. Despite the growing shortages of the currencies of these countries in the Fund, the use of the scarce currency clause was never considered by the Fund. Rather, it purchased additional quantities of such currencies with gold or borrowed them under the GAB. It was the rivalry between the United States and Western Europe which largely created this impasse. The United States had assumed the role of provider of reserve assets to the rest of the world and, to do so, ignored its overall payments situation. Western Europe, on the other hand, ignored its own surplus position and was reluctant to consider upward valuation of its exchange rates as a solution to the problem of its balance of payments surplus. A few upward revaluations (of the deutsche mark and the guilder in 1961 of 5 per cent) did occur but these were isolated events. Moreover, while the Europeans argued increasingly that adjustment should be made by the United States, they were not willing to prevent the growth of the Eurodollar market which occurred in the early 1960s and which aggravated the instability of the dollar.

A Eurodollar is a time deposit denominated in U.S. dollars placed in a bank located in another country, for example, in Britain. As a time deposit, it cannot be used by its owner during the period of the deposit but it can be lent out by the bank to others who may require dollars for transactions purposes. The rate of interest paid by the bank to the depositor of a Eurodollar will be higher than that obtainable for such a period in the United States and the rates charged by the bank to the borrowers will be lower than such borrowers can obtain in their own countries or in the United States. The relatively small gap between borrowing and lending rates in Eurobanks demonstrates the greater efficiency of such operations relative to domestic operations. The Eurodollar market appeared after the acceptance of non-resident convertibility by the major trading countries in 1958. Its size was to grow rapidly after the oil price increases in 1973–4, the oil exporters feeding dollars into the market and oil-importing countries becoming major borrowers. In addition, this market became an important source of funds for the major debtor nations of the 1980s. The growth of Western Europe, especially in the 1960s and 1970s, was partly financed with Eurodollars. By 1995, the market for Eurodollars had grown to around $4,000 billion. Other Euro-currencies, such as the deutsche mark, sterling, Swiss franc, and the yen have appeared and have grown in importance since the 1960s and, in 1995, the total was around

$2,000 billion. The introduction of the new European currency, the euro, has led to the dropping of the term 'euro-currencies' from reports in favour of cross-border bank claims and liabilities.

Another departure from the IMF system was the setting up of the Basle Arrangements and reciprocal swaps. The first was an agreement among European central banks to aid each other when flows of 'hot' (speculative) money produced pressures on their currencies. In several of the British payments crises of the 1960s, the Bank of England was able to maintain the value of sterling by borrowing extensively from continental central banks at the critical moment. Reciprocal swaps involved similar arrangements between Western European central bankers and those of the United States and Japan.

Despite the disagreement between surplus Europe and deficit United States concerning the source of the pressures that sometimes created uncertainty about the Fund system, tacit co-operation between them prolonged the life of the gold exchange standard. For example, the 'dollar overhang' (an excess of dollars held abroad over the value of the U.S. gold holdings) which developed in the early 1960s, could have forced the United States to suspend dollar convertibility if a rush by European central banks to convert their holdings of dollars into gold had developed, thereby ending the IMF system. Agreement among European central bankers not to upset the system in this way ensured its extension during the late 1960s. Secondly, eight Group of Ten countries formed a 'gold pool' in 1961 with the Bank of England as its agent, to hold the free-market price of gold at around $35 an ounce, the price established in 1934. The Bank would sell gold from the pool when upward market pressures appeared and buy gold if the price tended to fall. The arrangement worked well until the pound was devalued in 1967 when confidence in the key currencies weakened. France's withdrawal from the pool in 1968 led to severe upward pressures on the gold price and, to prevent the gold reserves of the pool from depletion, the Bank of England withdrew from the market, allowing the price of gold to increase. Thereafter, lack of confidence in the international monetary system forced the gold price to rise to a record height of over $900 an ounce in 1978. From 1968, a two-tiered system existed with the official gold price remaining at $35 an ounce, considerably below the free-market price.

Meanwhile, because of the declining United States competitiveness and its continuing heavy private foreign investment, which transferred production abroad and reduced domestic exports, its trade account moved into deficit late in the 1960s. Thus the United States 'deficit' policy in support of international liquidity became untenable. In August 1971, the U.S. President arrived at this conclusion and rendered the dollar inconvertible into gold and, to improve the U.S. balance of payments, placed a 10 per cent surcharge on all imports, a measure justified in the United States on the basis of the 'unfair' exchange rates existing at the time. Thus ended the gold exchange standard with its problems of liquidity, adjustment (or lack of it) and confidence.

Despite the claims that the Bretton Woods system came to grief in 1971, the system in force at that time paid no more than lip service to that system agreed upon in 1944. We cannot be certain therefore that the Bretton Woods system would have similarly failed because it was never implemented as its architects envisaged.

UNCERTAIN YEARS, 1971–6

As noted earlier, this five-year period witnessed an upheaval in the international economy. The commodity boom which ended in 1973, the world-wide high rates of inflation, exacerbated by the huge increase in the price of oil late in 1973, and government endeavours to curb inflationary pressures, led to a world recession in 1975 which had not been reversed by the signing of the Jamaica Agreement early in 1976. At the same time, the immense flow of financial resources to the oil-exporting countries led to large payments imbalances among the oil-importing countries. By the mid-1970s, a high degree of uncertainty existed in the world economy concerning its future development and it was against this background that reform of the international monetary system was attempted.

In response to the measures introduced by the United States in August 1971, namely, the inconvertibility of the dollar and the 10 per cent import surcharge, the Smithsonian Agreement of December 1971 produced what were to be temporary and marginal changes in the international monetary system. Although it was an agreement concluded within the Group of Ten, the IMF gave its blessing to the changes, which involved a re-alignment of exchange rates including a 10 per cent devaluation of the dollar against gold and the SDR, and a wider margin for fluctuation of the market value of a currency around the par value (now called the central rate) before the currency had to be supported by the central bank. As for the future, the growing solidarity among the developing country members of the Fund ensured that any substantial reform of the system would be conducted under the control of the Fund, which had much wider representation than the Group of Ten. With the setting up within the Fund of a Committee of Twenty in 1972 to produce proposals for the reform of the system, it would appear at first sight that the Fund had regained its central role in the system. In reality this was not entirely so. The chief reason for the failure of this committee to produce concrete proposals for reform was to be found in the lack of agreement between representatives of the industrial countries on the committee on a number of matters and, particularly, on the question of the need for both surplus and deficit countries to make balance of payments adjustments if the stability of the system was to be maintained.

In February 1973, the U.S. dollar was again devalued (by 10 per cent) relative to gold and the SDR in an attempt to improve the U.S. balance of payments which again had deteriorated badly. In March, the deutsche mark was revalued upward by 3 per cent, but the change was only a prelude to the introduction of the 'European snake', the joint floating of most of the EEC currencies relative to the dollar. This arrangement ensured that fluctuations in the values of these currencies were contained within prescribed limits relative to one another while they floated together relative to the dollar. The snake arrangements formed an integral part of the European Monetary System which came into effect in March 1979 with its ECU (European Currency Unit). Once again, Europe managed to set itself apart from the rest of the international economy.

The dismantling of the 'old' system continued in 1973 with the ending of the two-tiered gold policy, when the former gold pool members terminated their agreement not to sell gold in the private markets; with an increase in the size of the reciprocal swaps arrangements within the Group of Ten from $6,250 million to $17,980 million; and with a general movement within the industrial countries towards the 'managed floating' of their currencies—a considerable change from the rigid exchange rates of the immediate past.

In January 1974, the Committee of Twenty abandoned its two-year time-table for international monetary reform, agreeing that the altered conditions in the world economy, such as the oil price crisis and the movement into recession on a wide scale, required priority to be given to monetary arrange-ments which would solve or at least contain the new problems in the short term. When, in June 1974, the Committee concluded its deliberations, it advocated the setting up of an Interim Committee to continue with 'an evolutionary approach' to international monetary reform, the establishment of guidelines for the management of floating exchange rates, the establish-ment of a special oil facility within the Fund, and the valuation of the SDR on the basis of a standard weight of a basket of 16 currencies. The last was advocated to break the nexus between the SDR and gold (and the dollar). All these recommendations were put into effect in the months that followed. The Fund's oil facility allowed drawings by countries whose balance of payments was severely affected by the need to increase payments for oil imports. Such drawings were financed from funds provided largely by the oil-exporting members.

The creation of the Interim Committee ensured that there was virtually no cessation to the discussion on monetary reform. Early in January 1976, this committee produced the Jamaica Agreement which was to form the basis of the Second Amendment of the Fund Agreement and was to guide international monetary affairs through the next two decades. It brought to completion 'the first stage in the evolutionary reform of the international monetary system'. While the Jamaica Agreement stressed the need for mone-tary co-operation, it legalized the floating of the currencies of member coun-tries and the right of central bankers to interfere in the float. The IMF was to maintain surveillance over the managed floating of currencies and over the international liquidity policies of member countries. A 32.5 per cent general rise in quotas and larger increases in the quotas of oil-exporting countries were to bring the Fund's resources up to SDR39,000 million. The international monetary system was to move in an evolutionary manner towards an SDR system and gold was to be downgraded as a reserve asset. The Fund was to sell 25 million ounces (one-sixth of its gold holdings) by tender, and profits from these sales were to be used to set up a trust fund to assist developing countries with 1973 per capita incomes of no more than SDR300. The Second Amendment, incorporating these proposals, was effective from April 1978. Even so, another increase in quotas occurred in 1983, raising the total to almost SDR90 billion.

THE POST-JAMAICAN PERIOD, 1976–2000

The high inflation and unemployment of the second half of the 1970s continued into the 1980s, partly as a result of a second large increase in the price of oil. Serious international debt problems were created for many non-oil-exporting countries and these were perpetuated throughout the decade. Despite the fact that the floating of a number of currencies, freely or managed, reduced their demand for drawings from the Fund, the Fund gained a substantial amount of prestige over the years and its position in international monetary affairs tended to be enhanced. First, only 51 of the 181 currencies were floating independently, including (in March 1997) those of the United States, the United Kingdom, Japan, Canada, Australia, Italy, Sweden, Finland, Switzerland, New Zealand and several developing countries, including some eastern European currencies. The currencies of many other countries were tied to the SDR or leading key currencies and for them recourse to drawings was still necessary when their balance of payments deteriorated.

Second, increased quotas enlarged the Fund's facilities for granting drawings to countries with payments difficulties. Third, the total allocation of SDRs rose from 9.315 billion in 1976 to 21.5 billion in 1989 and the use of SDRs increased accordingly. Fourth, since 1976, a number of other financial facilities have been created in the Fund to enlarge its resources available to developing countries, especially the poorest of them. These included the SAF (structural adjustment facility) with commitments in excess of SDR1.7 billion, operational from 1987, and an ESAF (enhanced structural adjustment facility), commencing in 1989 on a renewal basis, which provides resources on concessional terms to support medium-term macroeconomic adjustment and structural reforms in low-income countries with heavy balance of payments problems. Loans drew an interest rate of 0.5 per cent a year and loans were to be repaid over five and a half to ten years. All SAF resources were allocated by 1995, but it was expected that an ESAF facility would continue, providing the revolving nature of the Fund's resources was maintained.

Provisions for funds to be made available under this facility were outlined in the mid-1990s, and included SDR3 billion a year for new loans and interest payments in the years 2000–2004, with extra funds coming from the self-financing nature of the ESAF.

In addition, a temporary STF (Systemic Transformation Facility) was established in April 1993 to provide financing to members with balance of payments problems associated with their change-over from non-market price setting to market-based pricing. With the collapse of the centrally-planned economies at the beginning of the 1990s, the Fund aided substantially the transition of these countries to market-based economies. After their admission to membership, large amounts of funds were made available to them, their use being subject to certain conditions regarding the monetary, fiscal, and other policies of the respective governments. The STF was primarily set up for this purpose while general drawings and stand-by credits were also used. Users were expected to switch to a stand-by arrangement of ESAF rapidly. Largely aimed at the countries in transition (CITs), it ceased to operate at the end of 1995.

Up to April 1997, these facilities had provided some SDR13 billion (SAF loans, SDR1.8 billion, ESAF, SDR7.1 billion, and almost SDR4 billion in STF). The CCFF continues to offer its own special type of aid. The need for adequate 'conditionality'[3] is taken into account whenever recourse to these facilities was requested. Finally, in December 1997, the Fund introduced a Supplemental Reserve Facility (SRF) to provide financial assistance to a member experiencing substantial payments difficulties owing to a large short-run financing need brought about by a sudden and disruptive loss of market confidence displayed by pressure on the capital account and the member's reserves. Korea was the first country to be offered aid under the SRF, early in 1998.

Fifth, through the profits from its gold sales ($4.6 billion), the Fund was able to set up a Trust Fund of SDR3,000 million out of which it could make loans to the poorest of the developing countries. Finally, to upgrade the prestige of the SDR to the position of major reserve asset, several abortive attempts were made to establish a substitution account by means of which key currencies held as official reserve assets could be exchanged for SDRs.

In the 1980s and 1990s the Fund's international reputation was further enhanced by a number of developments. In the 1980s it adopted a positive role in attempts to alleviate the large debt problems of a number of major developing countries. In the 1990s, its support helped to overcome the enormous economic problems faced by East European countries in their transition to market-based economic systems. Finally, in 1997, the Fund was called upon to assist Thailand, Indonesia, Malaysia, the Philippines and Korea in dealing with the sudden collapse of their economies.

It was against this background that the IMF quotas were raised by 45 per cent in 1998, the total reaching SDR212 billion (U.S.$288 billion). Moreover, by the mid-1990s, the Fund's powers to borrow from member countries increased substantially. The General Arrangements to Borrow (GAB) amounted to SDR17 billion from the 11 members (the Group of Ten and Switzerland[4]) and SDR1.5 billion under an associated agreement with Saudi Arabia. From the commencement of the GAB in 1962 up to 1997, the IMF took advantage of the arrangements to borrow nine times. Early in 1997, new borrowing arrangements were approved to enhance the Fund's ability to safeguard the international monetary system. These were included in the NAB (New Arrangements to Borrow), under which 25 members and institutions can lend to the IMF additional resources up to SDR34 billion (c$47 billion), to supplement its regular quota drawing rights to deal with unusual pressures in the international monetary system. The NAB did not replace the GAB, but became the facility of first recourse and remains in force initially for five years. Activation is similar to the GAB but is more flexible.[5] Such foresight concerning the need for such an innovation was undoubtedly accidental, for the massive Fund financial relief for countries such as Korea, Malaysia, Thailand, the Philippines and Indonesia, was possible later in 1997 only through the existence of the increased quotas and other facilities including the Fund's borrowing rights.

Meanwhile in the European Union there was a steady move towards full monetary integration within the region. The role of sterling as a key currency had been brought to an end in 1977 when the Bank of England arranged a Basle agreement with the central banks of eight industrial countries to ensure that end. Whereas Britain floated the pound sterling separately after 1973, the ECU also floated against the dollar but the members of the European Monetary System (EMS) had to adhere to an adjustable peg relative to the ECU (European Currency Unit). This EMS began in 1979 and covered the currencies of Belgium, Denmark, France, Germany, Ireland, Italy and the Netherlands. It had some success in its aims to achieve the downward convergence of the inflation rates of member countries and to insulate the exchange rates of member currencies against the fluctuations of the dollar. Nevertheless, from March 1979 to September 1992, there were 11 currency realignments within the EMS with a number of temporary withdrawals of currencies from the system, followed by an exchange market crisis which lasted from September 1992 to August 1993, when each currency was allowed to fluctuate in the market to a greater extent. However, in the Maastricht Treaty of December 1991, plans were developed for the full monetary integration of the EU, including the introduction of a European currency (the euro) and a European central bank (ECB) to replace the numerous national currencies and central banks of the member countries. A timetable was established, committing EU members to monetary integration by 1997 but it was later changed to 1999 when it became apparent that few countries would achieve the stringent European Monetary Union (EMU) entry conditions by 1997. Whether full monetary integration will result in higher levels of economic growth in the EU beyond the year 2000 than have been achieved so far in the 1990s will depend very much on the monetary policy pursued by the newly-created European Central Bank (ECB).

Because of the floating of a number of major world currencies, the consequent abundance of international liquidity, and the lack of demand for further SDR allocations, the expected SDR standard failed to materialize. At an IMF seminar in March 1996, it was accepted that the SDR was unlikely to become the main reserve asset of the international monetary system, nor would it become a fully-fledged world currency. Nevertheless, for several reasons, including a possible need for its use if the world economy got into serious difficulties, it was agreed that it should not be abolished.

Increasingly throughout the 1980s, and widespread during the 1990s, was the adoption of the 'new' economic stabilization philosophy mentioned earlier in this book.[6] It was adopted by the Fund at the Madrid meeting of the Interim Committee in October 1994, for inclusion in its advice to countries requiring financial aid. Unemployment did not enter into the equation because it was argued by macro-economists and accepted by the Fund that unemployment was largely a structural problem, the solution of which required labour market reforms. A steadfast belief within the IMF in macro-economic stabilization (maintaining low levels of inflation) and structural reform has influenced the Fund to take a greater interest in the internal affairs of its member countries.

In the 1990s some emerging markets experienced major monetary crises, especially Mexico in 1994 and ASEAN (Association of South Eastern Asian Nations) countries, Hong Kong, Taiwan and Korea in 1997, while Japan's long-term banking problems left much to be desired. With the expansion of the global financial system, certain weaknesses in it became more apparent. Greater freedom of movement of money from country to country enhanced the activities of speculators willing to shift funds very quickly at the first sign of trouble, thus compounding for the countries concerned whatever economic problems had appeared in them.

The opening up of capital markets on an international scale began after the adoption of floating exchange rates in the 1970s and later, thus accelerating the free movement of capital funds into and out of countries. Capital controls were lifted in the United States and Germany by 1975, in Britain in 1979, in Japan in 1980, and in the rest of Western Europe by 1990. By 1997, almost all of the advanced countries and 25 per cent of developing countries have dispensed with capital controls. These changes brought about capital account convertibility in the balance of payments and thus promoted the further globalization of financial markets. While such capital movements advanced the process of international economic integration, they also made economies vulnerable to outside shocks and, along with floating exchange rates, created the need for risk-avoiding instruments.

Floating exchange rates and a globally-free capital market undoubtedly intensifies international monetary crises by encouraging international currency speculation. At the same time, the large increase in the volume of portfolio capital in the international monetary system, combined with the rapid growth of derivatives, tends to emphasize the great uncertainty that exists over the future of the international monetary system. The accentuation of monetary problems will be most severe where the country's financial sector is fraught with a lack of responsibility, as has been most evident in the recent economic crisis in East Asia.

CONCLUDING REMARKS

The first stage in the development of the post World War II international monetary system came to an end in the early 1970s. Attempts at reform of the system have failed, which is not surprising, given that the shift towards more flexible exchange rates and the continuing use by many countries of the U.S. dollar as an international reserve asset, reduced the pressures for far-reaching changes in the international monetary area. There are several new problems confronting the system in the final years of the twentieth century. These include the enormous financial problems of the Countries in Transition and their need for massive amounts of investment funds—and the Asian financial crises—both products of floating exchange rates, easily obtainable investment funds searching for profitable avenues of investment, and 'hot money'. The introduction of the European single currency and its impact on the international monetary system, with the disappearance of the relevant national currencies and varying national monetary policies, along with the intense concentration of the Fund on developing countries with its conditionality approach, are further matters for concern. Finally, there is the obsession of the Fund with the rational economists' approach to economic policy from which, in the second half of the 1990s, without even a close approach to the full requirements of the new policy, major social unheavals have appeared in a number of countries because of the large unemployment such a policy engenders.

Nevertheless, the Fund has been equipped with new and massive sources of funds to maintain its operations for maintaining sound balance of payments positions in its member countries.

NOTES

1 This deficit resulted from a deteriorating trade balance, an expansion of foreign investment and a continuing high level of U.S. government outlays abroad.
2 Initially, the value of one SDR was equal to one U.S. dollar or 0.888671 grains of gold.
3 Under the conditionality approach, a country requesting a Fund drawing has to

satisfy the Fund that certain policies would be followed in an effort to eliminate the payments problem that caused the need for the required funds. Some countries regard conditionality as undue interference by the Fund in domestic affairs, whereas it is looked upon by the Fund as essential to the maintenance of the revolving nature of the Fund's financial resources. The conditionality rule was tightened during the 1990s.

4 Switzerland joined the GAB in 1982 after having had a loose arrangement with the IMF since 1962.

5 The countries included in the NAB were Australia, Austria, Belgium, Canada, Denmark, Finland, France, Germany, Hong Kong, Italy, Japan, Korea, Kuwait, Luxembourg, Malaysia, the Netherlands, Norway, Saudi Arabia, Singapore, Spain, Sweden, Switzerland, Thailand, the United Kingdom and the United States.

6 See p. 250.

SELECTED REFERENCES

Bank for International Settlements, *Annual Report*, various issues.

Garritsen de Vries, M., *Balance of Payments Adjustment, 1945–1986: The IMF Experience* (Washington: IMF, 1986).

International Monetary Fund, *Annual Report*, various issues.

International Monetary Fund, 'Financial Crises, Characteristics and Indicators of Vulnerability', *World Economic Outlook*, May, 1998, pp. 74–97.

MacBean, A. I. and Snowden, P. N., *International Institutions in Trade and Finance* (London: George Allen & Unwin, 1981).

Salvatore, D., *International Economics* (Englewood Cliffs, New Jersey: Prentice Hall, 1995), Ch. 21.

Valentine, T., 'Putting Derivatives in their Proper Place', *Agenda*, vol. 2, 1995, pp. 321–332.

Williamson, J., *The Lending Policies of the International Monetary Fund* (Washington: Institute for International Economics, 1982).

Chapter 19

The GATT, the World Trade Organization, and international commercial policy, 1947–2000

THE EARLY YEARS, 1947–60

Despite the diversity of interests among the contracting parties to GATT and the variety of commercial policies they pursued, GATT achieved considerable success in a number of areas during the 1950s. While the early success recorded in the 1947 tariff-reducing negotiations was not again repeated in the subsequent meetings at Annecy (1949), Torquay (1950–1), and Geneva (1955–6), some progress continued to be made and, by the mid-1950s, a net reduction in U.S. duties of 50 per cent had been achieved since 1934 by tariff concessions alone, the greater part of which had occurred after 1945. Even more striking, GATT membership grew from 23 signatories in 1947 to over 70 in 1960, covering over 80 per cent of total world trade. In addition, by providing a forum for conciliation and discussion, GATT resolved, often through arbitration or adjudication, commercial disputes which might otherwise have caused continuing bad feeling, reprisals, and even diplomatic breakdown.

Progress in dealing with quantitative trade restrictions was much slower than that with tariffs, partly because the economic difficulties of the late 1940s and 1950s led many countries to retain controls over their trade, and partly because GATT's powers over quantitative restrictions were weak, for it could only consult with members to persuade them to reduce these restrictive measures. But GATT's constant review of the individual commercial policies and its persistent attempts to reduce trade restrictions must have contributed something to the general, gradual, elimination of such restrictions which occurred in the late 1950s. Moreover, GATT's existence may have prevented the use of new preferential arrangements similar to those adopted in the 1920s, but this did not preclude the growth of regional trading blocs under the exceptions to the no-new-preferences rule which eroded GATT's powers to some extent.

The Advent of Regional Trading Blocs

A number of small customs unions, France–Monaco, Italy–San Marino, Switzerland–Liechtenstein and Belgium–Luxembourg, emerged unbroken from World War II.[1] After the war, the trend towards economic and/or political integration gathered pace. The first step had been taken with the formation of Benelux in 1944, when Belgium, the Netherlands, and Luxembourg agreed to establish a tariff community (Benelux) with a common external tariff as a prelude to complete economic integration in later years.

In 1950, the Schuman Plan to set up a European Coal and Steel Community (ECSC) under a waiver of GATT's no-new-preferences rule, was adopted by the Benelux countries, France, West Germany and Italy. The ECSC gradually removed duties on coal and steel, subsidies and other restrictions and discriminatory devices between member countries, under the guidance of a supranational authority. But it was only a forerunner of bigger things to come. In 1955, discussions began on the formation of a customs union by ECSC members, with far-reaching implications for the international economy as a whole. The structure of the European Economic Community (EEC) was agreed upon in March 1957 and incorporated in the Treaty of Rome, the provisions of which came into operation in 1958, after GATT's recognition of the regional trading bloc.

The aim of the EEC, by establishing a common market and by progressively harmonizing the economic policies of the member states, was to promote the development of economic activities in the region, increase economic stability, and accelerate improvements in the living standards of the population. Political unity formed a long-run aim even if it was only implied in the Treaty. Other features provided for the free movement of people, services, and capital within the region, common agricultural and transport policies, and the setting up of a Social Fund and an Investment Bank. The Treaty also provided for association of the EEC with the dependent overseas territories of the member states.

While the creation of permanent regional entities was an acceptable exception to the no-new-preferences rule at the time the General Agreement was signed in 1947, no one expected such unions to produce major trading blocs of the size of the EEC. In any case, it was considered that when formed they would prove beneficial to countries outside the union by improving the welfare of the participants and creating additional opportunities for trade. But with the establishment of large customs unions, it was found necessary to consider not only their trade-creating potentialities, but also the trade-diverting effects of such unions, that is, the extent to which the formation of a customs union will lead to a diversion of the trade of one member country from third countries to another member of the union. Moreover, while the rest of the world would benefit from the setting up of the customs union only if the creation of new trade opportunities exceeded the extent of trade diversion, the trade-creating aspects may also be perverse to the extent that only a few external countries could gain while the rest of the world did not. The big danger from a large union such as the EEC is the great temptation for it to become inward-looking and that, consequently, any benefits to be derived by external countries are only incidental.

The Haberler Report

The general improvement in trading conditions between the Western industrial nations evident in the second half of the 1950s led to increasing dissatisfaction among the primary producing countries. They were inclined to look upon GATT as an institution designed largely to allow commercial policies which favoured the richest industrial contracting parties. Consequently, a panel of experts was appointed to investigate and report on the working of the General Agreement since 1947. The Haberler Report was presented to GATT in 1958. It emphasized two major points: that agricultural protectionism in the industrial countries had minimized the benefits that the traditional food-exporting countries could have expected to receive from their membership of GATT, and that many of the developing countries had also been disadvantaged by the commercial and other policies of the industrial nations.

THE GATT, THE WTO AND COMMERCIAL POLICY, 1960–2000

After the Haberler Report

Out of the deliberations on the Haberler Report came the setting up of three committees to consider further tariff reductions, agricultural protectionism, and the specific trade problems of the developing countries. The first committee produced the Dillon and Kennedy Rounds of tariff negotiations in 1961 and 1964–7. The second committee, after much research, concluded that 'the extensive resort to non-tariff protection of agriculture had impaired or nullified tariff concessions or other benefits which agricultural exporting countries expect to receive from the General Agreement.' The third committee on the trade problems of the developing countries in 1964 achieved the incorporation of a new chapter in the General Agreement allowing discrimination in favour of developing countries. This paved the way for the establishment of the Generalized System of Preferences (GSP), introduced by most industrialized countries in the 1970s, for example, by the EEC in 1971 and the United States in 1976.

The Formation and Development of UNCTAD

As we have already seen, a major source of grievance within GATT in the 1950s was the relatively poor export performance of many primary-producing countries. Whereas some of the reasons for this state of affairs were to be found in the domestic policies of the primary-producing countries themselves, many of them, nevertheless, believed that the industrial nations had used the exceptions in GATT to protect their own relatively inefficient agricultural industries to the detriment of foreign primary producers. Furthermore, until the Kennedy round in the mid-1960s, agricultural products did not enter into discussions on tariff reductions. Rightly or wrongly, the less developed countries came to look upon GATT as a 'rich man's club' and, early in the 1960s, they turned to the United Nations, the only forum in which they had considerable voting strength, for an answer to their trade problems. The result was the first meeting of UNCTAD, the United Nations Conference on Trade and Development, in Geneva in 1964.

UNCTAD became institutionalized in much the same way as GATT, and conferences have been held in New Delhi (1968), Santiago (1972), Nairobi (1976), Manila (1979), Belgrade (1983), Geneva (1987), Cartagena (1992) and South Africa in 1996. UNCTAD membership includes most developing countries while developed nations maintain observers at all discussions. UNCTAD cannot force its recommendations on the industrial countries but, even so, by highlighting the inequities of the trade system and other aspects of international economic relations which favour the economically powerful, it has often influenced the richer nations into offering concessions that otherwise may not have been made. In the 1970s it highlighted the call for a 'new international economic order' and for a 'North–South' debate on the existing and mounting problems of the Third World. At Manila in 1979 (UNCTAD V) there was widespread support for the introduction of an integrated programme of commodities (IPC) and the establishment of a Common Fund, with a view to stabilizing primary product prices, thereby eliminating some of the uncertainties surrounding the export earnings of many of the developing countries. Despite the efforts of UNCTAD, however, progress towards solving some of the more pressing economic problems currently confronting the Third World has been very slow.

Discrimination in World Trade

From the early 1960s the undermining of one of the basic principles upon which GATT had been founded—non-discrimination in trade and no new preferences—was carried even further than it had been in the 1950s with the formation of the EEC.

The original six EEC members were joined by Denmark, Ireland and the United Kingdom in 1973, by Greece in 1981, by Portugal and Spain in

1986, and by Austria, Finland and Sweden in 1995, thus covering 15 European nations. There are plans for further expansion, but these plans will proceed more slowly, even though, in 1997, certain countries in central and eastern Europe were separated out for accelerated movement towards membership. By that time, some 14 countries had applied for membership. Along the way the Community has acquired the reputation of being a very powerful economic and political entity.

In 1960, as a counter to the EEC, the European Free Trade Association (EFTA) was formed by Austria, Denmark, Norway, Portugal, Sweden, Switzerland and the United Kingdom. EFTA was a much looser organization than the EEC for, while each member country was committed to reducing its tariffs on the other member countries' goods, each country could follow an independent policy with regard to its import duties on goods coming from non-member countries. While Finland became an associate member in 1961 and Iceland joined EFTA in 1970 and Liechtenstein in 1991, EFTA was weakened by the entry of Denmark and the United Kingdom into the EEC in 1973, followed by Portugal, and Austria, Finland and Sweden in later years.[2] However, EFTA gained somewhat from the free trade agreement with the EEC on non-agricultural goods in 1972 and by the creation of the European Economic Area (EEA) in 1994, again with the EEC (EU), a form of a Single Market. Switzerland (and Liechtenstein), however, opted to remain outside the EEA. With only four members (two of which are small), the reasons for the continued existence of EFTA remain vague. While bilateral trade agreements providing for progressive trade liberalization were arranged with the Czech and Slovak Republics, Poland and Romania in 1992, and with Hungary in 1993, similar arrangements by the EU with these countries and the formation of the EEA tend to downgrade these relations.

In addition to the expansion of the EU borders, internally, greater consolidation occurred with the introduction of the Single Market programme of 1986, ensuring the elimination of internal non-tariff barriers to trade in commodities and services, which was to be completed by the end of 1992. While it was estimated that the GDP of the EU would increase by some 4.5 per cent as the result of these measures and that non-member countries would gain because of the increased imports that higher incomes would generate, despite favourable comments from the EU Commission there have been negligible visible signs of such favourable influences up to 1998.[3]

As a result of the development of the 'Cold War', the Eastern European centrally-planned countries set up their own trading bloc, COMECON or CMEA (Council for Mutual Economic Assistance), comprising the U.S.S.R., Poland, Hungary, Romania, Czechoslovakia and Albania. This bloc operated successfully until 1990 when, as a result of the breakdown of the U.S.S.R. and the movement of central Europe towards the establishment of market economies, this interdependence weakened considerably. It is still not clear if these countries, and the new nations emerging from the U.S.S.R., will continue to follow independent economic policies. Already several of them have applied to the EU for membership. None has yet been accepted but several are on the waiting list.

As many as 17 trading blocs were established in other parts of the world in the 1960s—regional arrangements of varying degrees of integration covering more than 80 contracting parties. These included the Latin American Free Trade Area (LAFTA) of seven countries, set up in 1961, and the Central American Common Market (CACM) which was to become fully integrated by 1967. In Africa, the seven former French West African colonies formed a new trading bloc, and Chad, Gabon and the Central African Republic formed the Equatorial Customs Union. The successful Association of South East Asian Nations (ASEAN) covering Brunei, Indonesia, Malaysia, Philippines, Singapore and Thailand was set up in 1967. In 1992, ASEAN established the ASEAN Free Trade Area (AFTA), accepting Vietnam as a member in 1995 and Burma (Myanmar), Laos and Cambodia in 1997. The Australia–New Zealand Closer Economic Relations (CER) agreement commenced in 1965. Other preferential arrangements were established elsewhere but they were important only within their own region and many of them did not last for more than a decade.

LAFTA succumbed in 1968 when it was replaced by the Andean Pact, covering Bolivia, Chile, Colombia, Ecuador and Peru. This organization was in difficulties by 1975 and the CACM disintegrated in the 1970s after Honduras left it. Nevertheless, such regional groupings were revitalized in the 1990s. The CACM still exists with its original members although the presence of many quotas and other barriers prevent the full flow-on of benefits expected from such a union. CARICOM is an association of Caribbean states including Cuba; while, in South America, the Andean Group now comprises Venezuela and Colombia (between which two countries trade has increased rapidly), Ecuador, Peru and Bolivia. This group now favours free trade within its borders. But out of the former LAFTA has emerged the most successful Latin American group—MERCOSUR, introduced in 1991, comprising Brazil, Argentina, Paraguay and Uruguay, and which became a full customs union in January 1995 but with, however, a number of national exceptions, especially in sugar and motor vehicles, which must disappear by 2001. Early indications suggest that this region has benefited from the closer ties. Chile and Bolivia have made approaches on membership. Other regional groupings were negotiated in several continents during the 1990s. Their significance to the growth of world trade has yet to be determined.

At the instigation of France, the first Yaoundé Convention of the EEC in 1963 granted association status to the former French, Belgian, and Italian colonies in Africa. Under this Convention, these newly-emerging African countries received preferential treatment for their exports within the EEC and, also, a European Development Fund (EDF) was set up to offer them financial aid. These arrangements received a hostile reception from other developing countries which were discriminated against by the preferences granted. Subsequently, however, the adoption of GSP by the EEC in 1971 did much to reduce the degree of preferential treatment accorded to the former colonies. In 1975, the Yaoundé Convention was superseded by the Lomé Convention, which extended the preferential arrangements to include the former colonies of Britain and widened the area covered by including countries and colonies in Africa, the Caribbean and the Pacific (ACP countries). Given that the degree of trade preferences afforded under this agreement would be small, the major benefit to be derived by the countries in the ACP region from association with the EEC arose out of the STABEX scheme, under which these countries were to be compensated for any shortfall in their export earnings on several commodities sold to the EEC. Such compensation is financed out of the European Development Fund.

In addition to these conventions, the EEC negotiated preferential trade treaties with numerous other countries, especially in the Mediterranean area and in South America. In 1972, the preferential bilateral trade agreements which had been concluded by the EEC with individual Mediterranean countries after 1968 were multilateralized for the region and a highly preferential system was created. All these arrangements (including the free entry into the EEC of non-agricultural goods from EFTA members after 1972) show up the weaknesses of the GATT, more particularly its inability to prevent further erosion of one of the basic principles on which it was founded, non-discrimination in trade and no new preferences. They also illustrate the fact that the EEC had not accepted those basic principles even if it still paid lip service to the GATT. By 1973 fewer than half a dozen countries were confronted by the EEC's most-favoured-nation (MFN) duties under these arrangements.

While the EEC/EU has been a major offender in terms of discriminatory trade practices during the last four decades, the stalwart of non-discriminatory trade dealings, the United States, reacted in the 1980s to the EEC's disregard of the GATT rules by introducing tariff preferences on a list of commodities in favour of certain Caribbean countries and took the first steps towards a free trade area with Israel. Of major interest has been the formation of the North American Free Trade Area (NAFTA) by the United States, Canada and Mexico, commencing in January 1994, with the possibility of future extensions. In the East, ongoing discussions are occurring on the possibility of forming another important free trade area, APEC (Asian Pacific Economic Community), which is a wide grouping of countries set up in 1989, somewhat defensively, as an answer to the EU in the Pacific Area. It is described as embracing 'open regionalism', in which, according to the principles of the WTO, free and open trade and investment in the region will be introduced by 2010 by the developed members and by 2020 by the developing members. The whole exercise is an attempt to strengthen the multilateral trading system of the WTO. Side agreements such as NAFTA and ASEAN tend also to widen and strengthen economic co-operation within this vast region.

On the other hand, the EU wishes to cast a European flavour to the movement towards the globalization of trade. Negotiations with the Mediterranean countries not covered by other agreements led to the Barcelona Declaration of 1995 by means of which a gradual introduction of a free trade area, to be known as the Euro-Mediterranean Partnership, will be completed by 2010. In addition, in that year, an agreement was signed with South American states, the EU–Mercosur Inter-Regional Framework Agreement, which will lead to a free trade agreement and, finally, co-operation agreements have been signed with certain Asian nations.

Agricultural Protectionism

There are two other areas in which world trade has been even more distorted by the actions of the developed countries. By far the most damaging departure from the principles of GATT in the 1960s was the introduction of the common agricultural policy (CAP) by the EEC. The CAP aimed at ensuring that farmers in the Community would be able to enjoy incomes comparable with those obtained in other domestic industries. This was achieved through restrictions on the entry of foodstuffs from non-member countries, the use of support prices for agricultural products, and the disposal of agricultural surpluses when necessary. To restrict imports, a variable levy system was introduced and used in such a way that imports of foodstuffs were priced higher than the same commodities produced by EEC farmers. The levy could thus be used as effectively as quantitative restrictions on agricultural imports. The pricing policy was subject to annual review and, as applied to some commodities, it led to overproduction and the accumulation of surpluses, for example, in sugar and butter. One way of disposing of such surpluses was to dump them on world markets, financing such disposals out of an agricultural fund (the EAGGF or FEOGA) which was fed by financial contributions from the member governments.

Britain's accession to the EEC in 1973 created almost insuperable difficulties for several countries that had long-established markets in Britain for a number of primary products. They were compelled to rationalize their efficient agricultural sectors and/or cultivate new markets elsewhere in the world. Ironically, this search for new markets was hampered by the EEC's and, from the mid-1980s, by the U.S. policy of dumping agricultural surpluses in world markets.

Over the years the enormous costs associated with the Common Agricultural Policy (CAP) attracted substantial criticism even by member countries. As a result, in the early 1990s, a Farm Commissioner, Ray MacSharry, suggested radical reforms to the CAP to reduce its costs. At the same time, the agricultural discussions which took place in the Uruguay Round concluded that quantitative restrictions on imports of agricultural products should be 'tariffied'; that these tariffs should then be reduced by 36 per cent from the 1986–8 base over a period of six years from mid-1995; that some domestic support (which distorted production or trade) should be subject to 20 per cent reduction; and that export subsidies be reduced by 21 per cent from 1995. While MacSharry's suggested cuts in agricultural support were watered down somewhat by the European Commission when they were due for implementation, the Uruguay Round proposals should reduce substantially the excessive protection of agriculture within the EU and elsewhere and may ensure that agricultural trade flows much more freely in the future, thus granting efficient farmers reasonable access to wider markets for their produce.

Non-tariff Trade Restrictions

The second area of great concern arose in the 1970s when, for a number of reasons, frequent and widespread resort to non-tariff restrictions on imports by the industrial countries occurred. The types of measures used were varied in character but orderly marketing arrangements (OMAs) and voluntary export restraints (VERs) were the most common. The effectiveness of Japan's penetration of American and European markets was of major concern to those countries and was the initial reason for such restrictions. Later, the tariff reductions negotiated under the Kennedy round, and finalized early in the 1970s, were soon found to benefit the newly-industrializing countries (NICs), particularly in textiles, clothing and footwear, and some restrictions on these imports soon followed. Third, under the GSP introduced in the early 1970s, tariff preferences were extended to a wide range of exports from the developing countries but, at the same time, it became common to fix annual maxima to the quantities of the commodities allowed into the countries offering such preferential treatment. Finally, the worsening economic conditions which prevailed in all industrial countries after 1973 led to a general claim by domestic producers for greater protection against imports. As a result, despite the inauguration of the Tokyo round, in which some attention had to be paid to non-tariff restrictions, this form of protection became even more widespread.

Multilateral Trade Negotiations (MTNs) Since 1960

Since 1960, four rounds of multilateral trade negotiations (MTNs) have been concluded. The Dillon Round of 1961 achieved very little and it became apparent that the method of product-by-product negotiations had finally reached its practical limits and was no longer useful in bringing about substantial reductions in the levels of protection. As a result, the Kennedy round (1964–7) was notable because linear reductions in tariffs on a wide variety of products were negotiated which achieved an average reduction in industrial tariffs of between 36 and 39 per cent. At the same time, over 60 per cent of the reductions were in excess of 50 per cent. Thus, some tariff harmonization also occurred. The Kennedy round favoured the trade of the industrial countries, although it also benefited some developing countries to the extent that the lowering of tariffs on manufactured goods allowed the rapid growth of manufactured exports from the NICs such as Brazil, Taiwan, Korea, Hong Kong and Singapore. Although the terms of negotiation of the round required that some regard be paid to the reduction of agricultural protection, little progress was made. A new International Grains Agreement was the only concession to agriculture made by the EEC and the United States, and this Agreement lasted only three years.

The third round of MTNs since 1960 was the Tokyo round (1973–9). For the first time it appeared that, in addition to the usual reductions in tariffs on manufactures, the negotiators were committed to a consideration of ways of reducing the barriers to trade in agricultural products and non-tariff trade barriers, as well as a general consideration of the trade problems of developing countries. While a number of factors contributed to a delay in the commencement of the negotiations until 1977, the Trade Negotiations Committee had by then established that discussions would proceed along seven lines:

- tariffs on industrial products;
- non-tariff barriers to trade;
- the sectoral approach, that is, the technique of co-ordinated reduction or elimination of trade barriers within particular product groups;
- agricultural products;
- tropical products;
- the adequacy of the multilateral safeguards system;
- special differential treatment for developing countries.

In addition to the general hostility in Europe against the reduction of agricultural protectionism, the lower growth performances of industrial countries increased rather than reduced the prevalence of non-tariff trade barriers. Contracting parties outside the United States and the European Community took little part in the deliberations. The outcome included around 30 per cent reductions in tariffs on industrial products, including some tariff harmonization. The reductions were larger on finished goods than on raw materials or intermediate products and small reductions in tariffs occurred for temperate zone agricultural commodities on which non-tariff barriers remained unchanged. Agreement on relatively minor aspects of trade, which were of interest primarily to the EEC and the United States, was also achieved. Given the extent to which non-tariff barriers, in the forms of OMAs and VERs, had been introduced, particularly in Europe, to counter competition from Japan and the NICs, the relatively minor agreements reached highlighted the manner in which many of the fundamental trade problems which were supposed to receive the bulk of attention of the round were side-stepped in the negotiations.

Japan, the NICs, and some developing countries desired the introduction of a code of conduct to be followed by countries introducing import controls aimed at preserving orderly marketing on certain products in their domestic markets, but the EEC insisted on maintaining the right to implement such controls on a unilateral basis when they became necessary.

Given the rhetoric with which the Tokyo round was introduced, it was a failure. Little was achieved of direct benefit to contracting parties outside the industrial world and much that was achieved was peripheral to the major issues upon which the round was justified. Largely, the industrial countries, and especially the EEC, set out to protect their positions, but the round was necessary precisely because the policies then being followed by the EEC and other countries were contrary to the fundamental philosophy underpinning GATT.

The Uruguay Round

The Uruguay Round, the sixth round of GATT negotiations which commenced in 1986, was the most ambitious of them all, taking seven years of hard bargaining in areas of trade which, for decades, had been considered too difficult, namely, trade in agriculture and trade in services. It also aimed to reduce the prevalence of the new protectionism, popular after the early 1970s. The agriculture problem held back the completion of the Round for three years.

There were important successes. It was estimated that over $740 billion in tariff cuts were achieved and it was predicted that world trade would increase by some $270 billion a year and that the world would be over $500 billion better off by 2005. How such an improvement will be distributed throughout the world has not been estimated. The major features of the agreements included the replacement of GATT by the World Trade Organization, which would, however, remain in Geneva. The WTO was given a broader range of activities, including agriculture, the textile and clothing trades,[4] and the trade in services. The trade-related aspects of investment and the protection of property rights and some internal policy issues such as trade and the environment, competition policy, and labour standards, which may feature as protection issues, were also covered by the new body. For the settlements of disputes the WTO was offered greater power in that only a 66 or 75 per cent vote of contracting parties was required instead of GATT's 100 per cent.

In addition to the setting up of the WTO, tariffs on industrial products were reduced from an average of 4.7 per cent to 3 per cent while the percentage of goods with zero tariffs was to increase from between 20 and 22 to between 40 and 45 and no tariffs were to be placed on pharmaceuticals, construction equipment, medical equipment, paper products and steel. Quotas on the imports of agricultural commodities and of textiles and apparel (under the MFA) were to be replaced by less restrictive tariffs over a ten-year period—on agricultural products by 24 per cent in developing countries and by 36 per cent in developed countries. Tariffs on textiles were to be reduced by 25 per cent.

The volume of subsidized agricultural exports was to be reduced by 21 per cent in six years; government subsidies for industrial research were to be limited to 50 per cent of applied research costs. While the use of anti-dumping laws was not banned, faster and harder action was required to end disputes arising out of their use. On safeguards, the temporary use of trade restrictions was allowed if an increase in imports severely damaged a domestic industry, but using health and safety standards simply to restrict trade is not allowed. Such use must be substantiated by scientific evidence.

Finally, intellectual property such as patents, trademarks and copyrights were to have 20 years' protection, with a ten-year phase-in period for developing countries for patent protection of pharmaceuticals.

Despite these advances there are still many areas of concern. These include the need for further advances in liberalizing agricultural trade and the need for negotiations on banking and insurance. In addition, the poorest of the third-world countries need greater attention, as do the CEEC and CIS countries as they convert to Western-style market economies.[5]

The setting up of huge trading blocs in Europe, North America and the Asian–Pacific area will produce free trade internally but may also lead to protectionism, more bilateral trade, and interbloc disputes.[6]

The name change from GATT to WTO was effected in Geneva in January 1995. By then the WTO included 127 members. Its first meeting was held in Singapore in November 1996. It included in its agenda the working towards an agreement on labour standards, investment and competition policy, government procurement and an information technology agreement (ITA), an attempt to liberalize trade in computer-related products worth about one billion dollars a year, and, as in GATT, the emphasis was on items of special interest to North America and Europe. The possibility of talks with China concerning its entry into membership of WTO was discussed and the endorsement of talks aimed at removing agricultural trade barriers some time in the distant future occurred. Some developing countries were concerned about including new items into discussions, fearing that the industrial countries would favour these against the older more difficult issues important to the non-industrial world but peripheral to the developed countries. So far this appears to be true.

Commodity Agreements

Widely fluctuating export prices of primary products have posed a major problem for those developing countries with a narrow primary-product export base or those for whom these exports have provided a large part of their national incomes. Between the two World Wars, there were 72 commodity agreements signed and almost all faded away by 1945.[7] After World War II, several attempts were made to ensure orderly world marketing of primary products with international agreements covering such commodities as wheat, sugar, tin, coffee, cocoa and petroleum. These had limited success. Few lasted very long and those that survived produced only marginal improvements for the exporters of those commodities. Only OPEC (and illegal drug cartels) have had the right combination of factors allowing long-term survival. The many failures show only too well the tremendous difficulties surrounding any attempt to draw up such agreements, each of which must satisfy the many exporting and importing countries covered and with each country naturally concerned with the protection of its own interests.

As noted above, increased instability in world commodity markets in the 1970s led UNCTAD to press for an integrated programme of commodity control agreements (IPC) covering some 18 traded commodities to aid the financing of the buffer stocks of commodities to which these international commodity agreements would give rise. A Common Fund of $6,000m. was advocated. In 1979, a Common Fund of $6 billion was established but its role was less ambitious than that intended by UNCTAD, for its resources, made up of government contributions, were limited to $470m. In addition, as noted in Chapter 18, a modest compensatory finance scheme had already been set up by the IMF in 1963 in its CCFF (Compensatory and Continuing Financing Facility) and, later, a Buffer Stock Financing Facility was established for a similar purpose. The CCFF aided those developing countries whose exports in a particular year fell below their average value of the previous five years. In 1975 the EEC adopted a similar scheme to provide a $400m. fund for the 57 members of the ACP. Nevertheless, both of these compensatory schemes were only modest in their scope. On the whole, commodity agreements form one of the failures in the development of international economic integration.

CONCLUDING REMARKS

Immediately after World War II, a concerted effort was made to set up a multilateral trade system through the elimination of controls over trade and commerce and a reduction in the amount of protection afforded to domestic industries by contracting parties to the GATT. The most-favoured-nation principle and the no-new-preferences rule were intended to prevail in the tariff field. Discriminatory devices were to be rejected by all participants in Western trade, and non-tariff barriers to trade were considered objectionable by the GATT.

By 1960 the situation was, in practice, almost the complete reverse. As a result of the escape clauses in GATT and the inclusion of what was considered at the time to be a relatively minor exception to the general rules governing trade liberalization, the international economy was heading towards regionalization to such an extent that, within each regional free trade area, the most-favoured-nation principle and the no-new-preferences rule were side-stepped as individual member countries within them discriminated in favour of other member countries and against outsiders.

Since 1960 the international economic power which has come with the economic union of several of the major trading nations and others has led to many of the original rules of GATT becoming inoperative, and the failure of GATT negotiators to come to grips in the past with the major inequities which govern world trade demonstrates the fact that the record of GATT compared with its original basic objectives is one of failure. Yet the GATT was partially successful in that tariffs on manufactured imports were reduced substantially over the years by the advanced countries, and there was also the relaxation of the no-new-preferences rule as it affected the developing countries. Against the advantages for the developing countries of the receipt of GSP treatment, however, must be set the introduction and intensification of non-tariff barriers as they applied, mainly to manufactures.

The successes of the Uruguay round, when they are eventually carried through, and the setting up of the World Trade Organization will not solve the major trade problems. Whatever the new powers conferred on the WTO to meet 'modern trade conditions', its first meeting demonstrated no substantial shift in the positions of contracting parties. The topics under discussion were predominantly those which best served the interests of the major trading groups' intra-trade. Still, as in the past, the powerful are only interested in what concerns them; the rest of the world must patiently wait its turn in the distant future.

NOTES

1 A customs union involves the economic integration of a number of countries in such a way as to produce free trade among members of the union and a common external tariff levied against all non-members; a free trade area differs from a customs union in that member nations follow independent tariff policies with respect to other countries.

2 At the end of November 1994, Norway voted 52.2 per cent to 47.8 per cent against joining the EU.

3 One must note, however, the highly restrictive measures introduced in 1996 and 1997 to ensure the members met the Maastricht conditions of entry to the monetary union.

4 While several EU countries denied for years that agricultural trade was covered by the GATT, the deliberations of the Haberler Panel of the GATT (see above) negates such a contention. Agricultural trade was always covered by the GATT, even if some Europeans and Americans chose to ignore the fact.

5 See Dominick Salvatore, *International Economics*, 5th edn. (Englewood Cliffs, New Jersey: Prentice Hall, 1995), pp. 283–7, on some of these points.
6 See D. Salvatore, ibid, 286–7.
7 Peter Lindert, *International Economics*, 9th edn. (Burr Ridge, Illinois: Irwin, 1991), p. 250.

SELECTED REFERENCES

Davenport, M., *Trade Policy, Protection, and the Third World* (London: Croom Helm, 1986).

GATT/WTO, *International Trade*, annual, various issues.

Golt, S., *Developing Countries in the GATT System* (London: Trade Policy Research Centre, 1978).

MacBean, A. I. and Snowden, P. N., *International Institutions in Trade and Finance* (London: Institute for International Economics, 1981).

MacLaren, D., 'The Uruguay Round Agreement on Agriculture: A New Order?', *Agenda*, vol. 2, 1995, pp. 281–90.

Pomfrey, R., *Unequal Partners: the Economics of Discriminatory International Trade Policies* (Oxford: Blackwell, 1988).

Salvatore, D., *International Economics*, 5th edn. (Englewood Cliffs, New Jersey: Prentice Hall, 1995).

Trade Policy Research Centre, *Global Strategy for Growth* (London, 1981).

Chapter 20

Trade and growth in the international economy, 1945–2000

The developed countries

WORLD TRADE

Total Trade

Despite the restrictions on foreign trade which existed in one form or another from the end of World War II to 1960, the total value of the merchandise exports of the non-Communist countries rose from $53,300 million in 1948 to $112,300 million in 1960, or at an average annual growth rate of over 6 per cent. This was a remarkable achievement, especially when it is realized that the prices of traded commodities were about the same in 1960 as they had been in 1948. From 1960 to 1973, growth rates were even higher, at an average annual rate for the volume of exports of around 8 per cent. But 1973 marked the end of the rapid growth of exports, the annual increase dropping to average around 4.5 per cent from 1973 to 1979, to 1.5 per cent from 1980 to 1989, and then rising to 4.5 per cent in 1990–95. The rates were still high in most years, however, when compared with the rate of growth of world trade from the beginning of the nineteenth century to 1950. From 1950 to 1995, the volume of world trade fell in only three years, in 1958, 1975 and 1982.

Another important feature of world trade during this period was that, in almost every year, the increase in its volume exceeded the increase in the volume of world production. In other words, trade led economic growth. This also applied within the broad categories of products in most periods, as Table 27 illustrates.

The evidence provided on world trade and world output in Table 27 conflicts with the diminishing foreign trade hypothesis advanced during the 1930s.[1] In fact, during the relatively low growth period after 1973, trade was still expanding faster than production in most years.

The different regions of the world did not share equally in this rapidly rising trade. Excluding the centrally-planned economies, the rate of growth of the industrial countries of Europe, North America, and Japan was higher than the world average in the 1950s and, as a result, these countries increased

Table 27 World merchandise exports and production, total and by category, 1953–95

Period	Total increase in volume, per cent							
	Agriculture		Mining		Manufacturing		Total	
	Trade	Output	Trade	Output	Trade	Output	Trade	Output
1953–63	65	29	*	*	126	86	94	68
1963–79	96	47	101	99	282	149	200	120
1980–89	16	28	13	21	71	21	48	25
1990–95	25	8	25	10	37	5	34	8

Sources: GATT and WTO, International Trade, various issues.

Note
* Included in Agriculture.

their relative share of total exports from 61 to around 70 per cent. Other developed countries in Europe, Australasia and South Africa experienced a reduction in their share from 9 to 7 per cent and the share of the developing countries fell from 30 to 23 per cent. These changes largely reflected the different rates of growth in the output and exports of manufactures and primary products of the different regions.

Table 28 shows that the shares of all groups of countries in total world exports between 1963 and 1995 fluctuated from time to time. The industrial area, however, commanded around 70 per cent of the total towards the end of the period as the share of the countries in transition (including China), the former CPEs, fell substantially in their change-over to market economies. The share of developing countries fluctuated between 20 and 25 per cent

Table 28 World exports by major areas, 1953–95

Exporting region	Per cent of total						
	1953	1963	1973	1980	1985	1990	1995
Industrial area[a]	58.1	64.3	68.2	60.9	64.4	71.1	69.7
Australasia, South Africa	2.0	2.8	2.7	2.6	1.9	2.1	1.9
Developing countries[b]	39.5	20.7	19.2	28.8	22.9	21.9	22.2
CPEs/CITs[c]	0.3	12.1	9.9	7.7	10.7	4.9	6.1
Total	100.0	100.0	100.0	100.0	100.0	100.0	100.0

Sources: GATT and WTO, International Trade, various issues.

Notes: Discrepancies due to rounding.
a   Includes all Western Europe, United States, Canada and Japan.
b   Of which the oil-exporters recorded 5.9, 7.3 and 12.8 per cent in 1963, 1973 and 1980 respec-
    tively; while the newly-advanced Asian countries (Korea, Hong Kong, Taiwan and Singapore)
    recorded 4.7, 5.7 and 6.7 per cent from 1985 on (excluding re-exports).
c   From 1990, these were the countries in transition. China is also included here.

while, in the latest period, the inclusion in this group of Korea, Hong Kong, Taiwan and Singapore maintained the healthy share of this group of countries, contributing 4.7, 5.7 and 6.7 per cent respectively to the totals in years 1980, 1990 and 1995. The large increase in the share of developing countries in 1980 reflected the increased returns to the oil exporters of the Middle East as a result of the large oil price increases of the mid-1970s. The decline in the share of the CPEs to 1985 shows the lesser importance this group of countries placed on trade while the drastic fall in the 1990s shows some of the problems of switching from command-based to market-based economies.

The Direction of Merchandise Trade

The differences to be observed in the rates of growth in world trade recorded by the different groups of countries in Table 28 are reflected in the shifts that have occurred in the direction of trade (Table 29). Except for the rise of developing countries in the 1970s and early 1980s, as the oil-exporting countries gained larger shares, there were no major shifts in any of the series until the 1990s. The fall in the share of the CPEs/CITs in the 1990s occurred because of the major upheaval in production and trade as most of these countries changed to market-related economies. At the same time the rise in the developing countries' share in the 1990s not only reflected this fall but represented the substantial increases in the export trade of several east Asian countries, including China, as they industrialized.

When we examine the export performances of the chief industrial nations since 1937 (Table 30), we find that by 1960 the increase in the share of the United States was achieved largely at the expense of the United Kingdom, and that Germany and Japan by that year had barely regained their pre-war trading positions. From 1960 to 1973, the trade shifts became even more marked. Most striking was the doubling of the Japanese share and the large decline in the shares of the United Kingdom and United States. The continental European countries also increased their shares substantially. After 1973, however, comparatively few major changes occurred, except the ever increasing rise of the Japanese share. Moreover, since unification, the German share fell somewhat. The estimates for the EU suggest that there was little change in the share of the Union's export trade with the rest of the world between 1985 and 1995.

Outside these countries, the east Asian 'newly-advanced' countries (Korea, Hong Kong, Taiwan and Singapore) and the Asian NICs (including Malaysia, Thailand and Indonesia) improved their combined share of total manufactured exports from 3.9 per cent in 1973 to 6.7 per cent in 1995 if re-exports are excluded.

Table 29 Matrices of world exports for selected years 1953 to 1995 (per cent of the total)

Exports to from	Industrial countries	Developing countries	CPEs/CITs	Total[a]
1953				
Industrial countries	37.1	19.3	1.5	61.4
Developing countries	17.5	6.7	0.6	25.4
CPEs	1.1	0.4	8.0	9.6
Total	58.6	27.0	10.1	100.0
1963				
Industrial countries	44.6	14.7	2.3	64.1
Developing countries	14.2	4.5	1.7	20.8
CPEs	2.3	1.1	8.3	11.9
Total	63.6	20.8	12.3	100.0
1980				
Industrial countries	42.6	14.3	3.0	61.3
Developing countries	19.5	6.8	1.1	27.8
CPEs	2.9	1.6	4.5	8.9
Total	66.3	23.1	8.6	100.0
1990				
Industrial countries	55.4[a]	12.6	2.2	71.7
Developing countries	13.9	5.7	1.3	21.2
CPEs/CITs	2.6	1.7	2.5	7.1
Total	71.9	20.0	6.0	100.0
1995				
Industrial countries	51.0[a]	15.0	3.6	71.1
Developing countries	15.4	8.7	1.3	25.6
CPEs/CITs	2.0	0.5	0.7	3.1
Total	68.8	24.1	5.5	100.0

Source: As for Table 28.

Notes: Discrepancies due to rounding.
a   Includes Australasia and South Africa which, together, accounted for no more than 3 per cent of
the total and whose trade was principally with industrial countries.

Table 30 Distribution of the export trade of major industrial countries, 1937–95 (per cent of total)

Country	1937	1950	1960	1973	1980	1985	1990	1995
United Kingdom	20	20	14	9	10	9	9	8
United States	23	32	28	20	21	20	19	20
France	7	10	9	11	11	10	10	10
Germany[a]	16	6	15	19	18	20	20	17
Other W. Europe[b]	20	20	21	23	23	23	23	23
Canada	8	9	7	6	6	6	6	7
Japan	6	3	5	12	12	13	14	15
Total	100	100	100	100	100	100	100	100

Sources: A. Maizels, Industrial Growth and World Trade (Cambridge: Cambridge University Press, 1963), pp. 426–7; GATT/WTO, International Trade, various issues.

Notes: Discrepancies in totals due to rounding.
a   Germany experienced a reduction in geographical size from 1945 to 1991; only West Germany is considered during these years.
b   Includes Belgium, Luxembourg, the Netherlands, Italy and Sweden. On a similar basis, the EU$_{15}$ accounted for 37, 40 and 38 per cent of the total in 1985, 1990 and 1995 respectively. The figures presented are for the 15 members of the EU although some were not members in 1985 or 1990.

Table 31 Shares of commodity groups in world merchandise exports, 1937–95 (by value) (per cent of total)

Year	Primary products			Manufactures	Total Exports
	Food	Raw materials	Total		
1937	23	40	63	37	100
1950	23	34	57	43	100
1960	20	25	45	55	100
1973	15	23	38	62	100
1980	11	32	43	55	100
1985	11	26	37	63	100
1990	10	18	28	73	100
1995	9	17	26	74	100

Sources: P. Lamartine Yates, Forty Years of Foreign Trade, Table 16, p. 44; GATT/WTO, International Trade, various issues.

Note
Raw materials include fuels and non-ferrous metals.

Composition of World Trade

The trends in the direction of world trade ran parallel with the changes in the composition of total merchandise exports. As Table 31 and Figure 18 show, the increased importance of manufactures in world exports was matched by a

Figure 18 World trade in manufactures 1937–95 (commodity composition and country share)

Source: As for Tables 30 and 32.

corresponding decline in the importance of trade in food and raw materials, at least up to 1973 and again after 1979. In the late 1970s and early 1980s, the energy crisis brought about a marked but temporary increase in the share of raw materials in world export trade, but economies in the use of oil and a decline in its price in the 1980s reduced this share by 1990.

The changing composition of trade in manufactures followed the pattern established in the late nineteenth century and continued during the interwar period (see Table 32 and Figure 18). The shift away from textiles towards engineering products intensified, although the use of non-tariff import restrictions on textiles by the industrially advanced countries after 1970 accounts for some of the decline in the relative importance of this group. Since 1963 it has been motor vehicles which have contributed most to the increase in the share of engineering products in world trade in manufactures.

Table 32 Commodity pattern of trade in manufactures, 1937–95 (per cent of total)

Group/year	1937	1950	1963	1973	1980	1990	1995
Engineering products	26.5	34.9	51.8	54.2	54.2	50.4	52.2
Machinery	(16.0)	(20.7)	(43.0)	(42.8)	(42.6)	n.s.	n.s.
Transport[a]	(10.5)	(14.2)	(8.8)	(11.8)	(11.6)	n.s.	n.s.
Textiles, clothing	21.5	19.9	11.4	10.3	8.7	9.2	8.5
Metals [b]	15.3	12.9	9.1	8.2	7.0	4.4	4.1
Chemicals	10.6	10.5	11.9	12.0	13.9	12.2	12.8
All other	26.0	21.9	15.8	15.3	16.4	23.8	22.4
Total	100.0	100.0	100.0	100.0	100.0	100.0	100.0

Sources: Cairncross, A., 'World Trade in Manufactures Since 1900', Economia Internazionale, Dec. 1995, p. 244; GATT/WTO, International Trade, various issues.

Notes
a   From 1963, road motor vehicles.
b   Iron and steel from 1963; n.s. = not separated out.

The decline in metals (iron and steel) after 1963 is particularly evident while chemicals have continued to become more important. 'All other' manufactures lost ground in the 1960s but recovered somewhat from the late 1970s onwards. On the whole, there was a continuation and intensification of the movement away from consumer goods (and semi-manufactures) towards capital goods which had begun in the interwar years, a trend that is consistent with the greater trade among the industrial nations that occurred after World War II.[2]

In recent times interest has been increasingly focused on the trade in services which has always been an important aspect of the current account of a country's balance of payments. Table 33 illustrates the trends in this item since 1980. It shows the importance of Western Europe in the trade in commercial services, albeit a slightly declining one, as the current account figures for the region increased more slowly than those of other areas and countries. The share of the EU fell from 46.5 per cent in 1980 to 42.5 per cent in 1990. As the European share declined, that of North America, in particular, rose substantially.

Conclusions

It is apparent from the above account that the rich industrial countries were able to obtain greater benefits from the growth of international trade after 1950 than most other countries. The relative shift in the world demand away from foodstuffs and raw materials towards capital goods produced a change in the direction of total trade in favour of trade among the industrial countries and against the exports of developing countries to the industrial nations.[3] Even so, several developing countries were able to use the growth of world

Table 33 Trade in commercial services, 1980 to 1995 (US$ millions)

Country/region	1980	1985	1990	1995
World	402.0	405.0	802.2	1,198.0
North America	43.7 (11%)	64.3 (16%)	134.2 (17%)	210.6 (18%)
Western Europe	230.2 (57)	205.5 (51)	431.2 (53)	588.1 (49)
Japan	18.9 (5)	20.7 (5)	41.1 (5)	64.0 (5)
Singapore	6.0 (1)	6.3 (2)	12.7 (2)	29.3 (2)
Hong Kong	4.3 (1)	7.7 (2)	18.1 (2)	35.9 (3)
Australia	3.7 (1)	4.2 (1)	9.7 (1)	15.5 (1)
All other	95.2 (24)	96.3 (24)	155.2 (19)	254.6 (21)

Sources: GATT/WTO, International Trade, various issues.

trade in manufactures to achieve industrial take-off during the 1980s. These (mainly Asian) countries, despite the setbacks of the late 1990s, will undoubtedly continue on the path to advanced country status. The growth of trade within the industrial countries tends to contradict the predictions advanced by some economists in the 1930s that, as nations developed and their factor endowments became relatively more uniform, the need for trade based on the uneven distribution of factor endowments would decline. The historical record outlined above shows that trade in the post World War period grew at annual rates never before experienced and, what is more significant, it was the trade among the industrial countries which possessed similar ranges of factor endowments that rose the fastest. Several reasons have been advanced to explain this apparent divergence between economic theory and historical fact.

First, it has been argued that much of this increased trade between industrial countries was merely a return to a more normal rate of foreign economic relations following the lowering of restrictions on trade and payments introduced during the 1930s and in the early postwar years. Second, some of the expansion of trade within the group merely reflects the high rates of economic growth achieved by these countries. Increased per capita incomes, it is said, lead to a substantial diversification of consumer demand, while continuous advances in technological knowledge encourage widespread innovation. Because rapid and uneven technical innovations produce a continual process of adjustment in the comparative advantage enjoyed by any one industrial country in its many fields of manufacturing production, and because demand patterns become more diversified as incomes rise, a more complex and shifting pattern of commodity trade among industrial countries, as well as a growing trade, became possible. In other words, it appears that once technology is introduced as a type of factor endowment, it no longer follows that trade among industrial countries must necessarily decline because their factor endowments in other directions have become much more uniform over time.

Moreover, since patterns of domestic demand are influenced to an important degree by income, countries having similar income levels are likely to trade with each other more intensively than they are with countries having different income levels. Thus, a highly industrialized nation producing an output of manufactured goods in excess of its domestic requirements is more likely to find a market for its surplus production in other highly industrialized high-income countries than in countries with much lower income levels where the demand is for less sophisticated manufactures. There may be some overlapping, of course, since there will be some demand for sophisticated manufactures even in an undeveloped country. But, given the fact that per capita real incomes are growing faster in the industrial countries than elsewhere, the trade in manufactures could be expected to grow faster than the trade in primary products as a result.

It must not be forgotten, however, that agricultural protectionism in the industrial countries has substantially reduced the world trade in food products since the 1950s and, since the mid-1970s, the resort to quantitative restrictions on the imports of developing countries' manufactures into industrial countries has tended to preserve the status quo in manufactures trade. Nevertheless, the industrial countries' share of world trade in manufactures has fallen since the 1970s as the NICs increase their share. Despite the restrictions imposed on their exports, the Asian NICs, for example, have been able to increase their combined share of total trade in manufactures from 3.9 per cent in 1973 to 6.7 per cent in 1995. No doubt, this share will continue to grow over time, especially as international trade will become more liberalized following the conclusion of the Uruguay round of GATT negotiations, and once the Asian economies recover from the devastating blows they experienced late in 1997.

ECONOMIC GROWTH IN THE ADVANCED COUNTRIES, 1950–2000

The Record of Growth

World production was more severely affected by World War II than by World War I, but reconstruction in the years after 1945 was much more rapid and, in most countries, the 1938 levels of GDP had been exceeded by 1950. The major exceptions were West Germany and Japan, both of which did not better their pre-war economic performances until the mid-1950s. Beginning in the early 1950s, the industrialized countries[4] experienced over 20 years of sustained economic growth. They recorded an average annual growth rate of just over 5 per cent from 1950 to 1973. This compares favourably with averages of 2.6 per cent from 1870 to 1913 and 1.9 per cent from 1913 to 1950.[5] Between 1973 and 1980, however, the average annual growth rate fell to 2.9 per cent and even lower rates were recorded in 1980–90 and 1990–7 (Table 34 later and Figure 19).

1. Developed countries 2. Developing countries 3. Eastern Europe 4. U.S.S.R.

Figure 19 Average annual rates of growth in GDP and per capita GDP, 1955–98
(selected country groups)

Sources: As for Table 32; A. Maddison, *The World Economy in the 20th Century* (Paris, 1989); IMF,
World Economic Outlook (Washington, May 1998) Annex Tables.

Note: For 3 and 4, the Chart shows figures for 1980–88 for Eastern Europe and U.S.S.R. No
comparable figures are available for CEEC and Russia for 1980–88. For the CEEC and Russia
from 1990–98 the annual average growth rates of GDP are –2.8 per cent and –5.5 per
cent respectively.

The rate of economic growth was not uniform within this group of countries, however. During the 1950s and 1960s, Japan grew much more rapidly
than other countries, averaging 9.8 per cent annually, followed by West
Germany (6.3 per cent), Italy (5.6 per cent), and Finland and France (5 per
cent). The lowest growth rates were recorded by the United States (3.5 per
cent) and the United Kingdom (2.8 per cent). From 1973 to 1980, only a few
countries recorded 3 per cent or higher growth rates: Norway (4.9 per cent),
Canada (4.3 per cent), Japan (3.6 per cent), the Netherlands and Austria
(around 3 per cent). Switzerland recorded a slight decline in production
between these years.

The OECD countries as a whole recorded an average annual increase of 2.8

per cent and 2.7 per cent for the periods 1973–80, 1980–90 and 2.2 per cent for 1990–97. The leading growth countries of the 1980s were Japan (3.8 per cent), Finland (3.7 per cent), Ireland (3.4 per cent), Australia (3.3 per cent), Iceland (3.2 per cent) and Canada (3.0),[6] and in subsequent years to 1997, Ireland (6 per cent), Norway (3.7 per cent) and Australia (3 per cent) recorded average annual growth rates of 3 per cent or higher. At the same time, the newly advanced countries of Asia experienced much higher rates of economic growth: Singapore (8.2 per cent), Korea (7.1 per cent), Taiwan (6.5 per cent), Hong Kong (5.3 per cent) and Israel (4.6 per cent).

At the same time, the rate of change in both consumer prices and levels of unemployment in the industrialized countries altered substantially after 1973. The average rate of inflation in the OECD area from 1950 to 1970 was just over 5 per cent (largely influenced by the higher rates recorded towards the end of the 1960s). Between 1973 and 1980 it averaged 9.9 per cent. 1973 was the critical year when the rate of inflation rose to 7.3 per cent, followed by an even sharper rise to 12.5 per cent in 1974 as a result of the huge increase in oil prices. It was not until the mid-1980s that the industrial countries were able to pull inflation back to levels generally below 5 per cent. Despite another increase in the early 1990s, in the mid-1990s, for the first time since the 1960s, annual inflation rates of below 3 per cent were being recorded consistently in most advanced economies.

The economic downturn that followed the boom of 1973 also brought with it rising unemployment and, by 1975, it had become a major problem in the OECD area for the first time for over two decades. From 1975 to 1990, it remained persistently high in almost every industrial country, often exceeding 10 per cent of the workforce. While the average rate for the advanced economies for 1980–89 was 6.9 per cent and 7.1 per cent for 1989–97, it exceeded 10 per cent between 1993 and 1998. The respective figures for the EU were 9.1 per cent and 10.4 per cent, with Belgium, Finland, France, Germany, Greece, Ireland, Italy and Spain generally exceeding 10 per cent. These high unemployment rates stemmed mainly from low GDP growth rates and the new approach to government stabilization policies that has concentrated predominantly on controlling inflation, with unemployment a residual of such a policy requiring, it is argued, labour market structural reform for its solution. Altogether, from 1993 to 1998 the number of unemployed workers in the OECD exceeded 35 million of which over 18 million were recorded in the EU alone.

At the root of the extensive economic growth which occurred between 1950 and 1973 was a sustained increase in output per worker. Maddison's calculations suggest that, in 21 OECD countries, GDP per hour worked rose by 2.9 per cent a year. In industrial Europe it rose by 4.7 per cent, in Japan by 7.7 per cent and in the United States by 2.7 per cent a year over the same period.[7] Labour productivity did not improve as rapidly after 1973, the relevant figures for 1973–92 being 2.3 per cent for industrial Europe, 1.1 per cent for the United States and 3.1 per cent for Japan. During both periods, however, industrial Europe and Japan performed much better than the United States in this regard.

Productivity increases were higher in agriculture than in manufacturing in all countries except Japan and France, while they were decidedly lower in services than in the other two sectors. At the same time, employment in agriculture declined at an average rate of 3.3 per cent between 1950 and 1973, whereas employment in manufacturing and services rose at annual rates of 1 and 2.3 per cent respectively—trends which partly explain the relative changes in productivity.

Even more interesting are the changes that occurred in the average annual rates of growth in the major components of total output during the high growth period to 1973 and in the lower growth period after that year. Given the large differences from country to country in the components of demand for goods and services, the annual average rate of growth of real GDP for the industrial countries fell from an annual average of 5 per cent between 1963 and 1973 to 2.5 per cent (1973–9), 2.7 per cent (1980–89) and 2.2 per cent (1990–97). Consumption fell from an average growth rate of 5 per cent in the first period to 3 per cent in the second and third periods and to 2.8 per cent in 1989–98. In addition, the rate of investment expenditure during the 1980s remained at low levels until the last few years of the decade, when a revival began. An annual average of 2.8 per cent was recorded for gross capital formation from 1979 to 1988. This revival was relatively short lived, fading out by 1990. For 1989–98 an annual average of 2.6 per cent is estimated for the industrial countries, which rose after 1993. It is clear, therefore, given the relatively high rates of investment during the rapid growth period to 1973, that the decline in investment expenditure and a smaller proportionate decrease in real consumption expenditure both made a contribution to the lower growth rates in GDP after 1973.[8] Moreover, as Maddison notes, productivity, GDP per hour worked, between 1973 and 1992 was under half its value for 1950 to 1973.[9] But, as he points out, the performance of Western Europe in this regard was still better after 1973 than that of the United States, as the former caught up with the latter in terms of labour productivity. Nevertheless, the unacceptable levels of unemployment suggest that their overall growth performance up to 1998 was below what was possible.

In Europe, in order to improve the productivity and competitiveness of the European Community and to stimulate the region's technological achievements, the *Single European Act* was legislated in 1985. The thrust of the Act was to eliminate, by the end of 1992, the non-tariff trade restrictions the Treaty of Rome of 1957 had not addressed but which hampered intra-regional trade. The 1992 programme included the elimination of all barriers to trade and the offer of equal access for all member countries to the markets of the others. This reform was expected to raise the GDP of the EU by 4.5 per cent, largely as a result of the increased competitiveness the proposals were to produce. Despite the European Commission's favourable report on the progress being made, there was little evidence in 1998 to suggest any significant addition to the region's GDP growth after 1992. However, other changes, especially those adopted by member countries in their efforts to pass the criteria for admittance to the proposed European Monetary Union, may have had a braking effect on the EU's growth rate at the time.

It has already been noted that, in 1997, some Asian NICs were reclassified by the IMF as 'advanced economies', namely Hong Kong (returned to China in 1997 but allowed to continue to function as an independent entity), China–Taipei (or Taiwan), Korea, Singapore and Israel. These economies experienced very rapid economic growth and at annual rates much higher than those of other countries or regions. Much of this growth was concentrated in their export industries. In addition, they were very strongly tied to Japan by trade relations and by investment flows. The first major setback to their growth performance came with their stock exchange and currency crises which began in September 1997.

Factors Influencing Growth Rates

Economic growth in many parts of the world economy in the 1950s and 1960s was undoubtedly significantly influenced by the rapid expansion of industrial Europe and Japan, if only because the foreign trade of these countries rose faster than that of other countries and regions. At the same time, the foreign demand for the exports of industrial Europe and Japan was a major factor influencing the high growth rates in these countries. Progressive tariff reductions and the continuous elimination of other restrictive trade barriers, especially within Europe itself, also contributed a great deal towards the growth of this trade.

Another feature of the growth of industrial countries from 1950 to 1973 was the high ratio of investment to GDP. Directly and indirectly, investment generated substantial additions to GDP by raising demand in many sectors, increasing the amount of capital per worker, and allowing a high degree of innovation. But this high rate of investment itself cannot be treated as the primary cause or the all-determining factor of growth and improvements in productivity even if it was an important element. Continuously high investment was made possible by the existence of other factors, such as high levels of domestic and foreign demand, substantial supplies of relatively cheap domestic and foreign savings, a high degree of confidence in the continuation of prosperity, rapid changes in technological knowledge, which produced incentives to introduce new products or to modernize production methods, changes in the entrepreneurial capabilities of management, and a progressive approach towards the fostering of economic growth by the public sector.[10] It also appears that readily available supplies of low-wage labour in the form of the domestically unemployed, rural migrants and foreign migrant workers partly explain why output and exports grew more rapidly in Germany, Italy and Switzerland than in Britain, Belgium and the Scandinavian countries, where labour was in relatively short supply. The inflows of foreign workers also helped to maintain more stable wage levels and lower rates of inflation in the favoured countries. Furthermore, expectations of continued rising incomes and demand played an important part in maintaining the upward growth trends in all countries. Finally, in the period to 1973, it has been argued that the industrial countries were able to maintain their high growth rates by paying low prices to the developing countries for their raw materials, including oil—a feature of the times that was to change in the early 1970s.

Thus, many factors, reflecting both favourable demand and supply conditions, were responsible for the unprecedented growth rates experienced by most industrial European countries and Japan between 1950 and 1973. While many of these growth forces were domestic in origin, others had their origins in the international economy. In particular, the growth of foreign demand for manufactures was of considerable importance in stimulating an expansion of industrial capacity which, in turn, was partly sustained by an inflow of foreign capital (and its associated technology) and labour. Japan experienced explosive economic growth from the mid-1950s on, largely through unprecedentedly high levels of investment, a rapidly expanding labour supply, a shift out of low- into high-productivity industries, a growing foreign demand for Japanese exports, the ability of export industries to remain highly competitive, collaboration between the private sector and the public sector, an absence of economic waste through low military expenditure, and significant advances in education.

The United States and Canada recorded lower growth rates between 1950 and 1973 than most European countries, partly because they had experienced large increases in production from 1945 to 1950, before European recovery was complete. For this reason, European and Japanese economic growth in the 1950s and later involved an element of catching up with America. Moreover, to the extent that much American foreign investment supported import substitution in the capital-receiving countries, it may have hindered somewhat the expansion of American exports. Furthermore, in countries such as the United States and Canada, already with large national products and high per capita incomes, it became increasingly more difficult to sustain high rates of growth of output from year to year, for the incentive to do so may be less urgent than in countries that were attempting to raise per capita incomes. In Australia, New Zealand and South Africa, growth rates also fell below those of Europe and Japan. These countries grew rapidly in the years immediately following World War II and, in addition, 1950 was an exceptionally good year for them because of the high foreign demand for their primary exports. With such a high base year, it was difficult for these countries to maintain high average growth rates comparable with those recorded by other countries after 1950. Moreover, the spread of agricultural protectionism in later years had a depressing effect on the exports of the Australasian countries which was reflected to some extent in their lower growth rates.

After 1973, economic conditions deteriorated, average growth rates were lower than in the period before 1973, and investment proceeded at much lower levels for a number of reasons, including the decline in incomes in 1974–5; shortages of cheap investment funds; the uncertainty of reasonable profits given the high rate of inflation; the growth of real wages; government budget deficits, which placed strains on the capital markets as the deficits were financed from loans; the high cost of fuel; the ability to earn high interest income from financial investments; and government anti-inflationary policies. It was not until after 1985 that economic conditions favoured a return to higher levels of real investment in manufacturing capacity. The sharp fall in the productivity of labour and capital after 1973 also had a deleterious impact on economic growth.[11] In the 1990s the industrial countries were confronted with low and fluctuating rates of economic growth. While inflation was reduced to minimal rates and inflationary expectations tended to weaken, unemployment in most industrial countries remained a major problem.

Finally, the relatively low growth rates in most industrial countries during the 1980s and 1990s may suggest that, once countries achieve high levels of per capita income, the pressure for maintaining high growth rates may diminish as workers and others place a higher value on leisure. However, the appearance of economic rationalism and the emphasis placed upon globalization has widened the gap between the rich and the poor in society and has destroyed the leisure goals of much of the workforce of the industrial world, replacing them with uncertainty concerning the opportunities for future employment, especially in the unskilled area.

The lack of government attention in North America and much of Western Europe to economic growth has played a major role in anti-cyclical pressures during the 1990s, the movement towards globalization following the completion of the Uruguay round of the GATT/WTO, and the adherence to the new economic philosophy of economic rationalism, emphasizing the control of inflation above all other government economic objectives, especially in the United States, while the deflationary pressures in Western Europe, as countries attempted to conform with the procedures involved in passing the Maastricht tests, have possibly been the major causes of the aberrations of the late 1980s and the 1990s.

Economic Fluctuations

The high rates of economic growth attained by most advanced countries after 1950 substantially altered the character of the economic fluctuations they experienced. Between 1950 and 1960 the United States suffered three recessions but only in two of them, in 1953 and 1958, did GDP fall. Each setback, however, was followed in the succeeding year by higher than average increases in GDP. Western Europe, on the other hand, recorded recessions in only two years, 1952 and 1958. Moreover, it was in those two years alone that world trade declined, if only slightly.[12]

From 1960 to 1973, only three industrial countries recorded a reduction in GDP, Australia (1961), Germany (1967) and the United States (1970). In each case the decline was no greater than 0.3 per cent and, in each case, higher than average rates of growth were recorded in at least two of the next three years. Apart from their short duration and the fact that they were invariably followed by an immediate and substantial recovery, the recessions of this period were generally marked by changes in the rates of economic growth rather than fluctuations in absolute levels of economic activity characteristic of previous recessions and depressions. There was also a weak transmission of cyclical downturns between the United States and Europe. Thus, the recessions of this period contrasted markedly with those experienced during the interwar years. One of the reasons given for the weak transmission of downturns was that the cycles evident in the various countries differed in timing from one another, even within regions. For example, when Germany experienced its most severe recession in 1967, growth rates were rising or reaching a peak in Belgium, Denmark, Italy, the Netherlands and the United Kingdom.

In 1972 and 1973, however, and for the first time since the end of World War II, the economic cycles in the United States, Western Europe, and Japan roughly synchronized and by the end of 1973 all of the industrial countries slid into a recession which was worsened by the emerging oil crisis. In 1974, four countries, Japan, the United States, the United Kingdom and Denmark, experienced a fall in GDP while in 1975, the 'worst' year in the four decades from 1950 to 1990, ten industrial countries recorded declines in total output. Given the partial economic recovery in the OECD after 1975, few countries in the region experienced declining annual output until 1980 when another widespread recession was triggered by the oil price increases of 1979–80. In 1981, European countries collectively recorded a marginal increase in GDP while in 1982 the OECD as a whole experienced no growth.

Recovering in 1983, most countries experienced varying rates of growth during the remaining years of the 1980s. In 1990, the United States experienced a fall in its growth rate below 2 per cent for the first time since 1982, and went on to record a fall of 1 per cent in real GDP in 1992. In Europe, France, Italy, the United Kingdom, Austria and Belgium, in addition to Canada and Australia, followed the same path as the United States. In 1991, eight OECD countries recorded falls in their GDP. It was the worst year economically since 1982. After 1991, economic growth, for a number of reasons, has been spasmodic, but without more than a weak recovery throughout the whole OECD region up to 1998, at least. Of the major industrial countries, Japan has suffered most, in stark contrast to that country's performance in the 1960s.

The instability of the times, the greater uncertainty concerning the future, and the continuing presence of inflation along with high and rising unemployment ensured that more attention was paid to cyclical behaviour after 1973 than had been the case in the 1950s and 1960s. Moreover, more attention was directed from time to time towards the possibility that, during the second half of the twentieth century, the industrial world was experiencing the effects of a Kondratieff-type long wave in economic activity. Was the experience of the period from 1950 to 1973, with short and shallow recessions and high growth rates, evidence of the upward phase of a long wave in economic activity which peaked in 1973, and have the industrial countries been experiencing the downward phase of a long wave after 1973, with more protracted, more common, and deeper recessions, and lower overall growth rates, than before 1973? Without exploring these questions further, the appearance of another period of high and rising growth rates in the early years of the twenty-first century would increase the number of adherents to the possibility of Kondratieff-type long waves in economic activity.

NOTES

1 See p. 223 above.
2 During the interwar years when this trend first revealed itself, it was associated with a substantial decline in the volume of trade between roughly the same group of countries. Moreover, at the same time, the trade in capital goods was chiefly with the newly-industrializing nations.
3 Only the growing importance of the trade in fuels in the 1970s and early 1980s tended to go against this trend.
4 Includes the 16 most industrialized countries at the time: the EU_{15} (excluding Greece, Ireland, Portugal and Spain), Australia, Canada, Japan, Norway, Switzerland and the United States.
5 Estimates of Angus Maddison, 'Western Economic Performance in the 1970s: a Perspective and Assessment', *Banca Nazionale del Lavoro Quarterly Review*, Sept. 1980, pp. 247–89.
6 Estimates from *Economic Outlook* (Paris: OECD, Dec. 1989).
7 Angus Maddison, op. cit. and *Monitoring the World Economy, 1820–1992* (Paris: OECD, 1994), pp. 40–9. Also see GATT, *International Trade, 1979–80*, pp. 21–30.
8 Angus Maddison, 'Western Economic Performance', ibid. Note, however, in the 1980s, private consumption expenditure in the OECD rose at a rate of some 2.7 per cent, compared with 3.1 per cent in 1973–9, while private non-residential capital formation recorded an average annual increase of 4.1 per cent, compared with 2.2 per cent in the previous period. Most of the latter increase occurred after 1985. See IMF, *World Economic Outlook*, various issues.
9 This is stressed by Angus Maddison, *Monitoring the World Economy, 1820–1992* (Paris: OECD, 1994), pp. 45–8.
10 A. Boltho, *The European Economy: Growth and Crisis* (London, 1983). Also see

A. Maddison, 'Long Run Dynamics of Productivity Growth', *Banca Nazionale del Lavoro Quarterly Review*, Mar. 1979, pp. 3–44.
11 See Maddison, *Monitoring the World Economy, 1820–1992*, ibid.
12 See A. Lamfalussy, 'International Trade and Trade Cycles', in R. Harrod and D. C. Hague (eds), *International Trade Theory in a Developing World* (London, 1963), ch. XI.

SELECTED REFERENCES

Boltho, A. (ed.), *The European Economy: Growth and Crisis* (London: Oxford University Press, 1982).

Cairncross, A., 'World Trade in Manufactures Since 1900', *Economia Internazionale*, Dec. 1955.

Denison, E. F., *Why Growth Rates Differ: Postwar Experience of Nine Western Countries* (Washington: Brookings Institution, 1967).

General Agreement on Tariffs and Trade, *International Trade*, various issues.

International Monetary Fund, *World Economic Outlook*, various issues.

Maddison, A., *Economic Growth in the West* (London: George Allen & Unwin; and New York: Norton, 1964).

Maddison, A., *Phases of Capitalist Development* (London: Oxford University Press, 1982).

Maddison, A., *Monitoring the World Economy, 1820–1992* (Paris: OECD, 1995).

Olson, M., *The Rise and Decline of Nations: Economic Growth, Stagflation, and Social Rigidities* (Yale: Yale University Press, 1982).

Organization for Economic Co-operation and Development (OECD), *Economic Outlook*, various issues.

Postan, M. M., *An Economic History of Western Europe, 1945–1964* (London: Methuen, 1967).

Rostow, W. W., *The World Economy, History and Prospect* (London: Macmillan, 1978).

Chapter 21

Trade and growth in the international economy, 1945–2000

The developing economies, the centrally-planned economies and countries in transition

THE DEVELOPING ECONOMIES

Economic Growth

Table 34 shows that, in every period chosen, the rate of growth of production in the developing countries as a whole has been higher on average than in the developed countries. But so, too, has population increased more rapidly in the former group of countries than in the latter. As a result, the average rate of growth in per capita production or income in developing countries did not exceed that of the developed countries to the same extent as the growth of production. It is also interesting to note that the large increases in the average growth rates of GDP and per capita GDP of the developing countries in the 1990s are in stark contrast to the decline in each of these series for the advanced countries, which include some countries previously in the developing countries group.

These aggregate figures hide more than they reveal, however. On a regional basis, 'East Asia' has been by far the most successful in terms of increases in per capita income since 1955. While 'Europe, the Middle East and North Africa' recorded a high average rate of growth to 1973, thereafter the region's performance as a whole declined and, in the 1980s, it experienced little growth in per capita terms, largely due to the poor experience of the oil-exporting countries. A slight recovery occurred in the 1990s. 'Latin America and the Caribbean' exhibited a similar pattern of growth to that of Europe and the Middle East, while Sub-Saharan Africa consistently recorded the lowest growth rates of all the groups. Within the most successful group, 'East Asia', manufacturing production recorded much higher than average increases than it did for the developing countries as a whole.

It is common to classify developing countries into several groups such as: the newly-industrializing countries (NICs),[1] the least-developed, and the 'rest'. The last of these groups has been further distinguished as to whether its constituent countries are more or less industrialized. The 'heavily indebted poor countries' is another sub-group that has emerged in the literature as a

Table 34 Comparison of economic growth in developing and developed countries, 1955–98

	Average percentage growth rates					
	1955–60	1960–5	1965–73	1973–79	1980–88	1989–98
Developing countries						
Real GDP	4.6	5.5	6.6	4.9	4.3	5.8
Real GDP per capita	2.4	3.0	4.1	2.7	2.0	3.6
Developed countries [a]						
Real GDP	3.2	5.2	4.6	2.9	2.9	2.5
Real GDP per capita	2.0	3.9	3.5	2.2	2.3	1.8

Sources: World Bank, *Annual Report* and *World Development Report*, various issues; IMF, *World Economic Outlook*, various issues.

Note
a   Advanced economies from 1980–88, including Hong Kong, Israel, Korea, Singapore and Taiwan. Countries in Transition recorded 2.9 per cent and –2.9 per cent in real GDP in the last two periods, and 2.3 per cent and –3 per cent in real GDP per capita.

legacy of the large borrowing programmes of the 1980s. The highest rates of economic growth in the 1970s were recorded by the oil-exporting countries but, in the early 1980s, when oil prices began to decline, their growth rates were very low in per capita terms. The NICs, on the other hand, especially those in East Asia, became increasingly more industrialized, have experienced rapid economic growth, and have recorded high export performances despite the quantitative restrictions placed on their manufactured exports by the industrial countries. In essence, the NIC grouping is a half-way classification for emerging countries between 'developing' and 'advanced' status, and in 1997 the IMF 'granted' the latter classification to Hong Kong, Taiwan, Israel, Korea and Singapore.[2] China, Indonesia, Malaysia, Thailand and Vietnam recorded rates of growth of GDP generally in excess of 8 per cent during the 1990s, until the 'Asian Crisis' of 1997 affected their performances.

During the 1970s, inflation rates increased within the developing countries. If we exclude the six high-inflation countries—Argentina, Chile, Ghana, Israel, Turkey and Zaire, in each of which consumer prices rose at more than double the average for their groups—the oil exporters averaged an annual increase of 18 per cent in consumer prices from 1973 to 1980; the major exporters of manufactures, 33 per cent; the low-income countries, 17 per cent, and the remainder, 24 per cent. Inflation became a greater problem for most countries after 1978 when the second major oil price increase occurred. Averaging 25 per cent a year from 1973 to 1982, the inflation rate of developing countries as a group remained above 30 per cent until 1988, when it rose sharply. It was lowest in Asia, generally below 10 per cent, and highest in Latin America where in 1990 it peaked at over 440 per cent. By the mid-1990s, the average rate of inflation in developing countries had fallen from 68 per cent in 1990 to 10 per cent (1997), although it was still high at an average of 15 per cent in Africa and 22 per cent in the Middle East in that year.

Foreign Aid and Economic Development

As noted in Chapter 17, economic growth in the developing countries has been assisted by a massive inflow of foreign capital. In addition to the influx of long-term private capital, which has gone principally into mining, oil production, and manufacturing, a further $800 billion has been provided in the form of official foreign aid to these countries between 1950 and 1995. The aid offered recipient countries some help in their efforts to overcome two obstacles which might have frustrated their attempts to achieve sustained economic development. On the one hand, if a country's development pro-gramme entails greater investment expenditures than can be sustained by the level of domestic savings, it can undertake the additional expenditure with-out inflation only if the excess of domestic expenditure over current output is covered by external financing. On the other hand, a trade or foreign exchange gap will appear when a country's shortage of foreign exchange becomes an effective barrier to its economic development by denying it access to imported commodities, especially capital goods, essential for its economic growth. Foreign assistance is then needed to allow the projected investment of the development plan to take the desired form—that is, investment may require necessary imports that cannot be alternatively supplied from substitute domestic sources. If domestic saving does not result in an adequate increase in exports (through reducing the demand for domestically-produced goods, thus freeing them for export), or a reduction in imports of consumer goods so as to provide sufficient foreign exchange for the imports needed to support the higher rate of capital formation, foreign assistance will then be required for balance of payments reasons quite distinct from the need for aid as an adjunct to savings. Thus, a country in which savings are relatively abundant may still experience a foreign-exchange gap. It should also be pointed out that, whereas a savings gap requires a transfer of external resources in the form of aid, a trade gap may be filled by foreign exchange obtained in a number of ways, for instance, through aid receipts, improvements in the terms of trade and/or higher export earnings.

Fears have been expressed that developing countries will come to depend upon foreign capital assistance, and that this state of dependence will never end. But assuming that the foreign capital is used successfully to promote economic development, the consequent increase in productivity and income will create a source of potential saving that can at some point take over the burden of supplying the capital needed for continuing development. In order to achieve successful growth, the foreign capital should make a net contribution to a country's development. It must not lead to a diversion of domestic investment funds into inventory accumulation, luxury building, speculation, graft and corruption, or military expenditure. At the same time, a country's capacity to make effective use of foreign aid will depend on a wide range of conditions, including the stability and efficiency of government, the availability of complementary inputs, the size of the domestic market, the extent of social overhead capital—especially in transport and communications—so important for the mobility of goods and people, and finally, the prevailing social attitudes toward change and institutions and habits that influence growth. Even if successful economic development is achieved, however, a country's increased savings potential may be absorbed by population growth or by wasteful government expenditure.

The foreign aid policies adopted by donor countries can also influence for good or ill the way in which their financial assistance to the developing countries is used. Thus, tied aid—that is, loans and grants that can only be used to purchase goods in the donor country—may deny the recipient country the opportunity of buying its imports in the cheapest market or of obtaining the collection of goods most suitable for its development requirements. Untied aid, which has no restrictions on the uses to which it is put, is obviously to be preferred. When, in the 1950s, the Cold War made aid-giving an instrument of foreign policy for most donor countries, its economic effectiveness was reduced. Moreover, a large part of foreign aid advanced since 1945 has been in the form of military assistance and this has conferred few economic benefits on the countries receiving it. At times it was used to prop up dictatorships or military rule, with little of the money being used for economic purposes. Political considerations in the past have tended to produce gross distortions in the pattern of foreign aid. Thus, India, which has a high capacity to import capital, was, relatively speaking, starved of foreign funds because of its political policy of non-alignment.[3] On the other hand, certain other countries, because of their political stance, have obtained funds out of all proportion to their capacity to use them effectively. One way of overcoming this problem is to channel a greater part of the aid flow to developing countries through international agencies such as IDA rather than national governments.

Some aid to developing countries has been in the form of grants with no repayment but most aid has involved loans with or without interest payments, and with a short or long maturing period. Where interest has to be paid and where loans have to be amortized, these payments constitute a direct cost to the recipient country. To meet the service charges on foreign capital, the developing country must somehow generate a surplus of foreign exchange. If it achieves a rapid rate of economic development, the growth of new savings will ensure the release of a corresponding value of real resources which can be exported or can be substituted for imports. There will thus appear a similar surplus of foreign exchange receipts over payments for imports which can be used to cover debt service charges. If, however, development lags or if the population grows too rapidly, a borrowing country can only ensure that the debt charges will be covered by directing foreign capital into the production of exports or import substitutes, or by the imposition of restrictions on both imports and domestic consumption. The problem of debt-servicing has received much attention from the mid-1960s onward and a general movement towards debt restructuring and softer loans, incorporating lower interest rates and longer periods of grace and maturity, ensued. In addition, grants became more prevalent in the 1970s and 1980s. At the same time, however, the annual increases in the total amount of foreign aid in real terms tended to decline after the economic crises of the mid-1970s.

Increasingly during the 1980s when some relatively successful developing countries found their annual aid flows inadequate to finance their development projects, they turned towards the international loan market, in which many commercial banks in the United States and elsewhere were increasingly willing to lend to the governments of such countries. These were not 'soft' loans, however, and interest payments were quoted in U.S. dollars. The increasing international interest rates of the 1980s and the rise in the value of the U.S. dollar soon found several borrowing countries in payments difficulties. Thus, in 1982 (and again in 1994) Mexico experienced a debt crisis which had to be resolved with the aid of the international financial and foreign aid community. In addition, in the 1980s and increasingly in the 1990s, business firms and domestic banks in some of the 'richer' developing countries resorted to loans from financial institutions in the industrial countries.

Indeed, the foreign aid approach to financial assistance to developing countries altered in nature and in effect during the 1990s. From funding long-run economic development and reducing poverty, foreign aid has been directed increasingly towards emergency relief and peacekeeping activities. Traditional foreign aid has been reserved for the poorest countries and the heavily indebted poor countries in particular. On the other hand, given the opening up of world financial markets, foreign aid or official development finance, which fell from $56.3 billion in 1990 to $40.8 billion in 1996, has been increasingly replaced by private resource flows, which grew from $44.4 billion in 1990 to $243.8 billion. These private flows included direct foreign investment (an increase from $24.5 billion in 1990 to $109.5 billion in 1996), commercial bank debt ($3 billion to $34.2 billion), and bonds ($2.3 billion to $46.1 billion). Portfolio investment rose from $3.2 billion to $45.7 billion at this time. Thus, after the end of the Cold War in 1990, when the need for foreign aid as a political weapon disappeared, official aid gave way to foreign private borrowing on a large scale and official financial assistance began to wither.[4]

Foreign Trade and Economic Development

Because of the growing number of countries seeking aid and the ambitious targets set by development planners, it became increasingly clear to the developing countries from 1960 onwards that even a substantially increased volume of foreign assistance would still be grossly insufficient to meet all demands. The future prospect of a shortfall in aid, and the mounting debt-servicing problem in some countries, made the developing countries turn to trade as a possible solution to their external problems.

Several reasons were advanced in the 1960s to account for the relatively poor performances of primary producers in world trade during the 1950s and later. These included the change in the composition of industrial production in the industrial countries from light to heavy manufacturing (from industries normally demanding a high raw materials content in the finished product to those whose products have a low raw materials content); the relatively low income elasticity of consumer demand for many agricultural products; agricultural protectionism in the industrial countries; the substantial economies in the industrial uses of natural materials obtained through improved production methods; and the displacement of natural raw materials by synthetic and other man-made substitutes. Declining prices, due largely to falling demand brought about by these changes, also affected the export-earnings of many primary-producing countries. The resulting poor export performances of many developing countries placed severe constraints on their growth and, while foreign aid tended to alleviate these difficulties to a certain extent, by allowing the developing nations to import larger quantities of manufactures from industrial countries than their trading positions warranted, this offset to the relatively low growth of exports was far from complete for the group as a whole. As for a solution to their trade problems, although trends in demand and in technical progress cannot easily be reversed, the developing countries felt that the protectionist and fiscal policies of industrial countries could be moderated to allow greater rates of growth in at least some of their trade. At the same time they believed that a greater degree of stability in primary product prices could have been achieved through commodity agreements and other such arrangements.

The protection given by the advanced countries to their relatively inefficient domestic primary producers in the 1950s and 1960s was a major cause of discontent in the developing world. In addition, the levying of fiscal taxes in Europe on such agricultural products as tea, coffee and tobacco, also caused concern. Since these taxes were often more severe than the customs duties already imposed on the products, they had a very damaging effect on the exports of certain developing countries. But there was still more in contention. The developing countries felt that they were at a disadvantage in trying to raise their share of the world trade in manufactures. Particularly significant in this respect in the 1960s was the argument that their manufactured exports should receive preferential treatment by the industrial nations, since the most-favoured-nation clause included in the GATT was just only if all trading nations had reached the same level of economic development. More specifically, it was felt that the manner in which tariff reductions were agreed upon in GATT, namely, reciprocal reductions on the part of the negotiating countries, was inappropriate for the developing countries, since tariff reductions brought about in this way could adversely affect their development programmes. Moreover, the tariff structure of the developed countries was detrimental to the growth of manufactured exports of developing countries by being lowest on raw materials and highest on finished goods, favouring the last stages of manufacturing production to be carried out in the industrial world. In addition, the use of quantitative import restrictions by the developed countries to protect high-cost domestic producers against competition from developing countries tended to cover a number of commodities, such as leather and leather goods, jute and coir manufactures, electric motors, sporting goods and textiles, many of which the developing countries had been able to export in great amounts.

These trade difficulties led to a growing disenchantment in the developing countries with the GATT. As we have already seen, one outcome of all this activity was the establishment of UNCTAD, which held its first meeting in Geneva in 1964.[5] In addition, the new chapter written into the General Agreement, allowing preferential treatment by the industrial countries of the imports of products from the developing countries, led to the introduction of the Generalized System of Preferences (GSP) in the 1970s by most industrial countries.[6] However, despite the GSP, the tropical products agreement during the Tokyo round, and the movement towards the establishment of a Common Fund in relation to commodity agreements, it is highly questionable whether these innovations went far enough. In addition, the non-tariff barriers erected against the entry of manufactures into the industrial countries, especially in Europe, multiplied after 1973 and adversely affected the development performances of the NICs, some of which were among the most debt-ridden countries in the developing world. The negotiations under the Uruguay round in the early 1990s have, to some extent, reduced the effectiveness of many of these barriers to entry into the industrial countries.

Throughout much of the period during which the developing countries placed an emphasis on an expansion of trade with the rest of the world they experienced a deterioration in their terms of trade. Towards the end of the 1950s they found that their efforts at development were being undermined in this way. While little deterioration occurred for the non-oil developing countries from the early 1960s to 1972, adverse effects appeared once again during much of the 1970s when, despite an improvement of 7.5 per cent in the 1973 boom, a rapid decline in the next two years and a further fall after 1978 meant that, from 1972 to 1980, a deterioration of 11 per cent on average had occurred. A further 2 per cent decline in the terms of trade of the non-oil exporting developing countries was recorded between 1980 and 1989, but, thereafter to 1998, despite some annual fluctuations, on the whole little change occurred.

Despite the emphasis placed on trade by Third World countries over the years, it has been argued effectively that trade and aid are not alternative but rather complementary means to economic development. In particular, it has been increasingly recognized that a greater part of foreign aid should be allocated to improving export production in contrast to the earlier emphasis on industrialization through import substitution. Moreover, in recent times, there has been a growing emphasis on the argument that to switch from being aid-dependent on the rich countries to becoming trade-dependent was not enough because the rate of economic growth in developing countries then depended on the economic conditions in the rich nations and their demand for imports. While trade with industrial countries and the aid which is received from them go together and represent part of the requirements for more rapid development, there are other avenues of growth that should be explored to improve a country's development performance.

It has been argued, for example, that developing countries should trade more with each other, that primary producers should supply the NICs and other exporters of manufactures with raw materials in return for manufactured products. In fact, trade within the developing countries has fluctuated in relative terms over time but increased substantially in the 1990s. Second, it is increasingly recognized that a major drawback to development in many Third World countries is the lack of an efficient food-producing sector. Numerous countries quite often find it necessary to use valuable foreign exchange to purchase urgently needed food from the richer countries. An improved agricultural sector can not only provide a growing urban sector with its food requirements but can also act as a growing market for the output of the urban manufacturing sector of an economy.[7]

Long-run Economic Growth of the Developing Countries

Any concern about the slow rate of economic growth in the Third World is a continuation of a debate which developed at the end of World War II, concerning the long-run tendency for most developing countries to grow more slowly than the industrial world over the past century and a half. Broadly speaking, explanations of Third World economic underdevelopment have evolved in the form of two largely opposed theories: traditional society theories and world economy theories. The first set of theories sees the problem of slow growth and underdevelopment as originating within the Third World countries themselves, whereas the second set places emphasis on the economic domination of Third World countries by the industrialized West; that is, underdevelopment is a consequence of the way in which the international economy has evolved in the recent past.

In traditional society theories, the influence of the advanced countries on the underdeveloped economies is seen as basically development-promoting, and underdevelopment is analysed as a function of indigenous social, cultural and personality factors that block development. Thus, while the advanced countries may supply the economic preconditions for development, in the form of capital, technology and trade, and may also encourage the emergence of 'modernizing elites' concerned with promoting development in imitation of Western entrepreneurs and statesmen, underdevelopment persists, despite all this, because Third World societies are unable *because of their very nature*, to 'respond' adequately to the stimulus of industrialization. They may fail to encourage change and innovation, hampered as they may be by a rigid social structure or powerful and corrupt official bureaucracies or a dictatorial army-controlled and regimented political system. In short, these societies lack the existence or quick emergence of a political, social and institutional framework which exploits the impulses to expansion and development available to them. In sum, traditional society theories argue that underdeveloped countries are, by their very nature, insufficiently open to the development-promoting world economy created by the industrial nations.

World economy theories make precisely the opposite argument. They see underdevelopment as a result of the too great openness of the international economy. These theories attribute underdevelopment and slow growth to the 'dependent' position of Third World countries in an international economy that is constructed to benefit the Western industrial nations. In short, the influence of developed nations on the underdeveloped countries is seen as basically development-blocking, not development-promoting.

In terms of this set of theories, underdeveloped economies are seen as 'primary-producing satellites', providing a flow of cheap agricultural and mineral products to the West. Colonialism tended to reinforce this pattern of economic development, which often led to dependence on a limited range of primary products and the creation of 'enclave economies' brought about by foreign investment in the export sector. It is argued, moreover, that primary product export prices showed a long-run tendency to decline and this limited improvements in domestic living standards and seriously hindered industrial development by limiting the export earnings available to finance it. Industrial development in Third World countries was hampered in other ways. Colonialism involved the loss of autonomy in tariff protection, and the unrestrained competition of foreign manufactured goods often led to the collapse of native handicraft industries. Moreover, when industrial development did occur, it was often dominated by foreign-owned enterprises. In these and other ways the domination of the international economy by the industrially-advanced countries was seen as providing the major obstacle to economic development in Third World countries.

Neither set of theories outlined above is likely to provide the complete explanation of the problem of underdevelopment and slow economic growth. Intuitively, however, it does seem highly likely that the larger the country is in terms of population, resources, etc, for example, China, the more probable it is that underdevelopment is to be explained by internal political, social, and economic factors, with the economic impact of the West on the country between, say, 1840 to 1949, being of marginal significance. On the other hand, smaller countries, which have only recently gained political independence of their colonial governments, will certainly have felt the full impact of the forces which make up the core of the world economy theories. In short, no single theory or set of theories is likely to provide a sufficiently general explanation of underdevelopment. Only through a detailed study of the experience of individual countries will we be able to obtain satisfactory answers to the question of the origins of underdevelopment and slow economic growth in much of the Third World.

Finally, we must remember that not all developing countries have remained underdeveloped. Such countries as Korea, Hong Kong, Taiwan, Singapore, Indonesia, Malaysia and Thailand have all taken great strides towards becoming advanced countries. An investigation of the reasons for the success of some of these countries that have 'conquered' underdevelopment may also prove fruitful.

THE CENTRALLY-PLANNED ECONOMIES[8]

Economic Growth

In Europe, the CPEs emulated Western economic progress during the 1950s and 1960s. From 1951 to 1973, the U.S.S.R. recorded an annual average rate of growth of real GDP of 5 per cent and the other CPEs (excluding Albania) 4.7 per cent. Bulgaria (6.1 per cent) and Romania (5.9 per cent) were the fastest growing economies during these years.[9] In per capita terms, the U.S.S.R. averaged 3.6 per cent a year while the rest averaged 4 per cent. In China, GDP rose at around 6 per cent a year in the 1950s and 4 per cent per head of population.

After 1973, however, economic growth slowed down rapidly in the European CPEs. From 1974 to 1982, the Soviet Union's annual rate of growth of GDP averaged around 2 per cent and just under that figure from 1983 to 1988. The other European CPEs averaged 1.9 per cent between 1974 and 1982, and 2.7 per cent from 1983 to 1988. In per capita terms, the U.S.S.R. barely exceeded a growth rate of 1 per cent per annum after 1973, while the rest of East Europe was able to increase its per capita performance from 1.3 per cent a year (1974–82) to 2.3 per cent in the late 1980s. After 1982, however, only Poland (4.2 per cent) was able to record a GDP growth rate above 3 per cent. China, on the other hand, achieved an average annual growth rate of 5.2 per cent between 1965 and 1987. As a result of numerous economic reforms in the 1980s, including the encouraging of village–township small-scale manufacturing enterprises, the country was able to achieve an average of 9 per cent for the period 1979 to 1987. In addition, China opened its doors to direct foreign investment, and from 1979 to 1985 over $16 billion entered the country, principally from Hong Kong (61 per cent) and Japan (10 per cent).

A feature of the growth of the CPEs from 1960 to 1975 was the high rate of real investment, with the U.S.S.R. averaging 7.5 per cent a year and the other East European countries 10 per cent. The situation changed dramatically after 1975 with investment growth slackening to average 3.2 per cent to 1980 and 2.2 per cent from 1980 to 1985. Partly for this reason, the economic performance of industry (manufacturing and construction) worsened during the 1980s. While this sector grew at an annual average of 5 per cent from 1961 to 1980, over the next eight years this average fell to 2.5 per cent in the U.S.S.R. (about the same as in the Western industrial countries) and 1.3 per cent in other East European countries. As for agriculture, while it virtually stagnated in the U.S.S.R. in the 1980s, its growth in other CPEs rose from 1 per cent annually between 1961 and 1980 to 2.3 per cent a year from 1981 to 1988.[10]

Various reasons have been advanced for the relatively poor performances of the European CPEs from 1973 to 1988. While they were affected by the growth-inhibiting factors which also reduced growth rates in the Western industrial countries, it is also argued that the lack of competitive pressures prevented the growth of productivity and the drive towards greater efficiency within the industrial sector of the CPEs. In addition, the extreme difficulty in obtaining the immense amount of information required to ensure that central planning could be highly effective in all sectors of the economy also played an important role. During the 1980s, recognition of the defects of the economic system led to a move in each country towards the introduction of market-oriented structural reforms in an endeavour to correct the deficiencies of the planning system.

Foreign Trade

In conjunction with the goal of development through industrialization, the CPEs considered an autarkic trade policy to be most suitable for their purposes. Trading with the rest of the world was considered necessary only to obtain raw materials and other commodities which could not be produced domestically, and exports were considered essential only to the extent necessary to pay for the required imports and to dispose of surplus production. Even so, trade with the West was higher in the late 1940s than in the 1950s when, for several reasons, including the commencement of the Cold War in

1948 and the formation of Comecon (or Council for Mutual Economic Assistance—CMEA) in 1949, intrabloc trade expanded at the expense of trade with the West. By 1960, intrabloc trade was around four times the size of that undertaken with the Western industrial countries, the latter consisting largely of exchanges of food, fuel and raw materials for steel products and machinery and equipment.

The CMEA was set up to achieve broader economic co-operation within Eastern Europe, but it was not until 1955 that an elaborate scheme for the co-ordination of production and the development of a pattern of national export specialization was completed, which was designed to eliminate duplication of output and to achieve the benefits of large-scale production. But political difficulties in Hungary and Poland in 1956 and Romania's objection to being a supplier solely of primary products meant that, although intrabloc trade and commercial exchanges grew rapidly from 1957 to 1962, little progress was made toward the multilateralizing of planning and development.

At first the character of the foreign trade of the CPEs was bilateral, with each country attempting to balance its trade each year with each of its CPE trading partners. This practice, however, tended to ensure that trade within the region would not be maximized. To initiate a movement away from such bilateralism, the International Bank for Economic Co-operation (IBEC) was established in 1964 and a new trade currency, the 'transferable rouble', created. Each CMEA member country could then record deficits with some of its neighbours and surpluses with others, with the IBEC using transferable roubles to settle deficits and surpluses within limits. Trade with the West still tended not to be balanced bilaterally but an overall external balance was always a goal of the East European bloc.

In 1963, intrabloc trade accounted for 66 per cent of the total exports of CMEA members, trade with the Western industrial countries for 19 per cent and with developing countries for 12 per cent. From 1963 on, however, trade with the non-CPE world became much more important than it had been in the 1950s. This growing importance came about largely because the East European countries increasingly recognized that greater trade with the West could play an important part in their development programmes by providing additional supplies of scarce currencies and thus greater access to the benefits of modern industrial technology. By the 1980s, intra-area trade accounted for between 48 and 52 per cent of total exports, trade with the Western industrial countries for 27 to 33 per cent and with developing countries 14 to 17 per cent. But the expansion of trade with the West was fraught with problems, both political and economic.

In the 1970s, a widening trade deficit with Western countries emerged as the East European countries found it increasingly more difficult to expand their exports in line with their demand for technologically advanced machinery and equipment from the West. There were several reasons for this, including the adoption of the CAP within the EC which curtailed the exports of foodstuffs from Eastern Europe; the failure of CMEA countries to maintain continuity of supply of various exports; the general spread of trade restrictions in the West; and the depressed demand for imports in the industrial countries at various times. As a result, the East European countries changed their attitudes towards trading with the West and their methods of obtaining Western technology. First, they turned to the Western banking system for Euro-currency and other loans to finance their import surpluses. By 1980, total net borrowings of the CPEs had risen to $56 billion, with a net debt of $41.2 billion. The major borrowers were Poland, the U.S.S.R., and Hungary. In that year, it was clear that Poland was faced with a severe debt-servicing problem, for its debt–service ratio (interest commitment plus debt repayments as a percentage of exports) was over 100 per cent. During the early 1980s, attempts to reduce the bloc debt were successful but, after 1985, the debt began to rise again, and at the end of 1988 it exceeded $100 billion. The heaviest debtors were Poland and Hungary, each of which recorded a debt-to-GDP ratio of over 50 per cent.

Second, to conserve scarce foreign exchange and to obviate the need for extra loans from the West, many co-operative production agreements were arranged between Eastern and Western firms. These agreements took various forms but generally they involved the supply of the technology, often including plant and equipment, by the Western to the Eastern firm, with some of the output of the Eastern firm being supplied to the Western company in exchange for the supply of the technology. The supplier of the technology received the benefit of low-cost production while the recipient received the benefit of Western expertise and the right to sell part of its output in the CPE markets without competition from its Western partner. No foreign exchange was required to obtain the technology as it was paid for in commodities.

Foreign Aid and the CPEs

Foreign aid from the CPEs to the Third World dates from 1954, when the U.S.S.R. set up its first aid programme. By 1960, it was followed by other East European countries and China and total aid commitments of the CPEs reached some $3.6 billion, mostly in the form of loans. Over half this aid went to South Asia and about a third to the Middle East, with India and the United Arab Republic (Egypt) being the major recipients and together receiving about 40 per cent of the total commitments.

In the 1960s, total CPE aid commitments averaged around $1 billion a year and this grew in the 1970s and 1980s to an average from East Europe of almost $5 billion a year. The U.S.S.R.'s share declined in the 1960s relative to the shares of Czechoslovakia, China and the German Democratic Republic. Over time, the bulk of the aid went increasingly to other CPEs with Vietnam, Cuba and Mongolia, for example, receiving over 70 per cent of the total by the mid-1980s and other Communist developing countries around 12 per cent. Non-Communist Third World countries accounted for around 7 per cent.

Most of this aid was bilateral and repayments were often made in the currency of the recipient, in traditional export commodities, or in the form of goods produced by the projects aided. A high proportion of the loans went into the creation and modernization of enterprises in the non-farm sectors and, up to the mid-1970s at least, the ferrous metal industry received special treatment because it was held that this sector was vital to the industrialization of a developing country. In the 1970s much attention was also paid to the stimulation of export-oriented activities with an emphasis on those exports having a ready market in CMEA countries, particularly minerals and fuel. In the 1980s, specific projects of interest to the recipients were financed. There was a general hardening of the terms under which aid was supplied after the early 1970s and the loans were rendered less attractive to potential recipients. In addition to the financial aid, economic and technical assistance was provided to many of the developing countries over the years. China's foreign aid fluctuated substantially in the 1970s and 1980s but increased in size early in the latter decade, principally to sub-Saharan Africa, where emphasis was placed on agricultural development, transport and health. This aid was appreciated by the poorer recipients in that its technologies were adapted to their needs, especially in small-scale industries, such as agriculture and health.

While the bulk of the CPE's aid to developing countries was bilateral in form, a multilateral aid outlet for CMEA members was created in the mid-1970s when a Special Fund for development credits was established under the control of the International Investment Bank (IIB). A greater degree of co-ordination of the aid programmes of the CMEA countries also occurred. Nevertheless, by the 1980s, over 85 per cent of foreign aid from CMEA countries came from the U.S.S.R.

THE COUNTRIES IN TRANSITION (CITs)

The poor economic performances of the CPEs in the 1980s led, with the recognition of a need for change, to a concerted movement in all countries towards a market economy. Maddison's figures suggest an annual decline in the GDP of Eastern Europe from 1973 to 1992 of 0.8 per cent, with only Hungary holding its own. This contrasted with an annual average increase of 4.0 per cent from 1950 to 1973.[11] The years from 1989 have seen massive political, economic, and social changes in Eastern Europe and some parts of Asia. There was the break-up of the U.S.S.R. and its replacement by the Commonwealth of Independent States (CIS), comprising Russia, Belarus, Moldova, Ukraine, Estonia, Latvia and Lithuania, and the Transcaucasus and Central Asian states of Armenia, Azerbaijan, Georgia, Kazakhstan, Kyrgyz

Republic, Tajikistan, Turkmenistan and Uzbekistan, and, further east, Mongolia. The establishment of non-communist governments in Czechoslovakia (later to be divided into the Czech and the Slovak Republics), Hungary, Poland, Romania, Bulgaria, Albania, led to the classification of this group of countries as the *Central and East European Countries* (CEEC).[12] All of these *Countries in Transition* (CITs) endeavoured to convert from central-planning to market economy status. Out of the former Yugoslavia emerged Croatia, Bosnia-Herzegovina, Serbia, Slovenia and the former Yugoslav Republic of Macedonia (Macedonia FYR). All CEECs seek closer integration with the EU, initially through free trade agreements.

The beginning of this amazing transformation was associated with the dismantling of the former economic and political controls, the establishment of a Western-style banking system, including currency reform and the development of foreign trade and investment, the introduction of free market business legislation, and the privatization of the former state-owned enterprises. It was a formidable set of tasks and the process is ongoing. Aid from the West was essential to ensure progress could be rapid and that no backsliding would occur. At the same time, economic growth faltered as inefficient firms went into liquidation, trade ties with other CITs were broken, and the demand for exportable commodities fell rapidly. Inflation rose to untenable levels and so too did unemployment. Advice from the West, especially through the IMF, led to the introduction of stabilization programmes, including a rapid attack on inflation, the government deficit, the public debt, and the introduction of micro-economic reform. The IMF provided financial aid through its drawings and stand-by procedures, its EFF (Extended Fund Facility), ESAF (Enhanced Structural Adjustment Facility) and the new STF (Systemic Transformation Facility). The rapidity of change required by the West, which initially provided only a minimum of bilateral aid, led to some successes in those countries close to western Europe: Czechoslovakia, Hungary and Poland, but, for most, the tasks were far too great to guarantee immediate progress, in particular, the further the country was from Western Europe.

The 1990s have seen these countries struggle with the problems of economic transition, encouraged by the IMF and other bodies to introduce harsh stabilization programmes to achieve the short-term goals of balanced budgets, low inflation, monetary stability, and micro-economic reform, including the widespread privatization of industry, and all without any concern for the high levels of unemployment created as a result of these policies. By the mid-decade, inflation rates were being reduced in all but a handful of countries and economic conditions were beginning to improve in several of them. By 1996, all but five countries (including Russia) recorded positive growth, but all countries still had a long road to follow before they could emulate the Western industrial model. The most advanced of these countries, the Czech Republic, Hungary and Poland were granted associate status within the EU, and will no doubt be the first to gain full membership of the EU in the future.

Needless to say, little foreign aid issued from these countries during the 1990s. Indeed, financial resources tended to flow in the opposite direction, especially after 1995, from the IMF and mainly private sources in Western Europe.

NOTES

1 This group is a flexible one in the literature. The countries included in this grouping include China, India, Malaysia, Philippines, Thailand and Indonesia in Asia; Colombia, Argentina and Brazil in South America. Others, namely Hong Kong, Israel, Korea, Singapore and Taiwan have been elevated to the advanced category.

2 Strictly speaking, Hong Kong has become Hong Kong–China after the colony's return to China in 1997, and Taiwan is widely called China–Taipei.

3 While in terms of total aid received in the 1960s India was one of the most-favoured recipients, in terms of per capita aid it was close to the bottom of the list of recipient countries.

4 See pp. 261–2 above and World Bank, *Global Development Finance*, 1997, vol. 1, Washington, DC, p. 3.

5 See p. 287.

6 See pp. 286 and 292.

7 See W. Arthur Lewis, *The Evolution of the International Economic Order* (Princeton: Princeton University Press, 1977), p. 75.

8 This group includes the U.S.S.R., Czechoslovakia, Hungary, Poland, German Democratic Republic, Bulgaria, Romania, Albania (all in Europe), China, Laos, Mongolia, North Korea, Vietnam (in Asia) and Cuba. The European members, except Albania, were members of CMEA (Council for Mutual Economic Assistance), so were Cuba and Mongolia. Although Yugoslavia was centrally planned, it was normally excluded from the group of CPEs because of its more general economic relations with the West.

9 For this and the following paragraph, the information on the European CPEs appears in International Monetary Fund, *World Economic Outlook*, May, 1990, pp. 65–6, citing A. Maddison, *The World Economy in the 20th Century* (Paris: OECD, 1989).

10 For this paragraph and the following one, see International Monetary Fund, op. cit., pp. 66–75.

11 *Monitoring the World Economy*, p. 62.

12 The Czech and Slovak Republics formed a customs union in 1992 and also entered into free trade agreements with Hungary and Poland in that year.

SELECTED REFERENCES

Bhagwati, J. (ed), *The New International Economic Order: the North–South Debate* (Cambridge, MA: Harvard University Press, 1977).

International Monetary Fund, *World Economic Outlook*, various issues.

McBean, A. I. and Snowden, P. N., *International Institutions in Trade and Finance* (London: George Allen & Unwin, 1981).

Maddison, A., *The World Economy in the 20th Century* (Paris: OECD, 1989).

Maddison, A., *Monitoring the World Economy, 1820–1992* (Paris: OECD, 1994).

Organization for Economic Co-operation and Development, *The Impact of the Newly Industrializing Countries* (Paris: OECD, 1979).

OECD, *The Flow of Financial Resources to Less Developed Countries* (Paris: OECD), various issues.

United Nations, *World Economic Survey*, Washington, various issues.

United Nations Industrial Development Organization, *Industry and Development*, Washington, various issues.

Vienna Institute for Comparative Economic Studies, *CMEA Selected Economic Indicators*, various issues.

World Bank, *Development Co-operation*, various issues.

World Bank, *Global Development Finance*, various issues.

World Bank, *World Development Report*, Oxford, various issues.

Chapter 22

A summary: 1820–2000 and ahead

The evolution of the international economy during the period 1820 to 1998 has been largely a response to the changes that have occurred in the political, economic and technological environment within which economic relations between countries are conducted. The record demonstrates the slow but inexorable movement among the regions of the world economy towards greater integration. As a result of a number of developments, international trade increased dramatically in the second half of the nineteenth century, outstripping the growth of world output. Particularly important was the movement towards free trade up to the 1870s, even though it had faltered by the 1880s and was kept alive only by the United Kingdom and a few Continental countries, and the vast strides in steam transport technology which rapidly increased the flows of people and commodities across continents and from one continent to another by sea. This expansion of the international economy provided the mechanism for widespread economic growth in western Europe and its 'offshoots' abroad.

Apart from the vast transfer of population mainly from Europe to the continents of North and South America, capital funds were made available for economic development in the countries receiving these large inflows of migrants. The evolution of the foreign exchange market throughout the century and the widespread adoption of the gold standard after the 1860s, facilitated the international transfers of funds and commodities. The growth of world trade was also promoted by the slow spread of a multilateral trade network.

Europe exploited the vast land-intensive resources of the 'new' lands to help feed its growing population and to supply its growing manufacturing industries with many of the required raw materials. As a result, the nineteenth century witnessed the widespread growth of per capita income on a scale never before experienced.

A unique feature of the pre-1914 international economy is that it was dominated by one country, the United Kingdom. The first country to industrialize, to adopt the gold standard, and to accept free trade as its commercial policy, it set the pace for the growth of the world economy by providing the markets, capital and labour needed for the economic development of a large part of the world. After 1870, it is true, France, Germany and, to a lesser extent the United States, began to play a more important part in promoting the expansion of the international economy and shaping its character. Even so, Britain's continued pre-eminence in world financial affairs and her adherence to free trade, in a period when there was a general return to protectionism, gave her undisputed leadership in international economic affairs. It is perhaps for this reason that international agreements on financial and other matters were largely unnecessary before 1914. In so far as any guiding influences were exerted on the growth and functioning of the international economy in the nineteenth century, these originated chiefly in Britain, whose influence on world trade and finance was paramount.

Despite the long-run tendency towards international economic integration, the movement also contained the seeds for its destruction in the two decades following World War I. First, such integration depended to a large extent upon the British balance of payments, which became much more unfavourable after 1900, ensuring an inevitable collapse of the multilateral trade and payments network which had become evident in world trade from the 1870s. Second, the retreat from free trade by several important trading nations, including Germany, the United States, France and Russia placed additional strains on world trading patterns and trade by comparative advantage.

World War I altered the international economy dramatically. The subsequent decline in Britain's international economic position, the emergence of the United States as the world's leading industrial and financial power, and the economic difficulties experienced by Europe in general, and Germany in particular, made a simple return to the pre-war international economic system impossible. The attempt to restore the gold standard in the 1920s was a complete failure and, in the face of mounting economic difficulties, aggravated later by a worldwide depression and growing political insecurity, countries, or groups of countries, turned in on themselves in order to deal with their economic problems. Moreover, as governments were called upon to deal with these crises by playing a more active role in national economic affairs, international considerations were increasingly subordinated to domestic policies aimed at maintaining employment and output levels. With the collapse of the traditional framework of international economic institutions and the emergence of a more nationalistic approach to economic affairs, there was little hope of inter-governmental co-operation in the search for a multilateral solution to world economic problems and, while the demands of trade finally brought some international agreement to stabilizing exchange rates, attempts to deal with trade and financial problems in the 1930s either took the form of bilateral agreements or were made within a framework of discriminatory regional blocs.

The success in obtaining international agreement on a wide variety of economic matters from the early 1940s onwards contrasted sharply with the more nationalistic outlook prevalent during the interwar years, and the much more limited forms of international agreement characteristic of the period before 1914. But this did not come about because countries were less actively concerned in the 1940s with domestic levels of employment and rates of economic growth than they were in previous decades, rather the reverse. It was because governments would not allow domestic economies to be threatened by outside events that it became necessary to create, as an act of deliberate policy, an international economic system within which it was possible for individual countries to exercise economic sovereignty without endangering the welfare of other countries. Moreover, the fact that the attainment of national economic goals of full employment and high growth rates might be helped by the existence of a smoothly functioning world economy also contributed to making countries more willing to co-operate in the setting up of international economic institutions designed to eliminate the financial weaknesses and widespread impediments to world trade and commerce that had brought about the collapse of the international economy in the 1930s. In a sense, then, the emergence of a managed international economy after 1945 was largely the result of the spread of the managed economy at the national level characteristic of the period after 1920.

Added to these pressures, the severe disruptions to world trade and investment created by World War I and its aftermath ensured that little improvement in international economic relations occurred in the 1920s.

However, it was not until the 1950s that the trend towards greater 'globalization' was resumed, largely because of the initiation of a programme of freeing up world trade under the auspices of the GATT and a stable financial environment created by the establishment of the International Monetary Fund.

As a result of these and other international economic institutions set up by collective action or as a by-product of the efforts of the United Nations (or in spite of them), the era from 1950 to 1973 was the most prosperous of any such period in the history of the world economy. While it is possible to ascribe some of the favourable influences of this period to the existence of the international economic institutions, the recovery from the war played a part initially, while the acceleration in technological knowledge on a broad front was substantially responsible, alone and in combination with other forces, for much of the growth. In fact, one of the major growth-generating features of the post World War II era, even up to the present day, has been technological advance on a rapid and intensive scale. Never before have so many important discoveries been made on an annual basis, and this factor appears set to continue into the next millennium.

During the 1950s and 1960s, the main players were the industrialized countries of Western Europe, Canada, the United States, Japan and Australasia. While the developing countries as a group also benefited from the growing globalization, they still had a long way to go before they could claim equal status with the leaders. Large-scale foreign aid from the developed to the developing countries provided a great stimulus to those third world countries capable of adopting self-sustained growth. Countries that were centrally planned were also growing quite rapidly during these years.

This world economic system also contained the seeds of its own downfall. Both the GATT and the IMF operated according to the requirements of the EEC and North America. The IMF's exchange rate mechanism was the first to feel the strain in the early 1970s when the adjustable peg system was giving way to currency floating. At the same time, the reductions in tariffs under the guidance of GATT gave way in the 1970s to systems of quantitative import controls which were even more restrictive than the tariffs. At the same time, the movement towards customs unions and free trade areas, almost inevitably involving some trade discrimination, also inhibited the movement towards global free trade. In particular, Western Europe turned inward, increasingly so as the decades progressed, building up a large and growing trade bloc with many benefits for the participating countries and trade problems for other countries, especially in agriculture.

An international trading boom in the early 1970s led to ever-rising inflation rates, which were exacerbated in 1973 and 1974 by unprecedented increases in oil prices. In 1974, the world economy faltered, never again in the 20th century to return to the halcyon days of the 1950–73 period of low inflation and low unemployment. This marked the end of the international growth phase and the emergence of a difficult period which has lasted up to the late 1990s. After 1974, restrained economic growth occurred in the industrialized countries, generally with high inflation and intractably high unemployment.

Not that the world stood still during these years. On the contrary, it witnessed the appearance and growth of several newly-industrializng countries in Asia and elsewhere, including Korea, Hong Kong, Taiwan and Singapore (the 'four tigers'), Brazil, Argentina, Mexico, Israel, Spain, Greece and Portugal, to name but a few. Export-oriented growth strategies produced high rates of growth in most of these countries, but especially in the four tigers. By the early 1980s they had emerged as the coming industrial countries. In addition, within the already industrialized world, another phase of fundamental change was developing.

As Colin Clark predicted in his *Conditions of Economic Progress*, first published in 1943, in the industrially-advanced countries during the second half of the twentieth century, employment in, and the output of, manufacturing industry peaked and began a slow relative decline as the tertiary (services) sector rose to prominence. The change in employment began in the late 1960s and, especially, during the 1970s, while the net value added in manufacturing as a proportion of total output began to peak in the early 1980s, followed by a slow decline during the 1990s which looks set to continue into the next century.

In the 1980s, the four tigers of east Asia and Israel were also approaching their zenith as predominantly manufacturing countries and, although manufactured exports still dominated their trading patterns in the 1990s, the services sector has become increasingly more important in these economies. Thus, in sharp contrast to the experience of the industrially-advanced nations of Western Europe, North America and Japan, these newly-emerging countries have accomplished in a decade or two a development pattern it took the early developers much longer to achieve. Today we talk about 'advanced' countries instead of 'industrial' countries, and include Israel, Hong Kong (up to 1997), Taiwan, Korea and Singapore in the list. The world economy has changed its character significantly during the years since 1975 and will continue to do so, producing new trade and commercial patterns, and new commercially-powerful nations.

It is claimed that the pace of globalization in the world economy quickened considerably after the mid-1980s, with world trade rising almost twice as fast as world output, following the rapid liberalization of financial markets in many countries, and the acceleration of capital flows to many newly-industrializing countries.[1] This trend resulted in the speedy movement of some Asian countries into a higher group, while others, such as Malaysia, Thailand and China began to follow the Asian export-oriented path to their industrialization.

International economic integration will not be complete, however, while regionalism persists in Europe, where the Single European Market, the Maastricht monetary union, and the continued growth of membership of the European Union work against the efforts of more 'international' institutions such as the WTO and the IMF. Not until political union occurs in Europe, and the regional institutions established there become purely 'national' in character so that a 'United States of Europe' nation takes its place in the world economy, can the WTO and IMF operate as they are expected to and the rest of the world treat the European region in the same way as it treats the United States of America.

One economic problem to have become entrenched in the global economy during the 1990s is the widespread and unusually high level of unemployment. Short-term stabilization policies aimed at controlling inflation contain no mechanism for attacking unemployment, which has come to be regarded as basically 'structural' in nature and its solution requiring micro-economic reform and labour market reform. The net result of these policies when implemented, however, appears to have been more unemployment and lower wages. To overcome such structural unemployment, retraining and additional education are obviously required. How the new avenues of employment are chosen for such retraining, however, requires foreknowledge of the employment demands of the future and recent examples of retraining have led to further unemployment because of the lack of available positions in the fields of retraining. In 1998 there were some 18 million unemployed workers in the

EU and thus there is a substantial problem of placing so many even after retraining. These problems would be less apparent if growth rates were well above the poor performances of the 1990s. By keeping inflation down almost to zero and perpetuating high unemployment, a government is not only putting a cap on economic growth but is also creating enormous social problems which could lead to widespread political unrest, such as that experienced in Germany and France in 1997 and 1998.

Has this new emphasis on the integration of the international economy produced a widespread desire to accelerate the globalization process or should the natural evolutionary process be allowed to produce much greater world economic integration? So far the main results appear to be a greater gulf between the rich and the poor both within countries and between them and, as part of this, much greater unemployment than would have been tolerated previously by governments and unions. It is highly apparent that the world still has a long way to go before a much higher degree of integration of nations will be attained and the ultimate result of globalization, of 'one world, one people, one government', is still far into the distant future.

What of the immediate future, however? Few significant changes will occur in the relatively short term. Europe has adopted its common currency policy and the next stage towards political union will be set in motion. The former centrally-planned economies of central and eastern Europe will become increasingly more market-oriented and several of them will experience rapid economic growth. Their external economic ties will be largely with the EU and some of them will inevitably be absorbed into the Union. Russia, however, remains a serious economic problem in eastern Europe and could well revert to a political system under which the state plays a much greater role in the domestic economy than at present. While economic recovery in east and south-east Asia is likely to be slow, many of the countries in the region will continue to be major exporters of manufactured goods. China, in particular, should markedly improve its relative position in the international economy during the early decades of next century.

Other factors will undoubtedly play a part in the globalization process of the future. Productivity improvements based on a more efficient use of existing technology will be important in encouraging an increase in international trade but will be tempered by the extent to which such an approach leads to increased unemployment. New technological advances will continue to play as crucial a role in the development of world trade and production in the future as they have done in the past. The extent to which world trade responds to these changes will depend upon the nature of such technological advances, the linkages they will have with capital equipment and raw materials, and the changes which will occur in the comparative advantage in production enjoyed by the various regions of the world.

One worrying feature of the present time is the amount of mobile portfolio funds in the international monetary system, which could lead to severe financial strains of the type experienced by east Asian countries in the recent past. Shifts of these funds, similar to those of the late 1920s but on a much larger scale, could create almost insurmountable monetary crises for a number of countries and place severe strains on the international monetary system.

The next phase of world economic growth will witness an increasing concern about such issues as world population growth and its implication for food production, and a possible growing scarcity of certain raw materials and energy resources when manufacturing production again rises rapidly. Environmental issues may also impinge more heavily on world economic growth in the future than they have done in the past.

Perhaps above all, even if it is not apparent at the present time, advanced countries will be more concerned in the next few decades than hitherto with the raising of the living standards of an even greater proportion of the world's population. Although the trade advantages evident in recent decades have accrued largely to the industrial countries, this group includes some new members, and the case for international specialization remains as strong today as it was in the nineteenth century, while the indirect benefits that international trade can bestow upon today's developing nations exceed, both in size and variety, those which could have been expected a century ago. The number of industrialized countries is greater, the existing technology is far more advanced and diversified, and the opportunities for the international exchange of ideas and methods far more abundant today than they were 100 or even 60 years ago. Whether it will be possible, through more intergovernmental co-operation and a greater awareness of the need for more positive action on the part of the richer nations to ensure that the benefits of modern technology are more fully shared by the developing countries, remains one of the most challenging problems of the new millennium, and one that must be addressed if the advanced nations are to pay more than lip service to their newly-discovered globalization process.

NOTE

1 See IMF, 'Globalization, Opportunities and Challenges', *World Economic Survey* (Washington, May 1997), p. 72.

SELECTED REFERENCES

IMF, 'Globalization, Opportunities and Challenges', *World Economic Survey* (Washington, May, 1997), Chs. III–V and Annex.
Maddison, A., *Phases of Capitalist Development* (London: Oxford University Press, 1982).
Maddison, A., *Monitoring the World Economy, 1820–1992* (Paris: OECD, 1995). This publication includes many detailed statistical tables covering most of the period under discussion in this book.

Index